SPELLING CONNECTIONS

J. Richard Gentry, Ph.D.

8

Series Author
J. Richard Gentry, Ph.D.

Editorial Development: Cottage Communications

Art and Production: PC&F

Photography: George C. Anderson: cover, pages 1, 4, 6, 7, 254, 255, 256, 257; Corbis Bettmann: p. 12, © Werner H. Müller; p. 30, © Henry Diltz; p. 36, © Hulton-Deutsch Collection; p. 72, © Tony Arruza; p. 132, © Hulton-Deutsch Collection; p. 144, © Phil Schermeister; p. 216, © Joseph Sohm, Chromosohm Inc.; p. 268, © Kevin Schafer; p. 272, © The State Russian Museum; p. 273, © Hubert Stadler; p. 274, © Phil Schermeister; p. 275, © Gail Mooney; p. 280, © Patrick Bennett; p. 282, © Philip Gould; p. 286, © Phil Schermeister; p. 287, © Gianni Dagli Orti; p. 288, © Bettmann/CORBIS; p. 293, © Luca I. Tettoni; p. 296, © Charles. E. Rotkin; p. 298, © Bob Rowan; p. 299, © Peter Johnson; p. 300, © CORBIS; p. 301, © Hans Georg Roth; p. 302, © Francis G. Mayer; p. 304, © Tom Bean; p. 306, © Dave G. Houser; p. 311, © Roger Ressmeyer; p. 312, © Tony Arruza; p. 315, © Mimmo Jodice; p. 316, © Lee Snider; The Stock Market: p. 18, © LWA/Dann Tardif; p. 66, © John Paul Endress; p. 90, © Ken Straiton; p. 126, © Chris Hamilton; p. 138, © Tom Stewart; p. 168, © KJ Historical; p. 174, © Steve Terrill; p. 271, © Mark Gamba; p. 283, © Tim Davis; p. 310, © Wes Thompson; p. 313, © Mug Shots; SUPERSTOCK ©: p. 24, p. 156, p. 180, p. 192, p. 291, p. 294, p. 295; © Index Stock Imagery: p. 48, p. 54, p. 102, p. 108, p. 120, p. 198, p. 204, p. 210, p. 267, p. 277, p. 285, p. 292, p. 307, p. 308; Tony Stone Images: p. 60, © Simon Battensby; p. 84, © David Young-Wolff; p. 96, © David Frazier; p. 162, © Gary Braasch; p. 269, © Steve Taylor; p. 270, © Rich Frishman; p. 276, © Zigy Kaluzny; p. 278, © Darrell Gulin; p. 279, © Laurence Dutton; p. 281, © Ben Edwards; p. 284, © Stewart Cohen; p. 289, © Laurence Dutton; p. 303, Renee Lynn; p. 314, © Paul Edmondson

Illustrations: Laurel Aiello: pages 21, 34, 87, 146, 148; Dave Blanchette: pages 69, 110, 112, 113, 117, 129, 177; Len Ebert: pages 15, 16, 57, 74, 76, 77, 159, 160; Kate Flanagan: pages 93, 99, 105, 153, 165, 189, 201; Ruth Flanigan: pages 11, 17, 23, 29, 35, 47, 53, 59, 65, 71, 83, 89, 95, 101, 107, 119, 125, 131, 137, 143, 155, 161, 167, 173, 179, 191, 197, 203, 209, 215; Brian Lies: page 45; Bill Ogden: pages 10, 27, 51, 207, 218, 219, 224, 225, 226, 227, 229, 230, 231, 232, 233, 234, 238, 239, 240, 241, 242, 243, 244, 245, 246, 247, 248, 250, 251, 252, 253; George Ulrich: pages 38, 39, 63, 100, 123, 141, 171, 172, 182, 185, 195, 213

ISBN: 0-7367-0113-3

Zaner-Bloser, Inc., P.O. Box 16764, Columbus, Ohio 43216-6764 (1-800-421-3018)

Printed in the United States of America   00 01 02 03 04 QP 5 4 3 2

Contents

Spelling Study Strategy

Look ➡ **Say** ➡ **Cover** ➡ **See** ➡ **Write** ➡ **Check**

1 **Look** at the word.

2 **Say** the letters in the word. Think about how each sound is spelled.

3 **Cover** the word with your hand or close your eyes.

4 **See** the word in your mind. Spell the word to yourself.

5 **Write** the word.

6 **Check** your spelling against the spelling in the book.

Spelling and Thinking

1. inspector	*inspector*	A plumbing **inspector** checked the pipes.
2. abrupt	*abrupt*	Our bus came to an **abrupt** stop.
3. target	*target*	The archer missed the **target**.
4. criminal	*criminal*	Two witnesses identified the **criminal**.
5. dismal	*dismal*	It was a dark and **dismal** day.
6. astonish	*astonish*	This movie's ending will **astonish** you.
7. investigate	*investigate*	Please **investigate** that rattling noise!
8. entirely	*entirely*	Did the storm **entirely** destroy the crops?
9. escape	*escape*	They went to the beach to **escape** the heat.
10. shortage	*shortage*	The flood was followed by a food **shortage**.
11. emphasis	*emphasis*	She paused for **emphasis** during her speech.
12. victim	*victim*	One accident **victim** waited for help.
13. upheaval	*upheaval*	The hurricane caused **upheaval** in the city.
14. mustache	*mustache*	He decided to shave off his **mustache**.
15. startle	*startle*	A sudden noise might **startle** the baby.
16. eccentric	*eccentric*	An **eccentric** person is often interesting.
17. accomplice	*accomplice*	The thief must have had an **accomplice**.
18. budget	*budget*	We have money in our **budget** for the trip.
19. accessory	*accessory*	He was charged as an **accessory** to the crime.
20. incriminate	*incriminate*	This evidence will **incriminate** the accused.

SORT THE SPELLING WORDS

1.–2. An **open syllable** ends with a vowel sound. Write the spelling words in which the first syllable is open. Draw a line between the syllables in each word.

3.–20. A **closed syllable** ends with a consonant sound. Write the spelling words in which the first syllable is closed. Draw a line between the syllables in each word.

REMEMBER THE SPELLING STRATEGY

Remember that there are syllables that end with a vowel sound and syllables that end with a consonant sound. Find the pattern and spell each word by syllable.

Spelling and Vocabulary

Word Meanings

Write the spelling word that could best replace the underlined word or words in each sentence.

1. The earthquake created violent disruption in the entire region.
2. The governor was the object of criticism at the protest rally.
3. Our vacation offered us a temporary way of gaining freedom from our busy lives.
4. If I plan expenses well, I can save enough to buy a new pair of in-line skates.
5. Witnesses gave evidence that would clearly involve the accused.
6. Production slowed at the factory as a result of a deficiency of workers.
7. The reporter was an innocent one harmed because he believed the false story.

Word Groups

Write the spelling word that completes each series.

8. gloomy, dreary, hopeless, _____
9. observe, inquire, examine, _____
10. frighten, surprise, alarm, _____
11. unusual, odd, peculiar, _____
12. weight, importance, stress, _____
13. brusque, curt, rude, _____

USING THE Dictionary

Use a dictionary to help you write the spelling word that correctly completes each statement.

14. (Accessory, Incriminate) can be a noun or an adjective.
15. (Investigate, Inspector) has a root meaning "to look into."
16. (Astonish, Escape) begins with a schwa (ə) sound.
17. (Mustache, Accessory) has two acceptable pronunciations.
18. (Criminal, Incriminate) has two schwa sounds.
19. (Entirely, Abrupt) is an adverb.
20. (Emphasis, Accomplice) has the primary stress on the second syllable.

inspector	abrupt	target	criminal	dismal
astonish	escape	victim	startle	budget
investigate	shortage	upheaval	eccentric	accessory
entirely	emphasis	mustache	accomplice	incriminate

Solve the Analogies Write a spelling word to complete each analogy.

1. **Tourist** is to **travel** as **detective** is to _____.
2. **Patiently** is to **calmly** as **completely** is to _____.
3. **Truthful** is to **dishonest** as **gradual** is to _____.
4. **Uncertain** is to **sure** as **bright** is to _____.
5. **Paintbrush** is to **canvas** as **arrow** is to _____.

Complete the Sentences Write the spelling word that completes each sentence.

6. In words with several syllables, one syllable receives the greatest _____.
7. A family _____ helps to keep spending from going beyond income.
8. Failing to report the crime made her an _____ after the fact.
9. The three-year-old's musical genius will simply _____ you!
10. Locking yourself into a room to avoid germs is _____ behavior.
11. The thief refused to _____ his friend in the crime.
12. A sudden loud noise would _____ anyone.
13. I wasn't late on purpose; I was a _____ of circumstance!

Complete the Paragraph Write spelling words from the box to complete the paragraph.

Yesterday, a theft created an _14._ in the otherwise quiet Hastings Museum. A _15._, possibly aided by an _16._, stole several priceless paintings from the eighteenth-century collection. Arthur Trace, an _17._ for the police department, was called to the scene. Admitting a _18._ of clues, the officer noted one oddity. The thieves had drawn a _19._ on a nearby painting before making their _20._.

| inspector |
| shortage |
| accomplice |
| mustache |
| criminal |
| upheaval |
| escape |

Spelling and Writing

Proofread a Paragraph

Six words are not spelled correctly in this paragraph. Write the words correctly.

> Officer Trace was not entirelly convinced that the crime had been committed by outsiders. Any of the fifty museum employees might have been an accessery to the crime. The inspector decided to interview everyone in an attempt to incriminate someone. With time, the night watchman became the targit of the investigation. Other workers described him as an ekcentric. Suddenly, however, the case came to an abrubt end.

Proofreading Marks

≡	Make a capital.
/	Make a small letter.
∧	Add something.
ℓ	Take out something.
⊙	Add a period.
⌗	New paragraph
SP	Spelling error

Write a Paragraph

Narrative Writing

A good mystery keeps a reader asking, "And then what happens?" Usually, the plot involves several problems that the main character must solve before the mystery concludes. Write a paragraph that continues the mystery of the museum's missing paintings.

- Describe how Officer Trace solved the mystery. Add an interesting twist to the story that might surprise the reader.
- Remember to include a topic sentence supported by detail sentences.
- Follow the form used in the proofreading sample. Use as many spelling words as you can.

Proofread Your Writing During

Writing Process

Prewriting
⬇
Drafting
⬇
Revising
⬇
Editing
⬇
Publishing

Proofread your writing for spelling errors as part of the editing stage in the writing process. Be sure to check each word carefully. Use a dictionary to check spelling if you are not sure.

Vocabulary

Strategy Words

Review Words: Closed and Open Syllables

Write the word from the box that could best replace the underlined word or words.

adapt	biennial	compel	miniature	persist

1. Although Dad encouraged me to taste the anchovies, he did not <u>force</u> me to try them.
2. The class decided that the computer fair should be a <u>once-every-two-years</u> event.
3. Call the dentist if your toothache should <u>continue</u>.
4. Although <u>tiny</u>, these dollhouse pieces have all the details of full-size furniture.
5. Your puppy should <u>adjust</u> to its new environment within a few days.

Preview Words: Closed and Open Syllables

Write a word from the box to complete each sentence.

concept	detention	jasmine
pumpernickel		ultimatums

6. She ate a tuna sandwich on _____ bread.
7. The fragrant scent of _____ perfume filled the room.
8. To negotiate an agreement, the company president agreed to all the _____.
9. Failure to complete the assignment will result in a _____.
10. Some people are fascinated by the _____ of space travel.

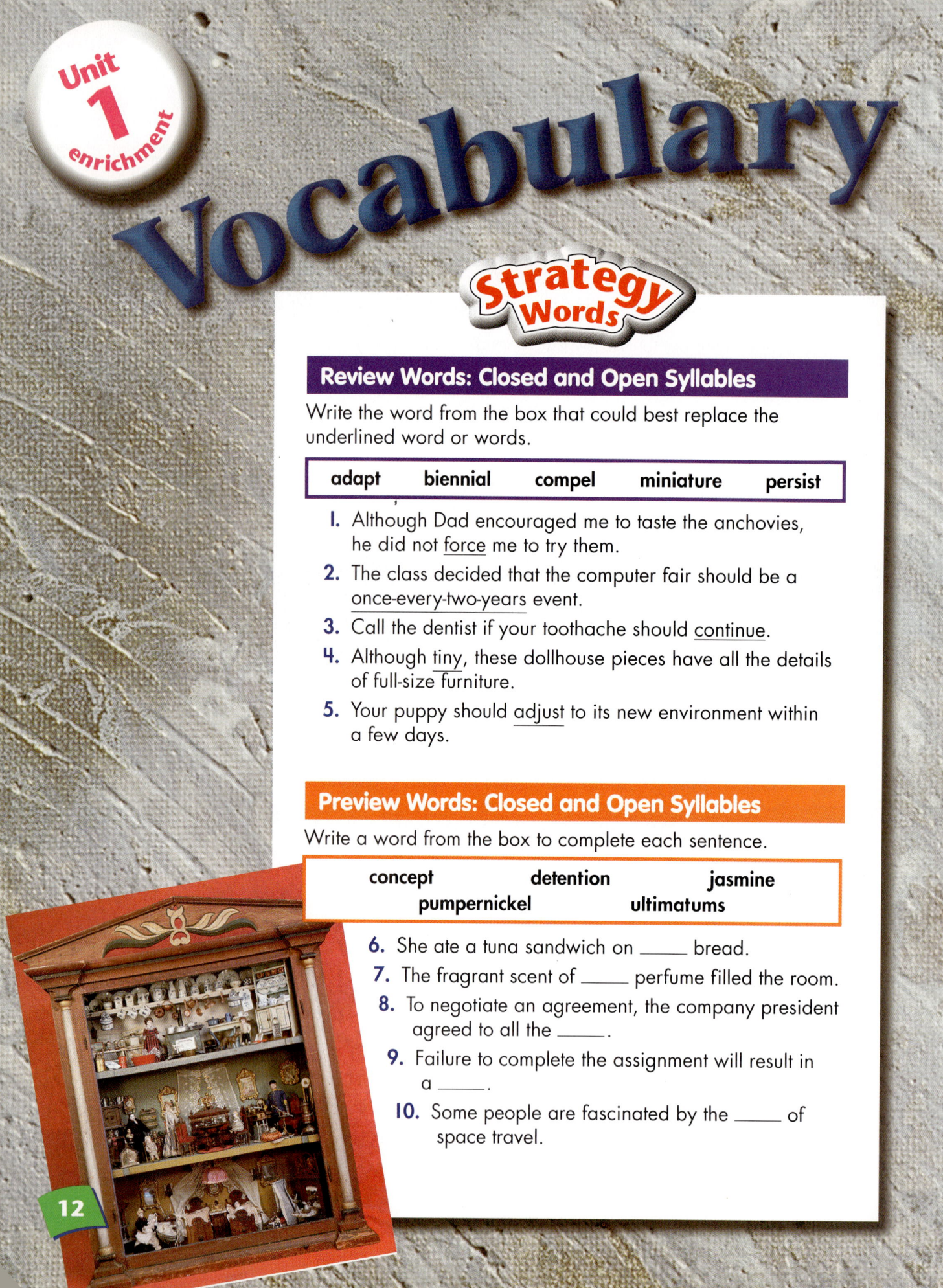

Connections

Science: Weather

Write words from the box that could best replace the word or words in parentheses.

destructive	forecast	hazard
meteorologist		precipitation

Pointing to the map, the ___1.___ (weather specialist) showed the path of the approaching hurricane. Her ___2.___ (prediction) warned people about ___3.___ (ruinous) high winds. Island residents were cautioned about the ___4.___ (danger) of being caught on the bridge during the height of the storm. The ___5.___ (rainfall) accompanying the winds would also present problems.

Social Studies: Farming

Write words from the box to complete the paragraph.

cultivate	drainage	irrigation	ravine	terrace

It can be a challenge to ___6.___ some farmland. Hilly terrain can be converted to usable land by forming a flat ___7.___ on the sloping hill. In particularly dry areas, ___8.___ is needed to bring water to growing crops. Too much water can present problems as well. The force of a river or stream can cause a deep ___9.___ to form. Proper ___10.___ prevents flooding.

Apply the Spelling Strategy

Circle the five content words you wrote that have an open first syllable.

Spelling AND Thinking

READ THE SPELLING WORDS

1.	caper	*caper*	Two students thought up that funny **caper**.
2.	utilize	*utilize*	I cannot **utilize** all of your suggestions.
3.	recycle	*recycle*	Save your bottles so we can **recycle** them.
4.	arena	*arena*	A big crowd gathered near the sports **arena**.
5.	debut	*debut*	Dad sent flowers when Alice made her **debut**.
6.	response	*response*	I wrote twice but never received any **response**.
7.	reprint	*reprint*	A publisher wants to **reprint** my sports column!
8.	diagnose	*diagnose*	Did Doctor Cutt **diagnose** your illness?
9.	aboard	*aboard*	Four families vacationed **aboard** the schooner.
10.	retrace	*retrace*	After I got lost, I had to **retrace** my steps.
11.	patiently	*patiently*	Alan paced around, but Rosa sat **patiently**.
12.	decipher	*decipher*	Can you help me **decipher** this scribbled note?
13.	utility	*utility*	This bill is from our local **utility** company.
14.	bias	*bias*	His **bias** against my ideas was clear.
15.	chaos	*chaos*	The flood caused **chaos** in the region.
16.	typhoon	*typhoon*	Luckily, the **typhoon** missed the island.
17.	credence	*credence*	Few people give **credence** to his wild theories.
18.	reimburse	*reimburse*	If you pay the bill now, I will **reimburse** you.
19.	violent	*violent*	That oak blew down during a **violent** storm.
20.	seasonal	*seasonal*	Each fall, I enjoy the **seasonal** color changes.

SORT THE SPELLING WORDS

1.–13. Write the spelling words that have one open syllable. Circle the open syllables.

14.–20. Write the spelling words that have two or more open syllables. Circle the open syllables.

REMEMBER THE SPELLING STRATEGY

Remember that an open syllable ends with a vowel sound. Note the spelling of the vowel sound.

Spelling and Vocabulary

Word Meanings

Write the spelling word that could best replace each underlined word or phrase.

1. A <u>severe tropical storm</u> hit Hawaii last week.
2. A dog ran through the room and created <u>total disaster</u> out of the neat stacks of paper.
3. My father wants to <u>go back over</u> the route that he and I hiked last summer.
4. Her <u>reaction</u> to the assignment was very creative.
5. To conserve natural resources, we <u>reuse</u> our plastic spoons and forks.
6. Can someone <u>decode</u> this secret message?
7. The <u>stadium</u> was crowded with excited sports fans.
8. We can <u>use</u> that sturdy carton to store heavy woolen blankets.

Word Definitions

Write the spelling word that matches each definition.

9. happening every fall, winter, spring, or summer
10. to pay back for money spent
11. usefulness
12. a first public appearance
13. to print again
14. identify a disease
15. severe or intense
16. calmly coping with delay

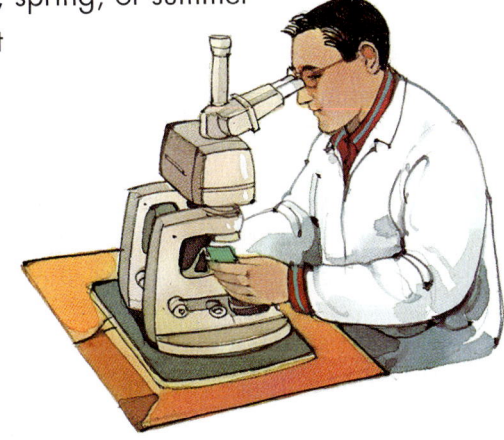

USING THE Dictionary

In a phonetic spelling, the **schwa** symbol, ə, indicates a **reduced vowel,** one that receives the weakest possible level of stress.

17.–20. Use the **Spelling Dictionary** to write all the two-syllable spelling words that have the **schwa** sound. Circle each reduced vowel.

15

caper	utilize	recycle	arena	debut
response	reprint	diagnose	aboard	retrace
patiently	decipher	utility	bias	chaos
typhoon	credence	reimburse	violent	seasonal

Solve the Analogies Write a spelling word to complete each analogy.

1. **Frugally** is to **frugal** as **seasonally** is to _____.
2. **Cloud** is to **cirrus** as **storm** is to _____.
3. **Equation** is to **solve** as **code** is to _____.
4. **Distress** is to **trouble** as **disorder** is to _____.
5. **Calm** is to **furious** as **serene** is to _____.

Complete the Sentences Write the spelling word that completes each sentence.

6. Are you able to _____ this new software?
7. In some states, you get a nickel for every soda can you _____.
8. An umpire should not show _____ toward any team.
9. Symptoms help a doctor _____ diseases.
10. The publisher will _____ that book in paperback.
11. Jocelyn made her stage _____ last September.
12. Her sincerity lent _____ to her story.
13. You might find your notebook if you _____ your entire route.
14. The gladiator entered the _____.
15. Gas service is one example of a public _____.

Complete the Paragraph Write spelling words from the box to complete the paragraph.

I climbed __16.__ the train but did not see Aaron. Perhaps he was in his cabin. I tapped on the door and waited __17.__ for several minutes. I tapped again but got no __18.__. Without him, our carefully planned __19.__ could not begin. Besides, I needed him to __20.__ me for all the unexpected expenses!

| response |
| patiently |
| caper |
| reimburse |
| aboard |

Spelling and Writing

Proofread a Paragraph

Six words are not spelled correctly in this paragraph. Write the words correctly.

The pirates did not need the black, rolling clouds to remind them that it was the time of year for that vilent, sesonal storm, the tiphoon. The air was stifling; the sea was gray-green and still. Ignoring the clouds, the pirates dug paitently in the rocky soil of the island. They knew that the loot from their last successful caper had to be buried before the storm struck. One pirate wondered aloud if they would finish before the storm reached them, but he got no rasponse. All the pirates had seen such storms before. They knew the danger and the caos that would follow.

Proofreading Marks

≡ Make a capital.

/ Make a small letter.

∧ Add something.

℘ Take out something.

⊙ Add a period.

⌗ New paragraph

SP Spelling error

Write a Paragraph · Narrative Writing

Write the opening paragraph of an adventure story of your own imagining, in which one person is pitted against the forces of nature.

- Select a dangerous force of nature.
- Consider where it occurs and the kind of character who might be exposed to it.
- Invent a reason why the character might ignore the danger.
- Follow the form used in the proofreading sample. Use as many spelling words as you can.

Proofread Your Writing During ▶

Proofread your writing for spelling errors as part of the editing stage in the writing process. Be sure to check each word carefully. Use a dictionary to check spelling if you are not sure.

Writing Process

Prewriting
⇩
Drafting
⇩
Revising
⇩
Editing
⇩
Publishing

Vocabulary

Strategy Words

Review Words: Open Syllables

Write a word from the box to match each clue.

climate	deductible	microphone
reality		vehicle

1. A sled is a simple one; a rocket is a complicated one.
2. This is the opposite of **fantasy**.
3. When people do their income taxes, they usually like to find expenses that are this.
4. It includes temperature, precipitation, and wind conditions.
5. If you use this, you will be heard above the sounds of conversation and laughter.

Preview Words: Open Syllables

Write a word from the box to complete each sentence.

gratitude	juxtapose	omnipotent
vivaciously		warranty

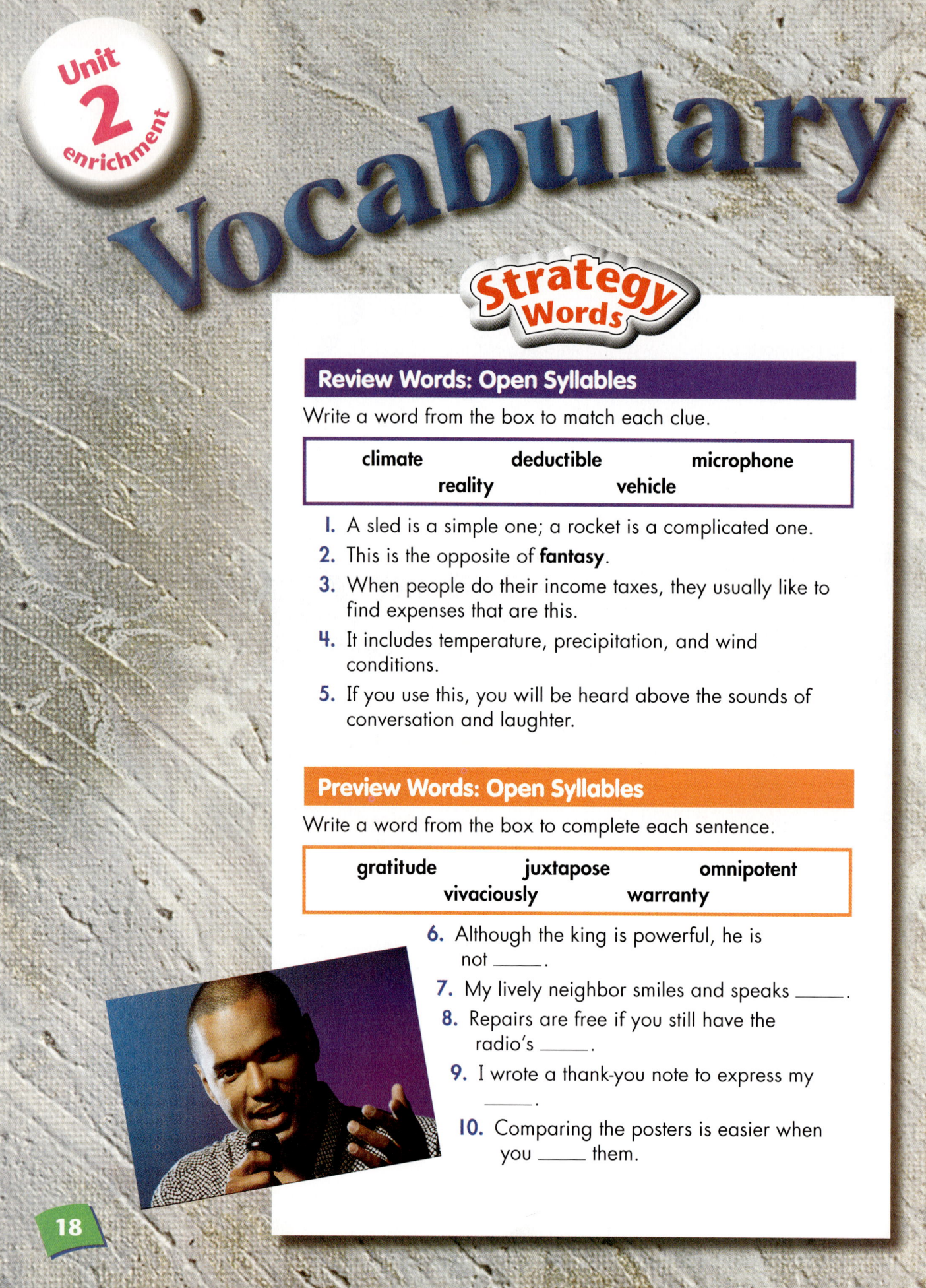

6. Although the king is powerful, he is not _____.
7. My lively neighbor smiles and speaks _____.
8. Repairs are free if you still have the radio's _____.
9. I wrote a thank-you note to express my _____.
10. Comparing the posters is easier when you _____ them.

Connections

Science: Physics

Write the word from the box that fits each meaning.

centrifugal	decelerate	friction
inertia	momentum	

1. the rubbing of one object or surface against another
2. the force of a physical object in motion
3. to slow down
4. moving away from a central point
5. the tendency of a resting body to stay at rest or a moving body to stay in motion

Language Arts: Literary Devices

Write words from the box to complete the paragraph.

allegory	foresight	illustration
proverb	virtue	

Before my long plane trip, I had the __6.__ to visit the library. I picked one book because I liked the colorful __7.__ on the cover. The first story was an __8.__, with each character representing either good or evil. The message was that people must have __9.__ to succeed. A well-known __10.__ states the same message: A good heart conquers bad luck.

Apply the Spelling Strategy

Circle the six content words you wrote that have open syllables.

Spelling and Thinking

READ THE SPELLING WORDS

1. feign	*feign*	Do not **feign** innocence for your mistake.
2. relieve	*relieve*	I will **relieve** you of that heavy box.
3. foreign	*foreign*	Can you speak a **foreign** language?
4. heir	*heir*	Who is the next **heir** to the throne?
5. retrieve	*retrieve*	We will try to **retrieve** the lost notebook.
6. sovereign	*sovereign*	Queen Mary was their **sovereign** ruler.
7. heirloom	*heirloom*	This antique clock is a family **heirloom**.
8. grieve	*grieve*	Don't **grieve** over the end of summer.
9. veil	*veil*	A black **veil** concealed her face.
10. reprieve	*reprieve*	I have a **reprieve** from homework tonight.
11. leisurely	*leisurely*	Visitors strolled **leisurely** along the beach.
12. beige	*beige*	His necktie was blue with **beige** stripes.
13. achievement	*achievement*	The rescue was a stunning **achievement**.
14. perceive	*perceive*	I **perceive** some changes in his appearance.
15. unwieldy	*unwieldy*	Help me move this **unwieldy** box.
16. forfeit	*forfeit*	We may be forced to **forfeit** the game.
17. counterfeit	*counterfeit*	Do not accept **counterfeit** dollar bills.
18. deceive	*deceive*	Will my disguise **deceive** anyone?
19. convenient	*convenient*	Call me when it is **convenient** for you.
20. weirdly	*weirdly*	The car spun **weirdly** out of control.

SORT THE SPELLING WORDS

1.–6. Write the words in which the letters **ie** spell the **long e** sound.

7. Write the word in which the **ie** spelling is in an unstressed syllable.

8.–9. Write the words in which the **ei** spelling pattern follows the letter **c**.

10.–12. Write the words in which the letters **ei** spell the **long a** sound.

13.–20. Write the other words that are exceptions to the **i** before **e** rule. Circle the **ei** vowel combination in the words you write.

REMEMBER THE SPELLING STRATEGY

Remember that the familiar **i** before **e** rule works for most words, but there are exceptions.

20

Word Meanings

Write a spelling word to match each definition.

1. to free from duty
2. self-governing
3. light tan color
4. treasured family possession
5. from another country
6. a delay of punishment
7. a face covering
8. something accomplished

Word Groups

Write the related spelling word that completes each group.

9. slowly, unhurriedly, not hastily, _____
10. regain, get back, fetch, _____
11. lose, give up, surrender, _____
12. fake, imitation, not genuine, _____
13. awkward, hard to handle, clumsy, _____
14. useful, suitable, helpful, _____
15. see, hear, sense, _____
16. mysteriously, strangely, oddly, _____

USING THE Thesaurus

A **thesaurus** provides synonyms and antonyms for words. When you use a thesaurus, be sure to choose a synonym that reflects the meaning you intend. Write a spelling word to replace each underlined word below. Check your answers in the **Writing Thesaurus**.

17. It is natural to <u>mourn</u> the loss of a pet.
18. Because he is an only child, he is the sole <u>beneficiary</u> of his father's estate.
19. Some animals <u>fake</u> death when they are in danger.
20. Don't let the color <u>mislead</u> you. These blue corn flakes are tasty.

feign	relieve	foreign	heir	retrieve
sovereign	heirloom	grieve	veil	reprieve
leisurely	beige	achievement	perceive	unwieldy
forfeit	counterfeit	deceive	convenient	weirdly

Complete the Sentences   Write the spelling word that best completes each sentence.

1. This vacation has been a welcome _____ from my troubles.
2. As the animal lover's only _____, she inherited several horses, dogs, and cats.
3. At what time will the next shift _____ us?
4. We wondered if the dog was sick, since she had been acting _____.
5. The salesperson tried to _____ us into thinking that the chair was a valuable antique.
6. The soccer player attempted to _____ injury in order to stall for time.
7. For nearly ten years, Texas was a _____ nation.
8. The police officer helped me _____ my lost wallet.

Solve the Analogies   Write a spelling word to complete each analogy.

9. **Difficult** is to **easy** as **inconvenient** is to _____.
10. **Capture** is to **seize** as **surrender** is to _____.
11. **Act** is to **action** as **achieve** is to _____.
12. **Laugh** is to **cry** as **rejoice** is to _____.
13. **True** is to **false** as **genuine** is to _____.
14. **Hand** is to **glove** as **face** is to _____.

Complete the Paragraph   Write spelling words from the box to complete the paragraph.

Elena sat on the floor of the dusty attic and __15.__ browsed through old photo albums. In one photo, she thought she could __16.__ a likeness between herself and her great-grandmother, who had come to the United States from a __17.__ country as a teenager. With some difficulty, Elena pulled an __18.__ trunk from under the eaves. Looking at the linens that had turned __19.__ with age, Elena hoped to find a family __20.__ by which to remember her great-grandmother.

> heirloom
> unwieldy
> beige
> perceive
> leisurely
> foreign

Spelling and Writing

Proofread a Book Summary

Six words are not spelled correctly in this book summary. Write the words correctly.

The Prince and the Pauper is a famous nineteenth-century novel by Mark Twain. Edward, hier to the English throne, and Tom, a young beggar, percieve that they are look-alikes. When the prince is mistakenly thrown out of the palace, Tom is forced to fayne the prince's identity. He is able to diceive the whole court, including his sovreign, Henry VIII. After many adventures, Edward is able to retrieve his throne and releive Tom of the responsibility of ruling.

Proofreading Marks

≡	Make a capital.
/	Make a small letter.
∧	Add something.
ℰ	Take out something.
⊙	Add a period.
⌗	New paragraph
SP	Spelling error

Write a Book Summary

Expository Writing

Choose a book that you know well. Write a summary.

- Be sure to spell the title of the book and the author's name correctly.
- Summarize the plot. Do not concentrate on small details. Try to capture the big picture.
- Follow the form used in the proofreading sample. Use as many spelling words as you can.

Writing Process

Prewriting
⇩
Drafting
⇩
Revising
⇩
Editing
⇩
Publishing

Proofread Your Writing During

Proofread your writing for spelling errors as part of the editing stage in the writing process. Be sure to check each word carefully. Use a dictionary to check spelling if you are not sure.

23

Vocabulary

Strategy Words

Review Words: ie, ei

Write the word from the box that matches each clue.

ceiling	fierce	receipt
shield	sleigh	

1. This word could describe the strong winds of a hurricane.
2. To return a purchase, you probably will need this.
3. Sunglasses do this for your eyes.
4. This is the surface opposite the floor.
5. A horse might pull this.

Preview Words: ie, ei

Write a word from the box to complete each sentence.

deficient	recipient	resilient
variegation	zombie	

6. My doctor told me that my diet is _____ in vitamins.
7. He is so _____ that his troubles never seem to get him down.
8. Notice the _____ in the coloring of the leaves on this plant.
9. You are the lucky _____ of first prize in the apple-picking contest.
10. The _____ in the movie scared my little brother.

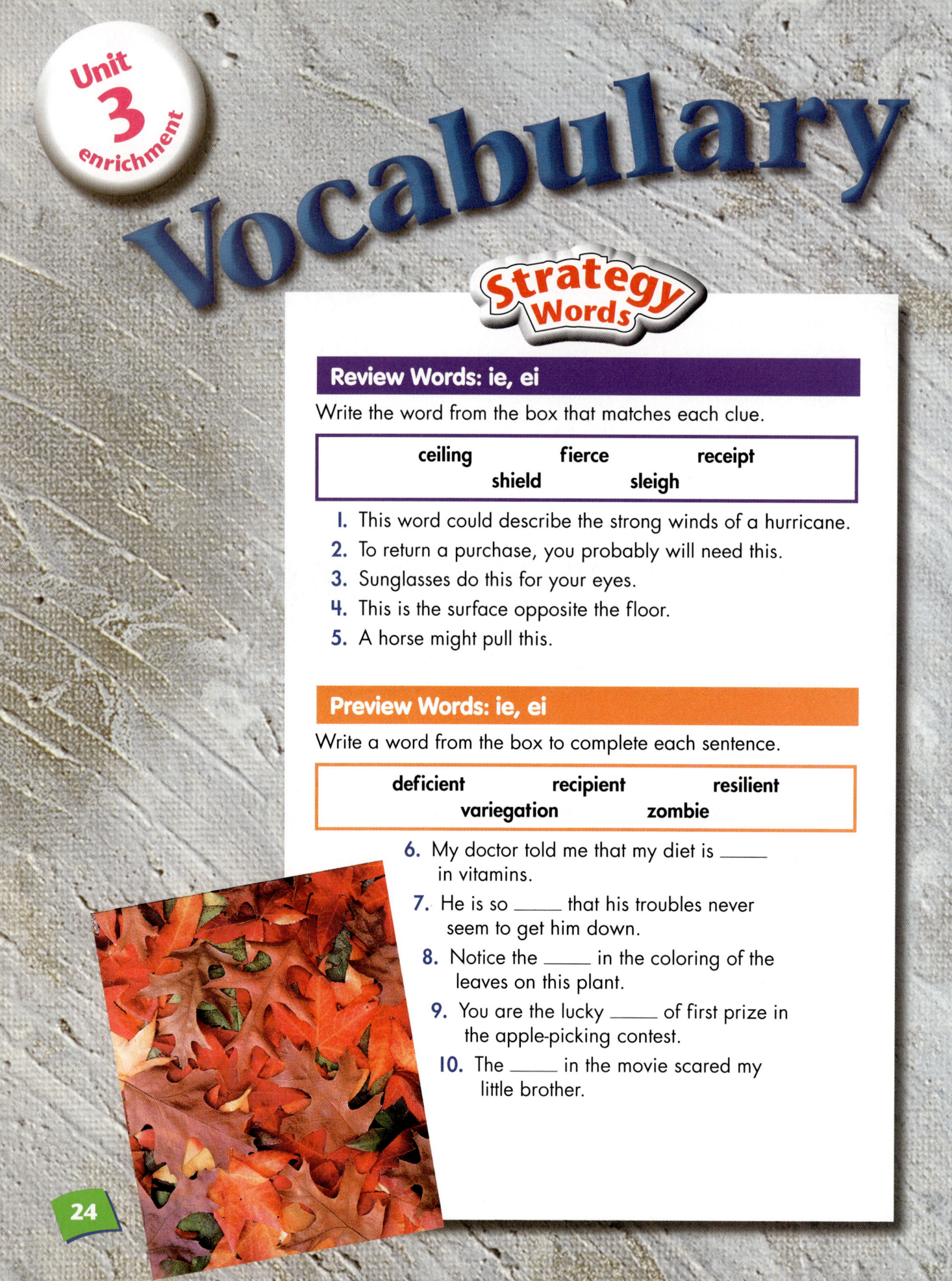

Connections

Social Studies: Archaeology

Write words from the box to complete the paragraph.

archaeologist	battlefield	excavation
fortified	traditional	

Ever since Homer's epic poem *The Iliad*, people have wondered whether the __1.__ story of the fall of the city of Troy to Greece was based on a real battle. In 1871, __2.__ Heinrich Schliemann began an __3.__ at a location in northwestern Turkey, in the hope of finding the site of the Trojan War. Although he did not find a huge __4.__, he did unearth several layers of a __5.__ city that may have been the site of Troy.

Social Studies: The Medieval Period

Write words from the box to complete the paragraph.

cathedral	crusade	medieval	pilgrimage	shrine

In the Middle Ages, travel was difficult and dangerous. A knight who fought in a holy war, or __6.__, could be away for years. The longest journey an ordinary person could make was a __7.__ to visit a religious __8.__. Many such trips ended at a __9.__, a large church in the center of a busy __10.__ city.

Apply the Spelling Strategy

Circle the **ie** spelling pattern in three of the content words you wrote.

Spelling and Thinking

READ THE SPELLING WORDS

1.	old-fashioned	*old-fashioned*	Her hat is **old-fashioned**.
2.	full-length	*full-length*	Buy a **full-length** mirror.
3.	problem-solving	*problem-solving*	Use **problem-solving** notes.
4.	out-of-date	*out-of-date*	It is an **out-of-date** style.
5.	best-selling	*best-selling*	Buy this **best-selling** book.
6.	well-informed	*well-informed*	Is she **well-informed**?
7.	up-and-coming	*up-and-coming*	He's an **up-and-coming** boy.
8.	long-distance	*long-distance*	Make a **long-distance** call.
9.	peace-loving	*peace-loving*	He's a **peace-loving** man.
10.	much-improved	*much-improved*	It's a **much-improved** box.
11.	play-by-play	*play-by-play*	Give **play-by-play** scores.
12.	world-famous	*world-famous*	It's a **world-famous** play.
13.	part-time	*part-time*	We want **part-time** work.
14.	far-reaching	*far-reaching*	I see **far-reaching** effects.
15.	matter-of-fact	*matter-of-fact*	Use a **matter-of-fact** tone.
16.	player-manager	*player-manager*	Is Pat a **player-manager**?
17.	decision-making	*decision-making*	Ask a **decision-making** body.
18.	up-to-the-minute	*up-to-the-minute*	Stay **up-to-the-minute**.
19.	thirst-quenching	*thirst-quenching*	Buy **thirst-quenching** milk.
20.	secretary-treasurer	*secretary-treasurer*	He is **secretary-treasurer**.

SORT THE SPELLING WORDS

1.–15. Write the compound words that are made up of two words.

16.–19. Write the compound words that are made up of three words.

20. Write the spelling word that is made up of four words.

REMEMBER THE SPELLING STRATEGY

Remember that compound words are made by joining two or more words. Some compound words are separated by a hyphen.

Word Meanings

Write the spelling word that best completes each phrase.

1. a _____ nation
2. a _____ phone call
3. a _____ drink
4. a widespread, _____ effect
5. a knowledgeable, _____ voter
6. an emotion-free, _____ attitude
7. a brainstorming, _____ approach

Word Replacements

Write a spelling word to replace each underlined word or phrase.

8.–10. In his first novel, *Pennant Fever,* Lefty Sanchez, the <u>universally known</u> <u>outfielder-coach</u> of the Beagles, pokes gentle fun at <u>out-of-date</u> ways of managing.

11. Sanchez uses a <u>sports commentary</u> style to make his points.

12. In real life, Sanchez credits his computer for the recent success of the <u>upgraded</u> Beagles.

13.–14. Loaded with <u>the most recent</u> information on each opposing player, Sanchez's trusty computer takes much of the guesswork out of the <u>verdict-passing</u> process.

15. Well on his way to becoming a <u>very successful</u> author, Sanchez still doesn't consider himself a writer.

16. "I'm strictly a <u>some-of-the-time</u> scribbler," he modestly insists.

17. However, fans know that soon Sanchez will need a <u>person to keep records and handle finances</u> for his fast-growing fan club.

USING THE Dictionary

Write the following spelling words. Then write the abbreviated part-of-speech label next to each one. Use the **Spelling Dictionary**.

18. out-of-date
19. full-length
20. up-and-coming

Spelling and Reading

Answer the Questions   Write the spelling word that best answers each question.

1. What kind of skill does a good detective need?
2. What would you call a coupon that expired last month?
3. What kind of description does a football fan like best?
4. What skills does an indecisive person lack?
5. How would you describe poor singing that gets a lot better?
6. Who can handle your club's financial records?
7. What would you call a reaction that is not emotional?
8. What would you call a book that is complete and not abridged?

Solve the Analogies   Write a spelling word to complete each analogy.

9. **Documentary** is to **award-winning** as **book** is to _____.
10. **Always** is to **sometimes** as **full-time** is to _____.
11. **Closed** is to **open** as **limited** is to _____.
12. **Food** is to **hunger-satisfying** as **water** is to _____.
13. **Violent** is to **nonviolent** as **war-loving** is to _____.
14. **Clumsy** is to **coordinated** as **ignorant** is to _____.
15. **Clinic** is to **doctor-owner** as **baseball** is to _____.

Complete the Paragraph   Write spelling words from the box to complete the paragraph.

In the early 1980s, Joan Benoit, not yet famous, was considered one of the __16.__ women in the world of sports. Then she ran a marathon and set a new world record for __17.__ running. Although Benoit is now a __18.__ athlete, she lives simply on an __19.__ farm in Maine. She trains for marathons and follows __20.__ trends in the sport.

Spelling and Writing

Proofread a Paragraph

Six words are not spelled correctly in this paragraph. Write the words correctly.

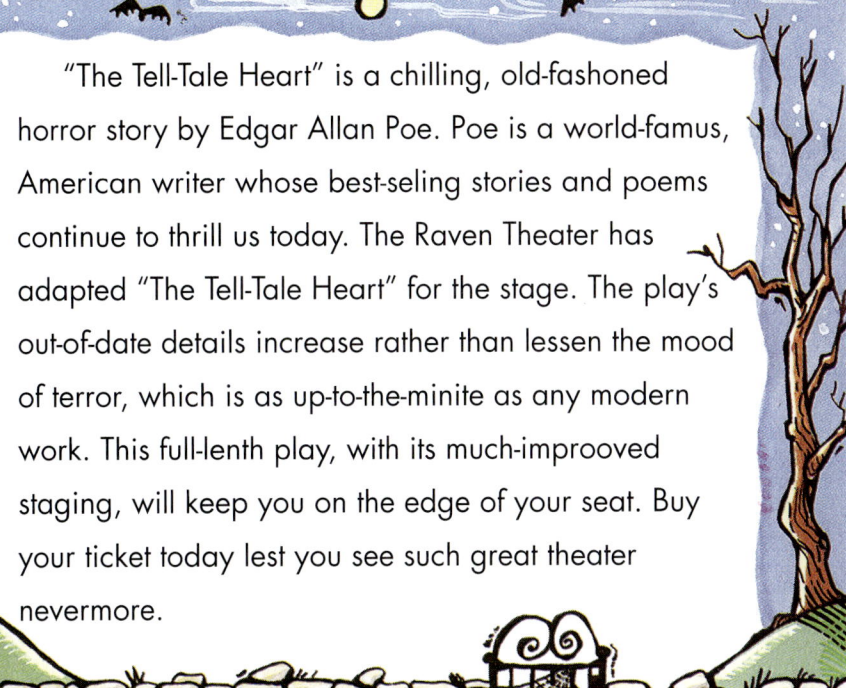

"The Tell-Tale Heart" is a chilling, old-fashoned horror story by Edgar Allan Poe. Poe is a world-famus, American writer whose best-seling stories and poems continue to thrill us today. The Raven Theater has adapted "The Tell-Tale Heart" for the stage. The play's out-of-date details increase rather than lessen the mood of terror, which is as up-to-the-minite as any modern work. This full-lenth play, with its much-improoved staging, will keep you on the edge of your seat. Buy your ticket today lest you see such great theater nevermore.

Write a Paragraph

Persuasive Writing

Write about a favorite play, book, movie, or television program. Be sure to tell exactly what you like and why.

- Give some background about the work or the author.
- Give specific details about what you liked or disliked.
- Encourage your readers to become familiar with the work.
- Follow the form used in the proofreading sample. Use as many spelling words as you can.

Proofread Your Writing During ➤

Writing Process

Prewriting
⇩
Drafting
⇩
Revising
⇩
Editing
⇩
Publishing

Proofread your writing for spelling errors as part of the editing stage in the writing process. Be sure to check each word carefully. Use a dictionary to check spelling if you are not sure.

Vocabulary

Strategy Words

Review Words: Compound Words

Write a word from the box to complete each sentence.

brother-in-law	far-fetched	quick-witted
self-esteem	well-known	

1. A _____ person could solve those riddles easily.
2. We are pleased to have such a _____ singer perform in our town.
3. I find it hard to believe such a _____ tale.
4. My sister's husband is my _____.
5. People benefit from being kind to themselves and having high _____.

Preview Words: Compound Words

Write a word from the box that matches each description.

blue-eyed	eye-opener	good-natured
hair-raising	hand-me-down	

6. a story that gives readers the shivers
7. a person who has a cheerful, easygoing personality
8. an icy glass of juice in the morning
9. what many Siamese cats are
10. your sweater that was once owned by your brother

Connections

Language Arts: Literary Devices

Write words from the box to complete the paragraph.

coincidence	foreshadow	flashback	repetition	reveal

Look for clues as you read. In mysteries, you can find clues that predict, or __1.__, events. In novels, look for a __2.__, or a return to a prior event, to __3.__ why someone acts in a certain way. The __4.__ of details is rarely a __5.__; the author may repeat specific details to make a particular point.

Science: Electricity

Write a word from the box that matches each definition.

electrical	generator	hydroelectric
turbine	transformer	

6. a machine that converts mechanical energy into electrical energy
7. a device used to transfer electrical energy from circuit to circuit
8. generating electricity by conversion of the energy of running water
9. of or pertaining to electricity
10. machine in which the energy of a moving fluid is converted to mechanical power

Apply the Spelling Strategy

Circle the content word you wrote that is a compound word. (Not all compound words are hyphenated.)

Spelling AND Thinking

READ THE SPELLING WORDS

1.	brilliant	*brilliant*	The flutist gave a **brilliant** performance.
2.	criticism	*criticism*	The art teacher offered helpful **criticism**.
3.	portrait	*portrait*	The **portrait** hung over the mantel.
4.	symbolic	*symbolic*	The dove is **symbolic** of peace.
5.	prelude	*prelude*	A **prelude** sets the key of a piece of music.
6.	texture	*texture*	Feel the silky **texture** of this fabric.
7.	impressive	*impressive*	The art exhibit is very **impressive**.
8.	interlude	*interlude*	The drama continued after the **interlude**.
9.	suite	*suite*	Listen to this **suite** of lively minuets.
10.	expressive	*expressive*	Her **expressive** paintings reveal her joy.
11.	sonata	*sonata*	Mozart wrote that superb piano **sonata**.
12.	operetta	*operetta*	Audiences enjoy this humorous **operetta**.
13.	romantic	*romantic*	He read a **romantic** poem at the wedding.
14.	romanticism	*romanticism*	His stories are filled with **romanticism**.
15.	repertoire	*repertoire*	Does your **repertoire** include early music?
16.	mythical	*mythical*	The unicorn is a **mythical** animal.
17.	ensemble	*ensemble*	A string **ensemble** played on the lawn.
18.	opus	*opus*	This is the fourth song in his **opus**.
19.	overture	*overture*	The opera began with a lovely **overture**.
20.	melodic	*melodic*	His music has a sweet, **melodic** quality.

SORT THE SPELLING WORDS

1.–7. Write the spelling words that are adjectives. Circle the adjective suffix **-al, -ant, -ic,** or **-ive.**

8.–20. Write the spelling words that are nouns. If the word ends in the noun suffix **-ism** or **-ure,** circle the suffix.

REMEMBER THE SPELLING STRATEGY

Remember that the English language includes many words that relate to the arts.

Word Meanings

Write the spelling words that match these definitions.

1. music played between parts of a long composition
2. a painting of a person, especially one showing the face
3. an instrumental composition having a succession of dances in the same or a related key
4. a group of supporting actors or musicians who perform together
5. a creative work, especially a musical composition or opera
6. the group of works that a player or company performs
7. the spirit and attitudes characteristic of romantic thought
8. a review expressing judgment or evaluation

Word Structure

Change each noun or verb into a spelling word that is an adjective. Write the spelling words.

9. symbol (*n.*)
10. myth (*n.*)
11. romance (*n.*)
12. express (*v.*)
13. melody (*n.*)
14. impress (*v.*)

USING THE Dictionary

The origin of a word, or its **etymology,** is often provided as part of a dictionary entry. The symbol < means "derived from." The etymologies below appear in the **Spelling Dictionary**. Write the spelling word that matches each etymology. Check your answers in the **Spelling Dictionary** if you are not sure.

15. Lat. **textura** < **textum,** that which is woven < **tegere,** to weave.
16. Ital., dim. of **opera,** opera < Lat., work produced < **opus,** work.
17. Ital. < fem. p.part. of **sonare,** to sound < Lat. **sonare.**
18. OFr. < Med. Lat. **praeludium** < Lat. **praeludere,** to play beforehand: **prae-,** before + **ludere,** to play < **ludus,** game.
19. ME < OFr. < Lat. **apertura,** opening < **aperire,** to open.
20. Fr. **brillant,** pr.part. of **briller,** to shine < Ital. **brillare,** perh. < **brillo,** beryl < Lat. **beryllus.**

brilliant	criticism	portrait	symbolic	prelude
texture	impressive	interlude	suite	expressive
sonata	operetta	romantic	romanticism	repertoire
mythical	ensemble	opus	overture	melodic

Solve the Analogies   Write the spelling word that best completes each analogy.

1. **Smell** is to **fragrance** as **touch** is to _____.
2. **Athlete** is to **athletic** as **melody** is to _____.
3. **Write** is to **novel** as **paint** is to _____.
4. **After** is to **conclusion** as **between** is to _____.
5. **Serious** is to **light** as **opera** is to _____.
6. **Create** is to **creative** as **express** is to _____.
7. **Impair** is to **repair** as **delude** is to _____.

Complete the Sentences   Write the spelling word that best completes each sentence.

8. The Greeks invented _____ tales to explain natural events.
9. You will enjoy the fanciful _____ of this adventure story.
10. An oak tree is _____ of strength.
11. The author's latest _____ is her finest book to date.
12. The orchestra played an _____ at the beginning of the opera.
13. People often send flowers as a _____ gesture of love.
14. The composer arranged several of her waltzes into a dance _____.

Complete the Paragraph   Write spelling words from the box to complete the paragraph.

Classical music lovers were treated recently to a
__15.__ concert by the legendary violinist Ilya Lakariakov.
His performance began with an __16.__ interpretation of a
Beethoven __17.__. This talented violinist has a vast __18.__
and performs as part of a string __19.__. The only __20.__ the
audience had of Mr. Lakariakov was that his performance
was not long enough. Although he played three encores,
the audience wanted more!

| repertoire |
| brilliant |
| sonata |
| ensemble |
| criticism |
| impressive |

Spelling and Writing

Proofread a Review

Six words are not spelled correctly in this music review. Write the words correctly.

I thoroughly enjoyed last night's immpressive recital by Anita Ruiz, a young pianist from Arizona. Although she has a varied reportoire, Ruiz is known to prefer music of the romantic period. Her brilliant interpretation of a Bach pralude, however, proved that she is also skilled at playing the music of earlier composers. My main critisism when Ruiz made her debut last year was that her music was stiff. Last night changed my opinion. Ruiz was so exppressive that her music cascaded with warmth and feeling.

Proofreading Marks

≡	Make a capital.
/	Make a small letter.
∧	Add something.
ℰ	Take out something.
⊙	Add a period.
#	New paragraph
SP	Spelling error

Write a Review

Expository Writing

An arts review reports on or evaluates a cultural event. Write a short review of an artistic production, such as a concert, play, movie, or piece of music.

- State your opinion and back it up with logical details.
- Remember that criticism can be both positive and negative.
- Follow the form used in the proofreading sample. Use as many spelling words as you can.

Writing Process

Prewriting
⇩
Drafting
⇩
Revising
⇩
Editing
⇩
Publishing

Proofread Your Writing During ➡

Proofread your writing for spelling errors as part of the editing stage in the writing process. Be sure to check each word carefully. Use a dictionary to check spelling if you are not sure.

Vocabulary

Strategy Words

Review Words: Fine Arts Words

Write words from the box to complete the paragraph.

applaud	artistic	rhapsody
symphonic		versatile

Ota Richter has a tremendous range of __1.__ expression. In fact, this pianist is so __2.__ that he can produce magnificent music either alone or with the accompaniment of a __3.__ orchestra. Whether he is playing a passionate Hungarian __4.__ or a playful piece of jazz, his performance always gives an audience reason to __5.__ enthusiastically.

Preview Words: Fine Arts Words

Write a word from the box to complete each sentence.

impresario	improvise	nocturne
reprise		romanticize

6. Some novels _____ love by ignoring the work required to establish and maintain a good relationship.

7. Rather than rely on written music, the jazz trumpeter Louis Armstrong tended to _____.

8. A _____ may be an exact repeat of the original music, or it may be a variation.

9. We were lulled to sleep by the dreamy Chopin _____.

10. Because of the illness of the lead soprano, the _____ has decided to cancel tonight's opera performance.

Connections

Content Words

Fine Arts: Music

Write a word from the box to replace the words in parentheses.

concerto	dedication	interpretation	soloist	virtuoso

Midori is a Japanese-born violin __1.__ (expert). Because of her __2.__ (devotion) to her art and what one major music critic calls her "truly astonishing technique," Midori enjoys a flourishing career as a __3.__ (solitary performer). At New England's Tanglewood Festival in 1986, her __4.__ (version) of *Serenade*, Leonard Bernstein's __5.__ (composition for an orchestra and solo instrument), brought down the house. Midori was only fourteen years old at the time.

Language Arts: Theater

Write the word from the box that best matches each definition.

dialogue	epilogue	monologue	prologue	soliloquy

6. the introduction to a play
7. a long speech or a series of stories delivered by one person
8. a short piece after a play's end, sometimes spoken directly to an audience
9. a conversational passage in a play or narrative
10. a speech given by an actor to himself or herself when alone on stage

Apply the Spelling Strategy

Circle the five content words you wrote whose etymology includes the Greek word **logos**, meaning "word" or "speech."

Assessment and Review

Assessment Units 1–5

Each Assessment Word in the box fits one of the spelling strategies you have studied over the past five weeks. Read the spelling strategies. Then write each Assessment Word under the unit number it fits.

Unit 1

1.–6. Remember that words are made up of syllable patterns. Find the pattern and spell the word by parts.

Unit 2

7.–10. Remember that an open syllable ends with a vowel sound. Note the spelling of the vowel sound.

Unit 3

11.–15. Remember that the familiar **i before e** rule works for most words, but there are exceptions.

Unit 4

16.–20. Remember that compound words are made by joining two or more words. Some compound words are separated by a hyphen.

Unit 5

Remember that the English language includes many words that relate to the arts.

lieu
tragic
well-groomed
bacon
sleight
hyena
convenience
figure
violence
full-scale
barren
underweight
washed-out
radar
chieftain
upside-down
tender
cross-examine
allergy
convey

Review

Unit 1: Closed and Open Syllables

target	dismal	investigate	entirely	escape
shortage	emphasis	victim	eccentric	budget

Write the spelling word that is a synonym for the underlined word or words in each sentence.

1. The accident was <u>totally</u> my fault.
2. Unique people often have <u>peculiar</u> lifestyles.
3. A surgeon must <u>pinpoint</u> the exact spot for an incision.
4. It may be impossible to <u>flee</u> from an angry bear.
5. The <u>injured person</u> had not been wearing a seat belt.
6. The sunlight is welcome after five <u>dreary</u> days.
7. Please <u>look into</u> the cause of the fire.
8. There may be a <u>deficiency</u> in the number of goods.
9. Use an <u>account of expenses</u> to plan the money you can spend or save.
10. The president stated his views with <u>forcefulness</u>.

Review

Unit 2: Open Syllables

utilize	arena	response	aboard	patiently
bias	chaos	reimburse	violent	seasonal

Write the spelling word that fits each set.

11. stadium, concert hall, auditorium
12. calmly, gently, kindly
13. answer, comeback, reply
14. troublesome, turbulent, disorderly
15. repay, compensate, settle up
16. timely, suitable, appropriate
17. use, employ, apply
18. disorder, jumble, disarray
19. slant, inclination, leaning
20. on, upon, within

Review   Unit 3: ie, ei

relieve	foreign	heir	sovereign	leisurely
achievement	perceive	forfeit	counterfeit	convenient

Write the spelling word that fits the description.

1. a noun that follows the "i before e" rule
2.–3. two verbs that follow the "i before e" rule
4. an adjective that follows the "i before e" rule
5. a verb or noun that has two syllables and doesn't follow the rule
6.–7. two words that have the same ending, a silent **g,** and don't follow the rule
8. a verb or adjective that has three syllables and doesn't follow the rule
9. a noun that has one syllable and doesn't follow the rule
10. an adjective or adverb that has three syllables and doesn't follow the rule

Review   Unit 4: Compound Words

old-fashioned	full-length	problem-solving	best-selling
long-distance	part-time	far-reaching	matter-of-fact
decision-making		secretary-treasurer	

Write the spelling word that means the opposite of these words.

11. modern
12. local
13. shortened
14. emotionally charged
15. insignificant

Write the spelling word for each of these clues.

16. often used to describe popular books or CDs
17. working ten hours a week
18. two jobs in one
19. something you do a lot in math class
20. deciding

 **Unit 5: Fine Arts Words**

brilliant	criticism	portrait	symbolic	texture
impressive	expressive	romantic	repertoire	ensemble

Complete the sentence by writing a spelling word. The word you write will add a suffix to the underlined word.

1. The <u>critic</u> reviewed the new play. Her _____ is sure to affect ticket sales.

2. Shannon wanted to <u>impress</u> her teacher, so she tried to do an _____ job on the first assignment.

3. I think the road in Frost's poem is a <u>symbol</u> of something, but I am not sure of its _____ meaning.

4. The actor was able to <u>express</u> the playwright's purpose. The final monologue contains some of the most _____ words I have ever heard on stage.

Write a spelling word that begins or ends with the same letters as the underlined part of the words below.

5. sympathe<u>tic</u>

6. <u>rep</u>etition

7. ass<u>emble</u>

8. mix<u>ture</u>

9. expect<u>ant</u>

10. <u>por</u>tray

 **Spelling Study Strategy**

Sorting by Number of Syllables

Sorting words is a good way to help you practice your spelling words. Here is a way to sort the spelling words with a partner.

1. Make four columns on a sheet of paper and label the top of each from **1 syllable** to **4 syllables**. Write a sample spelling word in each column, such as **heir** (1 syllable), **tragic** (2 syllables), **emphasis** (3 syllables), or **investigate** (4 syllables).

2. Take turns choosing words from the spelling list. Say the word aloud and then write it in the appropriate column.

3. If your partner agrees with your choice, it is then your partner's turn. Continue until all words have been sorted by number of syllables.

Grammar, Usage, and Mechanics

Prepositions and Objects of Prepositions

A **preposition** relates a word in a sentence to a noun or pronoun that follows it. This noun or pronoun is called the **object of the preposition**. The preposition, its object, and the words in between make a **prepositional phrase**.

Lakendra ran twice <u>around</u> the <u>track</u>.

preposition   object of the preposition

A. Write the preposition in each sentence.

1. My assignment had fallen between the desks.
2. The freed balloons lifted quickly over my head.
3. The puppies in the cages looked mournful.
4. We peered around the tree.
5. The scouts hiked quietly through the woods.
6. The actress co-starred with her husband.
7. Driving into a long tunnel can be frightening.

B. Complete the sentences by adding an object of the preposition. Try to use spelling words you reviewed.

8. Only two of Katelyn's arrows hit near the _____.
9. The EMT placed a blanket around the _____ of the accident to keep him warm.
10. The rodeo horses pranced into the _____.
11. Will and Tiara walked away from the _____ of the angry mob.
12. The reading of the will continued without the _____.
13. Sit near the _____ to hear the club minutes read.
14. Grandfather placed a light above his wife's _____.
15. The violinist was invited to play with a string _____.

WORKSHOP

Proofreading Strategy

Box It Up

Good writers always proofread their writing for spelling errors. Here is a strategy you can use to proofread your papers.

Cut a small hole or box in a piece of paper. Slide it over your work so that one or two words appear inside the box. You won't be able to see a whole sentence at one time. Instead of reading **Pecos Bill and Paul Bunyan are both characters in American tall tales,** you might see **Bill and Paul** or **in American tall**.

This may sound like a strange thing to do, but this strategy helps you focus on spelling, not meaning. Try it!

Electronic Spelling

Search Engines

Search engines are wonderful tools. They help you find information on the Internet, in encyclopedias, and in many programs. To use them, you simply type a word or phrase. However, you have to be sure you type this word or phrase correctly. There is a big difference between **border** and **boarder**. A search engine can't guess what you are looking for. If you are unsure of a word's spelling, look it up.

Look at these frequently misspelled words that are often used in searches. Which are misspelled here? Write them correctly. Write **OK** if a name is correct.

1. budjet
2. forin
3. medical
4. presidencial
5. catelog
6. international

Spelling and Thinking

READ THE SPELLING WORDS

1. bookkeeping	*bookkeeping*	Who does the company's **bookkeeping**?
2. appropriate	*appropriate*	Wear **appropriate** shoes with your suit.
3. acceptance	*acceptance*	Everyone liked Ira's **acceptance** speech.
4. disappearance	*disappearance*	The cat's **disappearance** was temporary.
5. essential	*essential*	Protein is **essential** to a good diet.
6. accuracy	*accuracy*	Check your answers for **accuracy**.
7. assistance	*assistance*	Thanks for your offer of **assistance**.
8. accelerate	*accelerate*	The rocket began to **accelerate**.
9. recommend	*recommend*	I can **recommend** someone for that job.
10. occasional	*occasional*	I enjoy an **occasional** slice of pizza.
11. occasionally	*occasionally*	Teachers **occasionally** show films.
12. dilemma	*dilemma*	How would you solve such a **dilemma**?
13. withholding	*withholding*	Is anyone **withholding** information?
14. accommodate	*accommodate*	This boat can **accommodate** six people.
15. vaccinate	*vaccinate*	A veterinarian will **vaccinate** our dog.
16. necessity	*necessity*	A computer is a **necessity** in this class.
17. successor	*successor*	Who will be my **successor** next year?
18. disapprove	*disapprove*	My parents **disapprove** of that movie.
19. accumulate	*accumulate*	How did I **accumulate** so many pens?
20. questionnaire	*questionnaire*	Fill in the **questionnaire** anonymously.

SORT THE SPELLING WORDS

1.–3. Write the words that have two sets of double consonants. Circle the double consonants.

4.–13. Write the words that have a single set of double consonants and three syllables. Circle the double consonants.

14.–20. Write the words that have a single set of double consonants and four syllables. Circle the double consonants.

REMEMBER THE SPELLING STRATEGY

Remember that a consonant sound may be spelled with two consonant letters.

Word Meanings

Write the spelling word that matches each definition.

1. the act of vanishing
2. infrequent
3. infrequently
4. to praise another as being worthy
5. the practice of recording a business's accounts
6. a printed form containing a set of questions
7. a requirement

Word Structure

When a prefix has been absorbed into a word root or a base word, a double consonant can result. For example, the word **accumulate** comes from the Latin prefix **ad-,** meaning "to," and the Latin noun **cumulus,** meaning "heap." Since **adc-** is hard to pronounce, the **d** was changed to **c** to make pronunciation easier.

8.–12. Write the spelling words in which the prefix **ad-** was absorbed into the word and changed to **ac-**.

13. Write the spelling word in which the prefix **ad-** was absorbed into the word and changed to **ap-**.

14. Write the spelling word in which the prefix **ad-** was absorbed into the word and changed to **as-**.

USING THE Dictionary

To determine whether a double consonant stands for one or two units of sound, check the phonetic spelling of the word in the **Spelling Dictionary**. For example, the phonetic spelling of **accept** /ăk sĕpt′/ tells you that the first **c** is pronounced as **k** and the second **c** as **s**. Write the spelling words that correspond to the following phonetic spellings. Circle the double consonants that represent two different units of sound.

15. /dĭs′ə prōōv′/

16. /dĭ lĕm′ ə/

17. /wĭth hōld′ ĭng/

18. /sək sĕs′ ər/

19. /ĭ sĕn′ shəl/

20. /văk′ sə nāt′/

vaccinate	accuracy	occasional	recommend	bookkeeping
necessity	successor	disapprove	appropriate	questionnaire
dilemma	assistance	acceptance	occasionally	accommodate
essential	accelerate	accumulate	withholding	disappearance

Replace the Words   Write a spelling word that is a synonym for each underlined word or phrase.

1. Doctors <u>inoculate</u> children against diphtheria and typhoid.

2. They also <u>urge</u> that children get a booster shot after a few years.

3. Scientists continue to work toward the <u>elimination</u> of childhood disease.

4. However, epidemics still occur <u>from time to time</u>.

5. Vaccination is often a <u>requirement</u> for tourists.

6. Before taking a physical exam, patients usually complete a <u>form</u> that asks about their previous medical history.

7. It is important that the questions be answered with <u>truth</u>.

8. It is <u>crucial</u> for the doctor to know the patient's medical history.

9. World hunger is a <u>problem</u> our society should resolve.

10. Social agencies can <u>provide services for</u> people who require medical help.

11. Medical record-keeping and <u>recording finances</u> systems are crucial.

Solve the Analogies   Write a spelling word to complete each analogy.

12. **Comply** is to **compliance** as **assist** is to _____.

13. **Precede** is to **follow** as **predecessor** is to _____.

14. **Unsuitable** is to **suitable** as **inappropriate** is to _____.

15. **Often** is to **seldom** as **frequent** is to _____.

16. **Fall** is to **rise** as **slow down** is to _____.

17. **Agree** is to **disagree** as **approve** is to _____.

18. **Reject** is to **rejection** as **accept** is to _____.

19. **Find** is to **discover** as **collect** is to _____.

20. **Generosity** is to **sharing** as **stinginess** is to _____.

Spelling and Writing

Proofread a Paragraph

Six words are not spelled correctly in this paragraph. Write the words correctly.

You probably know about Louis Pasteur because of pasteurization, the process he invented to make milk safe to drink. However, this French chemist also developed vaccines, including the one for rabies. By 1884, he had developed a way to vaxcinate dogs against rabies, but in 1885 a nine-year-old boy who had been bitten by a rabid dog was brought to him. Pasteur was in a dilema. He had not had time to acumulate the data he needed about using the vaccine on humans, but help for the boy Joseph was essential. Giving the vaccine would be risky, but witholding it might be fatal. The necessity for treatment won out; Joseph lived; the disapearance of rabies as a dreaded human disease was under way.

Proofreading Marks

☰	Make a capital.
/	Make a small letter.
∧	Add something.
ℒ	Take out something.
⊙	Add a period.
⌗	New paragraph
ⓢⓟ	Spelling error

Write a Paragraph

Narrative Writing

Write a paragraph about someone you know or know of who has contributed to the well-being of others in either a small or a large way.

- Select a person whom you admire.
- Do research to learn more about the person.
- Focus on one or two accomplishments in the person's life.
- Follow the form used in the proofreading sample. Use as many spelling words as you can.

Proofread Your Writing During

Proofread your writing for spelling errors as part of the editing stage in the writing process. Be sure to check each word carefully. Use a dictionary to check spelling if you are not sure.

Writing Process

Prewriting
⇩
Drafting
⇩
Revising
⇩
Editing
⇩
Publishing

Vocabulary

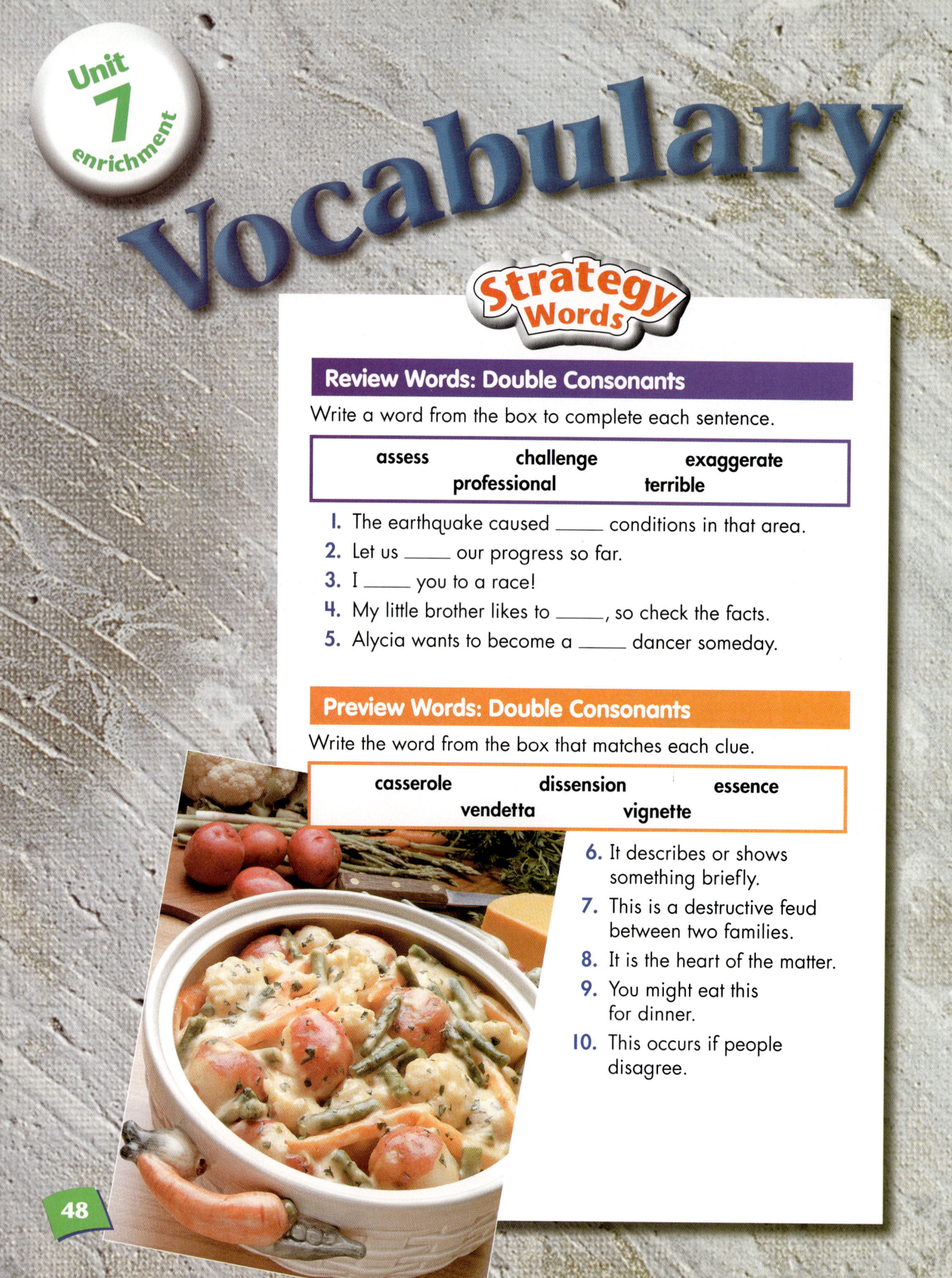

Strategy Words

Review Words: Double Consonants

Write a word from the box to complete each sentence.

assess	challenge	exaggerate
professional		terrible

1. The earthquake caused _____ conditions in that area.
2. Let us _____ our progress so far.
3. I _____ you to a race!
4. My little brother likes to _____, so check the facts.
5. Alycia wants to become a _____ dancer someday.

Preview Words: Double Consonants

Write the word from the box that matches each clue.

casserole	dissension	essence
vendetta		vignette

6. It describes or shows something briefly.
7. This is a destructive feud between two families.
8. It is the heart of the matter.
9. You might eat this for dinner.
10. This occurs if people disagree.

Connections

Social Studies: Royalty

Write a word from the box to match each definition.

> abdicate   lineage   majesty
>
> royalty   succession

1. the sequence in which people succeed to a throne
2. a person of royal rank
3. to formally give up power
4. the greatness and dignity of a ruler
5. direct descent from a particular person

Language Arts: Poetry

Write the word from the box that matches each clue.

> alliteration   allusion   assonance
>
> imagery   symbolism

6. vivid language that paints mental pictures
7. a red rose that stands for abiding love
8. l**a**te, f**a**ke, scr**a**pe, for example
9. a casual reference to a literary or historical figure or event
10. "The **h**all of **H**eorot rang **l**oud and **l**ong," for example (from *Beowulf*)

Apply the Spelling Strategy

Circle all of the double consonants in four of the content words you wrote.

Spelling and Thinking

READ THE SPELLING WORDS

1.	circuit	*circuit*	Do not touch a broken **circuit**.
2.	perforate	*perforate*	Use a nail to **perforate** the can.
3.	transform	*transform*	Wallpaper will **transform** the room.
4.	perplex	*perplex*	His complicated ideas **perplex** me.
5.	circulation	*circulation*	The fan provides good **circulation**.
6.	transparent	*transparent*	The **transparent** windows let in light.
7.	circumstance	*circumstance*	It was a preventable **circumstance**.
8.	persistence	*persistence*	His **persistence** brought him success.
9.	transition	*transition*	The move was a difficult **transition**.
10.	perpetual	*perpetual*	The **perpetual** drilling is annoying.
11.	circumvent	*circumvent*	We can **circumvent** the traffic.
12.	circumnavigate	*circumnavigate*	She will **circumnavigate** the globe.
13.	transfer	*transfer*	He will **transfer** to another school.
14.	persuade	*persuade*	Did his argument **persuade** the jury?
15.	transplant	*transplant*	We will **transplant** the bush.
16.	circulating	*circulating*	The news is **circulating** quickly.
17.	pertinent	*pertinent*	Tell me only the **pertinent** facts.
18.	transistor	*transistor*	Can you fix the radio's **transistor**?
19.	persevere	*persevere*	I will **persevere** to reach my goal.
20.	circumstantial	*circumstantial*	I reject the **circumstantial** evidence.

SORT THE SPELLING WORDS

1.–6. The prefix **trans-** means "across." Write the spelling words that begin with this prefix.

7.–13. The prefix **per-** means "through." Write the spelling words that begin with this prefix.

14.–20. The prefix **circum-** means "around." Write the spelling words that begin with this prefix or a form of it.

REMEMBER THE SPELLING STRATEGY

Remember that the Latin prefixes **trans-**, **per-**, and **circum-** may be added to roots and base words to change the meaning of the word.

Word Meanings

Write a spelling word to match each definition.

1. to uproot and put elsewhere
2. a closed circular path
3. movement of blood through blood vessels
4. a device used for amplification
5. dependent on circumstances
6. relevant
7. the process of changing from one form to another
8. moving about

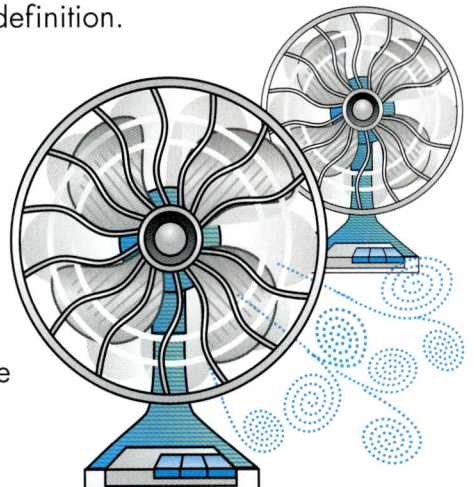

Word Replacements

Write the spelling word that best replaces each underlined word or words.

9. This is a difficult book to read, but you will be rewarded if you <u>persist</u>.
10. What <u>determining factor</u> led to his broken ankle?
11. On Main Street we have to <u>shift</u> to another bus.
12. With great <u>determination</u>, the runner completed the final lap of the race.
13. The <u>endlessly repeated</u> croak of the raven seemed to last forever.

USING THE Dictionary

An etymology traces a word to the language from which it came. Write a spelling word for each etymology. Use the **Spelling Dictionary** to help you.

14. Lat. **per** + **suadēre**, to urge
15. Lat. **circum**, around + **venire**, to come
16. Lat. **trans**, across + **forma**, shape
17. Lat. **per** + **plectere**, to entwine
18. Lat. **circum**, around + **navis**, ship + **agere**, to direct
19. Lat. **trans**, through + **parere**, to show
20. Lat. **per** + **forare**, to bore

Spelling and Reading

circumnavigate   perforate   transform   perplex   circulation
circumstance   transparent   persistence   transition   perpetual
circumstantial   circumvent   transfer   persuade   transplant
circulating   pertinent   transistor   persevere   circuit

Complete the Sentences Write the spelling word that best completes each sentence.

1. Our mail carrier walks the same _____ every day.
2. We have to _____ all your old files to your new computer.
3. They will _____ the trees when they put in the new sidewalk.
4. A _____ needs at least three electrical contacts.
5. The exciting news was _____ quickly within the school.
6. With this strong wind, we need two hours to _____ the lake.
7. My younger brothers made a smooth _____ from our old neighborhood to our new one.
8. I can think of no _____ that would have turned this banana blue.

Solve the Analogies Write the spelling word that best completes each analogy.

9. **Disturb** is to **bother** as **convince** is to _____.
10. **Calm** is to **impatient** as **unclear** is to _____.
11. **Lung** is to **respiration** as **heart** is to _____.
12. **Pull** is to **tug** as **pierce** is to _____.
13. **Deference** is to **deferential** as **circumstance** is to _____.

Complete the Paragraph Write spelling words from the box to complete the paragraph.

Throughout history, many inventors have dreamed of designing a __14.__ motion machine. One __15.__ fact, however, is that the device must permit __16.__, or constancy, of motion without the aid of an outside energy source. This situation continues to __17.__ scientists. But if inventors __18.__, they may manage to __19.__ the problem. They may __20.__ failure into success.

circumvent
perplex
transform
perpetual
persistence
pertinent
persevere

Spelling and Writing

Proofread a Paragraph

Six words are not spelled correctly in this paragraph. Write the words correctly.

My dream is to work for a natural history museum. Recently, I read about a group of museum workers who spent six weeks in a rain forest. They had to circumvant many problems as they took photographs and gathered pertinant information. It continues to purplex me how they later managed to transformm an empty exhibit room into a lifelike and life-size tropical rain forest. No one would have to persuede me to take part in such a project. If I persivere, I know I can make the transition from dreamer to one who helps others understand and respect the natural world.

Proofreading Marks

 Make a capital.

 Make a small letter.

 Add something.

 Take out something.

 Add a period.

 New paragraph

SP Spelling error

Write a Paragraph

Personal achievement requires dedication and perseverance. Write a paragraph describing your ambitions and hopes for the future.

- What would you like to accomplish? What kind of help or teamwork will be required for you to achieve your goals?
- Describe some of the hurdles you might have to overcome along the way.
- Follow the form used in the proofreading sample. Use as many spelling words as you can.

Proofread Your Writing During

Writing Process

Prewriting
⇩
Drafting
⇩
Revising
⇩
Editing
⇩
Publishing

Proofread your writing for spelling errors as part of the editing stage in the writing process. Be sure to check each word carefully. Use a dictionary to check spelling if you are not sure.

Vocabulary

Strategy Words

Review Words: Prefixes trans-, per-, circum-

Write a word from the box for each definition.

circumference	percolate	permissible
transmission	transmit	

1. to pass or ooze through
2. the boundary line of a circle
3. to send from one place to another
4. allowable
5. the act of transmitting

Preview Words: Prefixes trans-, per-, circum-

Write a word from the box to complete each sentence.

perambulate	perceptive	transcendental
transfusion	transom	

6. She probably knows how you feel, because she is very _____ about the moods of others.
7. The television program explored the nature of _____ experiences.
8. On nice evenings, tourists _____ along the river walk.
9. The bored students needed a _____ of enthusiasm.
10. The window will open once the _____ is repaired.

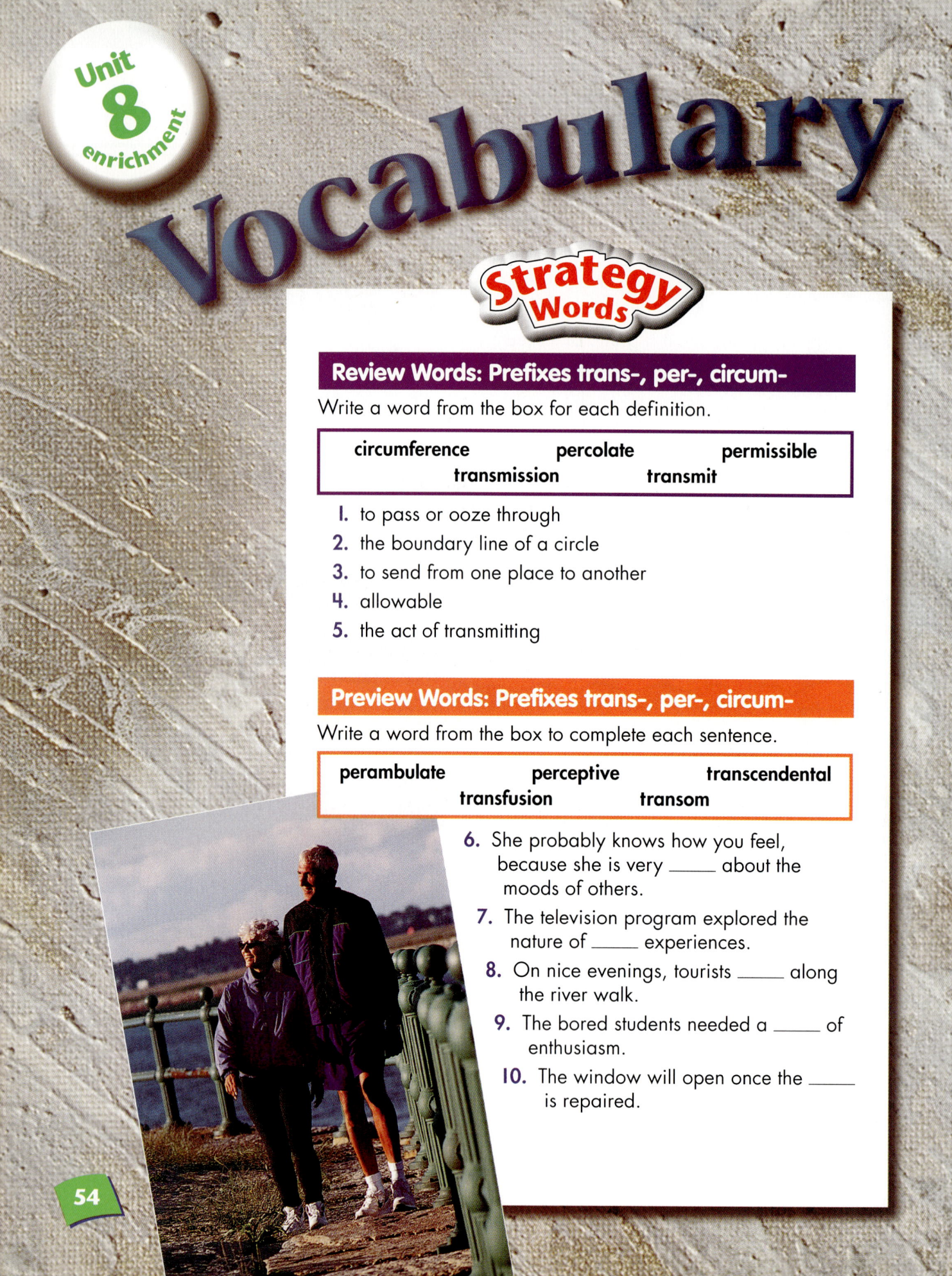

Connections

Math: Properties

Write words from the box to identify the statements
or definitions.

additive	closure	quantity
reflexive	transitive	

1. a = a
2. If a = b and b = c, then a = c.
3. a measurable amount
4. involving addition
5. the property of being mathematically closed

Science: Botany

Write words from the box to complete the paragraph.

conifer	deciduous	foliage
lichen	perennial	

   The botanist arrived at the Canadian border in early
September. Although the __6.__ trees were shedding their leaves
at the usual rate, the leaves were not as colorful as expected.
He intended to study the effects of the summer drought on the
fall __7.__ and on some __8.__ plants. He also planned to study
the __9.__, or "cone carrier." Removing a specimen of __10.__
from the bark of a pine tree, he would study it later in his lab.

Apply the Spelling Strategy

Circle the content words you wrote that begin with the prefix
trans- or **per-**.

Spelling and Thinking

1. alumna	*alumna*	My sister is an **alumna** of that school.
2. alumnae	*alumnae*	Pam and I are **alumnae** of Ivy College.
3. alumni	*alumni*	We are all **alumni** of state schools.
4. alumnus	*alumnus*	Dad is an **alumnus** of Park School.
5. stimulus	*stimulus*	The dog responds to a **stimulus**.
6. stimuli	*stimuli*	Bells and lights are the usual **stimuli**.
7. analyses	*analyses*	The two **analyses** differed.
8. analysis	*analysis*	Here is my **analysis** of that movie.
9. index	*index*	Many nonfiction books have an **index**.
10. indices	*indices*	We studied several types of **indices**.
11. criterion	*criterion*	Which **criterion** is most important?
12. criteria	*criteria*	We selected her, based on five **criteria**.
13. phenomena	*phenomena*	We witnessed awesome **phenomena**.
14. phenomenon	*phenomenon*	We focused on the odd **phenomenon**.
15. datum	*datum*	One wrong **datum** ruined the results.
16. data	*data*	You can present the **data** in chart form.
17. curricula	*curricula*	The **curricula** at those schools differ.
18. curriculum	*curriculum*	We offer music in our new **curriculum**.
19. memoranda	*memoranda*	Save all the **memoranda** on that topic.
20. memorandum	*memorandum*	Proofread the **memorandum** carefully.

SORT THE SPELLING WORDS

1.–10. Write the spelling words that are singular nouns.

11.–20. Write the spelling words that are plural nouns.

REMEMBER THE SPELLING STRATEGY

Remember that words from foreign languages often keep their foreign plurals.

Word Meanings

Write a spelling word to match each definition.

1. an item of information
2. a female graduate
3. a male graduate
4. in-depth studies and reports
5. things that cause reactions
6. particular courses of study, all in different, specialized fields
7. notes to remind
8. standards
9. more than one index
10. male graduates

Word Groups

Write a spelling word that is related in meaning to complete each group.

11. females, graduates, reunions, _____
12. message, note, reminder, _____
13. table of contents, preface, bibliography, _____
14. marvels, occurrences, happenings, _____
15. business subjects, science major, course, _____

USING THE Thesaurus

The following synonyms for spelling words are given in the **Writing Thesaurus**. Write the spelling word to which each list of synonyms applies.

16. event, happening, incident, marvel, miracle, occurrence, wonder
17. evidence, facts, information, statistics
18. model, norm, rule, standard, test, yardstick
19. examination, investigation
20. cause, impetus, motive

alumna	alumnae	alumni	alumnus	stimulus
stimuli	analyses	analysis	index	indices
criterion	criteria	phenomena	phenomenon	datum
data	curricula	curriculum	memoranda	memorandum

Answer the Questions Write the spelling word that answers each question.

1. What could you call in-depth discussions about news events?
2. Which word means "a female graduate"?
3. What might you call one specified fact?
4. What are the bells and buzzers that dog trainers use?
5. If you write a "memo," what are you writing?
6. Which word describes lists of topics found at the back of books?
7. On what standard might you base an important decision?
8. What could you call an unexpected tornado?
9. What describes the process of separating a subject into parts and studying those parts?
10. What term, which actually means "male graduates," is used today for both male and female graduates?

Solve the Analogies Write the spelling word that best completes each analogy.

11. **Cooking** is to **recipes** as **teaching** is to _____.
12. **Alumnae** are to **alumna** as **alumni** are to _____.
13. **Building** is to **directory** as **book** is to _____.
14. **Games** are to **strategies** as **decisions** are to _____.
15. **Note** is to **notes** as **memorandum** is to _____.

Complete the Paragraph Write spelling words from the box to complete the paragraph.

Maria Mitchell (1818–1899) was an American astronomer who studied sunspots, eclipses, and other solar __16.__. While gathering __17.__ for a government survey, Mitchell discovered a comet. Later, as a professor at Vassar College, she developed a radically new __18.__ in astronomy, which provided the __19.__ for many Vassar College __20.__ to pursue a career in astronomy.

phenomena
alumnae
data
curriculum
stimulus

Spelling ^{and} Writing

🔍 Proofread a Conversation

Six words are not spelled correctly in this telephone conversation. Write the words correctly.

Tonya called just before dinner. "Pablo," she said, "I'm supposed to gather dayta for a survey for science class. I'm finding out how people are affected by different types of weather phenomina. I'm looking forward to conducting the interviews, but would you like to discuss the analases with me afterwards? Ms. Tsao gave me several different criterea for determining which stimulae are most important."

"Sure," Pablo answered. "By the way, did you know that Ms. Tsao and my mom are both alumnas of Drake High School? Their names are in the index in the back of the 1979 yearbook. Check it out!"

Proofreading Marks

≡	Make a capital.
/	Make a small letter.
∧	Add something.
ℓ	Take out something.
⊙	Add a period.
#	New paragraph
SP	Spelling error

✏️ Write a Conversation

Write a conversation between two people talking on the telephone about a particular issue.

- Select or invent two characters.
- Choose the topic that they will discuss.
- Write the conversation between them.
- Follow the form used in the proofreading sample. Use as many spelling words as you can.

Writing Process

Prewriting
⇩
Drafting
⇩
Revising
⇩
Editing
⇩
Publishing

Proofread Your Writing During ➡

Proofread your writing for spelling errors as part of the editing stage in the writing process. Be sure to check each word carefully. Use a dictionary to check spelling if you are not sure.

Vocabulary

Strategy Words

Review Words: Irregular Plurals

Write a word from the box to complete each sentence.

bacteria	bacterium	oasis
parentheses	parenthesis	

1. Dashes or _____ could set off that comment within the sentence.
2. Scientists grow many kinds of _____ in petri dishes.
3. One _____ makes up half of a pair.
4. A traveler in the desert may unexpectedly come across an _____.
5. A _____ is one microorganism that can cause disease.

Preview Words: Irregular Plurals

Write the word from the box that could best replace the underlined word or phrase.

addenda	addendum	appendix
synopses	synopsis	

6. This book has several added parts that the earlier edition lacks.
7. The reviews should contain summaries of the plots.
8. Does this part to be added go with volume one or two?
9. The report begins with a brief outline of the contents.
10. The supplementary material at the back of the book contains exercises on the parts of speech.

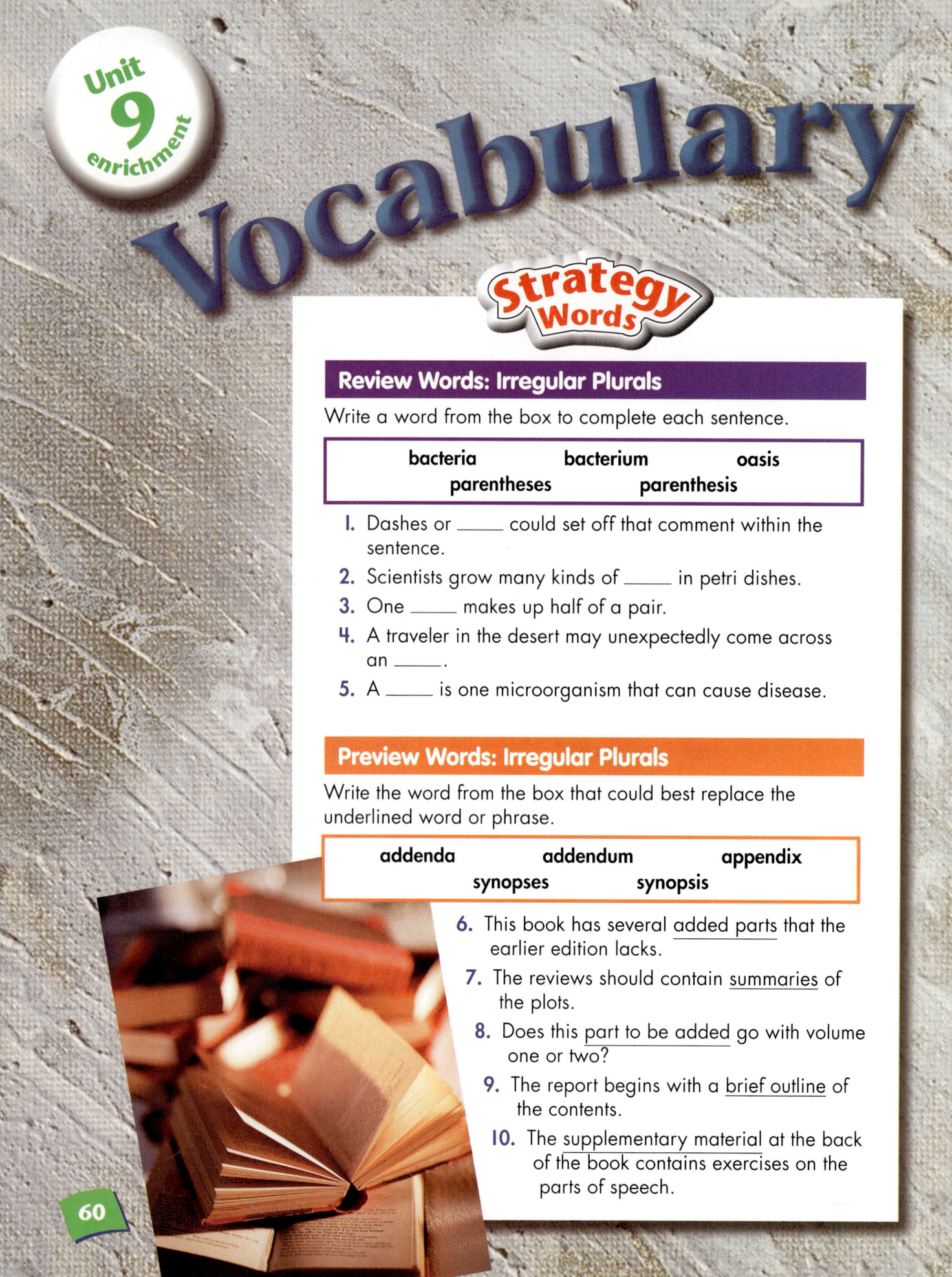

Connections

Content Words

Language Arts: Genres

Write a word from the box to identify each phrase.

epic	memoir	romance
genre	novella	

1. the style of fiction that idealizes love
2. an account of an author's personal experiences
3. a short novel
4. a long narrative poem about a traditional hero
5. a category of literature, such as poetry or drama

Language Arts: Literary Devices

Write words from the box to complete the paragraph.

cliché	exaggeration	parody
stereotype	trite	

When I read this story, I could not tell if it was a serious work or if it was intended as a ___6.___. Each character is a ___7.___ instead of an individual. Nothing that the hero says is original. Every phrase is a ___8.___. Besides always using ___9.___ expressions, this hero acts in extreme ways. He never walks; he always races around or charges. After a while, such ___10.___ becomes tiresome.

Apply the Spelling Strategy

Words borrowed from French often keep their French spellings and pronunciations. Circle the three words you wrote that kept their French spellings and pronunciations.

Spelling and Thinking

READ THE SPELLING WORDS

1.	superior	*superior*	This apple pie is **superior** to that one.
2.	superiority	*superiority*	The **superiority** of her baking is clear.
3.	inferiority	*inferiority*	The **inferiority** of this wood is evident.
4.	inferior	*inferior*	Do not purchase this **inferior** product.
5.	punctual	*punctual*	He is always **punctual** for appointments.
6.	punctuality	*punctuality*	How important is **punctuality** to you?
7.	visibility	*visibility*	Fog restricted **visibility** for days.
8.	technicality	*technicality*	A case was dismissed on a **technicality**.
9.	technical	*technical*	Mechanics take **technical** courses.
10.	flexibility	*flexibility*	Daily exercise improves **flexibility**.
11.	practicality	*practicality*	I like the **practicality** of your advice.
12.	personality	*personality*	The actor has an outgoing **personality**.
13.	fragile	*fragile*	This glass sculpture is very **fragile**.
14.	fragility	*fragility*	The **fragility** of sand castles is obvious.
15.	originality	*originality*	The artist is known for her **originality**.
16.	individuality	*individuality*	His **individuality** makes him interesting.
17.	liability	*liability*	Shyness can be a **liability** in this job.
18.	liable	*liable*	Who is **liable** for repairing the window?
19.	capability	*capability*	Your writing **capability** is enormous!
20.	availability	*availability*	The **availability** of brushes is limited.

SORT THE SPELLING WORDS

1.–6. Write the spelling words that are adjectives.

7.–20. Write the spelling words that are nouns.

REMEMBER THE SPELLING STRATEGY

Remember that the suffix **-ity** can be added to roots and base words to form nouns.

Word Meanings

Write the spelling word that could replace the underlined word in these sentences.

1. I questioned the <u>usability</u> of the sled in Florida.
2. Her <u>inventiveness</u> was apparent in her essays.
3. A good teacher understands the <u>uniqueness</u> of each student.
4. Generosity is a key element of one's <u>character</u>.

Word Structure

In spelling words ending in **-ble,** the **-ble** changes to **-bil** when the suffix **-ity** is added. Write the spelling words formed by adding **-ity** to the following adjectives.

5. capable
6. visible
7. flexible
8. available

USING THE Dictionary

When the suffix **-ity** is added to an adjective to form a noun, the primary stress in the word usually changes.

9.–20. Write the spelling words that are adjective and noun pairs. Circle the stressed syllable in each word, using the **Spelling Dictionary** if you need help. Notice the change in primary stress when the suffix **-ity** is added to the adjective to form the noun.

superior	superiority	inferiority	inferior	punctual
punctuality	visibility	technicality	technical	flexibility
practicality	personality	fragile	fragility	originality
individuality	liability	liable	capability	availability

Solve the Analogies Write the spelling word that best completes each analogy.

1. **Rough** is to **smooth** as **rigidity** is to _____.
2. **Able** is to **ability** as **fragile** is to _____.
3. **Late** is to **on time** as **tardy** is to _____.
4. **Musician** is to **musicality** as **technician** is to _____.
5. **Invisible** is to **invisibility** as **visible** is to _____.
6. **Norm** is to **normality** as **person** is to _____.
7. **Strong** is to **weak** as **tough** is to _____.
8. **Profit** is to **loss** as **asset** is to _____.
9. **Dual** is to **duality** as **individual** is to _____.

Complete the Sayings Write the spelling word that completes each famous saying.

10. Louis XVIII said that _____ (being on time) is the politeness of kings.
11. Eleanor Roosevelt said that no one can make you feel _____ (lower than others) without your consent.
12. Aristotle said that equals revolt to be _____ (better than others).
13. José Ortega y Gasset said that hatred is an outpouring of a feeling of _____ (the condition of feeling inferior).

Complete the Paragraph Write spelling words from the box to complete the paragraph.

technical
originality
practicality
superiority
liable
availability
capability

Many inventions are noted for their usefulness, or _____14._____. These have the __15.__ of making money for their inventors. Others, like an electric back scratcher for cats, are __16.__ never to find a market. The __17.__ of facts about inventions helps inventors to avoid copying others. The U.S. Patent Office requires that complete plans and detailed __18.__ drawings be included with each application. Every aspect is checked carefully to ensure __19.__ and to weed out any copies. Each applicant boasts of the __20.__ of his or her own idea.

Word Meanings ▬▬▬▬▬▬▬▬▬▬▬

Write the spelling word that matches each definition.

1. of the ears
2. at the current time
3. unconsciously performed
4. of the lungs
5. before the main part; introductory
6. required
7. first in importance
8. remarkable

Word Structure ▬▬▬▬▬▬▬▬

Write a spelling word by changing each of the following nouns and verbs into an adjective.

9. sense
10. circulate
11. element
12. legend
13. prepare
14. advise

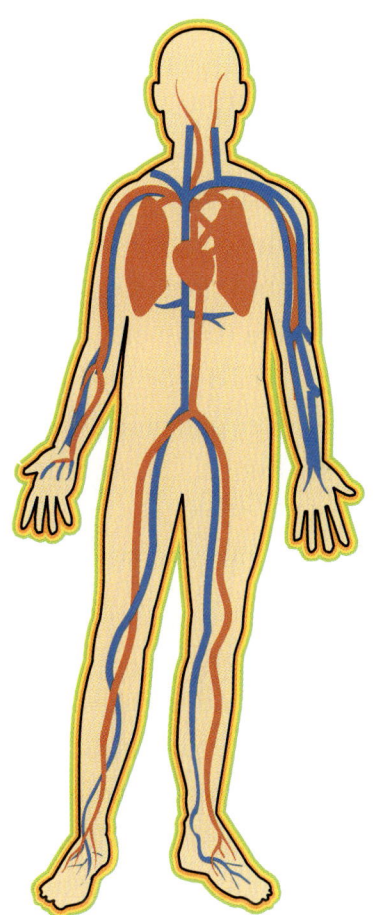

USING THE Dictionary

Note that the suffixes **-ary** and **-ory** both have two syllables. When one of these suffixes is added to a base word or root, one syllable in the new word often receives a secondary stress. Write each spelling word below. Underline the syllable with the primary stress and circle the syllable with the secondary stress. Use the **Spelling Dictionary** for help.

15. contrary
16. literary
17. migratory
18. satisfactory
19. complimentary
20. introductory

advisory	contrary	satisfactory	legendary	sensory
primary	mandatory	introductory	migratory	elementary
auditory	complimentary	contemporary	circulatory	involuntary
literary	preliminary	extraordinary	preparatory	pulmonary

Complete the Sentences   Write the spelling word that best completes each sentence.

1. That knee jerk is an _____ reflex.
2. The photo shows _____ birds in flight.
3. My little sister goes to an _____ school nearby.
4. We argue only because you have such _____ opinions!
5. Find a song about a _____ figure, like John Henry.
6. That author is well-known in _____ circles.
7. The _____ paragraph in the story immediately sets a mood of mystery.
8. I am suffering from _____ deprivation in this dark, silent cave!

Solve the Analogies   Write a spelling word to complete each analogy.

9. **Unkind** is to **kind** as **insulting** is to _____.
10. **Eye** is to **visual** as **ear** is to _____.
11. **Old** is to **modern** as **traditional** is to _____.
12. **Rule** is to **regulatory** as **advice** is to _____.
13. **Untidy** is to **tidy** as **unsatisfactory** is to _____.
14. **Willing** is to **voluntary** as **required** is to _____.

Complete the Paragraph   Write spelling words from the box to complete the paragraph.

The heart is the __15.__ organ of the __16.__ system. A __17.__ electrical impulse produced in this unique and __18.__ process triggers each contraction. The pumping action pushes blood loaded with carbon dioxide through the __19.__ arteries into the lungs. The heart rests briefly, __20.__ to beginning its next cycle.

preparatory
primary
circulatory
preliminary
extraordinary
pulmonary

70

Spelling and Writing

Proofread a Paragraph

Six words are not spelled correctly in this paragraph. Write the words correctly.

We are now inside the circulitory system. Our awditory sensors have picked up a rhythmic sound, but we cannot identify it. The system is filled with an extrordinary red fluid, whose primery function is still unknown. It seems to move in waves, but we are unsure whether the motion is involuntery or deliberate. We will provide a preliminary report shortly, and our intraductory section will include a diagram of this system.

Proofreading Marks

=	Make a capital.
/	Make a small letter.
∧	Add something.
ℓ	Take out something.
⊙	Add a period.
#	New paragraph
SP	Spelling error

Write a Paragraph

Narrative Writing

Imagine that you are the commander of a spaceship whose mission is to explore the function of one body system. Write a paragraph describing your journey through that body system. Try to mix fact and fiction.

- Imagine what you might see, hear, and feel.
- Invent a conflict or a situation.
- Follow the form used in the proofreading sample.

Use as many spelling words as you can.

Proofread Your Writing During

Proofread your writing for spelling errors as part of the editing stage in the writing process. Be sure to check each word carefully. Use a dictionary to check spelling if you are not sure.

Writing Process

Prewriting
⇩
Drafting
⇩
Revising
⇩
Editing
⇩
Publishing

Vocabulary

Strategy Words

Review Words: Suffixes -ary, -ory

Write a word from the box to match each definition.

customary	honorary	imaginary
momentary	secondary	

1. lasting a very short time
2. given as a mark of honor
3. of the second rank
4. usual
5. not real

Preview Words: Suffixes -ary, -ory

Write a word from the box to complete each sentence.

compensatory	directory	disciplinary
expository	inflammatory	

6. Her name is listed in the building _____.
7. The speaker refrained from making any _____ remarks.
8. We will give you a _____ gift for the time you wasted.
9. Your science report is a good example of _____ writing.
10. Reasons for detentions are given in the _____ code.

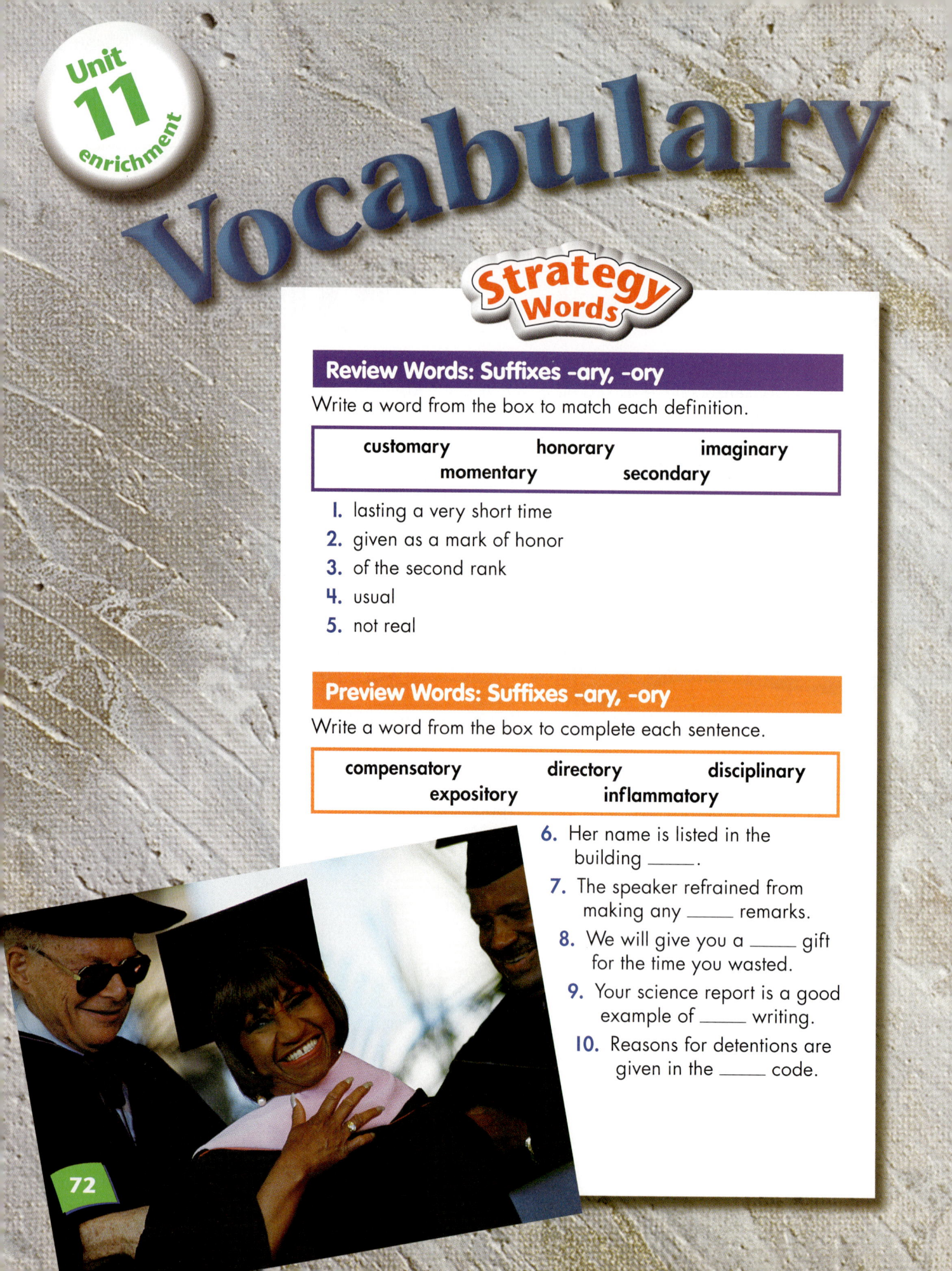

Connections

Math: Geometry

Write words from the box to complete the paragraph.

adjacent	complementary	corresponding
	interior	supplementary

Sometimes angles are given descriptive names. For example, when the sum of two angles is 90°, the angles are said to be __1.__ . The sum of __2.__ angles, on the other hand, is 180°. When angles have the same vertex and a common side, they are called __3.__ angles while __4.__ angles are the matching angles of congruent triangles. An __5.__ angle, finally, is the angle formed inside a polygon by two adjacent sides.

Social Studies: Geography

Write the word from the box that describes each of the following.

geographic	isthmus	peninsula
	plateau	tributary

6. a piece of land jutting out into water
7. a stream that flows into a larger body of water
8. a thin strip of land connecting two bigger pieces
9. having to do with the study of the earth
10. a high, level piece of land

Apply the Spelling Strategy

Circle the three content words you wrote that end in **-ary** or **-ory**.

Assessment and Review

Assessment

Units 7–11

Each Assessment Word in the box fits one of the spelling strategies you have studied over the past five weeks. Read the spelling strategies. Then write each Assessment Word under the unit number it fits.

Unit 7

1.–6. Remember that a consonant sound may be spelled with two consonant letters.

Unit 8

7.–11. Remember that the Latin prefixes **trans-**, **per-**, and **circum-** may be added to roots and base words to change the meaning of the word.

Unit 9

Remember that words from foreign languages often keep their foreign plurals.

Unit 10

12.–16. Remember that the suffix **-ity** can be added to roots and base words to form nouns.

Unit 11

17.–20. Remember that the suffixes **-ary** and **-ory** can be added to roots and base words to form adjectives.

senior

possessive

percussion

predatory

transatlantic

nationality

cellophane

grasshopper

transcontinental

accountant

finality

arbitrary

seniority

minority

warranty

circumvention

apparently

interplanetary

pertain

vapory

Review   Unit 7: Double Consonants

dilemma	accuracy	occasional	appropriate	bookkeeping
essential	assistance	recommend	occasionally	accommodate

Write the spelling words by adding the missing letters.

1. o__ __asion__ __
2. __o__ __ __e__pin__
3. a__ __istan__e
4. a__ __ura__y
5. __ile__ __a
6. e__ __ential
7. a__ __o__ __odate
8. a__ __ro__riate
9. __eco__ __end
10. o__ __asiona__ __y

Review   Unit 8: Prefixes trans-, per-, circum-

transparent	perforate	transform	circulation	circuit
circumstance	transfer	persuade	pertinent	transistor

Write the spelling word that completes each sentence.

11. I hope to _____ my dad to order pizza tonight.
12. You can _____ the file from a disk to your computer's hard drive.
13. Putting a sharp object in your ear could _____ your eardrum.
14. When the lightning blew out a _____, we lost our electrical power.
15. The investigator wanted only _____ information.
16. Your heart keeps your blood in _____.
17. The museum exhibited the valuable stones in a _____ case.
18. The invention of the _____ improved communication.
19. Under no _____ would he go to bed early.
20. How did Dr. Jekyll _____ into Mr. Hyde?

Unit 9: Irregular Plurals

alumna	alumnae	analyses	analysis	memoranda
indices	datum	data	index	memorandum

Write a spelling word for each clue.

1. a single fact
2. an alphabetical list or guide
3. a female graduate
4. a set of organized information
5. a reminder
6. a careful study of something
7. the plural of your last answer
8. female graduates
9. things that jog your memory
10. the plural of your answer to number 2

Review

Unit 10: Suffix -ity

superior	superiority	inferiority	inferior	technicality
technical	practicality	personality	fragile	fragility

Write the spelling words that best complete the sentence.

11.–12. Austin sometimes felt _____ to his more-skilled teammates. His feelings of _____ would lessen as he got better.

13.–14. The _____ of the crystal called for careful packaging and a large label reading _____.

15. The exuberant teacher has a lively _____.

16.–17. Because of a _____ error by the attorney, the judge ordered a new trial. Such a _____ can add weeks to the trial.

18. The mayor was questioned on the _____ of his idea to repave all the town streets in one year.

19.–20. The team made a _____ effort to beat their arch rivals. Winning would give them a sense of _____ for the entire school year.

Unit 11: Suffixes -ary, -ory

primary	literary	satisfactory	complimentary
circulatory	contemporary	introductory	preliminary
	extraordinary	preparatory	

Write the spelling words formed from these words.

1. satisfy
2. introduce
3. literature
4. circulation
5. prepare
6. compliment

Write a spelling word for each definition.

7. not ordinary
8. first, basic, or best
9. leading to the main event
10. of the same time

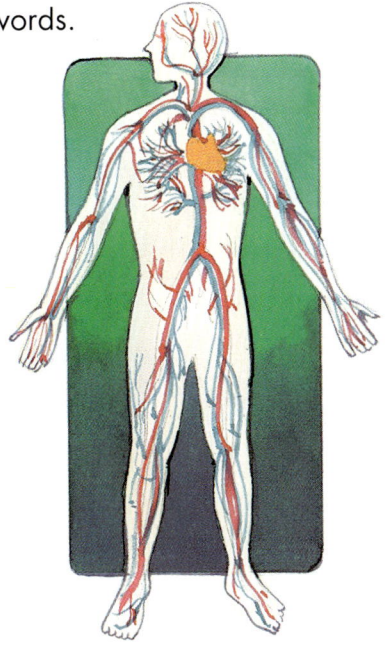

Spelling Study Strategy

Word Swap

Write words that you want to study on cards—one word to a card. Put your initials on each card. Give your cards to a partner. Your partner will give you a similar set of cards.

1. Read aloud a word from your partner's stack.

2. Your partner spells the word aloud. Check to see that the word is spelled correctly. If it is, give the card back to your partner. If it is not, give the correct spelling and keep the card.

3. Your partner will then say one of the words from your card stack for you to spell. If you spell it correctly, you get the card. If you don't, your partner tells you the correct spelling and keeps the card.

4. Continue taking turns until each of you has all of your own cards back.

Grammar, Usage, and Mechanics

Subject-Verb Agreement

The subject of a sentence may be singular or plural. The **verb** or verbs in the sentence must **agree** with the **subject,** meaning that a singular subject takes a singular verb and a plural subject takes a plural verb.

They **kick** the ball.   She **kicks** the ball.
They **hurry** away.   He **hurries** away.
They **go** home.   She **goes** home.

A. Write the subject of each sentence. If the subject is singular, write **S** next to it. If it is plural, write **P** next to it.

 I. The bookkeeper saves his records on two separate disks.

 2. Why should people vote to elect a president?

 3. Perhaps Bigfoot exists but is hiding from people.

 4. The alumnae gather each September to greet new students.

 5. Most apples ripen in the fall.

 6. A hot casserole tastes good on a cold night.

B. Choose and write the correct verb.

 7. The librarian (recommend, recommends) a new book each week.

 8. The arena (accommodates, accommodate) over five thousand fans.

 9. People usually (tries, try) to do their best.

 10. Everyone (think, thinks) it is a good idea.

 II. The city water (circulates, circulate) through numerous filters.

 12. Seat belts (prevents, prevent) many unnecessary injuries.

 13. A healthy baby (gain, gains) weight each week.

 14. Some snakes (hiss, hisses) as a warning.

 15. (Watch, Watches) the light turn on at dusk.

WORKSHOP

First and Last

Good writers always proofread their work for spelling errors. Here is a strategy you can use to proofread your papers.

Instead of reading in the regular way, look at one sentence at a time. Pay close attention to the first and last word. Make sure that the first word starts with a capital letter. Then make sure that the last word is followed by a punctuation mark.

This way of looking at a paper helps you focus on details, such as capital letters and punctuation, instead of ideas. It may sound funny, but it works. Try it!

Electronic Spelling

Computer Terms

Many computer terms are not really new words at all; they are just old words used in a new way. For example, the **mouse** was around for a long time before personal computers were invented, and so were **windows**.

It might be interesting to look up some of the following words in a recently published dictionary and see if both the old and new meanings are given.

menu: a list of commands that drops down from the menu bar

link: a way to get access to data between files

arrow: keys used to move the insertion point or select from a menu

driver: a special file that tells the computer how to operate

drag: to hold down the button while moving the mouse

Which of the following old words with new meanings for computers are misspelled? Correct the words that are spelled incorrectly and write **OK** if the word is correct.

1. docuement
2. hard drive
3. icon

4. hardwear
5. indecx
6. appilcation

READ THE SPELLING WORDS

1.	submit	*submit*	Please **submit** your report by Friday.
2.	submitted	*submitted*	She **submitted** a job application.
3.	commit	*commit*	Did he **commit** an error in the game?
4.	committed	*committed*	I am **committed** to learning to swim.
5.	committing	*committing*	She is **committing** herself to her work.
6.	transmitted	*transmitted*	They **transmitted** the news by phone.
7.	transmitting	*transmitting*	Are you **transmitting** the message?
8.	transmitter	*transmitter*	Is the radio **transmitter** still on?
9.	regret	*regret*	I **regret** that I must leave now.
10.	regretted	*regretted*	He **regretted** his decision to go home.
11.	regrettable	*regrettable*	The cancellation is **regrettable**.
12.	control	*control*	Please **control** your jumping puppy.
13.	controlled	*controlled*	The pilot **controlled** the plane well.
14.	uncontrollable	*uncontrollable*	I had an **uncontrollable** urge for pizza.
15.	forgetting	*forgetting*	She is always **forgetting** her pencils.
16.	unforgettable	*unforgettable*	Our camping trip was **unforgettable**.
17.	rebelled	*rebelled*	The child **rebelled** against naptime.
18.	rebellion	*rebellion*	Is compromise better than **rebellion**?
19.	forbid	*forbid*	I **forbid** you to wear my new pink hat.
20.	forbidden	*forbidden*	Swimming after dark is **forbidden**.

SORT THE SPELLING WORDS

1.–5. Write the spelling words that are base words ending in a vowel-consonant combination. Circle the stressed syllable.

6.–20. Write the spelling words that end in a suffix beginning with a vowel. Circle the doubled consonants.

REMEMBER THE SPELLING STRATEGY

Remember that a final consonant preceded by a single vowel is doubled when adding a suffix that begins with a vowel except when the accent is on or shifts to the first syllable.

Spelling and Vocabulary

Word Meanings

Write the spelling word that best replaces each underlined word or words.

1. Until recently, the radio station was <u>sending signals</u> for only a few hours a day.
2. She <u>was sorry about</u> her thoughtless words as soon as she had spoken them.
3. He has <u>dedicated</u> himself to finding a home for the gerbils.
4. They <u>sent</u> the news story electronically.
5. No one has <u>expressed strong rebellion</u> against the new school rules.
6. Entry into the building is <u>prohibited</u> during construction.
7. The state is <u>obligating</u> itself to spending the funds on new roads.
8. The captain of the ship <u>yielded</u> to the pirates.
9. I am always <u>unintentionally leaving behind</u> my bus pass.
10. The lunch monitor also <u>regulated</u> the playground.
11. On what day did he <u>carry out</u> the offense?

Word Structure

Add the following prefixes and suffixes to the base words indicated to write spelling words. Remember to double the final consonant of the base word before adding the suffix.

12. un + forget + able
13. rebel + ion
14. un + control + able
15. transmit + er
16. regret + able

USING THE Thesaurus

Write a spelling word that is a synonym for each set of words below. Use the **Writing Thesaurus** to check your answer.

17. direct, manage, regulate
18. offer, subject, surrender
19. ban, disallow, prevent
20. deplore, lament, repent

Spelling and Reading

uncontrollable	submitted	committed	commit	committing
transmitted	transmitting	transmitter	regret	regretted
regrettable	control	controlled	submit	forgetting
unforgettable	rebelled	rebellion	forbid	forbidden

Answer the Questions   Write a spelling word to answer each question.

1. How do you describe an event that you will always remember?
2. What do you call an act of defiance toward an authority?
3. What would you do with a completed school assignment?
4. What should you do with your temper?
5. What are you doing if you are sending a message?
6. What did people do if they went against authority?

Complete the Sentences   Write the spelling word that best completes each sentence.

7. After proper training, the dog was _____ by his owner.
8. Do you realize that you are _____ yourself to long hours of practice?
9. The architect _____ his playground plans to the city council.
10. I _____ my hasty decision as soon as I made it.
11. The storm knocked the radio _____ down.
12. Can you _____ these facts to memory?
13. Mosquitoes _____ the disease to people living in the area near the marsh.
14. I _____ you to wake me up before 7 o'clock.
15. Are you _____ who lent you the money?

Complete the Paragraph   Write spelling words from the box to complete the paragraph.

We __16.__ to inform you that, because of an __17.__ circumstance, swimming in Pilgrim Lake is strictly __18.__ . Although this is a __19.__ decision, we continue to be __20.__ to serving the needs of summer vacationers. Therefore, beginning July 4, Miller Pond will be open to all swimmers.

uncontrollable
regret
regrettable
committed
forbidden

Spelling and Writing

Proofread a Journal Entry

Six words are not spelled correctly in this journal entry. Write the words correctly.

Boston, December 17, 1773

The events of last night are unforgetable. It was necessary to forbidd three ships filled with tea to be unloaded. The British governor had forbiddin the ships to leave the harbor until a tax was paid. Other proud citizens and I could not submit to such an outrage. With some regrett, my friends and I decided to comitt an act of rebelliun. We heaved the tea into the water. The night of the Boston Tea Party was very exciting but also extremely frightening.

Proofreading Marks

☰	Make a capital.
/	Make a small letter.
∧	Add something.
ℓ	Take out something.
⊙	Add a period.
⌗	New paragraph
SP	Spelling error

Write a Journal Entry

Narrative Writing

Imagine what it would have been like to live through the events of the Boston Tea Party. Put yourself in the shoes of someone who took part in this event or some other important event in history. Write a journal entry describing your experience.

- Remember that a journal entry should include your thoughts and feelings.
- Follow the form used in the proofreading sample. Use as many spelling words as you can.

Proofread Your Writing During

Proofread your writing for spelling errors as part of the editing stage in the writing process. Be sure to check each word carefully. Use a dictionary to check spelling if you are not sure.

Writing Process

Prewriting
⬇
Drafting
⬇
Revising
⬇
Editing
⬇
Publishing

Vocabulary

Strategy Words

Review Words: Doubling Final Consonants

Write words from the box to complete the paragraph.

admitting	excelled	excelling
permitted		permitting

Although I am not very tall, I have always __1.__ at basketball. Last fall, our principal announced that the school was finally __2.__ eighth graders to join the basketball team. Until then, only ninth graders were __3.__ to be on the team. Now that our team is __4.__ in our league, my teammates are __5.__ that inviting us eighth graders was a good idea after all.

Preview Words: Doubling Final Consonants

Write a word from the box to replace the underlined word or words in each sentence.

acquittal	conferring	extolled
referral		transferred

6. The president is exchanging ideas with his advisers.

7. After her release, the falsely accused woman vowed to find the real criminal.

8. The committee praised his honesty.

9. The act of referring allowed the patient to see a skin specialist.

10. When our bus broke down, the driver shifted the luggage to another bus.

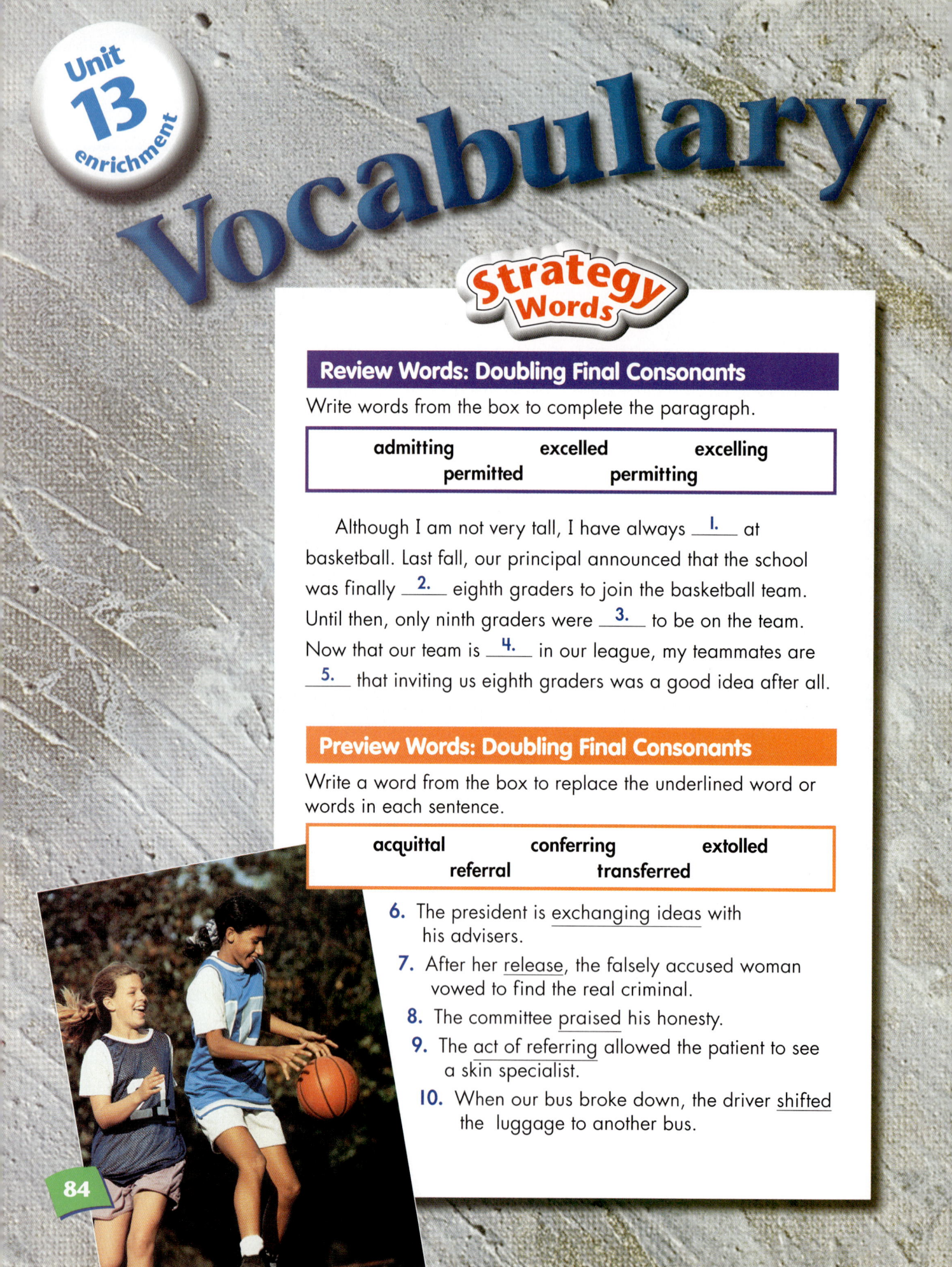

Connections

Science: Computers

Write words from the box to complete the paragraph.

| efficiency | framework | improvise | programmer | simulate |

Recent research into artificial intelligence suggests that computers may be able to ___1.___ thought someday. The challenge is to design a ___2.___ in which the computer can replicate the way humans ___3.___. A ___4.___ might suggest that the computer must be able to alter its program quickly to compete with the ___5.___ of the human brain.

Science: Acoustics

Write words from the box to complete the paragraph.

| acoustics | auditorium | carpeting | paneling | reverberation |

The next time you attend a program in an ___6.___ or a concert hall, consider the ___7.___, or the quality of the sound. In a large enclosed space, sound quality is determined by ___8.___, or sound bouncing off surfaces. Hard, firm surfaces, such as wood ___9.___, reflect sound and allow it to reverberate longer. By comparison, soft surfaces, such as ___10.___, absorb sound.

Apply the Spelling Strategy

Circle the content word you wrote in which the final consonant was doubled before adding the suffix **-er**. Underline the two words in which the final consonant was not doubled before adding the suffix **-ing**.

READ THE SPELLING WORDS

1. malice	*malice*	I feel **malice** toward no one.
2. benefit	*benefit*	The scholarships will **benefit** all of us.
3. equate	*equate*	Do not **equate** fruit candy with real fruit.
4. malady	*malady*	A doctor must first diagnose the **malady**.
5. equality	*equality*	The **equality** of the new law is clear.
6. beneficial	*beneficial*	Walking is **beneficial** to your health.
7. benign	*benign*	This **benign** treatment has no side effects.
8. malpractice	*malpractice*	Most doctors have **malpractice** insurance.
9. equivocal	*equivocal*	Were the instructions clear or **equivocal**?
10. malign	*malign*	I would never **malign** a decent person!
11. benefactor	*benefactor*	A secret **benefactor** gave me this pen.
12. equitable	*equitable*	An **equitable** solution is best.
13. beneficiary	*beneficiary*	Who is the **beneficiary** of this policy?
14. malfunction	*malfunction*	A light goes on if the brakes **malfunction**.
15. malignant	*malignant*	Researchers help cure **malignant** diseases.
16. equity	*equity*	The tests were graded with **equity**.
17. malnutrition	*malnutrition*	A junk food diet can cause **malnutrition**.
18. equilibrium	*equilibrium*	The ear infection affects my **equilibrium**.
19. benevolent	*benevolent*	Many **benevolent** families donated toys.
20. malicious	*malicious*	A **malicious** rumor can hurt people.

SORT THE SPELLING WORDS

1.–6. Write the spelling words that begin with **ben** or **bene**.

7.–14. Write the spelling words that begin with **mal**.

15.–20. Write the spelling words that begin with **equ** or **equi**.

REMEMBER THE SPELLING STRATEGY

Remember that knowing Latin forms like **ben(e), mal,** and **equ(i)** can give clues to the meaning and spelling of certain words.

Word Meanings

Write a spelling word with the Latin form **mal** that matches each definition.

1. poor nutrition
2. a disease, disorder, or ailment
3. to speak evil of
4. to function abnormally
5. deliberately harmful
6. threatening to life or health
7. the desire to harm others

Word Replacements

Write a spelling word that could replace the underlined word or words in each sentence.

8. A gymnast needs a good sense of <u>balance</u>.
9. The law promises <u>the state of being equal</u> to all.
10. The <u>intentionally misleading</u> meaning of the letter confuses me.
11. A vacation would be <u>advantageous</u> right now.
12. I am the <u>recipient</u> of her kindness.
13. Such rules help promote <u>fairness and justice</u>.
14. Was it an example of <u>improper treatment by a doctor</u>?
15. The kitten was rescued by a <u>kindly</u> firefighter.

USING THE Dictionary

Each group of scrambled letters is followed by the word history of a spelling word. Unscramble the spelling word and write it correctly. Check the answers in the **Spelling Dictionary**.

16. **gneibn,** from the Latin **bene + genus,** meaning "well-born"
17. **balequtie,** from the Old French **equite,** meaning "equity"
18. **tifeben,** from the Latin **benefactum,** meaning "good deed"
19. **teqaue,** from the Latin **aequus,** meaning "even"
20. **bacotenerf,** from the Latin **benefactio,** meaning "to do well"

malice   benefit   equate   malady   equality
beneficial   benign   malpractice   equivocal   malign
benefactor   equitable   beneficiary   malfunction   malignant
equity   malnutrition   equilibrium   benevolent   malicious

Solve the Analogies   Write the spelling word that best completes each analogy.

1. **Correction** is to **error** as **cure** is to _____.
2. **Unkind** is to **malevolent** as **kindly** is to _____.
3. **Hostile** is to **friendly** as **harmful** is to _____.
4. **Medicine** is to **disease** as **nourishment** is to _____.
5. **Spite** is to **spiteful** as **malice** is to _____.
6. **Incomplete** is to **complete** as **inequity** is to _____.
7. **Contribution** is to **donor** as **gift** is to _____.
8. **Succeed** is to **fail** as **operate** is to _____.

Complete the Sentences   Write the spelling word that best completes each sentence.

9. She is the _____ of her great-uncle's insurance policy.
10. Gossip and rumor can _____ innocent people.
11. The vet assured us that the cat's lump was not _____.
12. The speaker kept her _____ despite the breakdown of the sound system.
13. You hurt his feelings, even though you felt no _____.
14. This agreement seems fair and just to all parties; do you agree that it is _____?

Complete the Paragraph   Write the spelling words from the box to complete the paragraph.

The drafters of the United States Constitution believed in __15.__ for all. They thought a strong Constitution would be __16.__ to all citizens, and they were determined to __17.__ the political power and the people's will. The founders carefully avoided making any statements that were __18.__. For example, the steps for removing a government official found guilty of __19.__ are very clear. Today, more than two hundred years later, citizens still __20.__ from the founders' work.

equate
benefit
equality
equivocal
malpractice
beneficial

Spelling and Writing

Proofread a Paragraph

Six words are not spelled correctly in this paragraph. Write the words correctly.

We believe in the equalety of all students in this school. The current rules do not provide sufficient eqwity between sports teams and school clubs. We need an equitible distribution of support, supplies, and funds for every activity so that we can maintain an equilibreum among them. Students will not be the only benefissiary. Everyone will benefit. Rules will also be clearer and more consistent; right now the rules are sometimes equivacal.

Proofreading Marks

≡ Make a capital.

/ Make a small letter.

∧ Add something.

℮ Take out something.

⊙ Add a period.

⌗ New paragraph

SP Spelling error

Write a Paragraph — Persuasive Writing

Our U.S. Constitution is more than two hundred years old. Consider a student constitution for your school. Write a paragraph about this constitution, explaining its purpose and reason for existing.

- Clearly list the goals of the student constitution.
- Identify ways in which students would benefit.
- Explain additional benefits.
- Follow the form used in the proofreading sample. Use as many spelling words as you can.

Writing Process

Prewriting
⇩
Drafting
⇩
Revising
⇩
Editing
⇩
Publishing

Proofread Your Writing During

Proofread your writing for spelling errors as part of the editing stage in the writing process. Be sure to check each word carefully. Use a dictionary to check spelling if you are not sure.

89

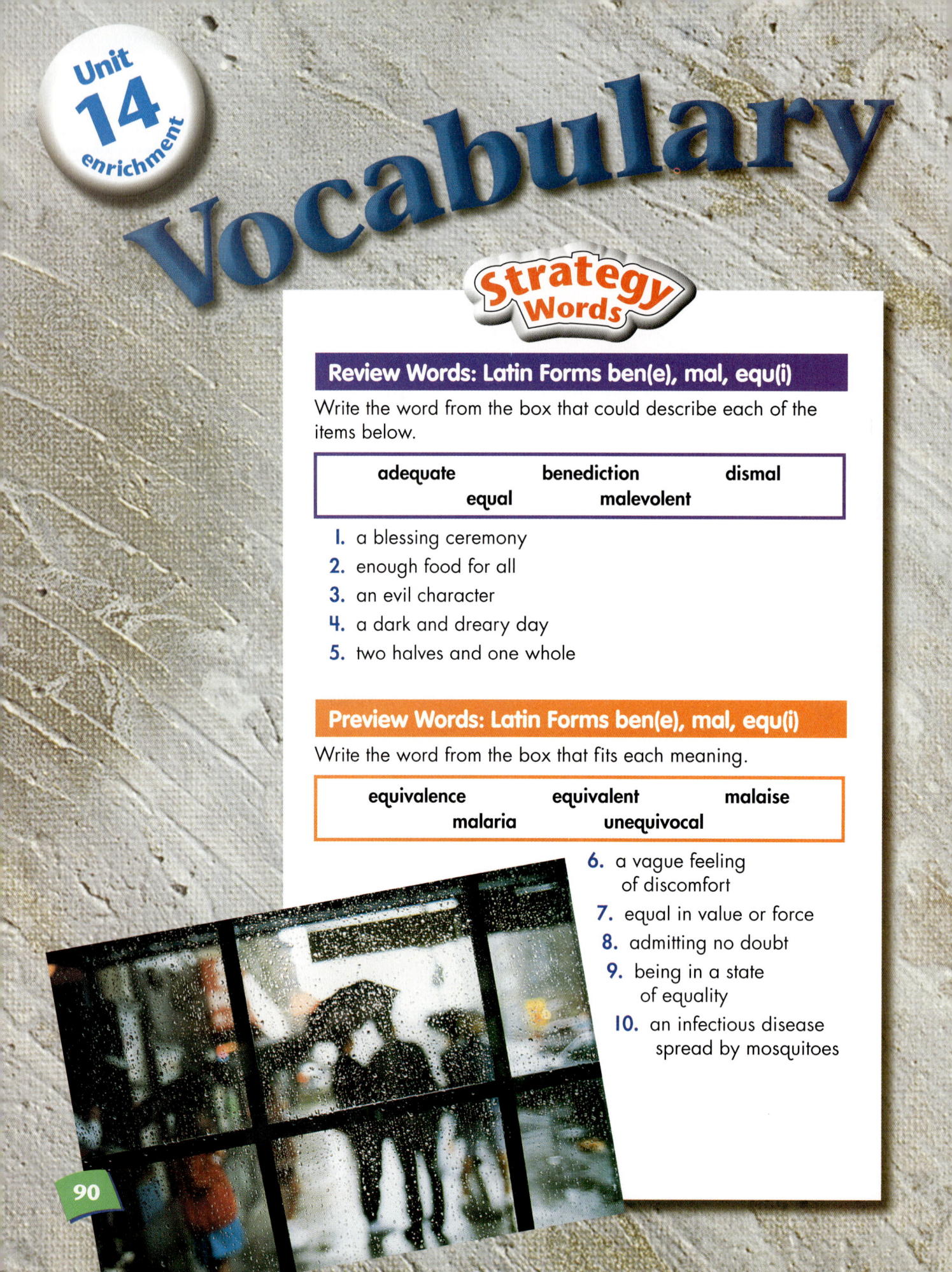

Vocabulary

Strategy Words

Review Words: Latin Forms ben(e), mal, equ(i)

Write the word from the box that could describe each of the items below.

adequate	benediction	dismal
equal	malevolent	

1. a blessing ceremony
2. enough food for all
3. an evil character
4. a dark and dreary day
5. two halves and one whole

Preview Words: Latin Forms ben(e), mal, equ(i)

Write the word from the box that fits each meaning.

equivalence	equivalent	malaise
malaria	unequivocal	

6. a vague feeling of discomfort
7. equal in value or force
8. admitting no doubt
9. being in a state of equality
10. an infectious disease spread by mosquitoes

Connections

Content Words

Math: Estimating

Write a word from the box to complete each sentence.

evaluate	inequality	inverse	opposites	substitution

1. numbers that are the same distance from zero on the number line (for example, −5 and +5)
2. the act of solving by replacing an unknown quantity with a real number
3. a word used to describe an operation that is opposite in effect from another operation
4. an algebraic statement that a quantity is greater than or less than another (for example, 5a > 52)
5. to calculate or set down the numerical value of

Language Arts: Dictionary

Write words from the box to complete the paragraph.

accentuation	definition	etymology
phonetic	pronunciation	

All dictionaries give the meaning, or ___6.___, of a word, and most dictionaries provide ___7.___ symbols to help you pronounce the word. A ___8.___ key interprets the phonetic symbols for you. The dictionary also indicates stressed syllables; this ___9.___ is shown by accent marks. Some dictionaries also provide the history of each word. A word's ___10.___ may be interesting or unexpected.

Apply the Spelling Strategy

Circle the content word that contains the Latin form **equ**.

91

Spelling and Thinking

READ THE SPELLING WORDS

1.	political	*political*	The **political** race for governor has begun.
2.	monarch	*monarch*	The queen has been **monarch** for years.
3.	democracy	*democracy*	Everyone plays a role in a **democracy**.
4.	academy	*academy*	He graduated from a military **academy**.
5.	anarchy	*anarchy*	The rebellion led to lawless **anarchy**.
6.	epidemic	*epidemic*	Doctors are worried about the **epidemic**.
7.	metropolis	*metropolis*	Chicago is a very busy **metropolis**.
8.	demography	*demography*	He is studying the **demography** of the city.
9.	patriarch	*patriarch*	Everyone listened to the family **patriarch**.
10.	academic	*academic*	The historian has an **academic** mind.
11.	acropolis	*acropolis*	The **acropolis** stood on a protected hill.
12.	democrat	*democrat*	A **democrat** has faith in the people.
13.	architecture	*architecture*	We studied **architecture** in college.
14.	politics	*politics*	I liked this book about European **politics**.
15.	bureaucracy	*bureaucracy*	The **bureaucracy** slowed the process.
16.	matriarch	*matriarch*	My grandmother is our family **matriarch**.
17.	metropolitan	*metropolitan*	We ride subways in **metropolitan** areas.
18.	autocratic	*autocratic*	The emperor was an **autocratic** ruler.
19.	politician	*politician*	The mayor is a skilled **politician**.
20.	cosmopolitan	*cosmopolitan*	The diplomat had a **cosmopolitan** view.

SORT THE SPELLING WORDS

1.–7. Write the words with the combining form **polis,** meaning "city."

8.–12. Write the words with the combining form **arch,** meaning "chief" or "highest."

13.–14. Write the words derived from the Greek word **Acadēmia.**

15.–20. Write the words with the combining form **demos,** meaning "people," and/or **crat,** meaning "strength" or "authority." Circle the two words that contain both combining forms.

REMEMBER THE SPELLING STRATEGY

Remember that knowing the Greek combining forms **arch, crat, demos,** and **polis** can give clues to the meaning and spelling of certain words.

Word Meanings

Write the spelling word that could best replace the underlined word or words.

1. I like the structural design of Victorian homes.

2. Scientists feared that an extensively spreading disease would follow the severe floods.

3. The female head of our family has influence over many of our decisions.

4. The professor wrote a lengthy scholarly article for a scientific journal.

5. Our neighbor expressed interest in getting involved in the activities of government.

6. She attends a private school in a neighboring town.

Word Clues

Write a spelling word for each definition.

7. one who is actively involved in government activities

8. government by the people, exercised through elected representatives

9. pertaining to a city

10. the study of the characteristics of human populations

11. a management system

12. pertaining to absolute or unrestricted power

13. dealing with the study, structure, or affairs of government

USING THE Dictionary

Write the spelling word for each etymology.
Use the **Spelling Dictionary** if you need help.

14. **monos,** single + **arkhein,** to rule

15. **patēr,** father + **arkhos,** ruler

16. **kosmos,** world + **politēs,** citizen

17. **mētēr,** mother + **polis,** city

18. **akron,** top + **polis,** city

19. **dēmos,** people + **kratia,** rule

20. **an-,** without + **arkhos,** ruler

political	monarch	democracy	academy	anarchy
epidemic	metropolis	demography	patriarch	academic
acropolis	democrat	architecture	politics	bureaucracy
matriarch	metropolitan	autocratic	politician	cosmopolitan

Complete the Sentences   Write the spelling word that best completes each sentence.

1. The Greek columns were crumbling on the _____.
2. Our city was once a small town, but now it is a thriving _____.
3. Government _____ is responsible for the delays in passing the bill.
4. We consider him the _____ of our community because he is so knowledgeable about the town's history.
5. A _____ believes that everyone should be represented by the government.
6. She has been the _____ of this family for several generations.
7. The newspaper is expanding to cover the entire _____ area.

Solve the Analogies   Write a spelling word to complete each analogy.

8. **Movie theater** is to **cinema** as **school** is to _____.
9. **Ocean** is to **oceanography** as **people** is to _____.
10. **Timid** is to **shy** as **sophisticated** is to _____.
11. **Water** is to **flood** as **illness** is to _____.
12. **Cheerful** is to **friendly** as **studious** is to _____.
13. **Musician** is to **music** as **architect** is to _____.

Complete the Paragraph   Write spelling words from the box to complete the paragraph.

The Greeks contributed greatly to __14.__, the art of governing. The cities of ancient Greece were ruled by a __15.__, or king. Often the king would be overthrown by a tyrant—an __16.__ ruler who kept all power for himself. The tyrant usually rose to power as a __17.__ who claimed to represent the poor. In time, a new __18.__ system emerged. The new form of government was a __19.__, in which the people held the power. Some philosophers, like Plato, feared that this form of government would lead to __20.__, in which no one could rule.

democracy
autocratic
politician
politics
monarch
political
anarchy

Spelling and Writing

Proofread a Paragraph

Six words are not spelled correctly in this paragraph. Write the words correctly.

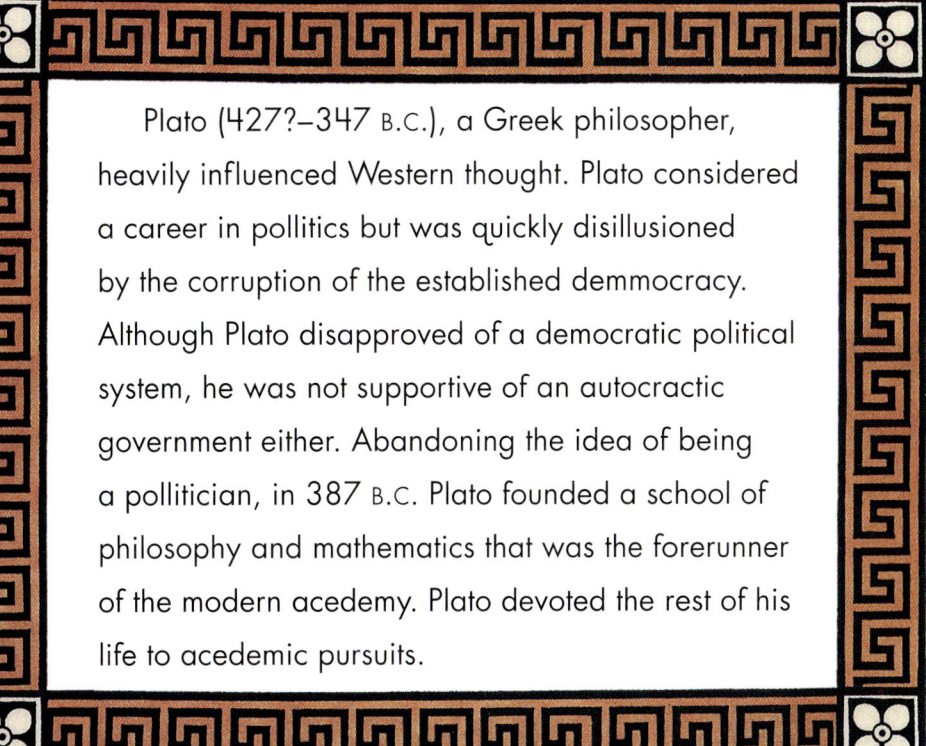

Plato (427?–347 B.C.), a Greek philosopher, heavily influenced Western thought. Plato considered a career in pollitics but was quickly disillusioned by the corruption of the established demmocracy. Although Plato disapproved of a democratic political system, he was not supportive of an autocractic government either. Abandoning the idea of being a pollitician, in 387 B.C. Plato founded a school of philosophy and mathematics that was the forerunner of the modern acedemy. Plato devoted the rest of his life to acedemic pursuits.

Proofreading Marks

☰	Make a capital.
/	Make a small letter.
∧	Add something.
℮	Take out something.
⊙	Add a period.
⌗	New paragraph
⑤ⓟ	Spelling error

Write a Paragraph

Expository Writing

Write a paragraph about someone in politics in your city or town, your state, or the country. Choose a particular focus.

- Focus on the person's career, accomplishments, or beliefs.
- Use reference sources, like encyclopedias, newspapers, magazines, or Web sites, to find accurate information.
- Follow the form used in the proofreading sample. Use as many spelling words as you can.

Proofread Your Writing During

Writing Process

Prewriting
⬇
Drafting
⬇
Revising
⬇
Editing
⬇
Publishing

Proofread your writing for spelling errors as part of the editing stage in the writing process. Be sure to check each word carefully. Use a dictionary to check spelling if you are not sure.

Vocabulary

Strategy Words

Review Words: Greek Combining Forms

Write a word from the box to match each definition.

aristocrat	democratic	oligarchy
	police	policy

1. believing in political equality
2. persons who keep order and enforce the law
3. a plan of action
4. a person who belongs to a privileged upper class
5. form of government in which only a few people have the ruling power

Preview Words: Greek Combining Forms

Write a word from the box to complete each sentence.

cosmopolitanism	democratically	hierarchy
	pandemic	theocracy

6. After many decades as a _____, the country now has a government that separates church and state.
7. The teacher deals with her students fairly and _____.
8. Although the disease was once confined to a small area, it is now _____.
9. Because of its _____, this city is attracting people from all over the world.
10. What is her rank in the political _____?

Connections

Social Studies: Elections

Write the word from the box that matches each definition.

congressional	gubernatorial	judicial
presidential	senatorial	

1. of or relating to a governor
2. having to do with a senate
3. pertaining to a congress
4. relating to the office of a judge
5. of or pertaining to the office of a president

Science: Computers

Write the word from the box that matches each definition.

analog	digital	electronic
magnetic	storage	

An ___6.___ computer represents data by measurable physical qualities. A ___7.___ computer, on the other hand, deals with the binary digits of a numerical code. Both computers use ___8.___ signals to power them. Permanent information is saved on a ___9.___ ___10.___ device called a hard disk.

Apply the Spelling Strategy

Circle the content word you wrote that comes from the Greek combining word **logos,** meaning "proportion."

Spelling and Thinking

READ THE SPELLING WORDS

1.	abundant	*abundant*	We have an **abundant** food supply.
2.	abundance	*abundance*	What an **abundance** of food you have!
3.	observant	*observant*	An **observant** person will see the nest.
4.	observance	*observance*	Our **observance** of the holiday is today.
5.	significant	*significant*	You show **significant** improvement.
6.	significance	*significance*	What is the **significance** of this mark?
7.	relevant	*relevant*	Please provide **relevant** information.
8.	relevance	*relevance*	What is the **relevance** of these data?
9.	evident	*evident*	His joy was **evident** in his face.
10.	evidence	*evidence*	Jurors will study the **evidence** today.
11.	confident	*confident*	I am **confident** that I passed the test.
12.	confidence	*confidence*	My parents have **confidence** in my skill.
13.	permanent	*permanent*	Will the address change be **permanent**?
14.	permanence	*permanence*	Granite is valued for its **permanence**.
15.	intelligent	*intelligent*	You made a very **intelligent** choice.
16.	intelligence	*intelligence*	Scientists study animal **intelligence**.
17.	competent	*competent*	They are both **competent** mechanics.
18.	competence	*competence*	Are you sure of his **competence**?
19.	inconvenient	*inconvenient*	No, this is not an **inconvenient** time.
20.	inconvenience	*inconvenience*	A leg cast is a major **inconvenience**.

SORT THE SPELLING WORDS

1.–4. Write the words with the suffix **-ant**.

5.–8. Write the words with the suffix **-ance**.

9.–14. Write the words with the suffix **-ent**.

15.–20. Write the words with the suffix **-ence**.

REMEMBER THE SPELLING STRATEGY

Remember that the suffixes **-ant**, **-ance**, **-ent**, and **-ence** change the part of speech of a word and how it is used in a sentence.

Word Meanings

Write the spelling word that could best replace each underlined word or phrase.

1. If this is an <u>awkward</u> time, we can meet later.
2. The jury should decide the case based on <u>physical proof</u>, not on rumors.
3. When the detective first saw the empty glass, she did not realize its <u>real importance</u>.
4. This state has an <u>extraordinary amount</u> of natural resources.
5. My birthday was yesterday, but the <u>celebration</u> will be on Friday.
6. We always have bouquets because wildflowers are <u>plentiful</u> in this area.

Word Definitions

Write a spelling word for each definition.

7. fixed and changeless
8. self-assured
9. quick to perceive
10. mentally acute
11. meaningful; noteworthy
12. capable
13. pertinent; appropriate
14. nuisance; something that is awkward or difficult

USING THE Dictionary

Write the spelling word for each dictionary respelling. Use the **Spelling Dictionary** if you need help.

15. /pûr′ mə nəns/
16. /ĕv′ ĭ dənt/
17. /kŏm′ pĭ təns/
18. /kŏn′ fĭ dəns/
19. /ĭn tĕl′ ə jəns/
20. /rĕl′ ə vəns/

abundant	abundance	observant	observance	significant
relevance	intelligence	significance	inconvenience	evidence
confident	confidence	permanent	permanence	intelligent
relevant	competent	competence	inconvenient	evident

Change the Parts of Speech   In each sentence, a spelling word is given in its noun or adjective form. First write the spelling word that appears; then write the spelling word that is the correct part of speech for the sentence.

1.–2. A good speller has confident at a spelling bee.

3.–4. You made a significance contribution to the project.

5.–6. Dolphins and whales are known for their high intelligent.

7.–8. You have more than enough competent to complete this challenging assignment.

9.–10. I hope my dropping in for dinner is not an inconvenient.

11.–12. The most helpful remarks in this discussion are the ones that have the most relevant.

13.–14. What gives you a feeling of permanent?

15.–16. I hope your life has an abundant of joy and fulfillment.

Complete the Paragraph   Write the spelling words from the box to complete the paragraph.

If you are an ___17.___ person, you can always spot wildlife when you go camping. The ___18.___ is everywhere, but it takes practice to recognize small details. Clues like footprints, burrows, and fur make it ___19.___ that animals are around. It goes without saying, of course, that ___20.___ of the rules not to feed or harm wildlife is critical to the safety and enjoyment of both the observers and the observed.

evident
evidence
observant
observance

Spelling and Writing

Proofread an Advertisement

Six words are not spelled correctly in this advertisement. Write the words correctly.

Person wanted: We seek someone who is observent, inteligent, and compitent. The person must have confidance and competence to deal with weather conditions. He or she must have a great tolerance for inconveneice, a sense of humor, and very quick reflexes. If you are qualified and have relevent experience, please apply for the school-bus-driving position today. Driving experience required!

Proofreading Marks

≡	Make a capital.
/	Make a small letter.
∧	Add something.
ℓ	Take out something.
⊙	Add a period.
⌗	New paragraph
ⓢⓟ	Spelling error

Write an Advertisement

Persuasive Writing

Write an advertisement for a position in your school, neighborhood, or community.

- Decide what skills and experience are needed for the position.
- Use humor and imagination to build up to the conclusion of your advertisement.
- Follow the form used in the proofreading sample.

Use as many spelling words as you can.

Proofread Your Writing During

Proofread your writing for spelling errors as part of the editing stage in the writing process. Be sure to check each word carefully. Use a dictionary to check spelling if you are not sure.

Writing Process

Prewriting
⇩
Drafting
⇩
Revising
⇩
Editing
⇩
Publishing

Vocabulary

Strategy Words

Review Words: Suffixes -ant, -ance, -ent, -ence

Write words from the box to complete the paragraph.

attendance	attendant	participant
residence	resident	

Next week, the Warren Institute is holding a music conference. Public __1.__ is encouraged at evening events, but the daytime workshops are meant to increase the skills of practicing artists. Every __2.__ is a well-known musician or singer. During the week, they will live in a __3.__ that the school will provide. They will have private rooms there, and each __4.__ will also have access to studio space. An __5.__ will help transport instruments to performances and practice sessions. The gala performance on Saturday night will include all performers. Tickets will be sold at the door, but advance reservations are recommended.

Preview Words: Suffixes -ant, -ance, -ent, -ence

Write the word from the box that fits each meaning.

effervescent	postulant	proponent
reminiscence	reminiscent	

6. an experience that is recollected

7. one who argues in support of something

8. bubbling or sparkling

9. tending to suggest something in the past

10. person submitting a request or application

Connections

Content Words

Science: Health

Write a word from the box to complete each sentence.

disinfectant	prevention	quarantine
	sanitation	aseptic

1. Some medicines, such as vaccines, are useful for _____ rather than for cure.
2. We scrubbed every surface with a powerful _____.
3. A crew of _____ workers helps keep the city clean.
4. Surgeons once spread germs, but now surgery takes place in an _____ environment.
5. Doctors used to _____ people who had scarlet fever.

Social Studies: Politics

Write the word from the box that matches each clue.

affiliate	constituent	convention
	delegate	nomination

6. _____ describes someone who lives in an elected official's district
7. _____ acts as a representative for another
8. _____ groups that join together do this
9. _____ act of submitting a name to be a candidate
10. _____ a formal meeting of members of a political party

Apply the Spelling Strategy

Circle the suffix **-ant** or **-ent** in two of the content words you wrote.

Spelling and Thinking

READ THE SPELLING WORDS

1. saga	*saga*	Rudy read the exciting **saga**.
2. antique	*antique*	Grandma's cameo is an **antique**.
3. opaque	*opaque*	No light penetrated the **opaque** window.
4. bonanza	*bonanza*	The best-selling novel was a **bonanza**.
5. snorkel	*snorkel*	The mask and **snorkel** fit well.
6. etiquette	*etiquette*	Polite people practice **etiquette**.
7. fiasco	*fiasco*	Meeting at 6 A.M. was a **fiasco**.
8. bungalow	*bungalow*	They are moving into a **bungalow**.
9. reservoir	*reservoir*	The **reservoir** is almost overflowing.
10. yacht	*yacht*	A **yacht** looks big beside a canoe.
11. surgeon	*surgeon*	A **surgeon** set Kate's broken arm.
12. motto	*motto*	Whose **motto** is "United We Stand"?
13. toboggan	*toboggan*	Ride the **toboggan** down the hill.
14. hickory	*hickory*	My walking stick is made of **hickory**.
15. faux pas	*faux pas*	No one noticed Lucy's **faux pas**.
16. brusque	*brusque*	Seth's **brusque** remark hurt her feelings.
17. kindergarten	*kindergarten*	Young children often go to **kindergarten**.
18. boulevard	*boulevard*	Traffic is heavy on the **boulevard**.
19. delicatessen	*delicatessen*	Mom bought food at the **delicatessen**.
20. lacquer	*lacquer*	The **lacquer** makes the table shine.

SORT THE SPELLING WORDS

Use the **Spelling Dictionary** to help you sort the words.

1.–7. Write the words derived from French.

8.–12. Write the words derived from Old Norse, German, and Dutch.

13.–16. Write the words derived from Hindi and Native American languages.

17.–20. Write the words derived from Italian and Spanish.

REMEMBER THE SPELLING STRATEGY

Remember that the English language includes many words from foreign languages.

104

Word Meanings

Write the spelling words that match these definitions.

1. an object valued for its age
2. a tube used for breathing underwater
3. a complete failure
4. a glossy finish
5. a large supply of water
6. discourteously abrupt in words or actions
7. a long, detailed story
8. a source of great wealth
9. accepted or required manners
10. impenetrable by light

Word Groups

Write a spelling word to complete each group.

11. lane, street, avenue, highway, _____
12. dinghy, kayak, motorboat, _____
13. pediatrician, dentist, dermatologist, _____
14. sled, sleigh, luge, _____
15. butcher shop, bakery, grocery store, _____

USING THE Dictionary

Write spelling words for the clues. Use the **Spelling Dictionary** if you need help.

16. German **child** + **garden**
17. Native American **pawcohiccora,** or "food from nuts"
18. French, meaning "false step"
19. Italian **motto,** or "word"
20. Hindi, meaning "house," from Bengali

saga	antique	opaque	bonanza	snorkel
etiquette	fiasco	bungalow	reservoir	yacht
surgeon	motto	toboggan	hickory	faux pas
brusque	kindergarten	boulevard	delicatessen	lacquer

Solve the Analogies   Write the spelling word that best completes each analogy.

1. **Sail** is to **schooner** as **motor** is to _____.
2. **Language** is to **grammar** as **behavior** is to _____.
3. **Saw** is to **carpenter** as **scalpel** is to _____.
4. **Rock** is to **marble** as **wood** is to _____.
5. **Automobile** is to **vehicle** as **belch** is to _____.
6. **Eat** is to **fork** as **breathe** is to _____.
7. **Building** is to **skyscraper** as **house** is to _____.
8. **Obvious** is to **transparent** as **impenetrable** is to _____.

Replace the Words   Write a spelling word that is a synonym for each underlined word or phrase.

9. Have you ever ridden on a <u>runnerless sled</u>?
10. At what age did you go to <u>the class before first grade</u>?
11. We send you a <u>large supply</u> of appreciation.
12. I am writing a poem based on a Norse <u>prose narrative</u>.
13. The discovery of gold was a <u>source of great wealth</u> for the miners.

Complete the Letter   Write the spelling words from the box to complete the letter.

Dear Tom,

   We are having a great time in Paris. Our hotel is on a tree-lined __14.__. I had hoped to see everything at the Louvre, but that was a __15.__ since the museum has more than 250,000 works of art. I especially enjoyed the galleries of __16.__ vases, some of which still have their original shiny __17.__. The Parisians are sometimes __18.__, but they do not hurt our feelings. I love the food. Once we even ate in an American-style __19.__. We've eaten a mountain of French pastry. This is a new twist on Marie Antoinette's __20.__ "Let them eat cake"! I miss you.

motto
antique
fiasco
lacquer
boulevard
delicatessen
brusque

Mai

Spelling and Writing

Proofread a Paragraph

Six words are not spelled correctly in this paragraph from a book about good manners. Write the words correctly.

A cruise on a yawt requires a special type of etikit. For example, because many boat decks are made of teak or hickery, passengers should wear shoes with rubber soles. These shoes protect the decks and also prevent people from slipping and breaking a bone. After all, a surgeon may not be onboard. Not using the correct names for the parts of the boat is considered a foe pas and may earn a brusqe comment from the captain. By knowing how to act on a boat, you can appear to be an experienced sailor rather than a kindergarden novice.

Proofreading Marks

≡ Make a capital.

/ Make a small letter.

∧ Add something.

℮ Take out something.

⊙ Add a period.

⌗ New paragraph

(SP) Spelling error

Write a Paragraph

 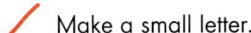
Expository Writing

As a travel agent, you have discovered that many of your clients are inexperienced travelers. Therefore, you have decided to give them some general information to help them know what to expect, no matter where they are going.

- Choose a specific way of traveling or a specific destination.
- Give suggestions about clothes to bring, based on climate or other considerations, and give advice about how to be prepared for particular situations.
- Follow the form used in the proofreading sample.

Use as many spelling words as you can.

Writing Process

Prewriting
⇩
Drafting
⇩
Revising
⇩
Editing
⇩
Publishing

Proofread Your Writing During ➤ Editing

Proofread your writing for spelling errors as part of the editing stage in the writing process. Be sure to check each word carefully. Use a dictionary to check spelling if you are not sure.

Strategy Words

Review Words: Words From Other Languages

Write a word from the box to complete each sentence.

avocado	chandelier	corsage
mirage	sombrero	

1. The crystal _____ sparkled above the dance floor.
2. The cowhand wore an enormous _____ to shield his face from the sun.
3. There was no water ahead; unfortunately, it was only a _____ in the distance.
4. We put cheese, tomato, and _____ on our tacos.
5. Grandmother wore an orchid _____ at her seventieth birthday party.

Preview Words: Words From Other Languages

Write the word from the box that matches each clue.

cassava	maelstrom	quinine
smorgasbord	veneer	

6. You should have a good appetite to attend one of these.
7. This can be a large and violent whirlpool—or a situation that feels like one!
8. This is a starchy root vegetable.
9. This can be used to treat malaria.
10. A thin layer of wood applied to a surface is called this.

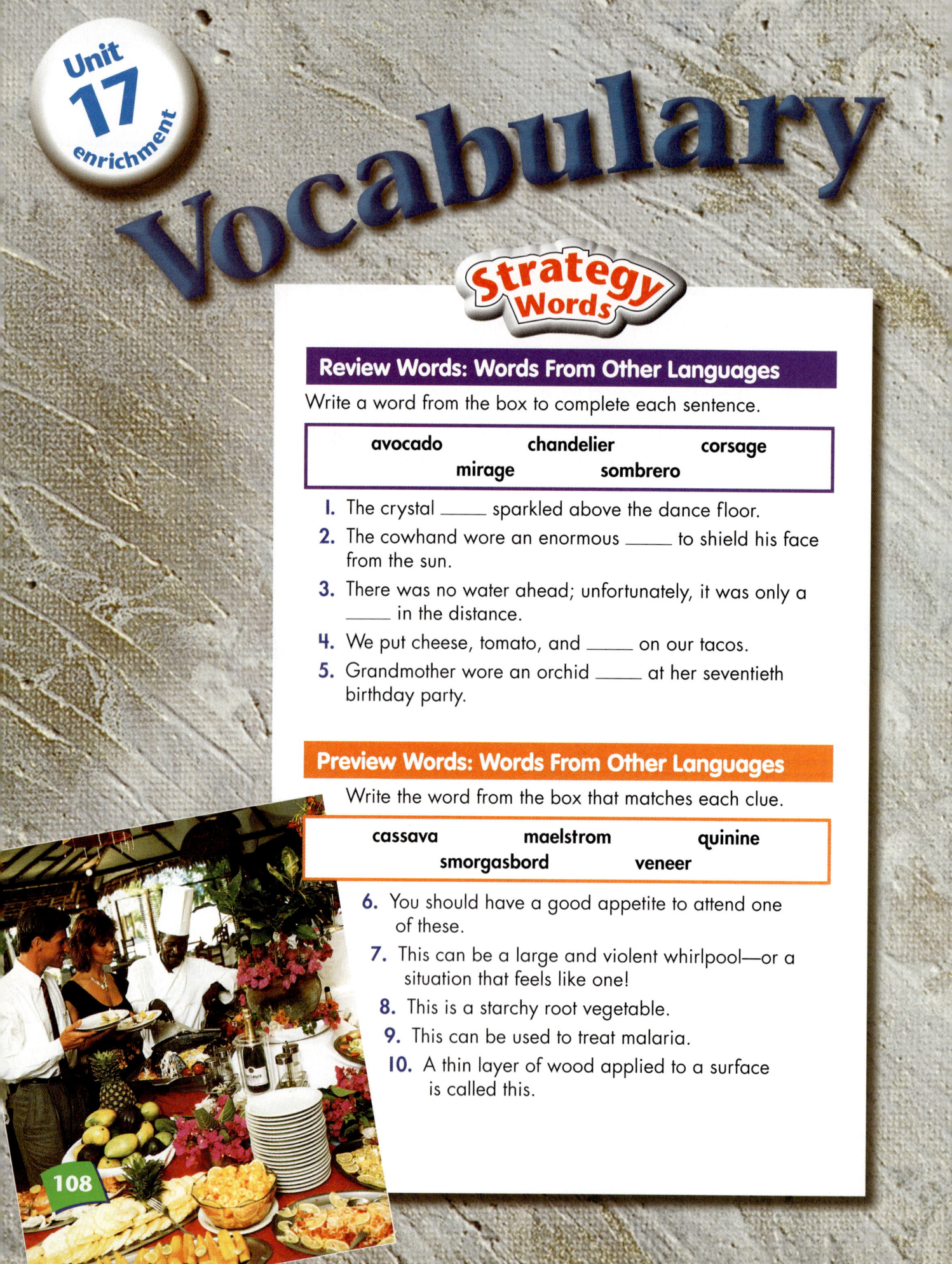

108

Connections

Content Words

Fine Arts: Furniture

Write the word from the box that fits each meaning.

baroque	elaborate	flourish	grandeur	ornamental

1. a European style of art, architecture, and music (1550–1700) that was highly ornamented
2. magnificence
3. serving as a decoration
4. to express in great detail
5. an embellishment or ornamentation

Social Studies: Commerce

Write a word from the box to complete each sentence.

entrepreneur	establish	innovative	venture	initiative

6. It takes _____, courage, and creativity to change your career path.
7. Ms. Parker's new _____ involves buying gifts for people who have no time to shop.
8. Carly would make a good _____; she has the ideas, know-how, and money to start her own business.
9. Both traditional-looking and _____ home pages are added to the Internet daily.
10. It may take a while for you to _____ an excellent reputation in your field of work, but you can do it.

Apply the Spelling Strategy

Circle the three content words you wrote that come from the French language.

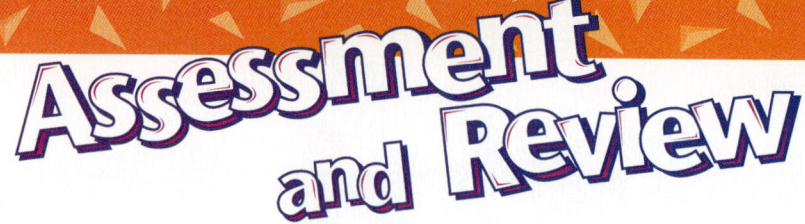
Assessment — Units 13–17

Each Assessment Word in the box fits one of the spelling strategies you have studied over the past five weeks. Read the spelling strategies. Then write each Assessment Word under the unit number it fits.

Unit 13

1.–5. Remember that a final consonant preceded by a single vowel is doubled when adding a suffix that begins with a vowel, except when the accent is on or shifts to the first syllable.

Unit 14

6.–11. Remember that knowing Latin forms like **ben(e)**, **mal**, and **equ(i)** can give clues to the meaning and spelling of certain words.

Unit 15

12.–14. Remember that knowing the Greek combining forms **arch**, **crat**, **demos**, and **polis** can give clues to the meaning and spelling of certain words.

Unit 16

15.–20. Remember that the suffixes **-ant**, **-ance**, **-ent**, and **-ence** change the part of speech of a word and how it is used in a sentence.

Unit 17

Remember that the English language includes many words from foreign languages.

unwrapping
insignificant
benefaction
aristocratic
malevolence
vehement
unwrapped
endemic
regretting
Neapolitan
transferring
vehemence
benefited
maliciousness
insignificance
inequity
forgettable
lenience
brilliance
equilibrist

Unit 13: Adding Suffixes/Doubling Final Consonants

forbidden	committed	regrettable	regret	control
controlled	forgetting	unforgettable	forbid	commit

Add the missing letters to write a spelling word.

1. c＿＿t＿＿l
2. r＿＿r＿t

3. co＿＿it
4. f＿rb＿d

Do the math to write a spelling word.

5. unforget + able =
6. forbid + en =
7. control + ed =

8. regret + able =
9. commit + ed =
10. forget + ing =

Unit 14: Latin Forms ben(e), mal, equ(i)

benevolent	equilibrium	equate	malady	equality
beneficial	malnutrition	benefit	malice	malicious

Write a spelling word for each definition. The spelling word will be the part of speech given in parentheses.

11. (adj.)   having a desire to harm others
12. (v.)   to consider or show as equal
13. (n.)   a stable, balanced, or unchanging system
14. (adj.)   promoting a favorable result
15. (n.)   the desire to harm others
16. (n.)   the same quality or value as another
17. (adj.)   kindly; characterized by kindness
18. (n.)   something that improves one's well-being
19. (n.)   a disease or disorder
20. (n.)   a condition caused by lack of food

Unit 15: Greek Forms arch, crat, demos, polis

metropolitan	epidemic	democracy	monarch	academic
architecture	politics	bureaucracy	political	politician

Write the spelling words by filling in the missing letters.

1. _ _ _ _arch
2. e_ _dem_ _
3. poli_ _ _ _ _l
4. poli_ _ _ _ _ _n
5. a_ _dem_ _

6. _u_ _ _ _ _cra_ _
7. arch_ _ _ _ _ _ _ _r_
8. poli_ _ _ _ _
9. demo_ _ _ _ _ _
10. _ _ _ _ _ _poli_ _ _

**Review**

Unit 16: Suffixes -ant, -ance, -ent, -ence

evident	abundance	significance	significant	abundant
evidence	permanent	permanence	competent	competence

Write a spelling word to complete each sentence.

11. The settlers celebrated having an _____ of food.
12. It is _____ that computer use is increasing.
13. No one questioned the _____ of the teenager when it came to computers.
14. After several moves, they finally settled in _____ housing.
15. Apples are so _____ this year that prices have gone down.
16. We noticed a _____ difference in the children's behavior.
17. They hope the mechanic is _____ to repair the transmission.
18. Never underestimate the _____ of a good appearance.
19. The detectives examined the _____.
20. Don't worry about the _____ of the grape juice stain.

Unit 17: Words From Other Languages

antique	delicatessen	etiquette	reservoir	surgeon
toboggan	kindergarten	boulevard	opaque	lacquer

Write the spelling word that belongs with each group.

1. ophthalmologist, orthodontist, _____
2. manners, graciousness, _____
3. avenue, street, lane, _____
4. ancient, old, aged, _____
5. storage, supply, reserve, _____
6. sleigh, ski, sled, _____
7. paint, varnish, _____
8. transparent, translucent, _____
9. café, bistro, _____
10. nursery school, preschool, _____

Spelling Study Strategy

Sorting by Suffixes and Root Words

One good way to practice your spelling words is to place the words into groups according to some spelling pattern. Here is a way to practice some of the spelling words you have studied in the past few weeks.

1. Make several columns on a large piece of paper or on the chalkboard.

2. At the top of each column write one of these suffixes or roots: **-ant, -ance, -ent, -ence, ben(e), mal, equ(i), arch, crat, demos, polis**.

3. Have a partner choose a spelling word from Units 14–16 and say it aloud.

4. Write the spelling word in the appropriate column.

5. For more practice, find additional words with these suffixes or roots and challenge the class.

Grammar, Usage, and Mechanics

Capitalization

Proper nouns, the **first word of a direct quotation,** and **important words in titles** must be capitalized in sentences.

Did you hear the announcement?
I think the announcer said, "**G**et your tickets for **S**aturday's performance of *The* ***M****an* ***W****ithout a* ***C****ountry.*"

A. Write the proper nouns in each sentence that should be capitalized.

  1. I bought the old chair at ruby's Antique Shoppe.
  2. Does Lake huron freeze over in the winter?
  3. We took the children to Patty's petting Zoo.
  4. The morgan horse is named after the man who developed it.
  5. The show begins at 7:00 in sterling Arena.

B. Write the word in each sentence that should be capitalized. If the sentence is already correct, write OK.

  6. Who said, "go west, young man, go west"?
  7. As Shakespeare wrote, "all the world's a stage."
  8. "Now, look," said Mrs. Lewis, "at the mess you've made."
  9. They sang the words, "happy birthday to you."
  10. "Please get your room cleaned," said Dad, "or I will be very unhappy."

C. Write the title words that should be capitalized.

  11. *The call of the Wild*
  12. *Spotty: The Story of a dalmatian*
  13. *under the Sea*
  14. *Green eggs and Ham*
  15. *Cat Named wonderful*

WORKSHOP

Circle and Check

Good writers always proofread their writing for spelling errors. Here's a strategy you can use to proofread your papers.

Instead of reading your paper the regular way, look at just the first three or four words. Are they spelled correctly? If you are sure that they are correct, go on and check the next three or four words. If you are not sure of the spelling of a word, circle it and keep going. Look at your whole paper this way—one small group of words at a time.

When you finish, get a dictionary and check the spelling of all the circled words. Looking up several words at once is faster than looking them up one by one. Try it!

Electronic Spelling

The Internet

There is a world full of information available through the Internet, and more is added each day. A knowledge of common Latin and Greek word roots will be helpful in spelling guide words correctly as you use the Internet.

Use your knowledge of the word roots **ben(e), mal, equ(i)** and the forms **arch, crat, demos,** and **polis** to find the incorrect spelling in these search topics. If a word is correct, write **OK**.

1. melignant tumors
2. retirement benifits
3. home equity loans
4. democratic countries
5. grassroots pollitics
6. artched bridges

Spelling and Thinking

READ THE SPELLING WORDS

1. regal	*regal*	The elegant film star had a **regal** look.
2. dominate	*dominate*	He tends to **dominate** a conversation.
3. urban	*urban*	New York City is a large **urban** area.
4. domineer	*domineer*	The tyrant always tries to **domineer**.
5. regime	*regime*	The new **regime** made daily life better.
6. suburb	*suburb*	We used to live in a **suburb** of Seattle.
7. regulate	*regulate*	Can they **regulate** rush-hour traffic?
8. civic	*civic*	Voting is a **civic** duty we appreciate.
9. docile	*docile*	I chose the most **docile** horse to ride.
10. indomitable	*indomitable*	Despite his illness, he was **indomitable**.
11. doctrine	*doctrine*	She teaches the **doctrine** of modern law.
12. suburban	*suburban*	They moved to a quiet **suburban** town.
13. regulation	*regulation*	The latest **regulation** protects the park.
14. republic	*republic*	He was president of the old **republic**.
15. civilization	*civilization*	Early Mayan **civilization** is fascinating.
16. dominant	*dominant*	What is the **dominant** theme of her art?
17. publicize	*publicize*	How will they **publicize** the new hotel?
18. predominant	*predominant*	What is the **predominant** language there?
19. documentary	*documentary*	We saw a **documentary** on space travel.
20. republican	*republican*	What is a **republican** form of government?

SORT THE SPELLING WORDS

1.–3.   Write the words with the root **urb**, meaning "city."
4.–6.   Write the words with the root **public**, meaning "people."
7.–10. Write the words with the root **reg**, meaning "rule."
11.–12. Write the words with the root **civ**, meaning "citizen."
13.–15. Write the words with the root **doc**, meaning "teach."
16.–20. Write the words with the root **dom**, meaning "to rule."

REMEMBER THE SPELLING STRATEGY

Remember that knowing Latin roots like **urb, public, reg, civ, doc,** and **dom** can give clues to the meaning and spelling of certain words.

Spelling and Vocabulary

Word Meanings

Write the spelling word that matches each definition.

1. to control or direct according to a rule
2. pertaining to a city or citizen
3. a rule or law designed to control or govern behavior
4. pertaining to a nation or state in which citizens elect government representatives
5. an objective presentation of facts, sometimes on film
6. a political order whose head is usually a president
7. a residential area outlying a city

Word Groups

Write the spelling word that completes each group.

8. manageable, obedient, agreeable, _____
9. invincible, unconquerable, fearless, _____
10. heavily populated, metropolitan, _____
11. government, administration, _____
12. belief, teaching, conviction, _____
13. make public, promote, make known, _____
14. royal, stately, majestic, _____

USING THE Dictionary

Write the spelling words for the dictionary respellings. Circle the syllable that receives the primary stress in each word. Underline the syllable (if there is one) that receives the secondary stress. Use the **Spelling Dictionary** if you need help.

15. prĭ **dŏm** ə nənt
16. dŏm ə **nîr**
17. **dŏm** ə nənt
18. sə **bûr** bən
19. sĭv ə lĭ **zā** shən
20. **dŏm** ə nāt

regal	dominate	urban	domineer	regime
suburb	regulate	civic	predominant	indomitable
doctrine	suburban	republic	regulation	civilization
dominant	publicize	docile	documentary	republican

Complete the Sentences   Write the spelling word that best completes each sentence.

1. It is against a school _____ to leave without permission.

2. When the dictator was overthrown, a new _____ took control of the government.

3. I enjoy living in a lively _____ area that is filled with shops, restaurants, and movies.

4. A major television network is filming a _____ about the world's largest dormant volcano.

5. She lives in a _____ of Los Angeles and commutes to work in the city.

6. Andorra is a small _____ between Spain and France in the Pyrenees mountains.

7. Having just moved from the city, he now has to adjust to _____ life.

Replace the Words   Write the spelling word that best replaces the underlined word or words in each sentence.

8. The king was known as someone who always needed to <u>tyrannize</u>.

9. His <u>unwavering</u> attitude helped the team to victory.

10. The <u>most prominent</u> theme in his books is the power of faith.

11. The production company will <u>advertise</u> its play in local newspapers.

12. He tried to promote his unique <u>philosophy</u> among the people in the community.

13. Can you <u>adjust</u> the volume on the television?

14. This <u>tame</u> dog is perfect for a family with children.

15. She had the <u>noble</u> bearing of a queen.

Complete the Paragraph   Write spelling words from the box to complete the paragraph.

predominant
dominate
republican
civilization
civic

Governmental theory was one of the great Roman contributions to modern __16.__. Under a __17.__ form of government, the Romans managed to __18.__ the ancient world. Our ideas about __19.__ responsibility are largely derived from the Romans, but the __20.__ effect of the Roman regime is the type of government we live under today.

Spelling and Writing

Proofread a Paragraph

Six words are not spelled correctly in this paragraph. Write the words correctly.

When I was growing up on a suburbin street, my two best friends were as different as night and day. My predominent memory of Alida is that she was even-tempered and docel, with an almost regal dignity about her. Lani, on the other hand, would barge into a room and immediately domanate the conversation. With great enthusiasm, she would take the dominent role in whatever activity we did or game we played. I was drawn to each friend for very different reasons: Alida for her easy and quiet grace and Lani for her cheerful and indomitible spirit.

Proofreading Marks

≡	Make a capital.
/	Make a small letter.
∧	Add something.
ℒ	Take out something.
⊙	Add a period.
⌗	New paragraph
⑤℗	Spelling error

Write a Paragraph

Expository Writing

Comparison shows the similarities between topics. **Contrast** shows the differences. Choose two people or topics that you can compare and contrast.

- Use a point-by-point focus to discuss each person or topic.
- Show the similarities and the differences, and comment on those points if you wish.
- Follow the form used in the proofreading sample. Use as many spelling words as you can.

Proofread Your Writing During

Writing Process

Prewriting
⇩
Drafting
⇩
Revising
⇩
Editing
⇩
Publishing

Proofread your writing for spelling errors as part of the editing stage in the writing process. Be sure to check each word carefully. Use a dictionary to check spelling if you are not sure.

119

Vocabulary

Strategy Words

Review Words: Latin Roots

Write the words from the box to complete the news story.

civil	document	public	publish	regular

MIDDLETOWN—City council meets on a ___1.___ basis, but last night it held a special meeting to discuss preserving historic buildings. Local historian Philip McDowell announced that he is about to ___2.___ a ___3.___ entitled "Dusting off Our Historic Treasures." McDowell announced that both private and ___4.___ contributions have brought the community together on this preservation effort and that all groups have been friendly and ___5.___ .

Preview Words: Latin Roots

Write a word from the box that best replaces the underlined word or words in each sentence.

civility	indoctrinate	publicist	regicide	urbane

6. The polite, refined architect presented his plans for the new museum.

7. He was arrested and accused of the act of killing a king.

8. The judge insisted on courtesy in the courtroom during the trial.

9. The sergeant's job was to train the new recruits in the military routine.

10. The popular singer hired a press agent to deal with the media.

Connections

Social Studies: Ancient Rome

Write words from the box to complete the paragraph.

chariot	coliseum	forum	gladiator	legion

In early Roman times, a temporary wooden amphitheater was erected in the public __1.__. Romans used it for entertainment and assemblies. Later, they constructed a massive __2.__ from concrete and stone. The ingeniously devised system of entrances, hallways, and staircases allowed for a __3.__ of spectators to come and go quickly. Here battles between men and wild beasts, __4.__ races, and other kinds of public entertainment took place. Trumpets would blare, and a __5.__ would enter the arena to thunderous applause. The activity in this remarkable building continued for more than four hundred years.

Science: Research

Write a word from the box that corresponds to each type of scientific study.

agronomy	botany	chemistry	physics	zoology

6. animals
7. plants
8. matter and energy

9. soil and plant management
10. composition, structure, and properties of matter

Apply the Spelling Strategy

Circle the content word you wrote that is derived from the Latin roots **carrus,** meaning "cart."

Spelling and Thinking

READ THE SPELLING WORDS

1. expose	*expose*	Do not **expose** the film to light.
2. intercede	*intercede*	He tried to **intercede** during their argument.
3. succeed	*succeed*	Their plan for the ballpark will **succeed**.
4. suspend	*suspend*	Please **suspend** judgment until tomorrow.
5. impose	*impose*	Our guests did not want to **impose** on us.
6. pendant	*pendant*	The **pendant** dangled from a gold chain.
7. exceed	*exceed*	You must not **exceed** the baggage limit.
8. supersede	*supersede*	These game rules **supersede** the old ones.
9. proceed	*proceed*	We will now **proceed** with the meeting.
10. recede	*recede*	Ocean waters **recede** at low tide.
11. depend	*depend*	We **depend** on them for a ride to school.
12. disposal	*disposal*	The ring is stuck in the garbage **disposal**.
13. suspense	*suspense*	She could not stand the **suspense** any longer.
14. transpose	*transpose*	Did you accidentally **transpose** two numbers?
15. posture	*posture*	The athletes had excellent **posture**.
16. concede	*concede*	I **concede** the chess match to my opponent.
17. impostor	*impostor*	The reporter proved to be an **impostor**.
18. precede	*precede*	Soup will **precede** the main course.
19. pendulum	*pendulum*	The clock's **pendulum** swung back and forth.
20. imposition	*imposition*	I am afraid this is an **imposition** on you.

SORT THE SPELLING WORDS

1.–3. Write the words that end in **ceed,** meaning "to go."

4.–7. Write the words that end in **cede,** meaning "to go" or "to yield."

8. Write the word that ends in **sede,** meaning "to sit."

9.–13. Write the words containing the root **pend** (or a form of it), meaning "to hang."

14.–20. Write the words containing the root **pos,** meaning "to place."

REMEMBER THE SPELLING STRATEGY

Remember that a final /sēd/ may be spelled **ceed, cede,** or **sede.** Knowing Latin roots like **ced, pend,** or **pos** can give clues to the meaning and spelling of certain words.

Word Meanings

Write the spelling word that matches each definition.

1. a burdensome or unfair demand
2. to rely or count on
3. to go beyond or pass
4. a swinging object suspended from a fixed support
5. a pretender or fraud
6. a position or attitude of the body
7. uncertainty or anxiety over an unresolved situation
8. something suspended from something else, especially a piece of jewelry attached to a necklace
9. the act of throwing something away

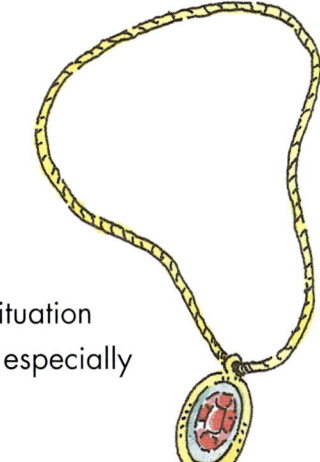

Antonyms

Write the spelling word that is an antonym for the underlined word in each sentence.

10. The lawyer attempted to <u>conceal</u> the most important evidence in the case.
11. The Senate voted to <u>remove</u> a tax on foreign imports.
12. A week after the storm, the floodwaters continued to <u>advance</u>.
13. Everyone hopes to <u>fail</u> in his or her first job.
14. The commander ordered his troops to <u>retreat</u>.
15. By the end of the conversation, she was willing to <u>deny</u> her mistake.

USING THE Dictionary

Write the spelling word that matches each etymology. Use the **Spelling Dictionary** if you need help.

16. **prae-,** before + **cedere,** to go
17. **sub-,** from below + **pendere,** to hang
18. **inter-,** between + **cedere,** to go
19. **trans-,** across + **ponere,** to place
20. **super-,** above + **sedēre,** to sit

Spelling and Reading

expose	intercede	succeed	suspend	impose
pendant	exceed	supersede	proceed	recede
depend	disposal	suspense	transpose	posture
concede	impostor	precede	pendulum	imposition

Answer the Questions   Write the spelling word that answers each question.

1. What might it be if weekend guests stayed for a month?
2. What is an important part of a grandfather clock?
3. What are you trying to improve if you stand tall and put your shoulders back?
4. What can help you get rid of garbage?
5. What do ocean waters do at low tide?
6. What hangs as an ornament or a piece of jewelry?

Replace the Words   Write the spelling word that best replaces the underlined word or words in each sentence.

7. We must be sure not to go beyond our budget for this vacation.
8. The new home run record will replace the old one in the record book.
9. When I failed to convince the coach, one of the other players offered to step in.
10. Be careful not to reverse the order of two numbers in figuring out the problem.
11. The sales clerk had to admit that he had miscalculated the bill.
12. The salesperson said she did not want to force her ideas on us.
13. They had to discontinue building until they raised more money.
14. A brief introduction by the producer will come before the play.

Complete the Paragraph   Write spelling words from the box to complete the paragraph.

To __15.__ in writing a mystery story, consider these points. First, to hold a reader's attention, you have to create a feeling of __16.__. Second, to try to predict the ending, the reader has to __17.__ on details that you provide. However, you should include several possible suspects, perhaps even an __18.__ or two, so that the mystery is not too easily solved. Finally, the characters have to __19.__ to __20.__ clues that eventually lead to an ending that, at best, is both surprising and logical to the reader.

expose
depend
succeed
impostor
suspense
proceed

124

Spelling and Writing

Proofread a Beginning

Six words are not spelled correctly in this beginning of a mystery. Write the words correctly.

> The unwieldy door clanged open. "You may procede to Room 13. Mr. Brodie is expecting you," the faceless voice ordered.
>
> Henry trembled as he stumbled down the dark hall. A faint gleam of light began to expose the form of a tall man with the straightest poschure Henry had ever seen. The man was clothed in black and wore a gold chain with a gleaming pendent.
>
> "I'm afraid I must impoze on you to tell me what you know about the project," Mr. Brodie demanded.
>
> "There must be some mistake," Henry stammered.
>
> "If there was a mistake," Mr. Brodie boomed, "it was yours. I must dipend on you to help me suceed in my quest."

Proofreading Marks

≡	Make a capital.
/	Make a small letter.
∧	Add something.
ℓ	Take out something.
⊙	Add a period.
⌗	New paragraph
SP	Spelling error

Write a Beginning

Narrative Writing

Write the beginning of a mystery.

- Start in the middle of the action so that you immediately capture the reader's interest.
- Use conversation to make the story lively.
- Follow the form used in the proofreading sample. Use as many spelling words as you can.

Proofread Your Writing During →

Proofread your writing for spelling errors as part of the editing stage in the writing process. Be sure to check each word carefully. Use a dictionary to check spelling if you are not sure.

Writing Process

Prewriting
⇩
Drafting
⇩
Revising
⇩
Editing
⇩
Publishing

125

Vocabulary

Strategy Words

Review Words: Latin Roots

Write words from the box to complete the paragraph.

expend	positively	oppose
position	suppose	

Where do you __1.__ my homework is? I __2.__ do not want to __3.__ any more energy looking for it. Now I am in a very difficult __4.__. I most strongly __5.__ your suggestion that I start the assignment over again!

Preview Words: Latin Roots

Write a word from the box to complete each sentence.

exceeding	independently	precedent
preceding	presuppose	

6. Mr. Tiberio set a _____ as the first teacher in our school to post homework assignments on his Web site.

7. This year, the wheelchair race will be _____ the runners in the marathon.

8. The contributions collected so far are _____ all estimates.

9. The lost hikers managed _____ to find their way back to the campsite.

10. Our teacher will _____ that we all learned basic mathematical concepts last year.

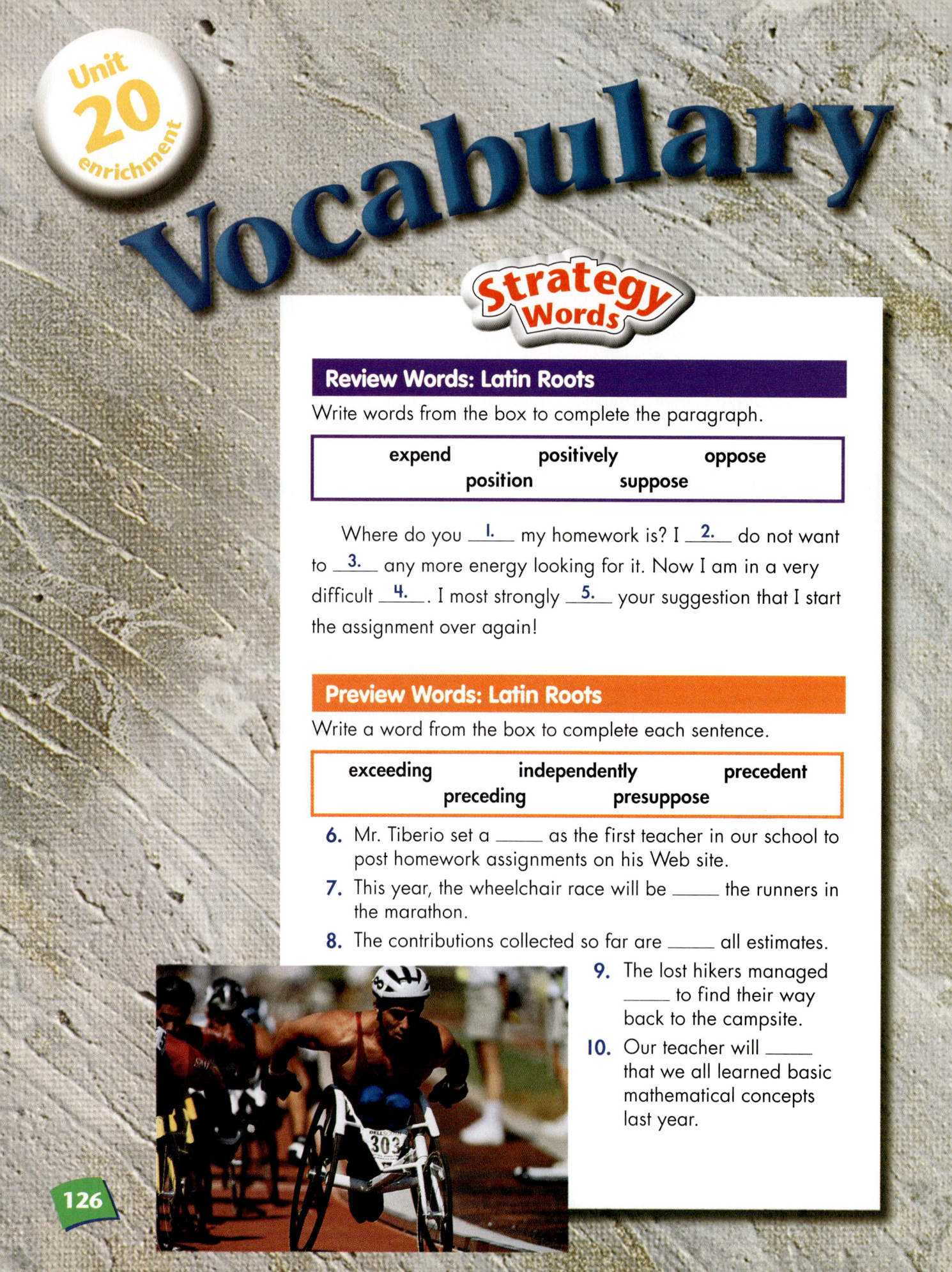

Connections

Content Words

Math: Statistics

Write a word from the box to complete each sentence.

> **dependent   independent   outcome   probability   random**

1. According to the weather forecast, the _____ of rain tomorrow is 90 percent.
2. The winners were chosen from a _____ sample of the population.
3. Two events are _____ if the occurrence of the first does not affect the occurrence of the second.
4. One possible _____ of tossing two coins in the air is that they will both land heads up.
5. Two events are _____ if the occurrence of one affects the occurrence of the other.

Social Studies: Diplomacy

Write words from the box to complete the paragraph.

> **aggression   concession   diplomacy   mediation   neutrality**

Unlike the situation in the rest of Europe during World War II, there was no need for an attempt at settlement, or __6.__, between Sweden and the warring nations. Sweden maintained its __7.__ by using __8.__ and by making more than one __9.__ to Germany. Although other European countries were put at risk by Nazi __10.__, Sweden was not a crucial country for the Germans.

Apply the Spelling Strategy

Circle the two content words you wrote that contain the Latin root **pend**.

Spelling and Thinking

READ THE SPELLING WORDS

1.	deduce	*deduce*	What do you **deduce** from the results?
2.	relocate	*relocate*	My family plans to **relocate** to Ohio.
3.	vocal	*vocal*	The soccer coach is **vocal** in her praise.
4.	allocate	*allocate*	They will **allocate** funds for a new school.
5.	vocalize	*vocalize*	The baby is happy to **vocalize** all day long.
6.	induct	*induct*	The club must **induct** the new members.
7.	dislocate	*dislocate*	This job change will **dislocate** our family.
8.	production	*production*	They worked hard on the play **production**.
9.	evoke	*evoke*	This scrapbook may **evoke** happy memories.
10.	reduction	*reduction*	Our city has seen a **reduction** in population.
11.	vocation	*vocation*	Her **vocation** is in the field of teaching.
12.	locomotion	*locomotion*	Flying is a common form of **locomotion**.
13.	revoke	*revoke*	Congress voted to **revoke** the tax law.
14.	deductive	*deductive*	Math requires **deductive** thinking.
15.	locality	*locality*	Many apartments are in this **locality**.
16.	induction	*induction*	His **induction** into the Hall of Fame is today.
17.	invoke	*invoke*	From whom shall we **invoke** assistance?
18.	induce	*induce*	Advertisements **induce** people to buy things.
19.	advocate	*advocate*	The group is an **advocate** for animal rights.
20.	vocabulary	*vocabulary*	Reading will improve your **vocabulary**.

SORT THE SPELLING WORDS

1.–8. Write the spelling words with the root **voc/vok,** meaning "voice."

9.–15. Write the spelling words with the root **duc/duct,** meaning "lead."

16.–20. Write the spelling words with the root **loc,** meaning "place."

REMEMBER THE SPELLING STRATEGY

Remember that knowing Latin roots like **voc/vok, duc/duct,** and **loc** can give clues to the meaning and spelling of certain words.

Spelling AND Vocabulary

Word Meanings

Write the spelling word that matches each definition.

1. to establish in a new place
2. all the words of a language
3. to express or say out loud
4. to withdraw or take back
5. a diminishing or lessening
6. to call forth or inspire
7. relating to reaching conclusions by reasoning

Word Replacements

Write the spelling word that best replaces the underlined word or words in each sentence.

8. From her letter, I <u>conclude</u> that she is happy at her new school.
9. The gymnast had to be careful not to <u>displace a bone in</u> his shoulder.
10. This afternoon we will <u>install</u> the new officers.
11. With increased sales of new cars, the company will speed up <u>manufacturing</u>.
12. I know we can <u>persuade</u> him to rollerblade with us.
13. The <u>installation</u> of the new governor will take place tomorrow.
14. You should <u>set aside</u> some of your allowance for your school trip.
15. The witness decided to <u>apply</u> the Fifth Amendment and not answer the question.

USING THE Thesaurus

Write the spelling word that is the synonym for each group of words. Use the **Writing Thesaurus** if you need help.

16. frank, outspoken, straightforward
17. area, district, site
18. recommend, support, champion
19. career, occupation, profession
20. mobility, movement, travel

deduce	relocate	vocal	allocate	vocalize
induct	dislocate	production	evoke	reduction
vocation	locomotion	revoke	deductive	locality
induction	invoke	induce	advocate	vocabulary

Complete the Sentences Write the spelling word that completes each sentence.

1. Phone repairs will be made in homes in your _____.
2. The company plans to _____ to a larger building.
3. With no concrete evidence, the detective used _____ reasoning to solve the case.
4. Many of the students _____ a longer lunch break.
5. The president decided to _____ his veto power.
6. To work as a veterinarian is her dream _____.
7. This book contains some difficult _____ words.
8. The army will _____ its new military recruits tomorrow.
9. Dr. Hernandez told me that I did not _____ my knee.
10. The club's _____ ceremony will take place in the auditorium.

Find the Antonyms Write the spelling word that is an antonym of each underlined word.

11. He will wait for a price increase before he buys that suit.
12. The first grader is quite reserved when playing with friends.
13. Students will withhold the money they made in the car wash.
14. Congress is voting on a bill that would restore the tax.
15. Teachers encourage students to suppress their opinions in class discussion.

Complete the Paragraph Write spelling words from the box to complete the paragraph.

The construction of an ant nest is an elaborate __16.__ . Each ant carries a load of soil five times its own weight and is in constant __17.__ as it helps dig a network of tunnels and chambers. The ants construct chambers for resting, food storage, nurseries, and, of course, the royal suite for the queen. From now on, an anthill will always __18.__ my admiration. As you can __19.__ from all I have learned, nothing would __20.__ me to destroy such a work of art and effort.

induce
deduce
evoke
locomotion
production

Spelling and Writing

Proofread a Paragraph

Six words are not spelled correctly in this paragraph. Write the words correctly.

Max is my loyal companion. We play games, go for walks, and spend time together whenever we can. I know he's happy to see me when he throws his seventy pounds at me to say hello. He can vocilize his needs with his extensive vocabulery, including unique barks for "Let's play," "I'm hungry," and "How about a walk?" Always in locamotion, he is able to evoake a smile from me even when I am grumpy, but every now and then I must invoke some of the ground rules we learned in puppy kindergarten. Most of the time, though, he can induse me to give him a treat just by looking at me with his warm, friendly eyes. You might diduce that Max has me wrapped around his big paw. You are probably right.

Proofreading Marks

≡ Make a capital.

/ Make a small letter.

∧ Add something.

℘ Take out something.

⊙ Add a period.

⌗ New paragraph

ⓢⓟ Spelling error

Write a Paragraph

Narrative Writing

Write a paragraph about a friend, a family member, or a pet.
- Begin with a general statement that is your main idea.
- Provide details and examples to develop that main idea.
- Follow the form used in the proofreading sample. Use as many spelling words as you can.

Writing Process

Prewriting
⇩
Drafting
⇩
Revising
⇩
Editing
⇩
Publishing

Proofread Your Writing During ▶ Editing

Proofread your writing for spelling errors as part of the editing stage in the writing process. Be sure to check each word carefully. Use a dictionary to check spelling if you are not sure.

Vocabulary

Strategy Words

Review Words: Latin Roots

Write words from the box to complete the school notice.

conduct	deduct	locate
location	provoke	

The Earth Club is looking for volunteers to help __1.__ its annual bake sale. We are trying to __2.__ the people who baked for the sale last year. The __3.__ of the sale has not yet been determined. We hope that the event will __4.__ interest in the club. After we __5.__ expenses, the profit will go toward supplies for our next beach cleanup day.

Preview Words: Latin Roots

Write a word from the box to complete each sentence.

advocacy	inductive	locomotive
nondeductible	reproduce	

6. This tape recorder will _____ sound very accurately.

7. George Stephenson created the first successful railroad _____.

8. The tax expert called the contribution _____.

9. Horace Mann was famed for his _____ of free public schools.

10. Inventors must use _____ reasoning in their work.

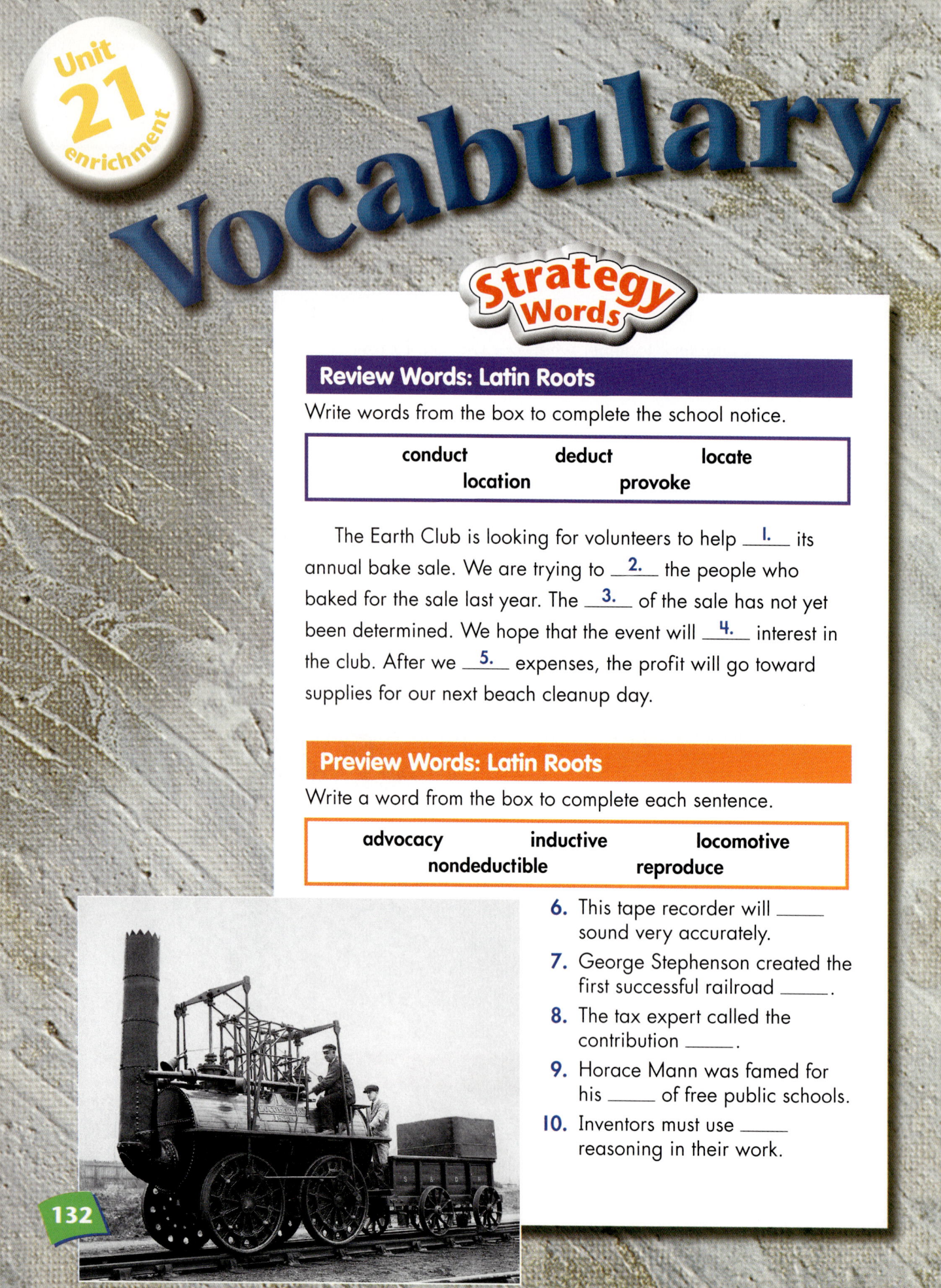

132

Connections

Science: Circulatory System

Write words from the box to complete the paragraph.

aorta	capillary	cardiac
	corpuscle	vessel

The heart is a living pump. Through muscle action, it pushes each tiny __1.__ out through the __2.__, a large blood channel attached to the heart. The cells move first into smaller arteries, and then each __3.__, a tiny blood __4.__, carries the corpuscles onward. The heart and these systems of tubes compose the __5.__ system.

Math: Algebra

Write a word from the box that matches each definition.

algorithm	coplanar	correlation
	counterexample	postulate

6. an example that refutes or disproves
7. an axiom, or statement taken to be true without proof
8. interdependence between two sets of numbers
9. a process or set of rules for calculating
10. points or lines on the same plane

Apply the Spelling Strategy

Circle the content word you wrote that comes from the Latin word **corpus,** meaning "body."

Spelling and Thinking

READ THE SPELLING WORDS

1. export	*export*	Grain is an important **export**.
2. diction	*diction*	Actors usually have excellent **diction**.
3. enact	*enact*	Did students **enact** a rule change?
4. dictator	*dictator*	The **dictator** ruled for ten years.
5. reject	*reject*	The committee might **reject** the plan.
6. react	*react*	How did you **react** to the play?
7. transport	*transport*	Refrigerated trucks **transport** fruit.
8. activate	*activate*	Push here to **activate** the blender.
9. contradict	*contradict*	Her story seems to **contradict** his.
10. portable	*portable*	He took the **portable** radio outside.
11. prediction	*prediction*	The weather **prediction** is for rain.
12. rejection	*rejection*	The **rejection** letter was expected.
13. transact	*transact*	They **transact** business by phone.
14. import	*import*	We **import** many foreign cars.
15. dictate	*dictate*	I will **dictate** the letter to you.
16. objective	*objective*	The **objective** is to score a goal.
17. reaction	*reaction*	What was her **reaction** to the idea?
18. transportation	*transportation*	Bus **transportation** will be provided.
19. unpredictable	*unpredictable*	The boy's reaction was **unpredictable**.
20. transaction	*transaction*	I recorded the business **transaction**.

SORT THE SPELLING WORDS

1.–6. Write the spelling words with the root **act,** meaning "do."

7.–11. Write the spelling words with the root **port,** meaning "carry."

12.–17. Write the spelling words with the root **dict,** meaning "say."

18.–20. Write the spelling words with the root **ject,** meaning "throw."

REMEMBER THE SPELLING STRATEGY

Remember that knowing Latin roots like **act, port, dict,** and **ject** can give clues to the meaning and spelling of certain words.

Spelling and Vocabulary

Word Meanings

Write the spelling word that best replaces the underlined word or words in each sentence.

1. Do not <u>set</u> the alarm until we are ready to leave the building.
2. We moved the <u>easily carried</u> television into the kitchen.
3. The student received three acceptances and one <u>refusal</u> from the colleges to which she had applied.
4. What is your <u>goal</u> in piling up all these rocks?
5. His letters <u>express the opposite of</u> the rumor that he is leaving town.
6. This speech class will help you with grammar and <u>enunciation</u>.
7. Her sweater is an <u>article shipped to this country</u> from Ireland.
8. If you <u>say</u> the words, I will type the letter.
9. Students in my history class will <u>act out</u> an original play about the American Revolution.
10. American companies <u>send abroad</u> many manufactured goods.

Word Structure

When the suffix **-ion** is added to a verb, a noun is formed. Write the spelling word pairs that match the definitions. The first word will be a verb, and the second word will be a noun.

11.–12. to act in response to a stimulus (verb); a response to a stimulus (noun)

13.–14. to carry out a business agreement (verb); the act of carrying out a business agreement (noun)

15.–16. to carry from one place to another (verb); the act of carrying from one place to another (noun)

USING THE Thesaurus

Write a spelling word that matches each group of words. Use the **Writing Thesaurus** if you need help.

17. haphazard, random, capricious
18. autocrat, tyrant, despot
19. forecast, prognosis, prophecy
20. deny, refuse, renounce

135

Spelling and Reading

export	diction	enact	dictator	reject
react	transport	activate	contradict	portable
prediction	rejection	transact	transportation	dictate
objective	reaction	import	unpredictable	transaction

Complete the Sentences   Write the spelling word that best completes each sentence.

1. The author understood the reason for the _____ of her manuscript.
2. The radio announcer spoke with clear _____.
3. Several witnesses were called to _____ the defendant's testimony.
4. Joseph Stalin was a _____ who ruled over the Soviet Union from 1929 to 1953.
5. Library patrons had a positive _____ to the new addition.
6. A tricycle cannot easily _____ a grown man.
7. Because we moved, we no longer _____ business at that bank.
8. The government will _____ new laws to improve highway safety.

Solve the Analogies   Write a spelling word to complete each analogy.

9. **Valid** is to **validate** as **active** is to _____.
10. **Heavy** is to **light** as **stationary** is to _____.
11. **Report** is to **account** as **forecast** is to _____.
12. **Recreation** is to **vacation** as **business** is to _____.
13. **Write** is to **speak** as **transcribe** is to _____.
14. **Obvious** is to **evident** as **uncertain** is to _____.

Complete the Paragraph   Write spelling words from the box to complete the paragraph.

export
react
transportation
import
objective
reject

   Most countries take part in the international conveyance, or __15.__, of goods. For example, if a country's climate prevents the production of a particular product, the country may choose to __16.__ the product from other nations. On the other hand, if a nation produces a product of outstanding quality or at a lower cost than other countries, the nation will probably __17.__ the product. Sometimes a country will place a quota on a particular product with the __18.__ of protecting domestic producers from foreign competition. Local producers __19.__ favorably to this idea, but most economists __20.__ the notion.

Spelling and Writing

Proofread a Product Review

Six words are not spelled correctly in this product review. Write the words correctly.

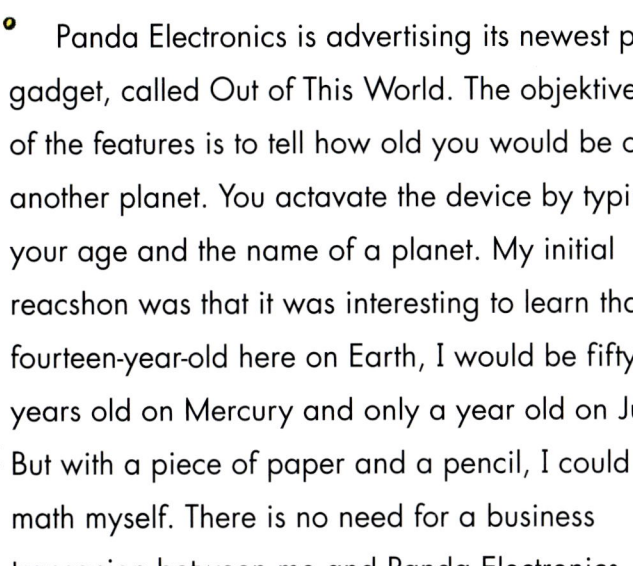

Panda Electronics is advertising its newest portible gadget, called Out of This World. The objektive of one of the features is to tell how old you would be on another planet. You actavate the device by typing in your age and the name of a planet. My initial reacshon was that it was interesting to learn that as a fourteen-year-old here on Earth, I would be fifty-eight years old on Mercury and only a year old on Jupiter! But with a piece of paper and a pencil, I could do the math myself. There is no need for a business transacion between me and Panda Electronics. My predicton is that other consumers will react as I did.

Proofreading Marks

☰ Make a capital.

/ Make a small letter.

∧ Add something.

℮ Take out something.

⊙ Add a period.

⌗ New paragraph

SP Spelling error

Write a Product Review

Expository Writing

New products come on the market all the time, and we all need to be critical consumers. Review a new product.

- Does the product do what the company claims? Is the product useful?
- Predict the product's chances for success.
- Follow the form used in the proofreading sample.

Use as many spelling words as you can.

Writing Process

Prewriting
⬇
Drafting
⬇
Revising
⬇
Editing
⬇
Publishing

Proofread Your Writing During ➤

Proofread your writing for spelling errors as part of the editing stage in the writing process. Be sure to check each word carefully. Use a dictionary to check spelling if you are not sure.

Vocabulary

Strategy Words

Review Words: Latin Roots

Write words from the box to complete the paragraph.

action	object	opportunity
predict	project	

As part of a science __1.__, our teacher asked us to imagine that we had the __2.__ to be on the moon. She asked us to __3.__ what would happen if we dropped a large rock and a small rock at the same time. I said that the result of this __4.__ would be that neither __5.__ would land before the other.

Preview Words: Latin Roots

Write a word from the box to complete each sentence.

actively	dictation	interject
rapport	valedictorian	

6. The _____ of the senior class presented a speech at graduation.

7. We take weekly _____ in Spanish class.

8. The interviewer was advised to _____ some humor in his "Meet the Stars" show.

9. She is _____ involved in many community service projects.

10. The soccer coach has good _____ with her team.

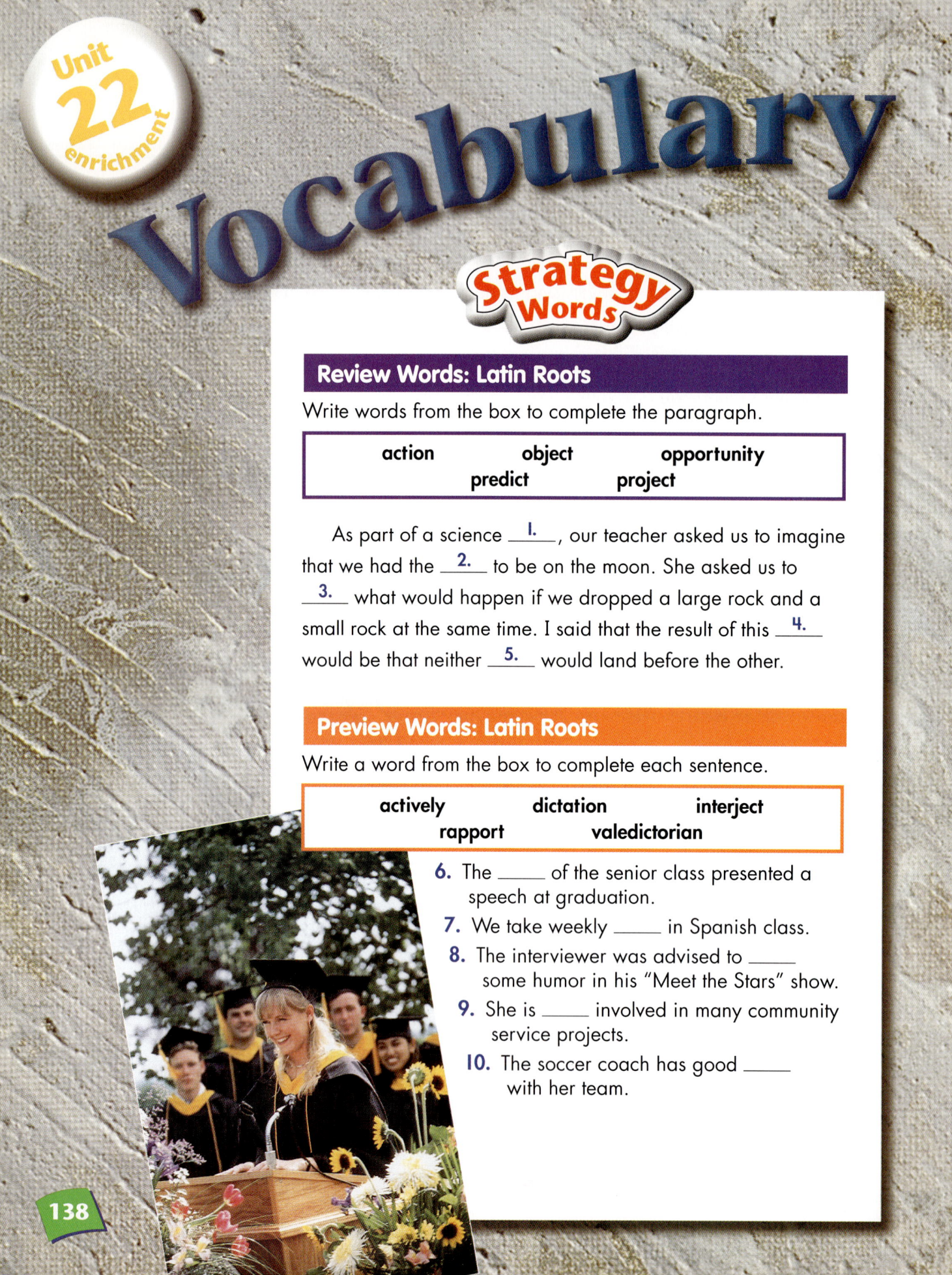

Connections

Language Arts: Grammar

Write a word from the box that identifies the part of speech of the underlined word or words.

conjunction	gerund	infinitive
interjection		participle

1. <u>Wow!</u> This floor is slippery.
2. The <u>barking</u> dog woke the entire neighborhood.
3. Please buy some bread <u>and</u> milk.
4. <u>Hiking</u> in the mountains was fun.
5. I tried <u>to memorize</u> the poem.

Social Studies: Law

Write the word from the box that best completes each sentence.

acquit	attorney	indictment
litigation		testify

6. The _____ over the disputed land lasted for months.
7.–8. A defense _____ asked the jury to _____ the accused couple.
9. A grand jury issues an _____, which charges a person with committing a crime.
10. Several witnesses came forward to _____ on behalf of the defendant.

Apply the Spelling Strategy

Circle the two content words you wrote that have the root **dict** or **ject**.

Spelling and Thinking

READ THE SPELLING WORDS

1.	peaceable	*peaceable*	My pets are both **peaceable**.
2.	inflexible	*inflexible*	Are the rules **inflexible**?
3.	disposable	*disposable*	Paper napkins are **disposable**.
4.	manageable	*manageable*	The problem was **manageable**.
5.	unmanageable	*unmanageable*	He tamed the **unmanageable** horse.
6.	sociable	*sociable*	She is friendly and **sociable**.
7.	unsociable	*unsociable*	A shy person can seem **unsociable**.
8.	admissible	*admissible*	Is it **admissible** to park here?
9.	honorable	*honorable*	We praised his **honorable** behavior.
10.	inadvisable	*inadvisable*	Swimming alone is **inadvisable**.
11.	irresponsible	*irresponsible*	The prank was **irresponsible**.
12.	accountable	*accountable*	We are **accountable** for our actions.
13.	hospitable	*hospitable*	They are **hospitable** toward guests.
14.	inaccessible	*inaccessible*	The road is **inaccessible** now.
15.	irreplaceable	*irreplaceable*	The antique cup is **irreplaceable**.
16.	irreversible	*irreversible*	Her final decision is **irreversible**.
17.	knowledgeable	*knowledgeable*	He is **knowledgeable** about sports.
18.	unimaginable	*unimaginable*	Is snow in July **unimaginable**?
19.	commendable	*commendable*	He has many **commendable** traits.
20.	interchangeable	*interchangeable*	These car tires are **interchangeable**.

SORT THE SPELLING WORDS

1.–15. Write the spelling words that end with the suffix **-able**.

16.–20. Write the spelling words that end with the suffix **-ible**.

REMEMBER THE SPELLING STRATEGY

Remember that the suffixes **-able** and **-ible** are added to roots or base words to form adjectives.

Word Meanings

Write the spelling word for each definition.

1. not inclined to be friendly
2. difficult to manage
3. fond of company
4. allowable
5. entitled to respect
6. receptive to guests
7. impossible to imagine

Word Structure

Write the spelling word formed by adding the suffix **-able** to each word.

8. knowledge
9. account
10. dispose
11. peace
12. interchange
13. manage
14. commend

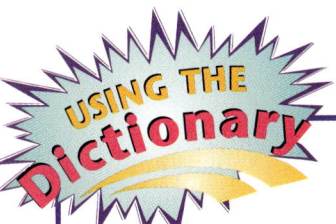

USING THE Dictionary

15.–20. The prefix **in-** changes to **ir-** when added to words beginning with **r**. Write the spelling words that contain the prefix **in- (ir-)** meaning "not." (Be careful. The prefix **inter-** means "between.") Circle the prefix in each word you write.

Spelling and Reading

sociable	hospitable	irreversible	manageable	commendable
inflexible	unsociable	inadvisable	irresponsible	unmanageable
peaceable	admissible	inaccessible	irreplaceable	knowledgeable
honorable	disposable	accountable	unimaginable	interchangeable

Replace the Words Write the spelling word that best replaces the underlined word or words in each sentence.

1. The sailboat was impossible to handle in the strong wind.
2. At first we thought he was unfriendly, but he was just timid.
3. Although summer is difficult, you will find it possible to manage.
4. Police say it is not recommended to drive on the icy roads.
5. Your final decision will be incapable of being changed back.
6. I am sure they would enjoy the movie, but your dogs are not allowable in this theater.
7. The mayor praised the students for their praiseworthy behavior.
8. If you find a wallet on the sidewalk, the admirable thing to do is to bring it to a police station.
9. The baker uses a mixing machine with exchangeable parts.
10. Neglecting to feed a pet is untrustworthy, undependable behavior.

Answer the Questions Write the spelling word that best answers each question.

11. What kind of plate do you throw away after you use it once?
12. How would you describe a box beyond your reach?
13. How would you describe a family heirloom that was broken?
14. If people settle an argument without angry words, how would you describe their agreement?
15. What kind of family is happy to welcome others into its home?

Complete the Paragraph Write spelling words from the box to complete the paragraph.

knowledgeable
accountable
unimaginable
inflexible
sociable

In 1883, an ___16.___ event occurred in professional baseball. A batter hit the ball, and then in his excitement he ran toward third base. Spurred on by what he thought was encouragement from the fans, he ran all the way home. Anyone ___17.___ about baseball knows that the rule is ___18.___ . Runners are held ___19.___ for touching the bases in the correct order, so the runner was out. No doubt, he did not feel very ___20.___ after that incident.

Spelling and Writing

Proofread a Letter to the Editor

Six words are not spelled correctly in this letter to a newspaper. Write the words correctly.

ZOO

To the Editor:

   I am in support of the commendible plan to create a more open and peacable existence for animals at our city zoo. I realize that we have come a long way from the irresponsable practice of keeping animals in bare cages with concrete floors, but more can be done. We are accountable for creating a managable environment in which creatures of different species live and interact much as they do in the wild. Our zoo should not only entertain but also help visitors become more knowledgable about how animals live in their natural habitat. As a frequent zoo visitor, I would find life without our city zoo unimagineable.

                                   Fred Marchione
                                   Springfield

Proofreading Marks

≡	Make a capital.
/	Make a small letter.
∧	Add something.
ℓ	Take out something.
⊙	Add a period.
#	New paragraph
SP	Spelling error

Write a Letter to the Editor

Persuasive Writing

Writing a letter to the editor is an opportunity for readers to air their views on an issue. Write a letter to the editor on an issue about which you feel strongly.

- State your opinion in your first sentence, which should be direct and specific.
- Support your opinion with facts or reasons.
- Follow the form used in the proofreading sample.

Use as many spelling words as you can.

Proofread Your Writing During →

Writing Process

Prewriting
⇩
Drafting
⇩
Revising
⇩
Editing
⇩
Publishing

Proofread your writing for spelling errors as part of the editing stage in the writing process. Be sure to check each word carefully. Use a dictionary to check spelling if you are not sure.

Vocabulary

Strategy Words

Review Words: Suffixes -able, -ible

Write a word from the box that is a synonym for each underlined word.

accessible	admirable	disagreeable
incredible	suitable	

1. Cheer up and don't be so <u>irritable</u>.
2. Costumes like this are not always <u>available</u>.
3. Red is a <u>becoming</u> color for you.
4. I know you will be an <u>unbelievable</u> hit at the party.
5. The teacher was honored for his many <u>praiseworthy</u> qualities.

Preview Words: Suffixes -able, -ible

Write a word from the box to match each definition.

disreputable	exceptionable	indescribable
susceptible	washable	

6. impossible to describe
7. having a bad reputation
8. objectionable
9. not harmed by washing
10. easily affected or influenced

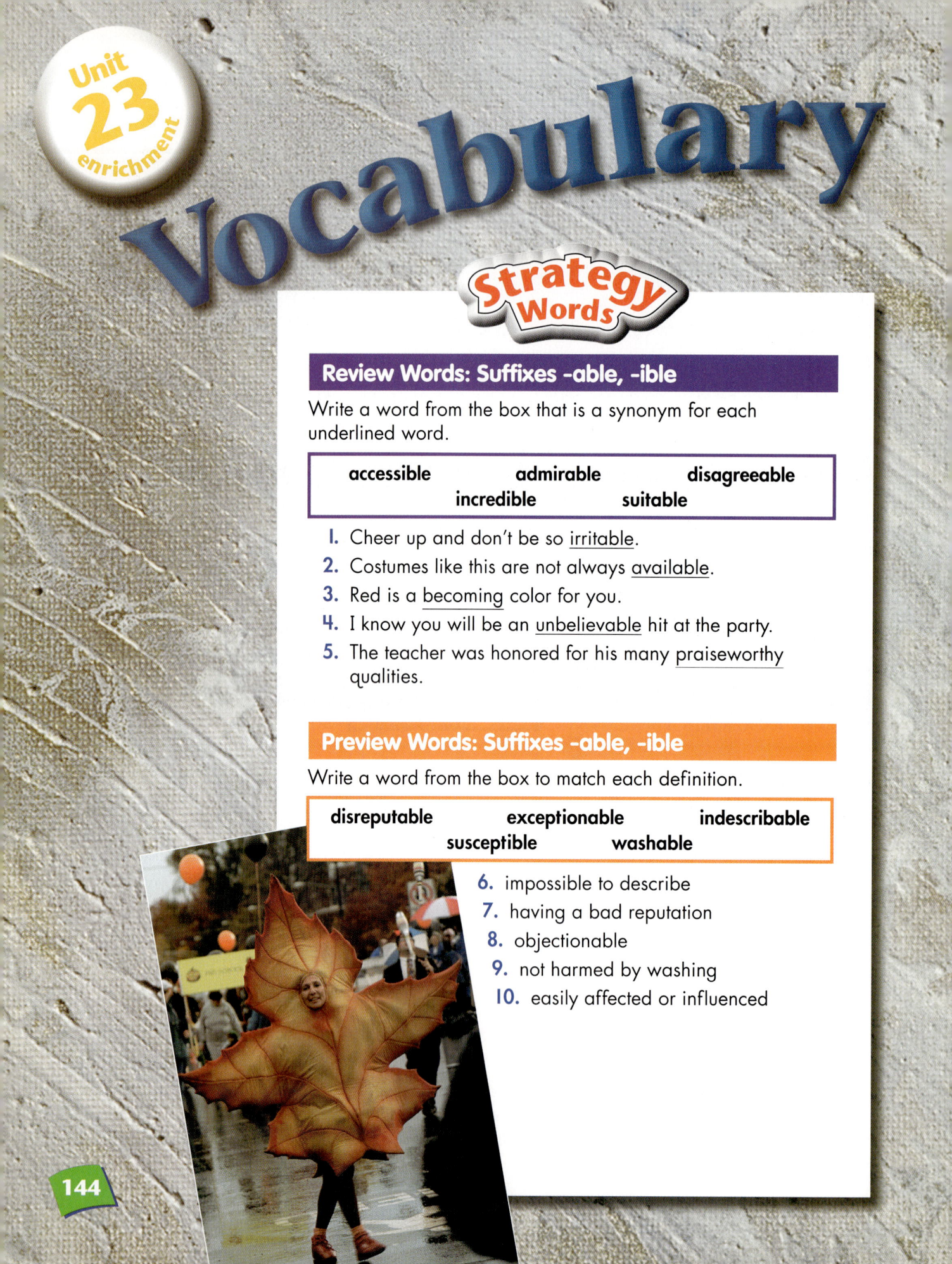

Connections

Philosophy: Logic

Write the word from the box that best matches each definition.

ambiguous	contradiction	incompatible
	paradox	fundamental

1. not compatible; not in harmony
2. an inconsistency or discrepancy
3. a seemingly contradictory statement that may be true
4. basic; essential
5. doubtful; uncertain; having more than one meaning

Math: Higher Arithmetic

Write the word from the box that completes each sentence.

algebra	coefficient	equation	radical	variable

$$2a + 3b = \sqrt{5}$$

6. A mathematical statement showing that two expressions are equal is called an _____.
7. The number **2** or **3** above is called a _____.
8. The letter **a** or **b** above is called a _____.
9. The number **5** above is called a _____.
10. The form of math in which (among other things) symbols, usually letters of the alphabet, represent numbers is called _____.

Apply the Spelling Strategy

Circle the two content words you wrote that end in the suffix **-able** or **-ible**.

Assessment and Review

Assessment   Units 19–23

Each Assessment Word in the box fits one of the spelling strategies you have studied over the past five weeks. Read the spelling strategies. Then write each Assessment Word under the unit number it fits.

Unit 19

1.–3. Remember that knowing Latin roots like **urb, public, reg, civ, doc,** and **dom** can give clues to the meaning and spelling of certain words.

Unit 20

4.–7. Remember that a final /sēd/ may be spelled **ceed, cede,** or **sede.** Knowing Latin roots like **ced, pend,** or **pos** can give clues to the meaning and spelling of certain words.

Unit 21

8.–11. Remember that knowing Latin roots like **voc, duc,** and **loc** can give clues to the meaning and spelling of certain words.

Unit 22

12.–15. Remember that knowing Latin roots like **act, port, dict,** and **ject** can give clues to the meaning and spelling of certain words.

Unit 23

16.–20. Remember that the suffixes **-able** and **-ible** are added to roots or base words to form adjectives.

domination
vocalist
actually
debatable
locale
regulatory
precedence
conductor
inactivity
projection
defensible
exposure
domain
inadmissible
indivisible
proposal
interaction
unavailable
secede
provocation

Review   Unit 19: Latin Roots urb, public, reg, civ, doc, dom

urban	regime	suburb	regulation	indomitable
civic	regulate	republic	civilization	dominant

Write a spelling word to complete each sentence. The word you write will contain the root shown in parentheses.

1. Some families live in a _____, and some live in the city. (urb)
2. His _____ spirit kept him going against all odds. (dom)
3. New York City is a huge _____ center. (urb)
4. Serving on a jury is your _____ duty. (civ)
5. Citizens elect their leaders in a _____. (public)
6. Our school has the _____ football team in the city. (dom)
7. For years parts of Europe lived under a communist _____. (reg)
8. The town will _____ water usage during the drought. (reg)
9. There is a _____ that dogs must be licensed. (reg)
10. The development of writing advanced _____. (civ)

Review   Unit 20: Latin Roots ced, sede, pend, pos

succeed	supersede	proceed	depend	disposal
suspense	posture	impostor	precede	pendulum

Find the misspelled word in each group and write it correctly.

11. superseed   depend   posture
12. disposal   impostor   suspens
13. pendulum   procede   supersede
14. suspense   precede   suceed
15. proceed   preceed   depend
16. depand   impostor   posture
17. disposal   pendulum   imposter
18. succeed   postur   suspense
19. pendulem   precede   depend
20. proceed   disposel   supersede

Unit 21: Latin Roots voc/vok, duc/duct, loc

vocal	allocate	production	reduction	locomotion
induce	locality	vocation	advocate	vocabulary

Write a spelling word for each definition.

1. a knowledge of words
2. a lessening or diminishing
3. done with the voice
4. to give out or set aside
5. the making of something
6. a calling to a certain work or way of life
7. a geographic place
8. a person who speaks on behalf of another
9. the power to move from place to place
10. to influence or persuade someone

Review

Unit 22: Latin Roots act, port, dict, ject

export	dictator	transport	activate	portable
prediction	import	objective	reaction	transportation

Replace the underlined letters with one or more letters to write a spelling word.

11. navi<u>g</u>ator
12. activi<u>ty</u>
13. imp<u>aired</u>
14. exi<u>t</u>
15. <u>lev</u>itation
16. <u>ad</u>jective
17. <u>pass</u>port
18. <u>re</u>apply
19. <u>contra</u>diction
20. <u>us</u>able

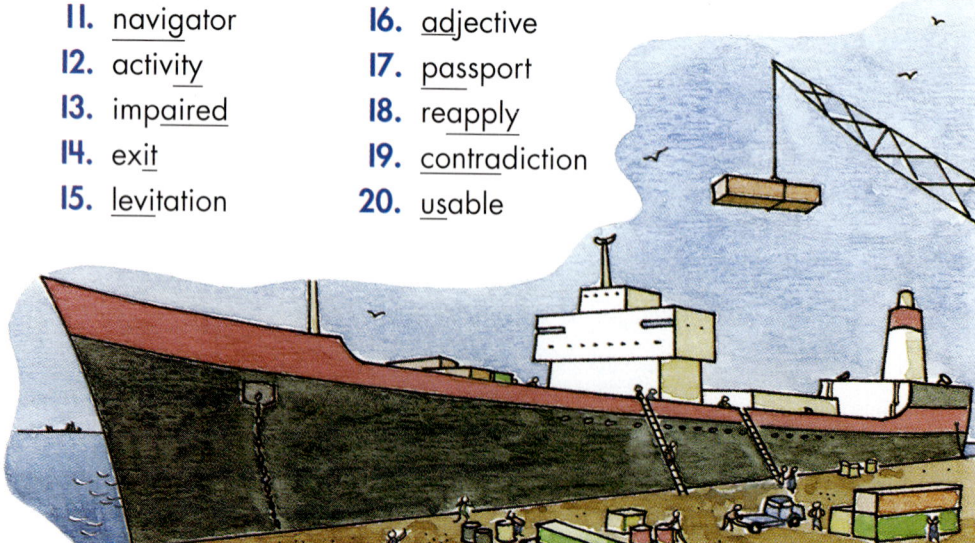

sociable	hospitable	admissible	inaccessible	irresponsible
peaceable	honorable	irreversible	manageable	interchangeable

Add the missing letters to write a spelling word.

1. p___ce__ble
2. h__n__r__ble
3. int___ch__ng___ble
4. ina___e___ble
5. adm_____ble

6. man__g___ble
7. i___esp__ns__ble
8. s_____ble
9. h__sp__t__ble
10. i___ev__rs__ble

Spelling Study Strategy

Ask a Question

Practicing spelling can be fun if you make it into a game. Here's an idea you can try with a partner.

1. Swap spelling lists with your partner. Be sure that you can each read the other's list.

2. Your partner should pick one of the words on your list, but not say it.

3. You may ask your partner three questions about the word. For example, you could ask, "Does it end with **able**?" If you guess the word in three questions or less, you get two points. Write the word.

4. Ask your partner to check your spelling. If you have the word spelled correctly, you get two more points. If not, ask another question. If you get the spelling right this time, you still get one point. If not, your partner will tell you the spelling, but you don't get any additional points.

5. If you haven't guessed the word, ask your partner to tell you the word. You don't get any points just now.

6. Now it is your partner's turn to guess a word and write it. Keep going until you have both practiced all the words. Add your points to see who is the winner.

WRITER'S

Grammar, Usage, and Mechanics

Using Subject Pronouns and Object Pronouns

A **pronoun** may take the place of a noun. The **subject pronouns** *I, you, he, she, it, we,* and *they* take the place of the subject of sentences. The **object pronouns** *me, you, him, her, it, us,* and *them* take the place of objects of verbs or of prepositions.

Lea gave the puppies a good home.

  ↑   ↑

subject   object

  ↓   ↓

She gave them a good home.

Practice Activity

A. Write **subject** or **object** for each underlined pronoun in these sentences.

  1. Joe and I walked in the locality of the school.

  2. Mom came by and offered us a ride.

  3. She and Dad were going to the store.

  4. We saw some friends and offered them a ride.

  5. They decided to walk instead.

  6. Help me open the door.

  7. Anna and he waved good-bye.

B. Write the correct pronoun to complete each sentence.

  8. Call (I, me) when the production is ready.

  9. Theresa and (I, me) will meet you there.

  10. I was hoping to see (them, they) soon.

  11. (We, Us) made a prediction about the film.

  12. Our parents saw (us, we) at the movies.

  13. The hot-air balloon was just above (he, him).

  14. You and (I, me) can always keep a secret.

  15. I made new sweaters for Sam and (they, them).

WORKSHOP

Proofreading Strategy

One at a Time!

Good writers always proofread their writing for spelling mistakes. Here's a strategy you can use to proofread your papers.

Look for one kind of mistake at a time. First, skim your paper and look at the spellings of word endings. Then, look for words that contain **ie** or **ei**. Go through again and check contractions.

This may sound like a lot of work, but it's not. You do not read many words each time. Instead, you focus on a small group each time. You look for particular problems. Try it!

Electronic Spelling

Computer Terms

Familiar terms are sometimes used differently when referring to computers. For example, a **hard drive** could mean a difficult car trip. But if you take a hard drive to the computer repair shop, you mean something else entirely.

Write the misspelled term that has a new meaning as a computer term.

1. You might see a menue in a restaurant or at the top of a computer screen.

2. You might see iecons at a museum or displayed on the screen.

3. A disck might be a toy or something that can hold encoded information.

4. A mous is a rodent or a device that moves the cursor on the screen.

5. A lynk might be part of a chain or a way to move between documents in a computer program.

Spelling and Thinking

READ THE SPELLING WORDS

1.	ascent	*ascent*	His **ascent** to the cliff top was slow.
2.	assent	*assent*	Did they **assent** to the plan?
3.	descent	*descent*	Our **descent** to the valley was easy.
4.	dissent	*dissent*	Such **dissent** among friends is unusual.
5.	canvas	*canvas*	The picture is painted on **canvas**.
6.	canvass	*canvass*	I need time to **canvass** the voters.
7.	moral	*moral*	The fable has a very clear **moral**.
8.	morale	*morale*	Team **morale** is high after the victory.
9.	bazaar	*bazaar*	We shopped at a colorful **bazaar**.
10.	bizarre	*bizarre*	The dancers wore **bizarre** costumes.
11.	eminent	*eminent*	Yo-Yo Ma is an **eminent** cellist.
12.	imminent	*imminent*	Their arrival home is **imminent**.
13.	emigrant	*emigrant*	Ruth is an **emigrant** from Poland.
14.	immigrant	*immigrant*	Any **immigrant** may study English here.
15.	confidently	*confidently*	A speaker strode **confidently** onstage.
16.	confidentially	*confidentially*	Speak to Dr. Kangas **confidentially**.
17.	continually	*continually*	That phone rings **continually**.
18.	continuously	*continuously*	Waves form in the ocean **continuously**.
19.	respectfully	*respectfully*	Both leaders bowed **respectfully**.
20.	respectively	*respectively*	List pets and breeds, **respectively**.

SORT THE SPELLING WORDS

1.–10. Write the spelling words with two syllables.

11.–14. Write the spelling words with three syllables.

15.–17. Write the spelling words with four syllables.

18.–20. Write the spelling words with five syllables.

REMEMBER THE SPELLING STRATEGY

Remember that words with similar spellings and meanings are often confused.

Word Meanings

Write the spelling word that matches each definition.

1. in the order given
2. concerned with correct or ethical conduct
3. strange and outlandish
4. heavy cloth used for sails and tents
5. movement downward
6. without interruption; unceasing
7. courteously
8. market lined with shops and stalls
9. to disagree
10. conduct a survey

Phrase Completion

Write the spelling word that best completes each phrase.

11. whispering the information _____
12. baby crying _____
13. showing _____ by nodding yes
14. popular candidate _____ waiting for Election Day
15. losses lowering the team's _____
16. long, tiring _____ to the summit

USING THE Dictionary

Etymologies can help distinguish between confusing word pairs. Use the **Spelling Dictionary** to look up etymologies for the following pairs of words. Write the spelling word that correctly completes each sentence.

emigrant, immigrant   eminent, imminent

17. The _____ came to the United States to begin a new life.
18. The _____ left Ireland during a severe food shortage.
19. We feared that a storm was _____.
20. The guest of honor was an _____ author.

153

Spelling and Reading

ascent	assent	descent	dissent	canvas
canvass	moral	morale	bazaar	bizarre
eminent	imminent	emigrant	immigrant	confidently
confidentially	continually	continuously	respectfully	respectively

Complete the Sentences   Write the spelling word that best completes each sentence.

1. My grandparents are of Chinese _____.
2. My parents provide financial and _____ support.
3. You can buy fresh fruit at the _____ on Saturday.
4. The mayor's _____ to a higher position was rapid.
5. I was disappointed, but a day's rest improved my _____.
6. Believe in yourself; go through life _____!
7. Make sure that you ask _____ rather than demand rudely.
8. Dr. Long is a beloved, _____ doctor in Dallas.
9. She is not a native but arrived as an _____ last year.
10. I read every volume of his autobiography and reported on each, _____.

Solve the Analogies   Write the spelling word that best completes each analogy.

11. **Occasionally** is to **seldom** as **regularly** is to _____.
12. **Announcement** is to **publicly** as **secret** is to _____.
13. **Past** is to **future** as **previous** is to _____.
14. **No** is to **refuse** as **yes** is to _____.
15. **Reveal** is to **disclose** as **poll** is to _____.

Complete the Paragraph   Write spelling words from the box to complete the paragraph.

   Louise Nevelson, an ___16.___ who left Russia in 1905, held on to her dream in the face of much ___17.___. This artist did not paint on ___18.___ but instead worked with wood and "found objects." At first, many thought that her sculptures were too ___19.___ to be accepted by the public. Believing in herself ___20.___, however, Nevelson was eventually recognized as a brilliant artist with a unique style.

continuously
dissent
emigrant
bizarre
canvas

Spelling and Writing

Proofread a Paragraph

Six words are not spelled correctly in this paragraph. Write the words correctly.

I see myself as a visual artist whose asent to fame is slow and difficult. Despite having to continualy defend my work, I maintain my high morale by reminding myself that many artists are misunderstood during their lifetime. Despite unfriendly critics, I continue to work confadently in oils, creating canvas after canvas of lifelike urban scenes. I believe that one day, while exhibiting at a local bizaar, my work will be discovered by an emminent art critic who then will publicize it. From that moment on, I will be treated respectfuly by the public, and I will be able to command the prices that my work deserves.

Proofreading Marks

 Make a capital.

 Make a small letter.

 Add something.

 Take out something.

 Add a period.

 New paragraph

 Spelling error

Write a Paragraph

Narrative Writing

What type of work would you find so satisfying that it would not seem like work? Explain the work that you dream about doing someday. Describe how you see yourself in the future.

- Decide what talents and abilities you enjoy using most.
- Consider various careers that use those skills.
- Choose one career and imagine how you might reach a satisfying position in the field.
- Follow the form used in the proofreading sample.

Use as many spelling words as you can.

Proofread Your Writing During

Writing Process

Prewriting
⇩
Drafting
⇩
Revising
⇩
Editing
⇩
Publishing

Proofread your writing for spelling errors as part of the editing stage in the writing process. Be sure to check each word carefully. Use a dictionary to check spelling if you are not sure.

Vocabulary

Strategy Words

Review Words: Commonly Confused Words

Write a word from the box to complete each sentence.

affect	device	devise
effect	formerly	

1. Muhammad Ali is the prizefighter who was _____ known as Cassius Clay.
2. One CD has an odd _____: it makes the dog howl.
3. Alyssa created a _____ that measures wind speed.
4. Luckily, the severe weather will not _____ our area.
5. I want to _____ a way to organize my papers.

Preview Words: Commonly Confused Words

Write the word from the box that matches each definition.

bullion	emigration	immigration
persecution	prosecution	

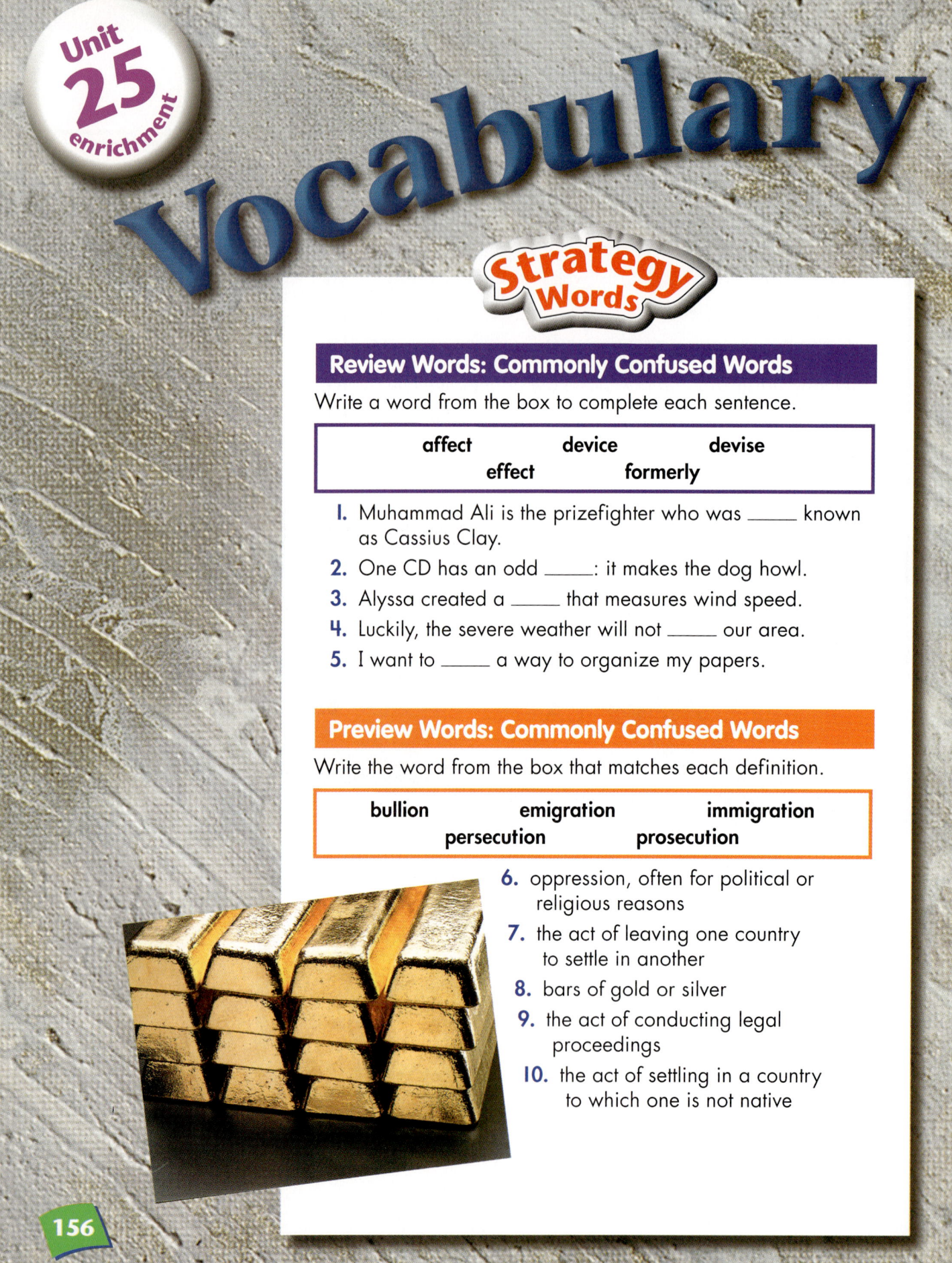

6. oppression, often for political or religious reasons
7. the act of leaving one country to settle in another
8. bars of gold or silver
9. the act of conducting legal proceedings
10. the act of settling in a country to which one is not native

Connections

Content Words

Science: Genetics

Write the word from the box that fits each meaning.

conform	evolution	extinct
inherited	mutation	

1. no longer existing
2. sudden structural change within a gene
3. to act according to customs or trends
4. received from an ancestor
5. gradual process of change

Social Studies: Diplomacy

Write the word from the box that matches each clue.

ambassador	consul	diplomatic
embassy	international	

6. a building you might be happy to see if you were traveling in a foreign country
7. someone sent to a foreign country to help other citizens living abroad
8. involving many countries of the world
9. describes a person who is tactful and sensitive
10. someone sent by a country to the United Nations

Apply the Spelling Strategy

Circle the content word you wrote that is commonly confused with **confirm**. Underline the word you wrote that is commonly confused with both **counsel** and **council**.

157

Spelling and Thinking

READ THE SPELLING WORDS

1.	campaign	campaign	The mayor ended her **campaign**.
2.	psychology	psychology	Behavior is studied in **psychology**.
3.	fascinate	fascinate	Lizards always **fascinate** Kim.
4.	undoubtedly	undoubtedly	He will **undoubtedly** recover.
5.	adjust	adjust	Toby must **adjust** to the schedule.
6.	miscellaneous	miscellaneous	Order the **miscellaneous** supplies.
7.	mortgage	mortgage	I got a **mortgage** to buy a house.
8.	adjoin	adjoin	The court will **adjoin** city hall.
9.	ascend	ascend	Please **ascend** the ramp in pairs.
10.	raspberry	raspberry	He made a **raspberry** dessert.
11.	subtle	subtle	Differences in color can be **subtle**.
12.	acquaint	acquaint	He will **acquaint** us with the plan.
13.	bankruptcy	bankruptcy	The store declared **bankruptcy**.
14.	pneumonia	pneumonia	Eli is ill with **pneumonia**.
15.	discipline	discipline	It takes **discipline** to eat properly.
16.	adjourn	adjourn	The court will **adjourn** for a day.
17.	acknowledge	acknowledge	It is best to **acknowledge** errors.
18.	adolescent	adolescent	He is no longer an **adolescent**.
19.	acknowledgment	acknowledgment	Please send an **acknowledgment**.
20.	acquaintance	acquaintance	Melinda is only an **acquaintance**.

SORT THE SPELLING WORDS

1.–9. Write the words with a silent **c** or **k**.

10.–12. Write the words with a silent **p**.

13.–15. Write the words with a silent **d** in the first syllable.

16.–17. Write the words with a silent **t**.

18. Write the word with a silent **g**.

19.–20. Write the words with a silent **b**.

REMEMBER THE SPELLING STRATEGY

Remember that some words have more letters than sounds.

Word Meanings

Write the spelling word that matches each definition.

1. the study of human behavior
2. a response in return for something done
3. not immediately obvious
4. to suspend until a later time
5. a person whom one knows slightly
6. a branch of knowledge
7. to make familiar
8. to admit the truth of

Synonyms

Write a spelling word that is a synonym for each of the following words.

9. assorted
10. teenager
11. adapt
12. rise
13. charm
14. attach
15. unquestionably

USING THE Dictionary

Write each of the following spelling words and draw a line between the syllables. Use the **Spelling Dictionary** if you need help.

16. pneumonia
17. campaign
18. bankruptcy
19. raspberry
20. mortgage

subtle	adjourn	mortgage	pneumonia	acknowledge
adjust	acquaint	campaign	psychology	acquaintance
adjoin	fascinate	raspberry	bankruptcy	miscellaneous
ascend	discipline	adolescent	undoubtedly	acknowledgment

Complete the Sentences
Write a spelling word to complete each sentence.

1. Some differences in cooking aromas are _____.

2. If _____ settles in the lungs, it causes breathing problems.

3. Studying math is good _____ for the mind.

4. Time and trust are required to turn an _____ into a friend.

5. Only a few _____ items were left on Sally's to-do list.

6. Does the dining room _____ the kitchen?

7. If you are an _____, you are almost an adult.

8. I accidentally dropped the string and was forced to watch the balloon _____ until I could see it no more.

9. If you _____ others with the game rules, they can learn to play the game.

10. Mara sent a thank-you note as an _____ of her gratitude.

11. Rather than _____ the meeting, we stayed past six o'clock.

Complete the Paragraph
Write spelling words from the box to complete the paragraph.

Tyler Wells would make a good case study for a __12.__ textbook. His repeated hard luck would __13.__ any scientist. For example, after losing his __14.__ bushes to mildew, he faced __15.__. Then he found a house he really liked but was refused a __16.__. He lost his __17.__ for mayor and was forced to __18.__ his defeat publicly. Tyler has __19.__ learned to __20.__ to misfortune.

> adjust
> raspberry
> fascinate
> acknowledge
> psychology
> bankruptcy
> mortgage
> campaign
> undoubtedly

Proofread a Journal Entry

Six words are not spelled correctly in this journal entry. Write the words correctly.

March 15

 Being new in town is lonely for me. I decided on the first day to wage a campain to make new friends, but most individuals barely acknoledge me on the street. My mom says to make the akwaintance of as many classmates as possible. I have used misselanious techniques to get to know people, including visiting a classmate in the hospital who has newmonia and staying at school meetings until they ajurn. When you are an adolescent, cliques are hard to break into, but I will not give up.

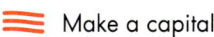
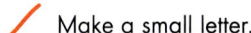

Proofreading Marks

≡ Make a capital.

/ Make a small letter.

∧ Add something.

℮ Take out something.

⊙ Add a period.

New paragraph

SP Spelling error

Write a Journal Entry

Narrative Writing

Writing in a journal helps you examine and reflect on your experiences. Choose an event in your life that affected you positively or negatively. Write a journal entry about it.

- Brainstorm a list of events to write about.
- Write a journal entry that includes the event you decide on and your thoughts about it.
- Follow the form used in the proofreading sample.

Use as many spelling words as you can.

Writing Process

Prewriting
⇩
Drafting
⇩
Revising
⇩
Editing
⇩
Publishing

Proofread Your Writing During

Proofread your writing for spelling errors as part of the editing stage in the writing process. Be sure to check each word carefully. Use a dictionary to check spelling if you are not sure.

Vocabulary

Strategy Words

Review Words: Words With More Letters Than Sounds

Write a word from the box to complete each sentence.

gnarled	hustle	resign
sought	wrestle	

1. We will have to _____ through this large crowd to buy our tickets.
2. The boys' team will _____ against Cayman High tonight.
3. Mr. Hayes plans to _____ as play director.
4. Many _____ trees with leafless branches surround the old house.
5. At the end of the dance, I _____ relief for my aching calf muscles.

Preview Words: Words With More Letters Than Sounds

Write the word from the box that matches each clue.

budgetary	khaki	pneumatic
psychological	psychiatry	

6. This color is often used for trousers.
7. Someone who studies this gets a medical degree.
8. Considerations like these help you decide how to spend your money.
9. This word describes processes relating to the mind or the emotions.
10. This word relates to using compressed air.

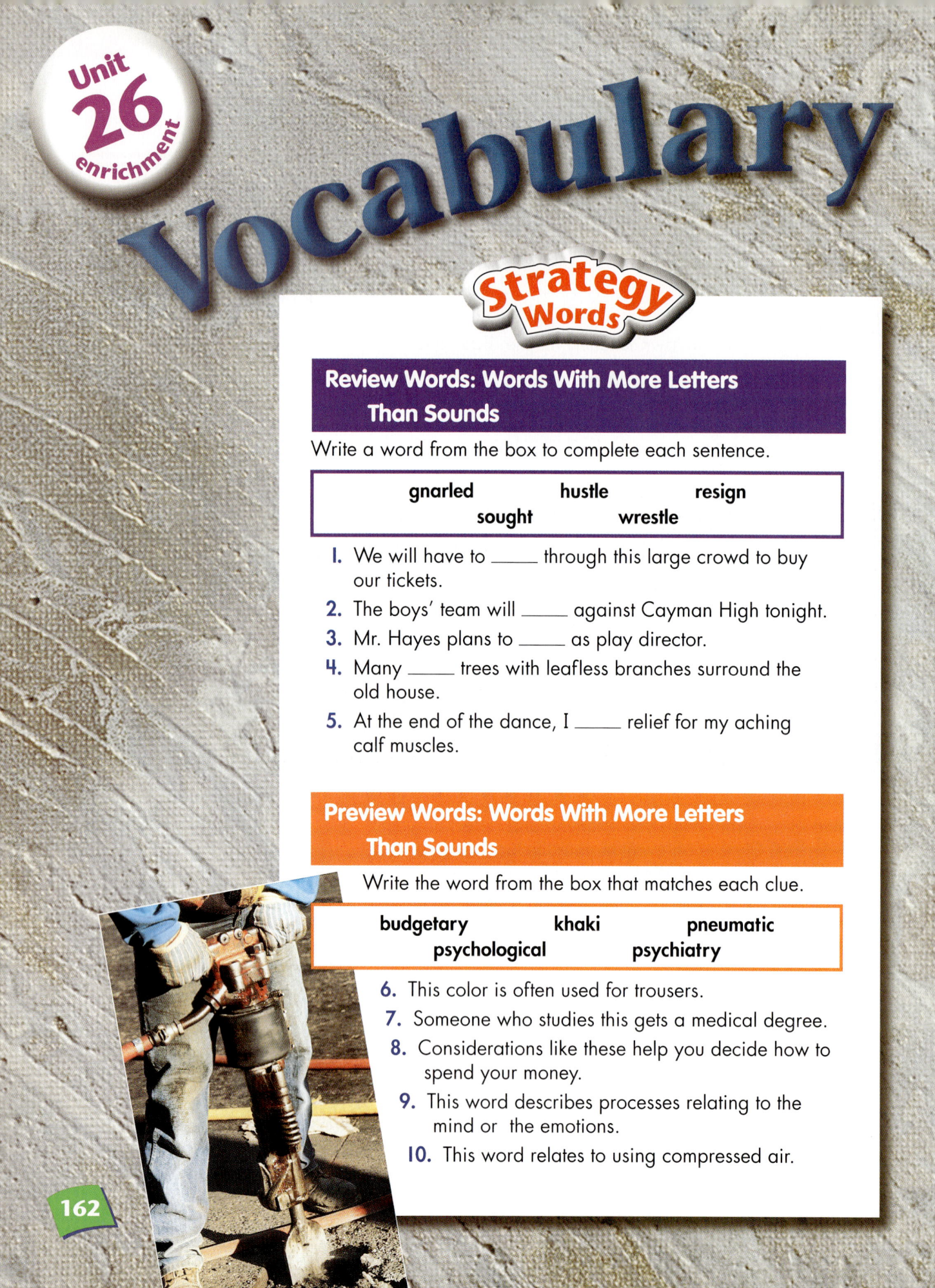

Connections

Social Studies: Medieval History

Write the word from the box that fits each meaning.

chivalry	joust	knighthood
pageantry		tournament

1. grand spectacle; gorgeous display
2. combat between two mounted knights with lances
3. a competition with a series of contests
4. idealized qualities, such as bravery
5. the rank or status of a knight

Language Arts: Style

Write a word from the box to complete each sentence.

convincing	essence	straightforward
synopsis		technique

6. Introducing a paragraph with a quotation is one _____ writers can use to capture the reader's attention.
7. When you write a _____ of a book, focus on the main events.
8. To be _____, a persuasive paragraph must supply reasons and examples.
9. Her writing style is concise, clear, and _____.
10. Family relationships are the _____ of every one of his novels.

Apply the Spelling Strategy

Circle the five content words you wrote that contain more letters than sounds.

READ THE SPELLING WORDS

1.	inscribe	*inscribe*	Who will **inscribe** the names?
2.	observe	*observe*	We can **observe** the race from here.
3.	translate	*translate*	Amal can **translate** that poem.
4.	prescribe	*prescribe*	The doctor will **prescribe** rest.
5.	reserve	*reserve*	I will call to **reserve** two seats.
6.	translator	*translator*	My sister is a bilingual **translator**.
7.	subscribe	*subscribe*	I want to **subscribe** to that paper.
8.	preserve	*preserve*	This varnish will **preserve** the wood.
9.	relation	*relation*	He is a **relation** by marriage.
10.	description	*description*	I read a **description** of that island.
11.	observation	*observation*	This report is based on **observation**.
12.	elated	*elated*	News of your prize **elated** us.
13.	inscription	*inscription*	Read the **inscription** on the back.
14.	reservation	*reservation*	Do we need a **reservation** for lunch?
15.	elation	*elation*	Only her grin revealed her **elation**.
16.	congratulate	*congratulate*	I want to **congratulate** the winners.
17.	preservation	*preservation*	We must promote land **preservation**.
18.	prescription	*prescription*	We had the **prescription** filled.
19.	congratulations	*congratulations*	An award merits **congratulations**.
20.	subscription	*subscription*	Send her a magazine **subscription**.

SORT THE SPELLING WORDS

1.–7. Write the words with the Latin root **scribe** or **script,** meaning "to write."

8.–13. Write the words with the Latin root **serve,** meaning "to watch."

14.–20. Write the words with the Latin root **lat,** from "carry" or "brought."

REMEMBER THE SPELLING STRATEGY

Remember that knowing Latin roots like **scribe/script, serve,** and **lat** can give clues to the meaning and spelling of certain words.

Word Meanings

Write the spelling word that best replaces each underlined word or phrase.

1. That woman, who knows sign language, will <u>make a translation of</u> the speech.
2. My cousins were <u>thrilled</u> to learn about your new twins.
3. Show me how to <u>protect</u> this finish from scratches.
4. A jeweler will <u>carve into the surface</u> the names of both people.
5. An ant farm allows you to <u>watch</u> the ants without disturbing them.
6. The traveler asked the <u>interpreter</u> to explain what the sign meant.

Word Structure

Write the spelling word that is a noun form of each verb.

7. inscribe
8. prescribe
9. subscribe
10. observe
11. reserve
12. preserve
13. elate
14. congratulate
15. describe

USING THE Dictionary

Write the spelling word for each dictionary respelling. Check your answers in the **Spelling Dictionary**.

16. /rĭ **zûrv′**/
17. /prĭ **skrīb′**/
18. /səb **scrīb′**/
19. /kən **grăch′** ə lāt′/
20. /rĭ **lā′** shən/

Spelling and Reading

elated   inscribe   prescribe   description   observation
elation   observe   subscribe   reservation   congratulate
reserve   preserve   translator   prescription   preservation
relation   translate   inscription   subscription   congratulations

Solve the Analogies   Write the spelling word that best completes each analogy.

1. **Hate** is to **love** as **depression** is to _____.
2. **Sculptor** is to **statue** as **engraver** is to _____.
3. **Image** is to **illustrator** as **language** is to _____.
4. **Funeral** is to **condolences** as **wedding** is to _____.
5. **Satellite dish** is to **own** as **cable TV** is to _____.
6. **Lose** is to **find** as **destroy** is to _____.
7. **Lawyer** is to **brief** as **doctor** is to _____.

Complete the Sentences   Write a spelling word to complete each sentence.

8. How many tickets did you _____ for the baseball game?
9. Let me be the first to _____ you on your award!
10. Dr. Valdez wants to _____ a new medication.
11. Who can _____ this song into English?
12. The officer asked for a written _____ of the accident.
13. Please cancel my _____ to your magazine.
14. We should _____ the winner's name on a brass plaque.
15. The restaurant will hold our _____ for half an hour.

Complete the Paragraph   Write the spelling words from the box to complete the paragraph.

Until the 1900s, Native Americans had no written language. They would keenly __16.__ nature and rely on word of mouth to teach their love of the land. A Cherokee named Sequoya watched white people read books. This __17.__ made him want to give his people the same advantage. Having grasped the __18.__ between symbols and sounds, Sequoya invented symbols for each sound in the Cherokee language. He tested the system on his daughter and was __19.__ when he realized that it worked. Sequoya's system made possible the __20.__ of a written record of Cherokee customs and history.

observation
preservation
elated
observe
relation

166

Spelling and Writing

Proofread a Paragraph

Six words are not spelled correctly in this paragraph. Write the words correctly.

Poets must obsurve details accurately to share them. Capturing a feeling, such as elaytion or pain, is difficult, yet the poet Dylan Thomas manages to do so in his poem "Fern Hill." When he writes, "And honored among wagons, I was prince of the apple towns," he is able to translait a child's joy into words and praserve it on paper. The speaker in the poem is elaited by his sun-filled, song-filled, carefree childhood. Only by his use of discription at the end of the poem do we find him making a less joyful observation about that time in his life. "Fern Hill" ends with the lines "Time held me green and dying/Though I sang in my chains like the sea."

POETRY

Proofreading Marks

 Make a capital.

 Make a small letter.

 Add something.

 Take out something.

 Add a period.

 New paragraph

SP Spelling error

Write a Paragraph

Expository Writing

Write a paragraph about a poem or a song that affected you in some way. Focus either on a particular line or on the whole work. Tell what element of the poem or song speaks to you and why.

- Select words and phrases that you find meaningful.
- Discuss what message the words send beyond their literal meaning.
- Quote or paraphrase from the work to support your ideas.
- Follow the form used in the proofreading sample.

Use as many spelling words as you can.

Writing Process

Prewriting
⇩
Drafting
⇩
Revising
⇩
Editing
⇩
Publishing

Proofread Your Writing During

Proofread your writing for spelling errors as part of the editing stage in the writing process. Be sure to check each word carefully. Use a dictionary to check spelling if you are not sure.

167

Strategy Words

Review Words: Latin Roots

Write the word from the box that best completes each sentence.

conserve	describe	postscript
relate	scribble	

1. I just want to _____ some ideas in my notebook fast; I know my writing will be messy.

2. We laughed when my little sister tried to _____ the neighbor's new dog.

3. Alan included his phone number, but only in a _____ at the bottom of the page.

4. Write on both sides to _____ paper.

5. The storyteller will now _____ a Peruvian folktale.

Preview Words: Latin Roots

Write the word from the box that fits each meaning.

ascribe	belated	conscription
preservable	transcriber	

6. compulsory enrollment in the armed forces

7. able to be saved

8. to attribute to a particular cause

9. one who makes a written copy

10. delayed; late

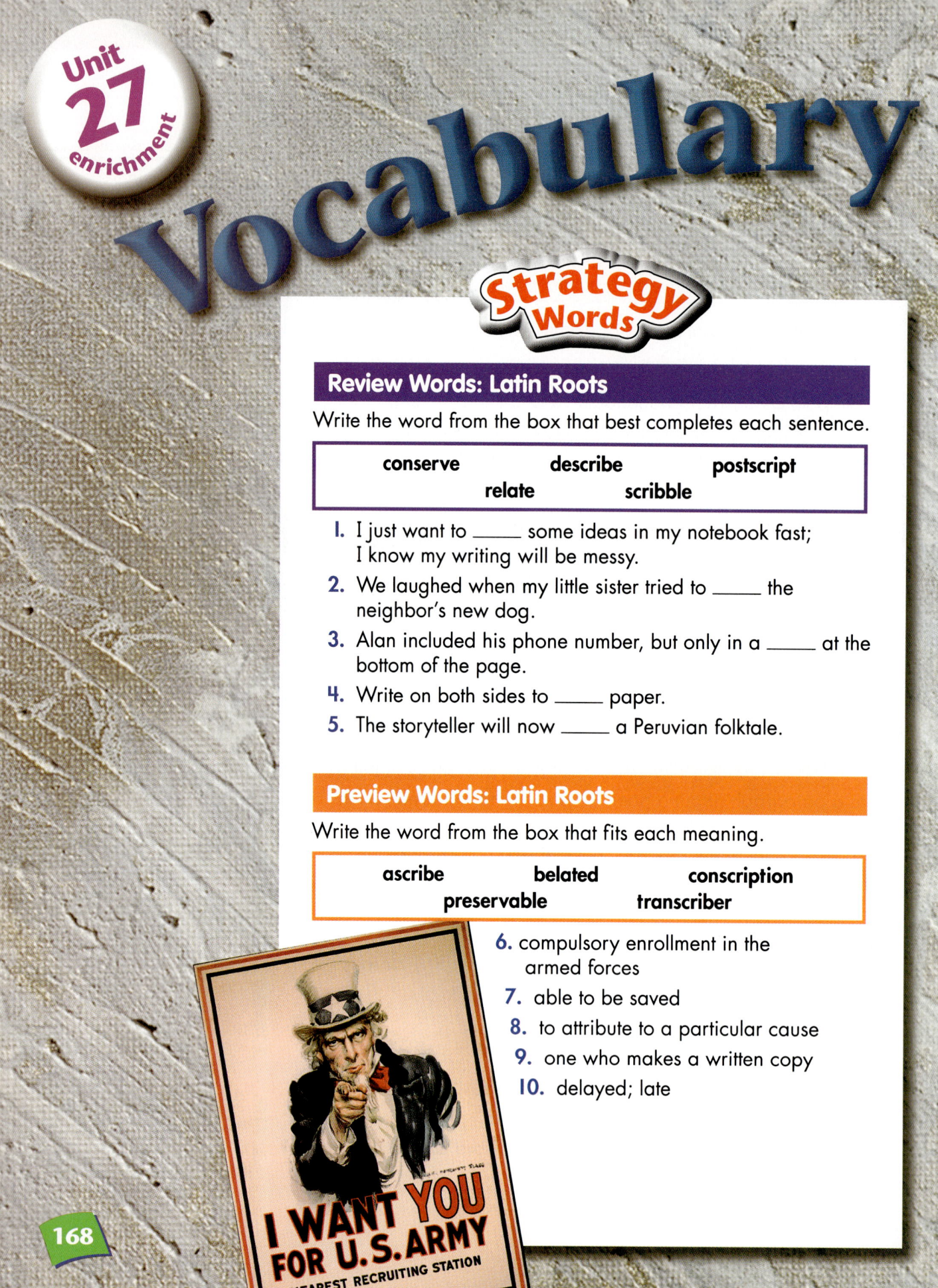

I WANT YOU FOR U.S. ARMY
NEAREST RECRUITING STATION

Connections

Social Studies: Manuscripts

Write the words from the box to complete the paragraph.

calligraphy	**illuminate**	**monastery**
parchment	**scribe**	

Many people believe that __1.__ was practiced only in the Middle Ages by a solitary __2.__ working in a __3.__. However, many modern artists still __4.__ manuscripts. They may apply gold leaf or brilliant colors to a page of writing. A few work on real __5.__, although more artists work on beautiful papers instead.

Math: Operations

Write the word from the box that matches each definition.

geometric	**reflection**	**rotation**
transformation	**translation**	

6. of or pertaining to geometry
7. shapes that are made up of corresponding points in the number plane
8. nonrotational movement
9. an angular displacement of coordinate axes with the origin remaining fixed
10. replacement of the variables in an algebraic expression

Apply the Spelling Strategy

One of the content words you wrote is a Latin root that you studied in this unit. Circle that word.

READ THE SPELLING WORDS

1.	odyssey	*odyssey*	Bill went on an Alaskan **odyssey**.
2.	jersey	*jersey*	Karen wore a baseball **jersey**.
3.	voltage	*voltage*	What **voltage** are these power lines?
4.	wattage	*wattage*	We need more **wattage** for better light.
5.	boycott	*boycott*	Thelma joined the 1970s lettuce **boycott**.
6.	limousine	*limousine*	Gary rented a **limousine** for the prom.
7.	galvanize	*galvanize*	Her speech will **galvanize** the class.
8.	panic	*panic*	A calm voice told us not to **panic**.
9.	turquoise	*turquoise*	In the Caribbean, the water is **turquoise**.
10.	platonic	*platonic*	Their **platonic** friendship grew stronger.
11.	macadam	*macadam*	Beneath the cement is a **macadam** road.
12.	jodhpurs	*jodhpurs*	Thea wore **jodhpurs** and riding boots.
13.	zeppelin	*zepplin*	The **zeppelin** floated over the stadium.
14.	rhinestone	*rhinestone*	Connie wore a **rhinestone** tiara.
15.	malapropism	*malapropism*	A **malapropism** is a misuse of a word.
16.	laconic	*laconic*	New Englanders are said to be **laconic**.
17.	pasteurize	*pasteurize*	We **pasteurize** milk to make it safe.
18.	maverick	*maverick*	Thom was the **maverick** in the group.
19.	spoonerism	*spoonerism*	A **spoonerism** is a reversal of sounds.
20.	mackinaw	*mackinaw*	A **mackinaw** is good for winter weather.

SORT THE SPELLING WORDS

Use the **Spelling Dictionary** to look up etymologies if you need help.

1.–13. Write the spelling words that come from the names of people.

14.–20. Write the spelling words that come from the names of places.

REMEMBER THE SPELLING STRATEGY

Remember that the English language includes many words taken from names and places.

Word Meanings

Write the spelling word that matches each definition or clue.

1. an electromotive force
2. tending toward the spiritual or ideal
3. to kill bacteria by heating
4. a "well-boiled icicle" for "a well-oiled bicycle"
5. to arouse to awareness or action
6. pavement made of compacted layers of stone, now bound with tar or asphalt
7. an imitation gem made of glass
8. a luxurious automobile

Word Groups

Write a spelling word related in meaning to complete each group.

9. azure, aqua, ultramarine, _____
10. jeans, leggings, shorts, overalls, _____
11. trek, journey, trip, voyage, expedition, _____
12. coat, parka, pea jacket, _____
13. strike, walkout, revolt, picket, _____
14. anxiety, apprehension, alarm, _____
15. brief, concise, reserved, terse, _____

USING THE Dictionary

Write the spelling for each dictionary respelling. Check your answers in the **Spelling Dictionary**.

16. /wŏt′ ĭj/
17. /zĕp′ ə lĭn/
18. /măl′ ə prŏp ĭz′ əm/
19. /jûr′ zē/
20. /măv′ ər ĭk, măv′ rĭk/

odyssey	jersey	voltage	wattage	boycott
limousine	galvanize	panic	turquoise	platonic
macadam	jodhpurs	zeppelin	rhinestone	malapropism
laconic	pasteurize	maverick	spoonerism	mackinaw

Fix the Malapropisms   Replace each underlined malapropism with the appropriate spelling word.

1. The chauffeur drove the <u>libertine</u> down Park Avenue.
2. We promised to <u>bucket</u> the company's products.
3. The chilly weather made me put on my <u>mackerel</u>.
4. She was wearing her <u>joggers</u> at the riding stable.
5. Each <u>rhinoceros</u> on her jacket was hand-sewn.
6. The lawyer put on her favorite <u>jury</u> sweater.
7. During their <u>oddity</u>, the adventurers encountered the Cyclops.
8. We may buy a light bulb according to its <u>waddle</u>.

Answer the Questions   Write the spelling word that best answers each question.

9. What kind of expression is "a blushing crow"?
10. What can cheering do for a losing team?
11. What kind of statement is "I was so hungry I gouged myself"?
12. What state of emotion do stampeding horses show?
13. What can you do to purify apple cider?
14. What transmits electric power over long distances?
15. What is both a color and a gemstone?
16. Which word is an antonym for **wordy**?
17. Which word can be made from the following scrambled letters: **mamadac**?
18. Which word is related to Greek philosophy?
19. What might be floating over the highway?
20. Which person would think and act independently?

Spelling and Writing

Proofread a Paragraph

Six words are not spelled correctly in this paragraph. Write the words correctly.

Betty is a mavwreck when it comes to clothes. One day, for example, she had on a plaid makignaw, a striped jersey, and a flowered skirt. On another day she wore joddpers with rinestone jewelry. Her silver and turkoise bracelets are beautiful, but they look silly when she wears fifty on one arm. Yesterday I saw Betty in a limozene; she was wearing a hat that looked like a zeppelin!

Proofreading Marks

≡	Make a capital.
/	Make a small letter.
∧	Add something.
ℓ	Take out something.
⊙	Add a period.
⌗	New paragraph
SP	Spelling error

Write a Paragraph

Descriptive Writing

Trends magazine has asked you to write about something new and exciting in your area.

- Choose a person, place, object, or idea that is gaining popularity. Use your imagination and a bit of flair.
- Compose a topic sentence that identifies your topic and explains its popularity.
- Organize your details in a logical order.
- Write a paragraph.
- Follow the form used in the proofreading sample.

Use as many spelling words as you can.

Proofread Your Writing During ➤ Editing

Writing Process

Prewriting
⇩
Drafting
⇩
Revising
⇩
Editing
⇩
Publishing

Proofread your writing for spelling errors as part of the editing stage in the writing process. Be sure to check each word carefully. Use a dictionary to check spelling if you are not sure.

Vocabulary

Strategy Words

Review Words: Words From Names and Places

Write a word from the box to complete each sentence.

angora	calico	cardigan
cheddar	suede	

1. Do you like melted _____ cheese on toast?
2. On casual Fridays, Dad wears a shirt without a tie and a _____ instead of a jacket to work.
3. Missy herself had gathered the rabbit fur that made her _____ mittens.
4. The singer wore soft, blue _____ shoes.
5. The country kitchen had red _____ curtains.

Preview Words: Words From Names and Places

Write a word from the box that matches each clue.

mausoleum	poinsettia	sequoia
serendipity	thespian	

6. This tree is also known as a redwood.
7. This is one little house you want to avoid while you are alive.
8. This plant often has showy, bright-red leaves.
9. This person might star in a play or a TV show.
10. An example of this would be running out of fuel in front of a gas station.

Connections

Content Words

Social Studies: Ancient Egypt

Write a word from the box to complete each sentence.

Egyptian	hieroglyphics	papyrus	pharaoh	sphinx

1. The first writing paper was _____.
2. Sandy always wanted to see the _____ pyramids.
3. Tutankhamen was the _____ whose tomb was unearthed.
4. The ancient Egyptians used _____, a system of writing in which symbols and pictures represent sounds.
5. A _____, with a lion's body and a woman's head, guards the pyramid.

Fine Arts: Theater

Write a word from the box to complete each sentence.

absurd	farce	melodrama	sensational	tragedy

6. The hero in a _____ often acts in a way that brings about his own downfall.
7. Soap operas are filled with _____, which includes unbelievable coincidences and emotion-filled conflicts.
8. Tabloid newspapers emphasize _____ events.
9. The philosophy that life is meaningless dominates the theater of the _____.
10. A comic play with a story and characters that are exaggerated to cause laughter is called a _____.

Apply the Spelling Strategy

Circle two content words you wrote that come from names of a person or place.

READ THE SPELLING WORDS

1. distinct	*distinct*	This milk has a **distinct** odor.
2. dissimilar	*dissimilar*	Fraternal twins are actually **dissimilar**.
3. lecture	*lecture*	The **lecture** on birds was fascinating.
4. harangue	*harangue*	The speaker's **harangue** lasted an hour.
5. obedient	*obedient*	Tad has an **obedient** puppy.
6. cooperative	*cooperative*	This job needs a **cooperative** effort.
7. commonplace	*commonplace*	Maples are **commonplace** in Maine.
8. conventional	*conventional*	Lee's idea was quite **conventional**.
9. paramount	*paramount*	Good health is a **paramount** concern.
10. prominent	*prominent*	She comes from a **prominent** family.
11. accountability	*accountability*	My **accountability** is to the boss.
12. responsibility	*responsibility*	Washing dishes is my **responsibility**.
13. tolerance	*tolerance*	We discussed the need for **tolerance**.
14. sympathy	*sympathy*	Meg expressed **sympathy** for our loss.
15. catastrophe	*catastrophe*	The airplane crash was a **catastrophe**.
16. calamity	*calamity*	The earthquake was a **calamity**.
17. anticipate	*anticipate*	Tennis players **anticipate** the next shot.
18. envision	*envision*	Dan could **envision** the winter scene.
19. consequence	*consequence*	My action had a serious **consequence**.
20. repercussion	*repercussion*	My remark had a sudden **repercussion**.

SORT THE SPELLING WORDS

1.–3. Write the spelling words that have two syllables.

4.–10. Write the spelling words that have three syllables.

11.–17. Write the spelling words that have four syllables.

18. Write the spelling word that has five syllables.

19.–20. Write the spelling words that have six syllables.

REMEMBER THE SPELLING STRATEGY

Remember that words with similar meanings are often confused.

Word Meanings

Write a spelling word to match each definition.

1. dutifully complying with commands
2. marked by a willingness to work together
3. answerability
4. a duty or obligation
5. an indirect result
6. an effect
7. the capacity for respecting the opinions of others
8. the act of sharing the feelings of another
9. having no remarkable characteristics
10. customary or traditional

Word Replacements

Write the spelling word that best replaces each underlined word or phrase.

11. The woman's <u>tirade</u> made everyone uncomfortable.
12. When will he <u>give a talk</u> about the new archaeological dig?
13. Skating in the Olympics was Gale's <u>primary</u> goal.
14. Kyle's deep voice was <u>readily distinguished</u>.
15. The house's most <u>noticeable</u> feature was its steep roof.
16. A typewriter and a computer are <u>unlike each other</u>.

USING THE Dictionary

Write the spelling word in each synonym pair that best completes each sentence. Use the **Spelling Dictionary** if you need help.

17. The development of transparent celluloid film would **(anticipate/envision)** the needs of motion pictures.
18. Eadweard Muybridge could not **(anticipate/envision)** the effect that his photographic work would have on the film industry.
19. The introduction of talkies was a **(calamity/catastrophe)** for actors with unsuitable voices.
20. A movie about a **(calamity/catastrophe)** is popular with many audiences.

Spelling and Reading

distinct	accountability	cooperative	harangue	obedient
lecture	commonplace	conventional	paramount	prominent
dissimilar	responsibility	catastrophe	sympathy	tolerance
calamity	consequence	repercussion	anticipate	envision

Solve the Analogies   Write the spelling word that best completes each analogy.

1. **Pat** is to **punch** as **speech** is to _____.
2. **Agree** is to **disagree** as **similar** is to _____.
3. **Market** is to **marketplace** as **common** is to _____.
4. **Audience** is to **attentive** as **group** is to _____.
5. **Flood** is to **deluge** as **catastrophe** is to _____.

Complete the Sentences   Write the spelling word that best completes each sentence.

6. Can you _____ a purple couch against this yellow wall?
7. A logical _____ of studying so hard will be an excellent grade on your math test.
8. The cyclone was a _____ that struck without warning.
9. Thomas Edison was a _____ inventor.
10. We expressed our _____ for the loss of their grandmother.
11. A good work of literature can teach _____ and understanding.

Complete the Paragraph   Write spelling words from the box to complete the paragraph.

Few tasks teach __12.__ the way taking care of a pet does. There are __13.__ benefits to assigning pet-care tasks even to toddlers. Learning to __14.__ and fulfill the needs of an animal without a parental __15.__ develops over time. Raising an __16.__, well-trained animal takes love and patience. Of __17.__ importance is consistent follow-through in feeding and training. Also, we live in days of __18.__, and owners must pay for any damage done by their animals. Children can learn to avoid any unexpected __19.__ resulting from the action of an unsupervised pet. Whether caring for a dog, a cat, a bird, or a less __20.__ pet, like a snake, a child can grow along with his or her animal.

repercussion
lecture
distinct
responsibility
anticipate
obedient
conventional
accountability
paramount

Spelling ᵃⁿᵈ Writing

Proofread a Letter to the Editor

Six words are not spelled correctly in this letter to a newspaper. Write the words correctly.

To the Editor:

It is time to look at our accountibelity rather than to practice toleranse in the following matter. Some of us, including a few prominant members of our community, do not want to antisipate the consequince of an upcoming decision. The attempt to discontinue leaf collection will have more than one serious repercushion. Let's not wait until a weather-related catastrophe forces us to reassess our priorities.

Yours truly,

Will U. Help

Proofreading Marks

≡	Make a capital.
/	Make a small letter.
∧	Add something.
ℓ	Take out something.
⊙	Add a period.
⌗	New paragraph
ⓢⓟ	Spelling error

Write a Letter to the Editor — Persuasive Writing

Write a letter to the editor about a problem in your school or community.

- State the problem.
- Discuss what might be done to solve it.
- Support your points with specific examples.
- Follow the form used in the proofreading sample.

Use as many spelling words as you can.

Proofread Your Writing During ▶

Proofread your writing for spelling errors as part of the editing stage in the writing process. Be sure to check each word carefully. Use a dictionary to check spelling if you are not sure.

Writing Process

Prewriting
⇩
Drafting
⇩
Revising
⇩
Editing
⇩
Publishing

Vocabulary

Strategy Words

Review Words: Synonyms

Write words from the box to complete the sentences.

display	exhibit	gigantic
	huge	immense

1.–3. The word _____ comes from the Greek **gigantikos** and is a synonym both for _____, which comes from the Latin **immēnsus,** and _____, which comes from the Old French **ahuge**.

4.–5. The word _____ comes from the Latin **exhibēre** and is a synonym for _____.

Preview Words: Synonyms

Write the word from the box that matches each clue.

accede	acquiesce	congenial
discordance		pugnacious

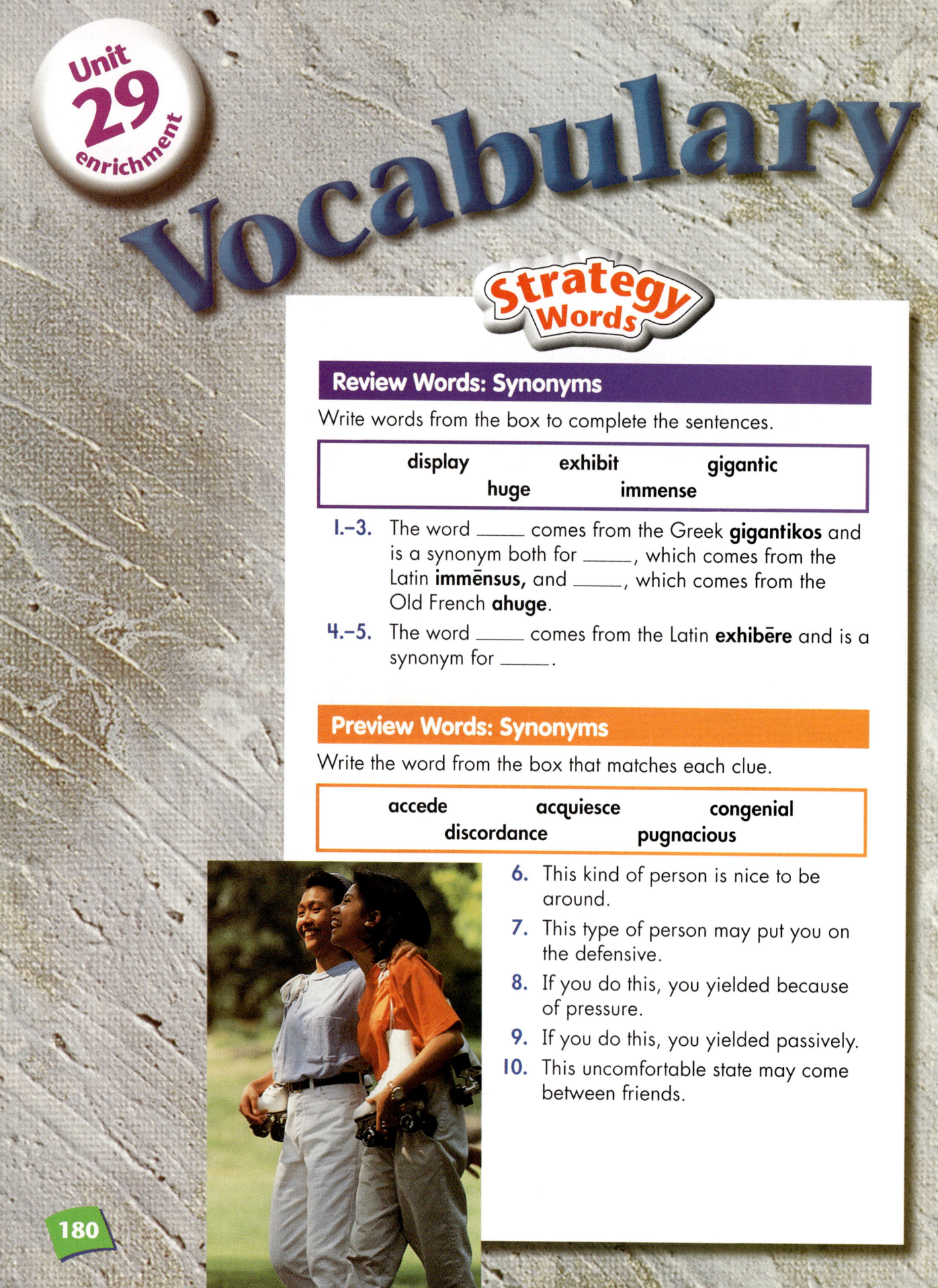

6. This kind of person is nice to be around.

7. This type of person may put you on the defensive.

8. If you do this, you yielded because of pressure.

9. If you do this, you yielded passively.

10. This uncomfortable state may come between friends.

Connections

Science: Chemistry

Write the word from the box that fits each meaning.

absorb	acidic	alkaline
dissolve	saturate	

1. related to any of various basic mineral salts found in natural water and in arid soil
2. to soak to capacity
3. to completely retain something taken in
4. having a characteristic sour taste
5. to cause to pass into a solution

Philosophy: Ideas

Write words from the box to complete the paragraph.

concept	derive	intellectual
intuition	philosophy	

The pursuit of knowledge by reasoning is the field known as __6.__. Philosophers use a rational, or __7.__, approach to investigate the causes and laws of reality. They obtain, or __8.__, each idea, or __9.__, through reason and logic, not through __10.__ or any other process that does not rely on logic.

Apply the Spelling Strategy

Circle the two content words you wrote that are related to **soak**.

Assessment and Review

Assessment   Units 25–29

Each Assessment Word in the box fits one of the spelling strategies you have studied over the past five weeks. Read the spelling strategies. Then write each Assessment Word under the unit number it fits.

Unit 25
1.–4. Remember that words with similar spellings and meanings are often confused.

Unit 26
5.–9. Remember that some words have more letters than sounds.

Unit 27
10.–16. Remember that knowing Latin roots like **scribe/script, serve,** and **lat** can give clues to the meaning and spelling of certain words.

Unit 28
Remember that the English language includes many words taken from names and places.

Unit 29
17.–20. Remember that words with similar meanings are often confused.

pneumonic
illicit
proscribe
preserved
comprehensible
circumscribe
scholar
preservative
irrevocable
elicit
unimportant
adjustment
descriptive
adolescence
unalterable
comprehensive
proscription
inconsequential
elatedness
acquainted

 **Unit 25: Commonly Confused Words**

ascent	assent	descent	continuously	continually
morale	moral	dissent	respectfully	respectively

Write the correct spelling word pairs to complete each sentence.

1.–2. After three days aloft, there was no _____ among the tired crew of the hot-air balloon when Captain Monroe said it was time for the _____.

3.–4. The _____ of the story is that if you can think positively and keep up your _____, you will get the job done.

5.–6. Please _____ to making the _____ of the mountain with my team and me.

7.–8. I _____ request that my first three job choices be listed as cook, farmhand, or landscaper, _____.

9.–10. It rained _____ for two days while the wind _____ banged the shutters.

 **Unit 26: Words With More Letters Than Sounds**

campaign	subtle	fascinate	undoubtedly	miscellaneous
adjust	adjoin	discipline	psychology	acknowledgment

Write a spelling word for each clue.

11. It has three syllables. It comes from the Latin word **discere**, meaning "to learn."

12. It ends with the Greek combining form **-logy**.

13. It begins with the prefix **un-** and ends with the suffix **-ly**.

14. A final **e** was dropped before the suffix **-ment** was added.

15. It has two syllables and a silent **b**.

16. It means "to change or adapt."

17. The long **a** sound is spelled **ai** and the **g** is silent.

18. It has three syllables and ends with **ate**.

19. There is a double **l** in the spelling.

20. It would come second in an alphabetical list of the words.

 **Review** Unit 27: Latin Roots scribe/script, serve, lat

observe	translate	reserve	relation
description	observation	reservation	congratulate
	prescription	congratulations	

Write a spelling word for each clue. The word you write will be the part of speech in parentheses.

1. to view carefully (verb)
2. to acknowledge someone's achievement (verb)
3. an acknowledgment of someone's achievement (noun)
4. to express in another language (verb)
5. an image or an account of something (noun)
6. the act of viewing and noting or recording a phenomenon (noun)
7. to keep back or save for future use (verb)
8. a connection between two or more things (noun)
9. land held for a particular purpose; a qualification (noun)
10. a written instruction from a doctor (noun)

 **Review** Unit 28: Words From Names and Places

| odyssey | voltage | boycott | limousine | galvanize |
| panic | turquoise | jodhpurs | pasteurize | maverick |

Write a spelling word to replace the underlined word or words in each sentence.

11. If the general could <u>arouse</u> the will of the troops, he might be victorious.
12. We hired a <u>long, fancy car</u> to go to the opera.
13. What an <u>incredible journey</u> we could take on that ship!
14. The silver necklace had <u>bluish-green</u> stones.
15. We brought in the <u>orphaned colt</u> after a long chase.
16. The <u>electrical force</u> in that fence is dangerously high.
17. The realistic suspense film gave me a jolt of <u>terror</u>.
18. For the horse show, you need to wear <u>riding pants</u>.
19. Be sure to <u>sterilize</u> that fresh goat milk.
20. In protest, we decided to <u>stop shopping</u> at that store.

distinct	dissimilar	obedient	cooperative	paramount
prominent	tolerance	sympathy	catastrophe	calamity

Add the missing letters to write spelling words.

1. __at__ __t__ __ph__
2. __ __ss__mi__ __ __r
3. di__ __ __n__t
4. __a__am__ __nt
5. c__la__ __t__

6. __y__ __at__y
7. __ol__ __ __n__e
8. __ __ __di__nt
9. __ro__ine__ __
10. __oo__ __r__ __ive

 **Spelling Study Strategy**

Spelling Capture

Swap spelling lists with a partner. On a sheet of paper, make five rows of dots with five dots in each row. Decide who is Player 1 and who is Player 2.

Player 2 says the first word on Player 1's list, and Player 1 spells the word. If it is correct, Player 1 uses a pencil to connect any two dots that are side-by-side. If Player 1 misspells the word, no dots are connected. If Player 2 spells the misspelled word aloud correctly, he or she connects two dots. Then it is Player 2's turn to spell the first word on his or her list.

Continue to take turns until all the words on each list have been spelled. Each time a player connects the final two dots to make a square, that player writes his or her initials in the square. That square is "captured." The player who has the most initialed squares at the end of the game wins.

Grammar, Usage, and Mechanics

Using Commas Correctly

A **comma** is used to separate parts of dates and addresses and to separate items in a series.

> On May 5, 1999, we saw planets, stars, and comets.
> Meet us in St. Louis, Missouri, next week.

A comma is also used to set off **appositives**.

An appositive follows a noun and gives more information about the noun.

> Ms. Jackson, the volleyball coach, arrived early.

Practice Activity

A. A comma is missing in each sentence. Write the word or number that precedes the missing comma and then write the comma.

(1.) The four pups were brown black, tan, and gray. **(2.)** They were born on December 4, 1998 in our yard. **(3.)** We named them Nero, Hero Lady, and Princess. **(4.)** The pups are part spaniel, part retriever part shepherd, and part collie. **(5.)** They were adopted on January 25 1999, by families nearby. **(6.)** The Jones family, our next-door neighbors took Princess, the brown pup. **(7.)** The gray pup Nero, went two houses down to the Johnsons. **(8.)** Lady the smallest of the four, moved across the street. **(9.)** Hero, the energetic black pup lives one block over. **(10.)** We kept Lucy the mother dog, who will see her pups often.

B. Write **one, two,** or **three** to tell how many commas are missing in a sentence. Write **OK** if none are needed.

11. We visited Williamsburg, Virginia on May 17 1998.

12. Toby, Todd, and Tyra the triplets, will soon be ten.

13. The play, *Our Town*, will be performed in March.

14. Pearl Harbor our base in Hawaii was bombed on December 7 1941.

15. Ashley bowled a 65, a 79, and a 104 her highest score ever.

WORKSHOP

Pair Up With a Partner!

Good writers always proofread their papers for spelling errors. Here is a strategy that you can use to proofread your writing.

Instead of proofreading all by yourself, pair up with a partner. Ask your partner to read your work aloud slowly. While your partner reads, you look at each word. Is it spelled correctly?

Hearing each word read aloud helps you focus on the word and its spelling instead of on the sentence. A second benefit is that a partner can help you fix misspellings. This strategy works. Try it!

Electronic Spelling

Spell Checkers

Computers have many programs and tools that help you proofread. Most word processors today have spell checkers that signal misspelled words. But even the most sophisticated spell checker won't find every mistake, so you must be alert for problems.

Sometimes the misspelling of the word you wanted will be the correct spelling of another word, but one you didn't want to use. A spell checker won't catch the mistake because it only recognizes a misspelling that isn't a real word.

A spell checker was used to correct the misspelled words in these sentences. Find the words it missed and write them correctly.

1. Camouflage made the hunter almost indivisible.
2. The assent of the mountain took nine days.
3. Bread dough is best if needed by hand.
4. The comedy show kept up the moral of the soldiers.
5. It was late when we fished doing the dishes.
6. Open the coral gate and let the horse out.

READ THE SPELLING WORDS

1.	spirit	*spirit*	The horse has a lively **spirit**.
2.	revive	*revive*	A short vacation will **revive** you.
3.	aspire	*aspire*	Does he **aspire** to win the gold medal?
4.	revival	*revival*	We enjoyed the **revival** of the old movie.
5.	vista	*vista*	The hikers admired the beautiful **vista**.
6.	inspire	*inspire*	The coach hoped to **inspire** the team.
7.	survive	*survive*	Will the crops **survive** the drought?
8.	inspiration	*inspiration*	His courage is an **inspiration** to others.
9.	survival	*survival*	Food and water are essential to **survival**.
10.	revision	*revision*	This is the third **revision** of the book.
11.	aspiration	*aspiration*	His **aspiration** is to be a playwright.
12.	survivor	*survivor*	The **survivor** was taken to the hospital.
13.	perspiration	*perspiration*	Vigorous exercise produces **perspiration**.
14.	vivid	*vivid*	I have **vivid** memories of our trip.
15.	supervisor	*supervisor*	The worker praised her **supervisor**.
16.	respiration	*respiration*	A bad cold can make **respiration** difficult.
17.	vital	*vital*	His skills are **vital** to our success.
18.	expiration	*expiration*	What is the **expiration** date on the milk?
19.	vitality	*vitality*	Good nutrition can improve **vitality**.
20.	supervision	*supervision*	Young children require adult **supervision**.

SORT THE SPELLING WORDS

1.–8. Write the spelling words with the root **spir,** meaning "to breathe."

9.–16. Write the spelling words with the root **viv** or **vit,** meaning "to live" or "life."

17.–20. Write the spelling words with the root **vis,** meaning "to see."

REMEMBER THE SPELLING STRATEGY

Remember that knowing Latin roots like **spir, viv/vit, vid,** and **vis** can give clues to the meaning and spelling of certain words.

Word Meanings

Write the spelling word that matches each definition.

1. ambitious goal
2. to remain alive
3. physical or intellectual energy
4. a restoration to life
5. to stimulate to action or creativity
6. animating force within living beings
7. to strive toward
8. motivation, incentive
9. the process of inhaling and exhaling
10. person who remains alive

Word Structure

Add the suffix to the base word to write a spelling word. Change the spelling of the base word as needed.

11. survive + al
12. expire + tion
13. supervise + ion
14. perspire + tion
15. revise + ion
16. supervise + or

USING THE Thesaurus

Write a spelling word that could replace the underlined word in each sentence. Check your answers in the **Writing Thesaurus**.

17. Some water should <u>rejuvenate</u> these dying plants.
18. The city council discussed issues of <u>critical</u> importance.
19. The discovery opened up a new <u>view</u> for medical research.
20. He painted the walls of his room a <u>bright</u> red.

spirit	revive	aspire	revival	vista
inspire	survive	inspiration	survival	revision
aspiration	survivor	perspiration	vivid	supervisor
respiration	vital	expiration	vitality	supervision

Replace the Words   Write the spelling word that best replaces the underlined word or phrase in each sentence.

1. Exercise helps maintain <u>vigor and energy</u>.
2. They were fortunate to <u>live through</u> the devastating hurricane.
3. His yoga instructor taught him to control his <u>breathing</u>.
4. The speaker hoped to <u>restore</u> their interest in ancient Greek history.
5. Her <u>active and specific</u> imagination helps her write creative stories.
6. The <u>view</u> from the top of the mountain was worth the climb.
7. The <u>manager</u> checked on production as she walked around the factory.
8. He hoped that his editorial would <u>motivate</u> readers to write letters.

Complete the Sentences   Write the spelling word that best completes each sentence.

9. Proper training and supplies are important to a hiker's _____ in the wilderness.
10. Of all the rose bushes he planted, this is the lone _____.
11. The _____ date on the mailing label indicates that this magazine is the last issue you will receive.
12. Because the book dates back to 1983, it is time for a _____.
13. Runners were soaked with _____ as they crossed the finish line.
14. People who love to write sometimes _____ to a career in journalism.
15. Students worked in the science lab under their teacher's _____.

Complete the Paragraph   Write spelling words from the box to complete the paragraph.

At the age of sixty-eight, Lillian Carter created her own "sixties" __16.__ and joined the Peace Corps. Her __17.__ was to help others. "Miss Lillian" spent two years in India tending to the __18.__ needs of people afflicted with disease. Her strong __19.__ was an __20.__ to others, including her own children, one of whom became president of the United States.

inspiration
vital
revival
spirit
aspiration

Spelling and Writing

Proofread a Paragraph

Six words are not spelled correctly in this paragraph. Write the words correctly.

> I believe that one of the most vitle roles we can play in the lives of young children is to inspire them to grow into confident, caring adults. As a volunteer in an after-school program, I provide more than supervishion. I play games, do arts and crafts, and talk with the children. Their greetings when I walk through the door are an inspuration to me. I espire to a teaching career so that I can continue to help children develop and maintain their vitalaty and spiret.

Write a Paragraph

Expository Writing

Write a paragraph about one of your life goals. It may be something you would like to do later in life, or it may be a short-term goal.

- Explain the reasons for your goal.
- Describe how you might go about achieving it.
- Follow the form used in the proofreading sample.

Use as many spelling words as you can.

Proofread Your Writing During

Proofread your writing for spelling errors as part of the editing stage in the writing process. Be sure to check each word carefully. Use a dictionary to check spelling if you are not sure.

Writing Process

Prewriting
⇩
Drafting
⇩
Revising
⇩
Editing
⇩
Publishing

Vocabulary

Unit **31** enrichment

Strategy Words

Review Words: Latin Roots

Write a word from the box to complete each sentence.

invisible	perspire	supervise
television	video	

1. We watched a _____ on how to handle the sails of a sailboat.
2. My favorite _____ program is going off the air!
3. The room was so hot that he began to _____.
4. Her summer job was to _____ children at the town playground.
5. Some insects are so small that they are nearly _____.

Preview Words: Latin Roots

Write words from the box to complete the paragraph.

conspire	inspiring	providence
provision	visualization	

For centuries, people had visions of flying. A __6.__, however, was just not the same as reality. Because of their __7.__ as hardworking bicycle mechanics, Orville and Wilbur Wright were able to develop the first "aeroplane." The brothers were aware that snow or sleet might __8.__ against them, but they were hopeful. They made a __9.__ for the __10.__ moment to be photographed. On a cold and windy December day in 1903, Wilbur Wright, in fact, piloted the first powered flight in history.

192

Connections

Content Words

Science: Light

Write the word from the box that matches each definition.

| filament   infrared   incandescent   luminescent   ultraviolet |

1. emitting light from a nonthermal source
2. pertaining to wavelengths greater than those of visible light
3. a fine wire that can be heated electrically until it gives off light
4. pertaining to radiation wavelengths that range from beyond the violet in the visible spectrum to the border of the x-ray region
5. emitting light as a result of being heated

Language Arts: Literary Devices

Write the word from the box that completes each sentence.

| expressed   implied   metaphor   simile   similarity |

6. "The road was a ribbon of moonlight" is a _____.
7. The literary device in question 6 expresses a _____ between a road and a ribbon.
8. "Her face was like a light" is an example of a _____.
9. The comparison directly _____ in question 8 is between a face and a light.
10. Sometimes a comparison is _____ rather than stated directly, as in "The moon . . . tossed upon cloudy seas."

Apply the Spelling Strategy

Circle the content word you wrote that has the Latin root **lumen**, meaning "light." Underline the word with the Latin root **filum**, meaning "thread."

READ THE SPELLING WORDS

1. familiar	*familiar*	Are you **familiar** with this ancient city?
2. liaison	*liaison*	He is our **liaison** with the student council.
3. postpone	*postpone*	Rain forced us to **postpone** the game.
4. exhaust	*exhaust*	The five-mile hike did not **exhaust** us.
5. exhilarating	*exhilarating*	A ride down a slide is **exhilarating**.
6. committee	*committee*	The **committee** met to plan the parade.
7. reliable	*reliable*	I chose a **reliable** person for the job.
8. jealousy	*jealousy*	Do not let **jealousy** end a friendship.
9. frivolous	*frivolous*	I bought a **frivolous** and impractical gift.
10. spontaneous	*spontaneous*	His joyful answer was **spontaneous**.
11. prejudice	*prejudice*	She has a **prejudice** against traveling.
12. procedure	*procedure*	What is your message-taking **procedure**?
13. lightning	*lightning*	The power went out when **lightning** struck.
14. numerous	*numerous*	She had **numerous** phone calls to make.
15. irrelevant	*irrelevant*	Her question was **irrelevant** to the topic.
16. genuine	*genuine*	Is this necklace **genuine** gold?
17. forehead	*forehead*	His hair partially covers his **forehead**.
18. luxury	*luxury*	His life is filled with comfort and **luxury**.
19. minimum	*minimum*	I need a **minimum** of seven hours of sleep.
20. aluminum	*aluminum*	This picnic chair is made of **aluminum**.

SORT THE SPELLING WORDS

 1. Write the word that is a noun, an adjective, and a verb.

 2.–3. Write the words that are both nouns and verbs.

 4.–5. Write the words that are both nouns and adjectives.

 6. Write the word that is a verb only.

 7.–13. Write the words that are adjectives only.

 14.–20. Write the words that are nouns only.

REMEMBER THE SPELLING STRATEGY

Remember that it is important to know the spellings of words that are frequently misspelled.

Spelling and Vocabulary

Word Meanings

Write the spelling word that matches each definition.

1. a silvery-white metallic element
2. a flash of light in the sky
3. something that is not essential but that gives pleasure
4. a channel of communication between different groups
5. silly; trivial
6. the part of the face above the eyes
7. a group of people delegated to perform a function
8. an irrational preconceived judgment
9. envy, resentment
10. a method of doing things

Antonyms

Write a spelling word that is an antonym for each word below.

11. maximum
12. relevant
13. undependable
14. uncommon
15. planned
16. gloomy

USING THE Thesaurus

Write the spelling word that is a synonym for each group of words. Use the **Writing Thesaurus** to check your answers. (For item 19, follow the **See also** reference.)

17. countless, infinite, abundant
18. deplete, fatigue, tire
19. adjourn, defer, delay
20. authentic, real, true

familiar	liaison	postpone	exhaust	exhilarating
committee	reliable	jealousy	frivolous	spontaneous
prejudice	procedure	lightning	numerous	irrelevant
genuine	forehead	luxury	minimum	aluminum

Complete the Sentences   Write the spelling word that best completes each sentence.

1. She was bundled up against the cold so that only her eyes and _____ were exposed.
2. His _____ stands in the way of his enjoying friendships with everyone.
3. A _____ of students will help plan the class trip.
4. Eighteen is the _____ age for voting in the United States.
5. The library has a new _____ for checking out books.
6. The frightened deer ran with _____ speed.
7. Be careful not to _____ your energy before the trip is over.
8. The school principal was the _____ with the statewide educators' organization.

Solve the Analogies   Write the spelling word that best completes each analogy.

9. **Careless** is to **careful** as **unknown** is to _____.
10. **Tiny** is to **enormous** as **few** is to _____.
11. **Dull** is to **boring** as **invigorating** is to _____.
12. **Wood** is to **oak** as **metal** is to _____.
13. **Give** is to **donate** as **put off** is to _____.
14. **Confidence** is to **uncertainty** as **necessity** is to _____.
15. **Hectic** is to **calm** as **related** is to _____.

Complete the Paragraph   Write spelling words from the box to complete the paragraph.

   True, or __16.__, friendship is free of __17.__. Friends can depend on each other; by definition, they are __18.__. Communication between friends can be serious, or it can be trivial, even __19.__. Whether you feel silly or somber, though, you can always act naturally with a friend, and your conversation and activities can be either carefully planned or delightfully __20.__.

reliable
jealousy
frivolous
spontaneous
genuine

Spelling and Writing

Proofread a Recollection

Six words are not spelled correctly in this recollection. Write the words correctly.

I woke up with a start and immediately felt my forhead. It did not feel hot. I knew I was trying to postpone the inevitable, my first day at a new school. Would the students be friendly? Would I encounter predgudice?

The morning was uneventful, though it was hard not seeing one familier face. Later, though, in the cafeteria, a boy walked up to me and said in a very spontanious way, "You look confused. Can I show you the proceedure for buying lunch?"

That was two years ago. Now I feel genuin interest in new students, and I try to help them through that difficult first day.

Proofreading Marks

≡ Make a capital.
/ Make a small letter.
∧ Add something.
℮ Take out something.
⊙ Add a period.
New paragraph
SP Spelling error

Write a Recollection

Narrative Writing

Write about a time when someone befriended you or you gave a friend a helping hand.
- Explain how you felt.
- Describe any lessons you learned.
- Follow the form used in the proofreading sample.

Use as many spelling words as you can.

Proofread Your Writing During → Editing

Proofread your writing for spelling errors as part of the editing stage in the writing process. Be sure to check each word carefully. Use a dictionary to check spelling if you are not sure.

Writing Process

Prewriting
⇩
Drafting
⇩
Revising
⇩
Editing
⇩
Publishing

Vocabulary

Strategy Words

Review Words: Frequently Misspelled Words

Write words from the box to complete the paragraph.

bouquet	courtesy	maneuver
picnicking		pursue

We have to plan each __1.__ carefully as we __2.__ our goal of keeping our surprise a secret. First, we will present her with a __3.__ of beautiful flowers. Then, with baskets of special foods, we will take her __4.__ at her favorite lakeside spot. We treat Grandma with __5.__ every day, but on this special birthday, we will treat her royally!

Preview Words: Frequently Misspelled Words

Write a word from the box to complete each sentence.

annihilate	chiropractor	chrysanthemums
clientele		dysfunctional

6. Every fall, he plants _____ in the garden.

7. The patient's _____ kidney had to be replaced.

8. A _____ does not usually use surgery or medicine to treat back problems.

9. Most of the store's _____ live within walking distance.

10. The fierce storm might _____ that fleet of fishing boats.

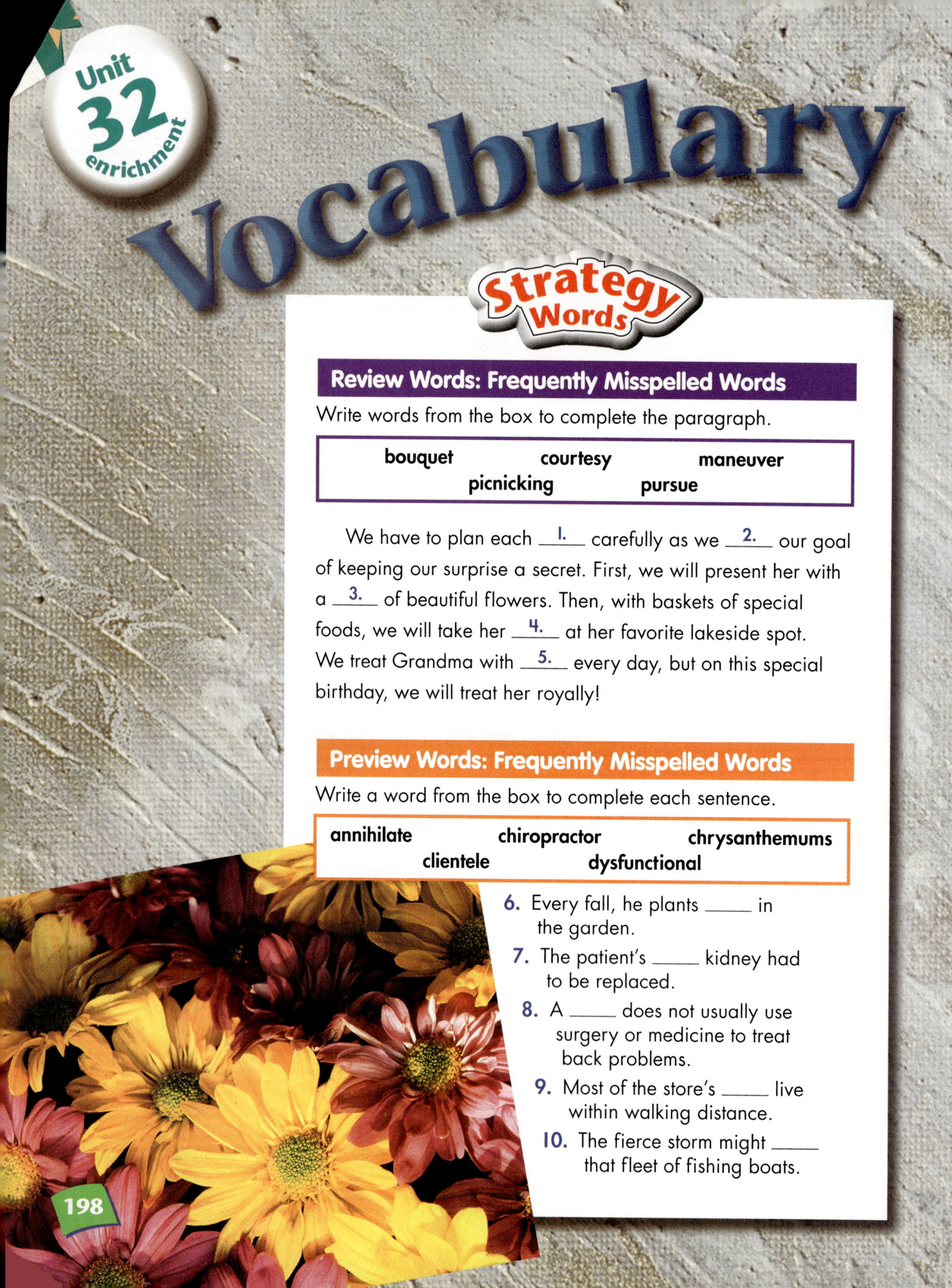

Connections

Math: Geometry

Write words from the box to identify lines and points on the graph.

abscissa	axes	intercept
negative	ordinate	

1. C, D or A, B
2. A or C
3. B or D
4. x and y
5. C

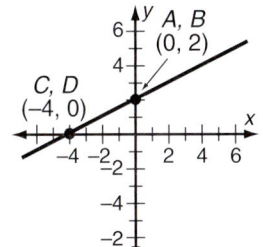

Science: Biology

Write words from the box to complete the paragraph.

chlorophyll	conversion	inorganic
organic	photosynthesis	

   All things can be classified as plants, animals, or minerals. Plants and animals are living, or __6.__ . Minerals are not living; they are __7.__ . Green plants use sunlight and __8.__ in the __9.__ of carbon dioxide to sugars that feed the plant. This chemical process of __10.__ also produces oxygen as a by-product.

Apply the Spelling Strategy

Circle the two content words you wrote in which the letters **ph** are pronounced /**f**/.

Spelling *and* Thinking

READ THE SPELLING WORDS

1.	obstacle	*obstacle*	No **obstacle** will block our path.
2.	submerge	*submerge*	You cannot **submerge** this life jacket.
3.	surpass	*surpass*	I hope to **surpass** this year's record.
4.	incorporate	*incorporate*	The logo will **incorporate** our name.
5.	occupy	*occupy*	Who will **occupy** these rooms?
6.	succinct	*succinct*	Tell the moral in one **succinct** phrase.
7.	surface	*surface*	How smooth the water's **surface** is!
8.	offend	*offend*	That comment will not **offend** him.
9.	immerse	*immerse*	Do not **immerse** the handle in water.
10.	occupation	*occupation*	What **occupation** interests you most?
11.	suppress	*suppress*	I tried to **suppress** a nervous giggle.
12.	implicate	*implicate*	These clues **implicate** the defendant.
13.	sustain	*sustain*	Food and water help to **sustain** life.
14.	incentive	*incentive*	High satisfaction is a work **incentive**.
15.	offensive	*offensive*	He criticizes without being **offensive**.
16.	immaterial	*immaterial*	What you wear is **immaterial** to me.
17.	surplus	*surplus*	Will you sell your **surplus** squash?
18.	oppressive	*oppressive*	The heat here can be **oppressive**.
19.	supplement	*supplement*	I take a vitamin **supplement** daily.
20.	impressionable	*impressionable*	The film scared **impressionable** tots.

SORT THE SPELLING WORDS

1.–6. Write the words with the prefix **ob-** (meaning "toward, against") or one of its assimilated forms, **oc-, of-,** or **op-**.

7.–11. Write the words with the prefix **sub-** (meaning "under, below") or one of its assimilated forms, **suc-, sup-,** or **sus-**.

12.–14. Write the words with the prefix **sur-** (meaning "over, above").

15.–20. Write the words with the prefix **in-** (meaning "into, not") or its assimilated form, **im-**.

REMEMBER THE SPELLING STRATEGY

Remember that the prefixes **ob-, sub-, sur-,** and **in-** may be assimilated into the spelling of a base word or a root.

200

Spelling and Vocabulary

Word Meanings

Write a spelling word that matches each definition.

1. to cause to merge into a united whole
2. to involve or to connect incriminatingly
3. of no importance or relevance
4. to involve completely or absorb
5. readily or easily influenced; suggestible
6. something, as in the fear of punishment or the expectation of reward, that incites to action or effort
7. the outer or topmost boundary of an object
8. being in excess of what is required

Word Structure

An assimilated prefix may result in a double consonant. Answer each question with a spelling word that begins with an assimilated form of **ob-** or **sub-** and doubles the consonant. Circle the doubled consonants.

9. What is a synonym for **dwell**?
10. What is added to complete a thing or make up for a deficiency?
11. What do you do when you cause resentment?
12. What is another word for **tyrannical**?
13. What is another way to say **terse**?
14. What is a synonym for **vocation**?
15. What is another way to say **subdue**?
16. What is an antonym for **defensive**?

USING THE Dictionary

Write the spelling word for each etymology. Use the **Spelling Dictionary** to check your answers.

17. **sur-**, over + **passer**, to pass
18. **sub-**, below + **tenere**, to hold
19. **sub-**, under + **mergere**, to plunge
20. **ob-**, against + **stare**, to stand

Spelling and Reading

obstacle	submerge	surpass	incorporate	occupy
succinct	surface	offend	immerse	occupation
suppress	implicate	sustain	incentive	offensive
immaterial	surplus	oppressive	supplement	impressionable

Complete the Sentences   Write the spelling word that best completes each sentence.

1. We can _____ our new apartment next week.

2. Try to _____ just your face and not your entire head when you swim.

3. The film has been edited to delete any _____ content.

4. Wet cement is _____, but it does not stay that way for long.

5. Whether we go tonight or Saturday is _____ to me.

6. During first period, I tried to _____ my yawns, but I was very sleepy.

7. This solution will _____ everyone's ideas into one plan.

8. Write a short, _____ statement of your goals.

9. They hope that this year's sales will _____ last year's.

10. The first prize is a trip to Paris, which is a strong _____ for many people.

11. That joke is funny, but it might _____ some people.

12. Your teacher did not _____ you; in fact, he defended you.

13. Those goldfish swim just below the _____ of the pond.

14. If the heat becomes _____, turn on the air conditioner.

15. I would like some ribbon, if you have any _____.

Complete the Paragraph   Write spelling words from the box to complete the paragraph.

My soccer coach works evenings to __16.__ her income and buy extras for her family. Coaching is not her regular __17.__; she works in a bank during the day. However, she has a passion for soccer. Coaching allows her to __18.__ this interest, even though she cannot play anymore. As a teen, she would __19.__ herself in the sport. Later, she injured her leg. However, she would not allow her injury to become an __20.__ that would keep her from something she cared about so much.

obstacle
immerse
occupation
sustain
supplement

Spelling and Writing

Proofread a Memo

Six words are not spelled correctly in this business memo. Write the words correctly.

M E M O

To: All employees

From: Francis

Subject: Business letters

Recently, two customers complained about letters from us that they considered ofensive. They felt that the letters were too informal. Although I do not want to implacate any one person or to surpress creativity, I feel I must offer a few guidelines for future correspondence. Business letters should create and sustane good relations with clients. The letters should never offend. They must be sucsinct and courteous, and they should incorperate business terms and concepts.

Proofreading Marks

☰	Make a capital.
/	Make a small letter.
∧	Add something.
ℒ	Take out something.
⊙	Add a period.
⌗	New paragraph
ⓢⓟ	Spelling error

Write a Memo

Expository Writing

Memos are messages used in business institutions for interoffice communication. Create a business situation, or write a memo to a teacher about a concern that you think needs attention.

- Decide to whom you will send the memo.
- Determine the problem and the desired outcome.
- Explain the situation briefly but completely.
- Follow the form used in the proofreading sample.

Use as many spelling words as you can.

Proofread Your Writing During

Writing Process

Prewriting
⇩
Drafting
⇩
Revising
⇩
Editing
⇩
Publishing

Proofread your writing for spelling errors as part of the editing stage in the writing process. Be sure to check each word carefully. Use a dictionary to check spelling if you are not sure.

Vocabulary

Strategy Words

Review Words: Latin Prefixes ob-, sub-, sur-, in-

Write a word from the box to complete each sentence.

inheritance	obtaining	obvious
submarine	subtotal	

1. A small _____ was sent to search the ocean floor.
2. This swamp is the _____ source of our mosquitoes.
3. First, you must _____ each column of numbers.
4. Although your parents might leave you money, your real _____ is your sense of humor and love of puns.
5. My sister is at the town hall, _____ a fishing license.

Preview Words: Latin Prefixes ob-, sub-, sur-, in-

Write the word from the box that matches each clue.

institutional	obsession	submerse
surfeit	surmount	

6. Better hold your breath when you do this!
7. Overfeeding your pet is one example.
8. A person with trunks full of baseball cards might be said to have this.
9. Do this to overcome an obstacle.
10. This might refer to a bank, a school, or a corporation.

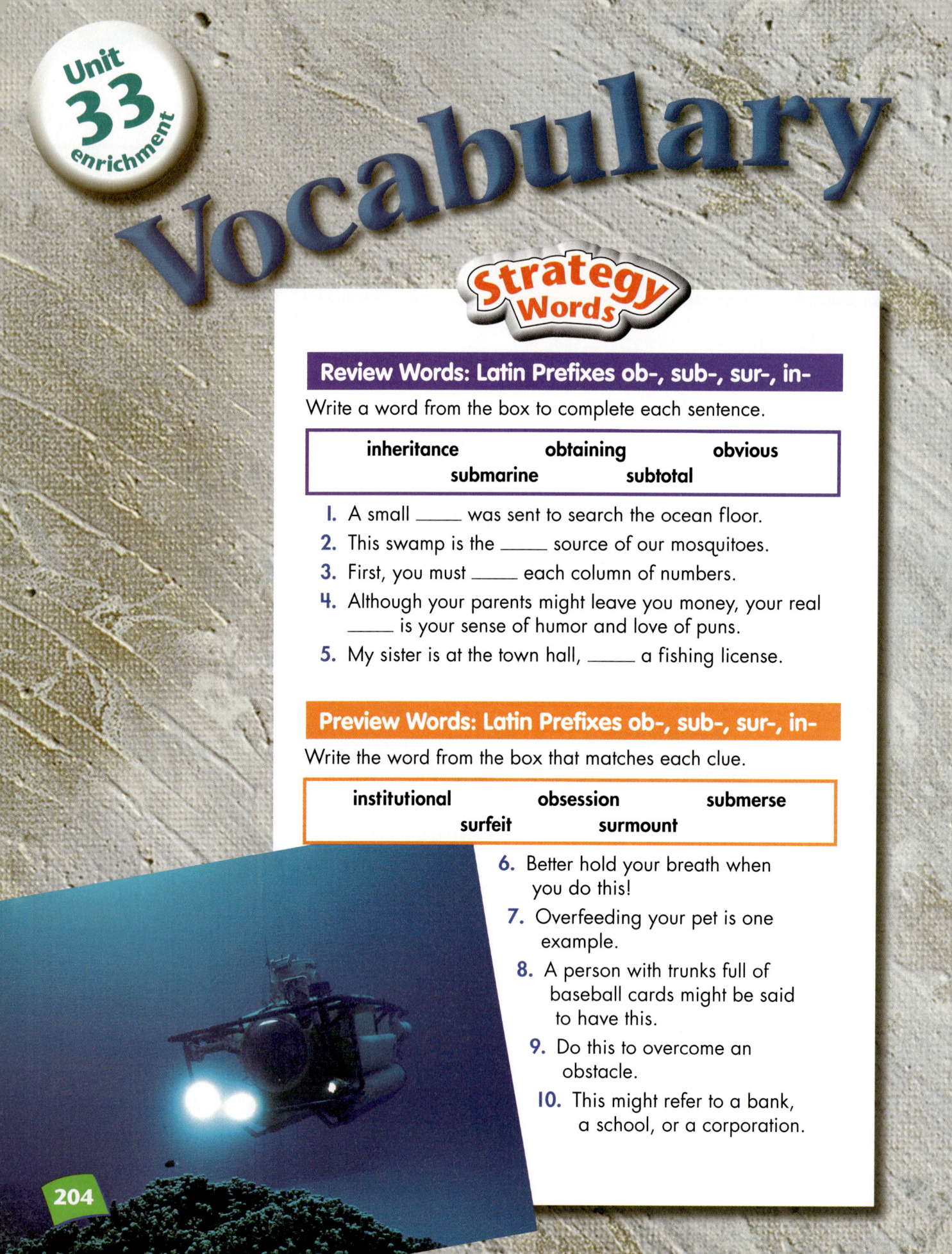

Connections

Content Words

Language Arts: Style

Write words from the box to complete the paragraph.

| discrepancy | fulfillment | incongruous | irony | sarcastic |

The novel was certainly not the ___1.___ of this reviewer's dreams. Although the author aimed at ___2.___, he succeeded only in making ___3.___ remarks that wounded without compassion or humor. Sadly, there was a vast ___4.___ between the author's intentions and the finished product. For example, the funny scene between the parents was ___5.___, since the people were supposed to be angry at each other.

Math: Reckoning

Write the word from the box that fits each meaning.

| calculus | factorial | finite | infinite | progression |

6. describing a sequence that does not have a last term
7. a method of mathematical analysis using special symbolic notations
8. the product of all positive integers from one to a given number
9. describing a sequence that has a last term
10. a series of numbers, each derived from the one preceding by adding a constant

Apply the Spelling Strategy

Circle the two content words you wrote that begin with the Latin prefix **in-**.

READ THE SPELLING WORDS

1.	televise	*televise*	The local station will **televise** the game.
2.	itemize	*itemize*	I will **itemize** a grocery list.
3.	authorize	*authorize*	Ms. Lin will **authorize** the field trip.
4.	alphabetize	*alphabetize*	Please **alphabetize** your bibliography.
5.	symbolize	*symbolize*	A rose might **symbolize** beauty.
6.	rationalize	*rationalize*	Gwen tries to **rationalize** her behavior.
7.	enterprise	*enterprise*	The Smiths' new **enterprise** is successful.
8.	visualize	*visualize*	Can you **visualize** a beach and palm trees?
9.	familiarize	*familiarize*	Sam will **familiarize** himself with the music.
10.	standardize	*standardize*	The designer will **standardize** the layout.
11.	penalize	*penalize*	Many companies **penalize** rule breakers.
12.	harmonize	*harmonize*	That couple can **harmonize** effectively.
13.	franchise	*franchise*	Dad wants to buy a chicken **franchise**.
14.	economize	*economize*	We will **economize** by shopping at sales.
15.	sympathize	*sympathize*	I **sympathize** with the refugees' plight.
16.	emphasize	*emphasize*	Did you **emphasize** the need for hard work?
17.	reorganize	*reorganize*	Kay will **reorganize** these cabinets.
18.	apologize	*apologize*	I must **apologize** for my dog's behavior.
19.	monopolize	*monopolize*	They try to **monopolize** the conversation.
20.	compromise	*compromise*	It took a while to reach a **compromise**.

SORT THE SPELLING WORDS

1.–4. Write the spelling words that end in **-ise**.

5.–20. Write the spelling words that end in **-ize**.

REMEMBER THE SPELLING STRATEGY

Remember that the endings **-ize** and **-ise** may be added to roots and words.

Word Meanings

Write a spelling word to match each definition.

1. a business organization; an undertaking
2. to acknowledge regretfully a fault or offense
3. to broadcast by television
4. to serve as a representation of
5. authorization granted by a manufacturing firm to sell its products or services
6. to settle by concessions
7. to punish or place at a disadvantage
8. to arrange according to the customary order of the letters of a language
9. to dominate by excluding others
10. to grant power or permission to

Word Groups

Write a spelling word to complete each group.

11. excuse, justify, defend, _____
12. picture, imagine, daydream, _____
13. scrimp, save, budget, _____
14. console, commiserate, comfort, empathize, _____
15. enumerate, list, inventory, _____

USING THE Dictionary

Write the spelling word for each dictionary respelling. Check your answer in the **Spelling Dictionary**.

16. /stăn′ dər dīz′/
17. /ĕm′ fə sīz′/
18. /här′ mə nīz′/
19. /rē ôr′ gə nīz′/
20. /fə mĭl′ yə rīz′/

Vocabulary

Strategy Words

Review Words: Endings -ize, -ise

Write a word from the box to complete each sentence.

civilize	criticize	fertilize
generalize		specialize

1. If you can _____ from a regrettable incident, you can learn from your mistake.
2. To _____ young children, you might teach them table manners.
3. Your tomatoes will be bigger if you _____ them.
4. My cousin is planning to _____ in pediatric medicine.
5. Give your speech, and then the class will _____ it.

Preview Words: Endings -ize, -ise

Write the word from the box that matches each clue.

hypothesize	neutralize	sensationalize
sensitize		tranquilize

6. A zookeeper might do this to an unruly animal.
7. The tabloid newspapers do this with the news.
8. Do this before you carry out an experiment.
9. Sometimes parents have to _____ their children to the feelings of others.
10. A chemist may do this to an acidic solution.

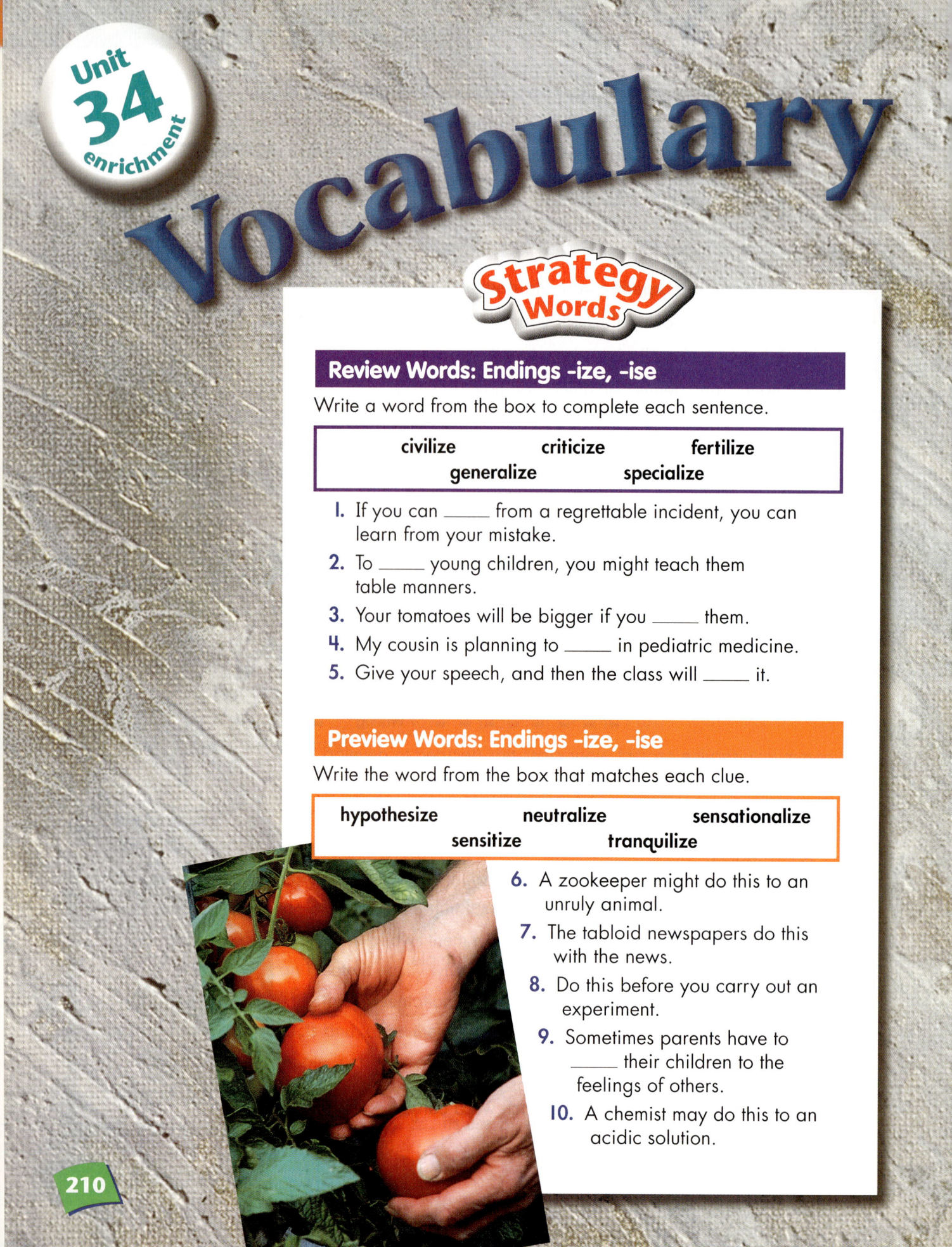

Connections

Language Arts: Word Choice

Write the word from the box that fits each meaning.

colloquial	concise	idiom
precise	jargon	

1. definite; exact
2. expressing much in few words
3. relating to conversation
4. the specialized or technical language of a group
5. an expression with a meaning beyond the meaning of the words themselves

Science: Scientific Investigation

Write a word from the box to complete each sentence.

analyze	category	classification
resemble	systematic	

6. In biology, the classification of living things is done by _____ .
7. A genetic researcher would be interested in the ways in which children _____ their parents.
8. An orderly or _____ method is key in scientific investigation.
9. Geologists _____ the structure of rock crystals.
10. The _____ of plant species is important in botany.

Apply the Spelling Strategy

Circle the two content words you wrote that have the **-ise** ending pronounced differently from the **-ise** in the spelling words **televise, enterprise, franchise,** and **compromise**.

Spelling and Thinking

READ THE SPELLING WORDS

1.	agenda	*agenda*	Today's meeting has a full **agenda**.
2.	administer	*administer*	The teacher will **administer** the test.
3.	itinerary	*itinerary*	Our **itinerary** will take us to Canada.
4.	technician	*technician*	The computer **technician** made repairs.
5.	revenue	*revenue*	The state must increase its **revenue**.
6.	invoice	*invoice*	Please send me an **invoice** for the work.
7.	corporation	*corporation*	The **corporation** has offices worldwide.
8.	industrial	*industrial*	He works in a busy **industrial** area.
9.	patent	*patent*	A **patent** will protect her rights.
10.	advertisement	*advertisement*	The radio **advertisement** airs frequently.
11.	construction	*construction*	When will the **construction** begin?
12.	executive	*executive*	A principal has an **executive** position.
13.	investment	*investment*	Buying the land was a good **investment**.
14.	merchandise	*merchandise*	A shipment of **merchandise** arrived.
15.	consumer	*consumer*	A wise **consumer** thinks before buying.
16.	promote	*promote*	Stores will **promote** their new fall line.
17.	endeavor	*endeavor*	Baby-sitting is a new **endeavor** for her.
18.	employer	*employer*	His **employer** gave him the day off.
19.	income	*income*	Expenses should not exceed **income**.
20.	negotiate	*negotiate*	The countries will **negotiate** for peace.

SORT THE SPELLING WORDS

1.–4. Write the words that can be a noun or a verb.

5. Write the word that can be a noun or an adjective.

6. Write the word that is an adjective only.

7.–17. Write the words that are nouns only.

18.–20. Write the words that are verbs only.

REMEMBER THE SPELLING STRATEGY

Remember that the English language includes many words that relate to commerce.

Spelling and Vocabulary

Word Meanings

Write the spelling word that matches each definition.

1. goods that may be bought or sold
2. an amount of money coming in for one's labor or service
3. to contribute to the growth or progress of
4. an expert in certain skills
5. a detailed list of goods shipped or services rendered
6. a person who carries out or manages the affairs of an organization

Word Structure

Add or subtract the suffix to write a spelling word. You may need to drop a letter, add a letter, or do both.

7. advertise + ment
8. construct + ion
9. administrate – ate
10. employ + er
11. invest + ment
12. industry + al
13. corporate + ion

USING THE Dictionary

Write a spelling word that matches each etymology. Use the **Spelling Dictionary** if you need help.

14. from Latin **consumere,** meaning "to take"
15. from Latin **itinerarium,** meaning "course of travel"
16. from Old French **devoir,** meaning "duty"
17. from Latin **negotium,** meaning "business"
18. from Latin **revenire,** meaning "to come back"
19. from Latin **agere,** meaning "to do"
20. from Latin **patere,** meaning "to be opened"

agenda	administer	itinerary	technician	merchandise
invoice	corporation	industrial	patent	advertisement
consumer	executive	investment	revenue	construction
promote	endeavor	employer	income	negotiate

Complete the Sentences   Write the spelling word that best completes each sentence.

1. She used to work for the president of a large _____.
2. The principal handed out the _____ for the meeting.
3. He is training to be a _____ in a dentist's office.
4. The government is discussing ways to increase the _____ it collects from toll roads.
5. This _____ carpeting is designed to withstand very heavy traffic.
6. The singer's agent will _____ a new contract for him.
7. Her _____ asked if she could return to the job the following summer.
8. Thomas Edison had a _____ for more than a thousand devices and processes.

Replace the Words   Write the spelling word that best replaces the underlined word or words in each sentence.

9. Leave your travel plan so that we can reach you if necessary.
10. The plumber gave her a detailed bill for the repair work.
11. The company is looking for someone with managerial experience.
12. The building of the new tunnel is an amazing engineering feat.
13. He was hired to supervise the credit department.

Complete the Paragraph   Write spelling words from the box to complete the paragraph.

Ever since the first __14.__ appeared in a newspaper in 1704, businesses have been using magazines, billboards, radio, television, and the Internet to __15.__ their __16.__. A company allocates a certain amount of its __17.__ to advertising. The goal of this __18.__, of course, is to influence the __19.__ to buy its products or services. A successful ad campaign is a wise __20.__ for any company.

promote
merchandise
consumer
advertisement
income
investment
endeavor

Spelling and Writing

Proofread a Classified Ad

Six words are not spelled correctly in this classified ad. Write the words correctly.

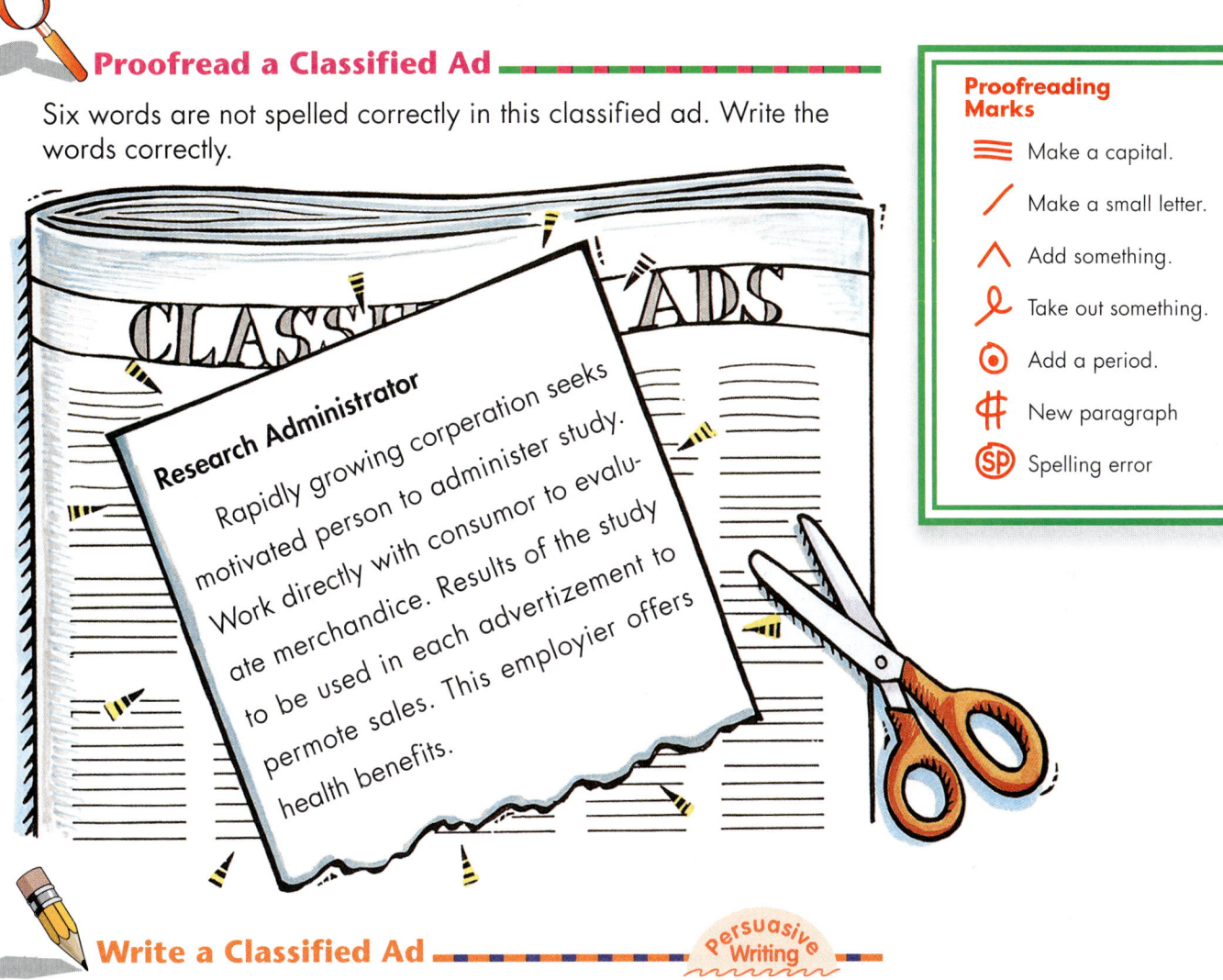

Research Administrator

Rapidly growing corperation seeks motivated person to administer study. Work directly with consumor to evaluate merchandice. Results of the study to be used in each advertizement to permote sales. This employier offers health benefits.

Write a Classified Ad _Persuasive Writing_

Many people turn to the classified ads in the newspaper or on the Internet to find a job. Write a classified ad for a job you would like to have.

- Give specific details about the employee's responsibilities.
- Keep in mind that people scan ads rather than read every word. Be brief and to the point.
- Follow the form used in the proofreading sample.

Use as many spelling words as you can.

Writing Process

Prewriting
⇩
Drafting
⇩
Revising
⇩
Editing
⇩
Publishing

Proofread Your Writing During ➤ Editing

Proofread your writing for spelling errors as part of the editing stage in the writing process. Be sure to check each word carefully. Use a dictionary to check spelling if you are not sure.

215

Vocabulary

Review Words: Words From Commerce

Write a word from the box to complete each sentence.

agent	applicant	assistant
engineer		merchant

1. The insurance _____ assessed the storm damage.
2. A local _____ is holding a sidewalk sale.
3. The building contractor consulted an _____ about the crack in the foundation of the house.
4. I am an _____ for the counselor opening at Camp Happykids.
5. The kindergarten teacher has an _____ to help with the large class.

Preview Words: Words From Commerce

Write words from the box to complete the paragraph.

electronics	mechanizing	millionaire
technological		tycoon

I have an idea for an __6.__ specialist. With all of the __7.__ advances today, someone should be working on __8.__ the task of room cleaning. Anyone who invents such a machine is sure to make enough money to become a __9.__ . I would personally thank this business __10.__ for making my life easier.

Catastrophe Claims

Connections

Content Words

Science: Astronomy

Write words from the box to complete the paragraph.

astronomer	**celestial**	**terrestrial**
planetarium	**satellite**	

We saw the planets, stars, and other __1.__ bodies in the __2.__ at the science museum. Then the __3.__ said, "Now, if you __4.__ beings will follow me outside, I will point out some constellations. Perhaps we will even see a __5.__ cross the night sky."

Math: Trigonometry

Write a word from the box that matches each definition.

cosine	**function**	**sine**
tangent	**trigonometry**	

6. the science of triangles
7. a set of ordered pairs that for each value of **x** there is only one value of **y**
8. the ratio of the adjacent side to the hypotenuse in a right triangle
9. the ratio of the opposite side to the adjacent side in a right triangle
10. the ratio of the opposite side to the hypotenuse in a right triangle

Apply the Spelling Strategy

Circle the content word you wrote that names someone's job title.

Assessment and Review

Assessment   Units 31–35

Each Assessment Word in the box fits one of the spelling strategies you have studied over the past five weeks. Read the spelling strategies. Then write each Assessment Word under the unit number it fits.

Unit 31

1.–5. Remember that knowing Latin roots like **spir, viv/vit, vid,** and **vis** can give clues to the meaning and spelling of certain words.

Unit 32

Remember that it is important to know the spellings of words that are frequently misspelled.

Unit 33

6.–13. Remember that the prefixes **ob-, sub-, sur-,** and **in-** may be assimilated into the spelling of the base word or word root.

Unit 34

14.–20. Remember that the endings **-ize** and **-ise** may be added to roots and words.

Unit 35

Remember that the English language includes many words that relate to commerce.

oblong
imprison
visitation
formalize
moisturize
surreal
impeach
subside
visor
popularize
obstruct
vivacity
obliterate
surround
personalize
expire
materialize
idolize
evidently
crystallize

Review   **Unit 31: Latin Roots spir, viv/vit, vid, vis**

revision	survive	inspiration	spirit	aspiration
perspiration	vivid	supervisor	vital	expiration

Write the spelling word that fits the definition.

1. absolutely necessary
2. to endure, live on
3. a desire for achievement
4. the animating force of living things; the dominant mood
5. moisture given off by the skin
6. coming to the end
7. a person in charge
8. a stimulation of the mind or emotions
9. bright and distinct; brilliant
10. an updated version

Review   **Unit 32: Frequently Misspelled Words**

familiar	liaison	committee	procedure	lightning
numerous	irrelevant	forehead	minimum	aluminum

Find the misspelled words. Write each word correctly.

11. The principal served as the liason between teachers and parents.
12. Wrap the meat and vegetables in aluminium foil.
13. Florida has more lightening than any other state.
14. There is a minnimum charge of ten dollars for all television repairs.
15. Snow is not a familar sight in southern Texas.
16. All requests for tickets must follow a certain proceedure.
17. We've made numerus attempts to locate the missing heirs.
18. The commitee members couldn't agree on anything.
19. The fact that some viewers liked the movie is irrevelant to our review.
20. The doctor felt the forhead of the sick child.

| supplement | incorporate | occupy | succinct | surface |
| occupation | incentive | offensive | surplus | obstacle |

Write a spelling word for each clue.

1. You must go around this to get where you're going.
2. It's the top layer.
3. It could be the opposite of **defensive** or a synonym for **rude**.
4. This is how one earns a paycheck.
5. It's one way to form a business.
6. A good speech is usually this.
7. Having this will make you want to work harder.
8. The base word is the opposite of **minus**.
9. It's the verb form of **occupant**.
10. Replace the prefix in **implement** to make this word.

| compromise | authorize | symbolize | enterprise | visualize |
| standardize | franchise | emphasize | apologize | televise |

Write the spelling word that has the same meaning as the underlined phrase.

11. Providing Internet services can be a promising <u>business venture</u>.
12. They bought a <u>right to own and operate</u> for a well-known fast-food restaurant.
13. The president can <u>give permission for</u> emergency spending.
14. The local station is going to <u>broadcast on television</u> our band concert.
15. We had to <u>each give up something</u> to reach an agreement.
16. Our school decided to <u>put special importance on</u> math this year.
17. What does the Statue of Liberty <u>stand for</u>?
18. I want to be the first to <u>say I am sorry</u>.
19. Can you <u>form a mental picture of</u> the redecorated room?
20. The café needs to <u>define a certain standard for</u> the size of each serving.

 **Unit 35: Words From Commerce**

corporation	industrial	advertisement	consumer	promote
construction	endeavor	merchandise	employer	income

Change a prefix, a suffix, or both to write a spelling word.

1. employment
2. destructible
3. consumed
4. advertised
5. industrious

Write a spelling word to complete each analogy.

6. **Achieve** is to **accomplish** as **attempt** is to _____.
7. **Meditate** is to **meditation** as **corporate** is to _____.
8. **Working** is to **work** as **merchandising** is to _____.
9. **Demotion** is to **demote** as **promotion** is to _____.
10. **Work** is to **employment** as **salary** is to _____.

Spelling Study Strategy

Sorting by Prefixes and Suffixes

One good way to practice spelling is to place words into groups according to some spelling pattern. Here is a way to practice some of the words you studied during the past few weeks.

1. Make two columns on a large piece of paper or on the chalkboard.

2. At the top of one column, write **Prefixes: ob-, sub-, sur-, in-, im-, cor-, con-, ad-, pro-**. At the top of the other column, write **Suffixes: -ise, -ize, -sion, -tion, -ation, -ive**. (You can make the sorting activity more precise by making separate columns for *each* prefix and suffix and including additional prefixes or suffixes that have been studied this year.)

3. Have a partner choose a spelling word from Units 31, 33, or 35 and say it aloud. You may wish to include appropriate words from other units as well.

4. Take turns saying the spelling word and writing it under the prefix or suffix column.

WRITER'S

Identifying Modifiers: Adjectives and Adverbs

Adjectives are words that modify, or describe, nouns or pronouns. An adjective tells *how many, what kind,* or *which one.*

<u>Those</u>   <u>three</u>   <u>red</u>   <u>wagons</u> are sold.
(which one)   (how many)   (what kind)

Adverbs modify verbs, adjectives, or other adverbs. An adverb tells *how, when, where,* or *to what extent.*

The blue bike <u>sold</u>   <u>quickly</u>   <u>yesterday.</u>
                          (to what extent)   (when)

Practice Activity

A. Write **adjective** or **adverb** to identify each underlined word.

1. Please move <u>forward</u>.
2. My room is <u>nearly</u> cleaned.
3. The apples look <u>ripe</u>.
4. *Black Beauty* is a very <u>good</u> book.
5. Be ready in <u>fifteen</u> minutes!
6. The lioness roared <u>loudly</u>.
7. The bath water feels <u>warm</u>.

B. Write the word that is modified by each underlined **adjective** or **adverb**.

8. I performed <u>poorly</u> in yesterday's game.
9. The bear growled <u>gruffly</u> and charged.
10. Have you seen my <u>blue</u> jacket?
11. The clouds overhead looked <u>dark</u> and threatening.
12. That box of books should <u>soon</u> arrive.
13. I don't feel very <u>well</u> today.
14. This restaurant is known for its <u>delicious</u> food.
15. Coins are <u>often</u> tossed into a fountain for luck.

WORKSHOP

Read it Backwards!

Good writers always proofread their writing for spelling errors. Here's a strategy that you can use to proofread your papers.

Usually, you read a paper from the first word to the last. This time, try reading it backwards. In other words, read it from the last word to the first. You would read the sentence **They desperately wanted freedom.** like this:

freedom. wanted desperately They

It sounds like a funny way to proofread, but reading backwards helps you think about the spelling of each word instead of the meaning of the sentence. Try it!

Electronic Spelling

Computer Graphics

Using a computer, you are able to make many types of diagrams, graphs, and charts to accompany your reports and essays. You can also cut and paste photographs and drawings from other files into your own work and even create your own original illustrations and artwork.

Remember that most diagrams, graphs, charts, and illustrations are accompanied by text, such as labels and captions. When you are creating a graphic, it is important to check the spelling of these words. The effect of even the most complex and impressive diagram or chart can be ruined by misspelled labels.

Find the misspelled word in each of the diagram titles or labels below and write it correctly. Write **OK** if all words are correct.

1. Prewriting, Writing, Revizion
2. States With the Most Lightening Strikes
3. Percentage of Students Bying Lunch
4. A Comparison of Occuepation to Income
5. Tipes of Homes
6. Expiration Dates of Fruits and Vegetables

Challenge Activities

extent	excessive	sinister	sporadic
vicinity	semester	erratic	tacit

A. Write the challenge word that fits each "What Am I?" statement.

1. Sometimes I work quickly and well, and at other times I do not. I am definitely not dependable!

2. Now you see me, now you don't! I appear here and there or now and then in scattered instances.

3. I promise trouble and suggest an evil motive.

4. I go beyond what is reasonable or necessary. I am quite extreme!

5. I am not spoken or written, but I am implied.

6. I am a nearby or surrounding place.

7. I am the scope or range of something.

8. I am one of two terms that make up a school year.

B. Write a challenge word that belongs in each row.

1. harmful, evil, corrupt

2. understood, silent, unexpressed

3. outrageous, extreme, extravagant

4. measure, range, limit

5. neighborhood, area, locality

6. occasional, incidental, unpredictable

7. undependable, wandering, inconsistent

8. time period, quarter, school year

C. For each challenge word that is an adjective, write a noun that it could describe. For example, "a **sinister** look" or "a **tacit** agreement." Choose one of your word pairs to incorporate in an interesting topic sentence for a composition. Then complete your composition.

Challenge Activities

enable	feisty	diploma	recreation
hasten	trivia	riotous	lenient

A. Write the challenge word that completes each analogy.

1. **Harsh** is to **mild** as **strict** is to _____.
2. **Peaceful** is to **calm** as **turbulent** is to _____.
3. **Trifles** are to _____ as **basics** are to **essentials**.
4. **Graduation** is to _____ as **treaty** is to **document**.
5. **Delay** is to **dawdle** as _____ is to **hurry**.
6. **Unenergetic** is to **sluggish** as **frisky** is to _____.
7. **Game** is to _____ as **coin collecting** is to **hobby**.
8. **Empower** is to **power** as _____ is to **ability**.

Diploma

B. Write the challenge word that completes each sentence.

1. These puppies are playful and _____.
2. We must _____ to the store before it closes.
3. Modern cars _____ people to travel great distances easily.
4. These facts deal with _____, or nonessential matters.
5. The crowd turned into a mob and became _____.
6. What sport do you play or watch for _____?
7. My mother framed her _____ when she graduated from college.
8. A _____ judge does not deal with criminals harshly.

C. Write eight trivia questions about your school or about your favorite sport or hobby. Use a synonym, or a synonymous phrase, for a challenge word in each question. Then exchange papers with a partner and substitute a challenge word for each synonym.

Challenge Activities

skein	conceive	grievous	unbelievable
sienna	inconceivable	inefficient	resilience

A. Write the challenge word that answers each question.

   1. What color is a yellowish brown or a reddish brown?

   2. How would you describe a machine that wastes time and energy?

   3. What quality does rubber have that helps it spring back?

   4. What is a small, coiled bundle of yarn called?

   5. How would you describe something that causes great pain or suffering?

   6. What word means *imagine* or *think up*?

   7.–8. Which two challenge words mean the same as **incredible**?

B. Write the challenge word that would be found on a dictionary page with each pair of guide words.

   1. senile | sierra

   2. sierra | skin

   3. conceit | concentrate

   4. inconclusive | inelastic

   5. incomplete | inefficiency

   6. grief | income

   7. resign | siege

   8. unable | unequal

C. Imagine a machine that can do anything and everything. What are some things it can do? What does it look like? Describe your fantastic machine. Use some of the challenge words in your description.

Challenge Activities

| cross-reference | well-defined | masterpiece | postmaster general |
| self-assured | all-purpose | mastermind | president-elect |

A. Word elements are mismatched in the challenge words below. Write the challenge words correctly.

1. all-piece
2. postmaster elect
3. self-defined
4. cross-piece

5. well-assured
6. masterpurpose
7. masterreference
8. president-general

B. Write a challenge word to replace the underlined words that match it in meaning.

1. The rules of the game are accurately described.
2. Are you sure of yourself?
3. This piece of art done by a great artist is priceless.
4. The main person who planned the scheme of the operation is never revealed.
5. The unlimited-use brush is selling well.
6. The statement referring the reader from one part of the book to another reads, "See TEETH for diagram."
7. Who is the person at the head of our postal system?
8. The recently chosen highest executive officer of that country will be sworn in later this month.

C. Suppose that you have just been elected President of the United States. What qualities would you look for in choosing a person to fill each post in your cabinet? Write your answers using some of the challenge words.

227

Challenge Activities

| Renaissance | surrealism | allegro | cantata |
| Impressionism | portraiture | fortissimo | a cappella |

A. Answer each question about music with a challenge word.

1. How would you sing if you had no instrumental backup?

2. What word on a music sheet would indicate a quick, lively tempo in a piece of music?

3. What word on a music sheet would indicate that the music should be played loudly?

4. What is one kind of musical composition that tells a story that is sung by a chorus?

B. Answer each question about art with a challenge word.

1. What style of European art and architecture is representative of Europe during the 1300s, 1400s, and 1500s?

2. Which modern art movement is characterized by unusual arrangements and distortions of images?

3. Which style of painting gives the effect of light striking and reflecting from a surface?

4. What word refers to a picture of a person, especially a person's face?

C. Write the challenge word or words that . . .

1.–2. begin with a capital letter.

3. is made from the base word **real**.

4. is made from the base word **portrait**.

5.–8. come from the Italian language.

D. Suppose that both an art show and a concert were to be held at your school. Write a program guide describing either one of the events. Include a list of imaginary musical performers or artists and their works. Use the challenge words in your program guide.

Challenge Activities

| affirmative | allergic | appreciative | incessant |
| accentuate | appraisal | illustrious | succulent |

A. Write a challenge word to answer each question.

   1. What kind of person might you read about in the newspaper?

   2. How might a person describe a juicy tomato or a pear?

   3. What kind of noise or chatter might give you a headache?

   4. How might the person for whom you did a great favor feel toward you?

   5. What kind of reaction is hay fever?

   6. What kind of vote would you make if you were in favor of something?

   7. What would you need to get if you wanted to know how much your house was worth?

   8. What would you do regarding your skills at a job interview?

B. Look at each base word in parentheses. Write a challenge word that is the part of speech shown next to the base word to complete each sentence.

   1. Are you (**allergy,** *adj.*) to tomatoes?

   2. The bank's (**appraise,** *n.*) set the value of the jewel at over one thousand dollars.

   3. The (**appreciate,** *adj.*) crowd stood up and applauded.

   4. Is your answer to my question negative or (**affirm,** *adj.*)?

   5. Her long eyelashes (**accent,** *v.*) her blue eyes.

C. Write the challenge word that fits in each group.

   1. accomplished, famous, distinguished

   2. moist, juicy, delicious

   3. unceasing, nonstop, continuous

D. Write two tongue twisters. In the first, use words beginning with the letter **a** and include two challenge words. For example, your tongue twister could make a statement about an **appraisal** of your school or of your talents. In the second, use words beginning with the letter **i** and include two challenge words. You could write a statement about an **illustrious** person you know about.

Challenge Activities

circumlocution	transient	transcribe	perpetrate
circumspect	transcend	translucent	persuasion

A. Write the challenge word that fits each definition.

1. a wordy or roundabout expression
2. to go outside the range of
3. a winning-over; a convincing
4. letting light through in such a way that the images are blurred
5. watchful; cautious
6. fleeting; not lasting
7. to do or commit something bad or foolish
8. to copy in writing or typewriting

B. Write the challenge word that would complete each sentence.

1. The guard was always _____ near the prisoners.
2. The "wife of my father's brother" is a _____ for "my aunt."
3. The top salesman had great powers of _____.
4. Beauty and wealth are sometimes _____.
5. The detective knew who could _____ the crime.
6. The benefits of that medicine _____ words.
7. Please _____ my shorthand notes.
8. Waxed paper is not transparent, but it is _____.

C. Think of eight different people each of the challenge words fits in some way. For example, a prankster would **perpetrate** a practical joke, or a secretary would **transcribe** notes. Then write a sentence for each challenge word.

Challenge Activities

oases	antennae	diagnosis	appendices
errata	antennas	diagnoses	hypotheses

A. Write the challenge word that is the plural form of each singular noun below.

1. appendix
2. oasis
3. hypothesis

4. diagnosis
5.–6. antenna
7. erratum

B. Write the challenge word that best completes each analogy.

1. _____ are to **deserts** as **waterholes** are to **wastelands**.
2. _____ are to **books** as **postscripts** are to **letters**.
3. **Symptom** is to _____ as **fact** is to **conclusion**.
4. _____ are to **editors** as **corrections** are to **teachers**.
5. _____ are to **scientists** as **theories** are to **professors**.
6. _____ are to **TV sets** as **cables** are to **telegraph machines**.
7. **Nerves** are to **people** as _____ are to **insects**.

C. Write the two challenge words that are the singular and plural forms of the same word. Circle the letters that differ in each word.

D. We all make mistakes, but many of them are unnecessary. How could you prevent certain mistakes or correct them? Write a short report explaining what you would fix and how you would fix it. Use some of the challenge words in your report.

eventual	generosity	formality	hospitality
eventuality	generality	informality	eligibility

A. Write the adjective that fits each definition below. Add the noun-forming suffix **-ity** to make the related challenge word. Write the challenge word.

1. willing to share with
2. without ceremony
3. fit to be chosen
4. not specific
5. according to set customs or rules

B. Write a challenge word to answer each question.

1. What could someone thank you for if you held a reception in his or her honor?
2. What might the judges of a contest consider if they wanted to know whether you were properly qualified?
3. What might someone accuse you of making if you gave a vague or indefinite statement?
4. What could someone compliment you on if you showed unselfish behavior?
5. What might you be prepared for if you knew a certain occurrence was a possibility?
6. What is a synonym for **inevitable**?
7.–8. Which words are antonyms of each other?

C. Write the challenge word that . . .

1. is a synonym for **cordiality**.
2.–3. is based on the word **event**.

D. Write a thank-you note to the parents of your friend for an imaginary weekend stay at their home. Use as many challenge words as you can in your note.

Challenge Activities

subsidiary	monetary	exemplary	parliamentary
revolutionary	savory	unsavory	exploratory

A. Use the clues in each statement below to identify the challenge word that describes the person or thing. Write the challenge word.

1. I am a most agreeable roasted turkey.
I am especially pleasing in taste and smell.

2. I am worth imitating, so follow my example.

3. My procedure is according to the rules and customs of a high lawmaking body.

4. I'm coins and currency valued in terms of the money of a country.

5. I have my own company, but it's controlled by another company.

6. People find me unpleasant in taste and smell.

7. I am an invention that brought about great changes.

8. I am a kind of surgery that examines a part of the body.

B. Write a challenge word that is an antonym for each word below.

1. imperfect

2. unappetizing

3. pleasant

4. uninquiring

C. Write a challenge word that is a synonym for each word below.

1. sweeping; radical

2. branch

3. financial

4. according to parliament

D. Use challenge words to write detailed descriptions of two or more of the items below. Try to paint a vivid word picture of each item. Write complete sentences.

1. a baked apple

2. an expensive toy

3. a search or an examination

4. an idea with far-reaching effects

Challenge Activities

| tranquil | dispel | repel | deter |
| tranquillity | dispelled | repellent | deterred |

A. Write the challenge word that fits each definition.

1. **a.** to make disappear as if by scattering
   b. driven away

2. **a.** to drive away or ward off
   b. something that wards off

3. **a.** calm; quiet
   b. peacefulness

4. **a.** to discourage or hinder
   b. kept back

B. Write the challenge word that best completes each sentence. Next to each word you write, write the letter **a** or **b** to match the meaning given in Activity A.

1. I love the calmness, or _____, of this mountain cabin.

2. The telephone call from a friend helped to _____ his loneliness.

3. The electronic gate _____ any trespassers.

4. Will the dog's barking_____ you from petting it?

5. This disgusting odor would _____ even skunks.

6. The early hours of the morning are quiet and _____.

7. The friendly and informative dentist _____ my fear.

8. This jacket has been sprayed with a water _____.

C. Picture a real or imaginary place where things are calm and beautiful. Then picture a place where just the opposite conditions exist. What words would you use to describe each place? Write a comparison of the two places. Use some of the challenge words.

Challenge Activities

beneficent	equatorial	equivalency	malcontent
equalize	equinox	equivocate	maladroit

A. Write a challenge word that is more exact than the underlined words in each sentence.

1. At first, the young dancer made <u>awkward and clumsy</u> movements.

2. Candidates who want to please both parties <u>speak in a way that can be interpreted in two ways</u>.

3. I recently read about <u>the time of year when the day and night are about equal in length</u>.

4. This person is <u>rebellious and not satisfied with the rules of the house</u>.

5. This person is <u>kind and does good deeds</u>.

6. The weather was so hot and humid that it was <u>like conditions at or near the equator</u>.

7. The scientist tried to <u>make even or uniform</u> the pressures inside and outside the tank.

8. A balance will determine whether two objects have <u>the condition of being equal</u> in weight.

B. Write the challenge word that best describes each person or place.

1. a benefactor or a do-gooder
2. a bungler or an oaf
3. a rebel or a faultfinder

C. Write the challenge word that means "to avoid making an explicit statement."

D. Write the five challenge words that are based on the Latin root *aequus* meaning "equal."

E. Write a short science fiction story in which a person rebels and wants to change the weather and the length of days and nights on Earth. Use as many challenge words in your story as you can.

235

Challenge Activities

aristocracy   megalopolis   demagogue   archenemy
anarchist   archaic   archives   archetype

A. Who would you be if you possessed each set of characteristics below? Write the challenge word that is the answer.

1. has leadership qualities but appeals to people's emotions and prejudices to win them over

2. rejects all forms of organization or authority

3. shows hostility toward others or toward a chief opponent

4. is the original model after which others will be patterned

5. is old-fashioned and not modern

B. Where would you be if you were in a place that possessed each set of characteristics below? Write the challenge word that is the answer.

1. is enormous and contains several large cities

2. has wealth, status, and often titles

3. is organized and is full of documents or records

C. Write the challenge word that contains **arch** and best completes each sentence.

1. The laws were so outdated that they were _____.

2. The _____ wants to destroy governments and laws.

3. We'll find the historical documents stored in the _____.

4. In cartoons, the cat is the _____ of the mouse.

5. The Model T Ford was the _____ of other cars.

D. Write the challenge word that comes from the Greek roots *dēmos,* meaning "common people" and *agōgos,* meaning "leading."

E. Create a political comic strip about leadership. For example, you may want to show two characters—a demagogue and an anarchist—as archenemies. Each panel should show and tell a story. Write speech balloons using some of the challenge words.

Challenge Activities

jubilant	exuberant	extravagance	prevalent
prudent	eloquence	negligence	effervescence

A. Write the challenge words that complete this story.

The case against the negligent shopkeeper finally went to court. Sam, who fell on a banana peel outside Mike's Vegetable Store, was suing Mike for __1.__ . Sam claimed that Mike should have swept the sidewalk in front of his store. Mike's lawyer argued that litter—even a banana peel—is __2.__ in busy shopping areas. Sam's lawyer argued his case with grace and force, or __3.__ . She also had a certain __4.__ , or liveliness. She was even __5.__ enough to supply photographs of the scene of the accident.

The judge and jury listened quietly throughout the trial. Then the jury found Mike guilty as charged. Sam and his lawyer were __6.__ and __7.__ . Sam thought that the money he spent for legal fees was not an __8.__ after all.

B. Write the challenge word for each definition below.

1. high spirits; liveliness; animation

2. a failure to act with care or concern

3. careless or excessive spending

4. speech that is persuasive and expressive

5. shrewd in management; sensible

6. widespread; commonly occurring

C. Write the two challenge words that have a similar meaning.

D. Write about a real or imaginary dispute or court case. Tell both sides of the argument. Give the outcome and describe how each person felt about it. Use challenge words in your description.

237

Challenge Activities

caucus	finesse	joie de vivre	mediocre
desperado	ingenious	mammoth	origami

A. Write the challenge word that fits each set of clues.

1. paper, art, flowers, folding
2. so-so, not bad, average, not great
3. bandit, Old West, dangerous, desperate
4. tact, delicacy, restraint, subtlety
5. huge, elephant, extinct, tusks
6. meeting, closed, politics, plan
7. attitude, life, joy, pleasure
8. creative, clever, talented, skilled

B. Write the challenge word that answers each question.

1. Who might have challenged the sheriff in the Old West?
2. What might you attend along with other members of a political party to choose a candidate?
3. What art form would you be practicing if you folded paper to make birds or flowers?
4. What expression might apply to a person who has a keen enjoyment of life?
5. What quality might a diplomat or an ambassador need to handle a delicate situation skillfully?
6. How might you describe an inventor?
7. How might you describe a performance that is neither good nor bad?
8. What word can mean "an extinct elephant" or "gigantic"?

C. Pretend that you are judging an art contest. The contestants have created different kinds of artwork. Some of the works of art are very creative, and some are average. Describe the winning entry and explain why you chose it above all the other entries. Use some challenge words in your answer.

uncivilized	irregularity	regimen	urbanite
documentation	regalia	publicly	suburbia

A. What is missing in each situation below? Write the appropriate challenge word.

1. "Where did you get these quotations and names in your report?" the teacher asked the student. The student needs to provide _____.

2. "You forgot to sew special symbols onto my dress uniform," the emperor said to the tailor. The emperor wants additional _____.

3. "You forgot to put me on a course of treatment," said the patient to the doctor. The patient wants a _____.

4. "You forgot to announce the players over the loudspeaker," said the coach to the sportscaster. The sportscaster needs to announce their names _____.

5. "You forgot to mention in our ad that the sale item has an imperfection," said the salesclerk to the newspaper editor. The editor needs to include that the sale item has an _____.

B. Write a challenge word that is an antonym for each word.

1. suburbanite
2. privately
3. steadiness
4. refined

C. Write a challenge word that is a synonym for each word.

1. method
2. emblems
3. sources; evidence
4. outskirts; environs

D. Write the three challenge words whose meanings relate to how and where people live.

E. Pretend that you are a real estate broker in suburbia. What would you say to convince an urbanite to move to the suburbs? Try to be persuasive. Write your sales pitch using some of the challenge words.

239

Unit 20

Challenge Activities

| antecedent | proposition | dependable | appendicitis |
| supposition | impending | expenditure | expendable |

A. Write the challenge word that matches each statement.

1. I am used up or sacrificed if there is something to be gained by it.
2. I am a noun or noun phrase to which a pronoun refers.
3. I am trustworthy.
4. I am likely to happen soon.
5. I am money spent.
6. I might require that a person have the appendix removed.
7. I am offered for consideration.
8. I am guesswork, if you ask my opinion.

B. Write the challenge word that best completes each sentence.

1. **Cat** is the _____ of **that** in "The cat that is climbing the tree is gray."
2. The weather forecasters warned of an _____ storm.
3. The _____ to extend the school year is before the city council.
4. As we grew older and no longer played with our toys, we decided that the toys were _____.

C. Write the challenge word that best completes each analogy.

1. **Tonsillitis** is to **tonsil** as _____ is to **appendix**.
2. **Cost** is to **payment** as **expense** is to _____.
3. **Theory** is to **hypothesis** as **assumption** is to _____.
4. **Wasteful** is to **preserving** as **unreliable** is to _____.

D. Write a persuasive ad for a major household appliance. Describe what might happen if someone bought a different brand. Use some of the challenge words in your ad.

Challenge Activities

vocational	relocation	productivity	deduction
revocable	dislocated	conducive	inducement

A. Write the challenge word or words formed from each base word below. Underline the prefixes and/or suffixes in each challenge word you write.

1. deduct
2.–3. locate
4. vocation
5. revoke

6. productive
7. induce
8. conduct

B. Go **duc/duct** hunting! Find the challenge words you wrote in Activity A that contain the root **duc** or **duct**. Circle this root in these words.

C. Write the challenge word that relates to the clues in each group.

1. moving van, new home, new address
2. occupation, trade, business
3. raise, bonus, trophy
4. shoulder, bone, socket
5. subtraction, inference, conclusion
6. results, harvests, dividends
7. license, law, promise
8. causing, contributing to

D. Think about how workers in a car factory could be encouraged to work more efficiently. What would make these people feel happy or proud about their work? Write your comments and suggestions using some of the challenge words.

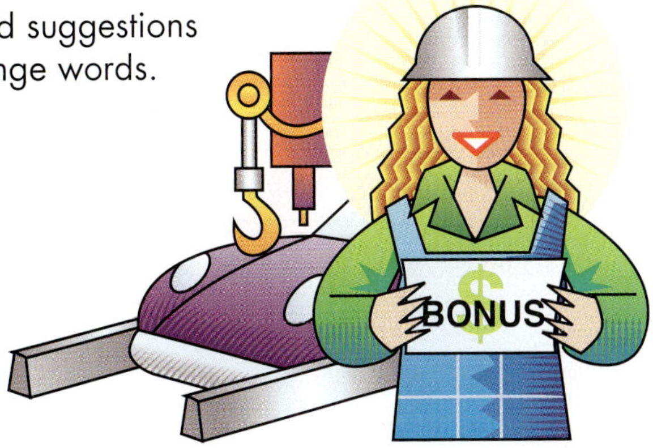

BONUS

Challenge Activities

impact	portfolio	jurisdiction	conjecture
actualize	edict	contradictory	subjective

A. Write the challenge word that matches each set of definitions. Write *n.*, *v.*, or *adj.* to indicate the part of speech for each meaning.

1. **a.** a conclusion reached by guessing
   b. to guess
2. **a.** a collision
   b. a forceful or dramatic effect
3. **a.** authority or power
   b. a thing or place over which authority extends
4. **a.** a briefcase
   b. a list of investments owned
5. **a.** existing in the mind
   b. personal
6. **a.** to realize in action
   b. to describe or portray realistically

B. Complete these sentences using the two challenge words not identified in Activity A.

This public order, or __1.__, is __2.__ to the decree that the king sent out last week about spending more and being a better consumer. Now he wants everyone to be frugal and economical.

C. Write the challenge words in alphabetical order.

D. Pick a real or imaginary trouble spot in the world. Then, as the newly appointed secretary of state, take an imaginary trip to that place. Introduce yourself to the head of that government. Tell him or her what your mission is. Write the speech you would give as the secretary of state. Use challenge words in your speech.

Challenge Activities

pliable	inevitable	gullible	indelible
affable	immeasurable	inaudible	discernible

A. Write the challenge word that best completes each sentence.

1. We couldn't listen to the couple's conversation because they were whispering. Their conversation was _____.

2. There was nothing Fran could do about the falling leaves. The change of seasons was _____.

3. Poor Julie! She always makes the mistake of believing people's fantastic stories. Julie is _____.

4. It was a bright, cloudless day. The mountains were _____ from miles away.

5. Julio didn't mind telling the principal his hopes and dreams. The principal was pleasant and _____.

6. There is no doubt that we could bend the strips of willow. The wood is _____.

7. We made sure that our signatures could not be erased or removed. We wrote our names in _____ ink.

8. The parents' love for their child is boundless. Their love is _____.

B. Write the challenge word that belongs with each pair of words.

1. approachable, sociable
2. distinguishable, perceivable
3. flexible, adaptable
4. inescapable, unavoidable
5. permanent, irrevocable
6. naive, inexperienced
7. indistinguishable, silent
8. bountiful, boundless

C. Pretend you have just discovered an island. Write several journal entries of what and whom you saw during the first few days. What impressions did the people and the natural surroundings have on you? Use some challenge words in your journal entries.

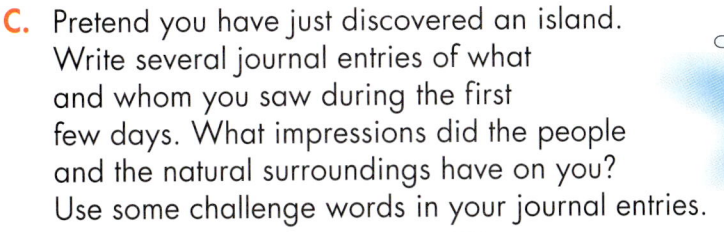

Challenge Activities

credible	disburse	discreet	emerge
creditable	disperse	discrete	immerge

A. Write the challenge word that fits each definition.

1. **a.** to scatter   **b.** to pay out
2. **a.** separate   **b.** careful
3. **a.** to come into view   **b.** to plunge
4. **a.** believable   **b.** honorable

B. Write the challenge word in parentheses that correctly answers each question.

1. **a.** How might you describe a person who shows good judgment? **(discreet, discrete)**
   b. Which word describes units that are distinct from one another? **(discreet, discrete)**
2. **a.** Which word describes an action that applies to leaves blowing in the wind? **(disburse, disperse)**
   b. Which word describes an action that a treasurer or a bank teller might do? **(disburse, disperse)**
3. **a.** Which word describes an action that a bookworm might do with a good book? **(emerge, immerge)**
   b. Which word describes an action that the sun might do to come out from behind a cloud? **(emerge, immerge)**
4. **a.** Which word describes the kind of acceptable excuse you might give a teacher for being late? **(credible, creditable)**
   b. Which word describes the kind of career that a popular and effective governor might have? **(credible, creditable)**

C. Write four or more short directions telling how to do something successfully. Use one challenge word in each direction.

Challenge Activities

apropos	asthma	ascertain	rescind
qualm	savvy	succumb	acquisition

A. Each word below is misspelled. Write the challenge word correctly. Underline the letter or letters that you had to add.

1. apropo
2. aquisition
3. quam
4. recind

5. savy
6. sucum
7. asma
8. acertain

B. Write the challenge word that best completes each sentence.

1. When I suffer from _____, I take medicine to help me breathe.
2. He had a _____ about walking into the haunted house.
3. As far as she could _____, the evidence pointed to two logical conclusions instead of one.
4. When space for new businesses became so difficult to find, the council voted to _____ the zoning law.
5. Your answer was certainly _____ to what you were asked.
6. That painting is the collector's latest _____.
7. I could not help but _____ to my fatigue and fall asleep.
8. Your outfit demonstrates that you are very _____ about fashion.

C. A neighbor asks you to solve the case of the missing milk. The clues you found in your neighbor's kitchen are: an empty pitcher with traces of milk, paw prints, and an open window. What can you ascertain from these clues? Add details and describe the situation. Then write your conclusions using some of the challenge words.

Challenge Activities

transcript	observatory	observable	undulate
transcription	conservatory	superlative	relatively

A. Complete the story using challenge words.

Teddy walked into the __1.__ to take a music lesson. The music room was __2.__ quiet because the other students hadn't started to practice yet. The grand piano in the middle of the room was the first thing that caught his eye. It was __3.__ even when the room was crowded. He noticed the fish tank and touched the surface as the water began to __4.__.

The class soon started. After the practice, the teacher said that the students' performance needed much work because it was far from __5.__. She had recorded their music and explained that it was not good enough for public broadcasting.

"Maybe I should be an astronomer and find work in an __6.__ instead," Teddy thought sadly.

B. Add one or more prefixes or suffixes to each base word below to form challenge words. Write the challenge words.

1. relate   **4.** conserve

2.–3. script   **5.–6.** observe

C. Write the challenge words that match each meaning.

1.–2. written record

3. to move in a wavelike manner

4. superb; extremely accomplished

D. In Activity A, Teddy had doubts about where he should be and what he should be. Would you rather work in an **observatory** or a **conservatory**? Explain your choice using some of the challenge words.

Challenge Activities

bedlam	herculean	nocturnal	iridescent
epicure	mesmerize	guillotine	vandalism

A. Write the challenge word that comes from each proper noun described below.

1. Epicurus was a Greek philosopher who taught that pleasure is the highest good.

2. Hercules was a Greek hero who was famous for his great strength.

3. Franz Mesmer was an Austrian physician who experimented with hypnotism.

4. Joseph-Ignace Guillotin was a Frenchman who championed a law requiring that all sentences of death be carried out by "means of a machine."

5. Bedlam was a popular name for the medieval Hospital of St. Mary of Bethlehem, a London insane asylum.

6. The Vandals were a Germanic people who robbed and looted Rome when they captured the city in A.D. 455.

B. Read the meaning of each Latin form. Write the challenge word that comes from it.

1. *iris* means "rainbow"

2. *nox* means "night"

C. Write the challenge word that belongs with each pair of words.

1. damage, destruction

2. lustrous, colorful

3. gourmet, gourmand

4. disordered, wild

5. mammoth, overpowering

6. darkness, night

7. hypnotize, captivate

8. decapitate, execute

D. Think of several other famous people and create new words using their last names. Write a definition for each word that relates to something this famous character did.

Challenge Activities

| colossal | declaration | opposition | prosperous |
| ponderous | proclamation | competitor | flourishing |

A. Write the challenge words that are adjectives and could describe the things below.

    1. the Colosseum, an ancient stadium in Rome

    2. a vegetable garden that is growing well

    3. a hippo or other heavy and clumsy animal

    4. a person whose business is successful

B. Write the challenge words that are nouns and are described below.

    1. a contestant entered in a chess tournament

    2.–3. an official, public announcement

    4. action against

C. Write the challenge word that best completes each analogy.

    1. Small is to **tiny** as **large** is to _____.

    2. Light is to **feathery** as **heavy** is to _____.

    3. Education is to **educator** as **competition** is to _____.

    4. Unfruitful is to **thriving** as **undeveloped** is to _____.

    5. Unfortunate is to **well-to-do** as **unsuccessful** is to _____.

    6. Assistance is to **resistance** as **cooperation** is to _____.

    7.–8. _____ is to **proclaim** as _____ is to **declare**.

D. Think of a monument honoring a hero who would rival any competitor. For example, the Colossus of Rhodes was a huge statue, honoring Apollo, that was one of the seven wonders of the ancient world. Imagine that the monument of your choice is to be unveiled soon. Write a proclamation about the monument. Use some of the challenge words.

Challenge Activities

visionary	inspirational	transpire	revitalize
advisable	conspiracy	vivify	convivial

A. Write the challenge word that matches each statement.

1. I am fond of eating and of socializing with friends.
2. I can take place.
3. I am an unlawful plot against someone.
4. I am to be recommended.
5. I am a dreamer.
6. I can bring new life to something.
7. I am a strong influence on thought and feeling.
8. I can enliven or animate.

B. Write the challenge word that is an antonym for the word in the first column and a synonym for the word in the second column.

1. unexciting   stimulating
2. unwise   worthwhile
3. realist   idealist
4. antisocial   friendly
5. not happen   take place
6. bore   energize

C. Write the challenge word that . . .

1. contains the word **piracy**.
2. contains the word **vital**.

D. Think about a kind of fund-raising event, such as a concert, that would draw together thousands of people for a common cause. Write about what might transpire at such an event. Use some of the challenge words in your report.

Challenge Activities

| idiosyncrasy | pedestrian | labyrinth | cancellation |
| rendezvous | ebullient | condominium | remuneration |

A. Write the challenge word that goes with each statement.

1. It is hard to find your way through this network of paths.
2. This person goes on foot.
3. This is a payment for services.
4. This names a peculiar trait.
5. This is an appointment to meet at a certain time or place.
6. This is an apartment building owned by tenants of the apartments.
7. This means "high-spirited" and "enthusiastic."
8. This statement means services are not wanted.

B. Substitute a challenge word for the underlined word or words in the sentence. Write the challenge word.

1. Don't you have a meeting with your friends today?
2. The passageways of the cave were like a maze.
3. The voiding of the order was due to the customer's indecision.
4. Where is my reward for delivering these goods?
5. The fans of the winning team were full of bubbling excitement.
6. The car stopped to let the walker cross the street.
7. Eating popcorn for breakfast is an unusual form of behavior.
8. How many people own their own apartments in the apartment building?

C. Think of humorous idiosyncrasies that people might exhibit in different places or situations. Then write a funny short story in which the main character possesses these peculiar traits. Use challenge words in your short story.

Challenge Activities

---

obligatory	obsolete	impromptu	supplant
obnoxious	obstruction	infuriate	surmise

A. Write the challenge word that matches each expression.

1. make one see red
2. on the spur of the moment
3. behind the times; old hat
4. put two and two together
5. a fly in the ointment
6. step into someone else's shoes
7. a must-do
8. a pain in the neck

B. Write the challenge word that best completes each sentence.

1. The odor was so _____ that I couldn't stand it any longer.
2. If the bullfighter waves the red cape, it will _____ the bull.
3. In the United States, formal education is _____ for children under a certain age.
4. Since the speaker had no time for preparation, her speech was _____.
5. Latin is an _____ language in terms of everyday use.
6. Who will _____ the dictator?
7. Although there is no proof, I _____ that someone who attends the school turned off the lights.
8. The fallen tree was an _____ in the road.

C. Write a list of things you would associate with each challenge word. For example, a dam might be an obstruction on a river, or a column might be an obstruction in a theater.

Challenge Activities

| antagonize | patronize | scrutinize | despise |
| computerize | minimize | chastise | demise |

A. Write the challenge word that fits each group of words.

1. support, do business with, shop at
2. fall, collapse, ruin
3. inspect, examine, investigate
4. reduce, lessen, gloss over
5. discipline, punish, correct
6. defy, combat, oppose
7. dislike, abhor, cannot abide
8. mechanize, integrate with technology

B. Write the only challenge word that is not a verb. Write its part of speech.

C. Write a challenge word that tells what the superhero in a cartoon must do in each situation.

1. The superhero is instructed to earn the dislike of his enemy by tweaking his nose.
2. The superhero must punish the criminal for robbing the bank.
3. The superhero must electronically store the information of how many peanuts and acorns the squirrels gathered for the winter.
4. The superhero is required to regard the guard dog with contempt as it scurries by.
5. The superhero must reduce the amount of damage done to the house before the owners get back.
6. The superhero must support his friend's lemonade stand as a steady customer.
7. The superhero must examine the land deed carefully before signing and returning it to the sly villain.

D. Pretend you are a movie director. Direct each of seven actors to act in different ways. Write your directions using the challenge words. You may want to use Activity C for ideas.

Challenge Activities

requisition	arbitration	authorization	pension
compensation	administration	retirement	promotion

A. Write the challenge word that matches each statement.

1. This happens when you reach a certain age and withdraw from work.

2. This is given to make up for a loss or injury.

3. As a proper noun, it refers to the President of the United States, the cabinet, and their departments.

4. This gives one official permission.

5. This is a formal, written request.

6. This is paid regularly as a retirement benefit.

7. If an employee earns this, he or she gets more responsibility and a salary increase.

8. Employees and employers might seek this if they cannot settle an important dispute.

B. Write the challenge word that is related to each word below.

1. requisite

2. promote

3. author

4. arbitrate

5. administrate

6. retire

C. Write the two challenge words that are from the Latin word *pendere,* meaning "to pay."

D. You are the personnel director of a large company. Suppose a long-time employee wants to speak to you about retiring. Write a list of helpful suggestions to make this person's retirement as pleasant and profitable as possible. Use some of the challenge words in your list of suggestions.

WRITER'S HANDBOOK
Contents

Spelling Strategy
When You Take a Test

1 **Get** ready for the test. Make sure your paper and pencil are ready.

2 **Listen** carefully as your teacher says each word and uses it in a sentence. Don't write before you hear the word **and** the sentence.

3 **Write** the word carefully. Make sure your handwriting is easy to read. If you want to print your words, ask your teacher.

6 **Circle** any misspelled parts of the word.

4 **Use** a pen to correct your test. Look at the word as your teacher says it.

7 **Look** at the correctly written word. Spell the word again. Say each letter out loud.

5 **Say** the word aloud. Listen carefully as your teacher spells the word. Say each letter aloud. Check the word one letter at a time.

8 **Write** any misspelled word correctly.

Spelling Strategy
When You Write a Paper

1 **Think** of the exact word you want to use.

2 **Write** the word, if you know how to spell it.

3 **Say** the word to yourself, if you are not sure how to spell it.

4 **Picture** what the word looks like when you see it written.

5 **Write** the word.

6 **Ask** yourself whether the word looks right.

7 **Check** the word in a dictionary if you are not sure.

SPELLING AND THE Writing Process

Writing anything—a friendly letter, a paper for school—usually follows a process. The writing process has five steps. It might look like this if you tried to draw a picture of it:

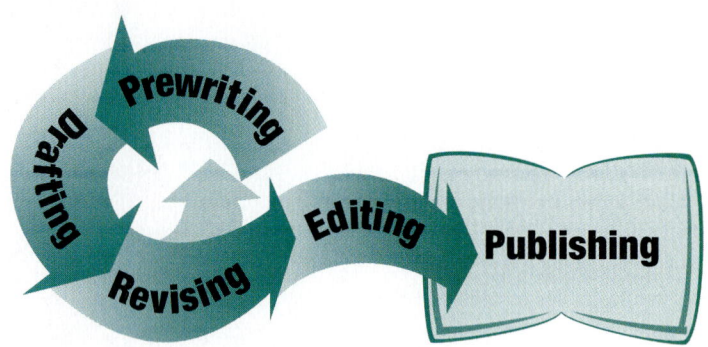

Notice that part of the writing process forms a loop. That is because not every writing task is the same. It is also because writers often jump back and forth between the steps as they change their minds and think of new ideas.

Here is a description of each step:

Prewriting This is thinking and planning ahead to help you write.

Drafting This means writing your paper for the first time. You usually just try to get your ideas down on paper. You can fix them later.

Revising This means fixing your final draft. Here is where you rewrite, change, and add words.

Editing This is where you feel you have said all you want to say. Now you proofread your paper for spelling errors and errors in grammar and punctuation.

Publishing This is making a copy of your writing and sharing it with your readers. Put your writing in a form that your readers will enjoy.

Confident spellers are better writers. Confident writers better understand their own writing process. Know the five steps. Know how they best fit the way you write.

SPELLING AND Writing Ideas

Being a good speller can help make you a more confident writer. Writing more can make you a better writer. Here are some ideas to get you started.

Ideas for Descriptive Writing

You might…

- describe a profession you might be interested in or a career you might choose.
- describe a busy train station or airport. Choose details that involve all of your five senses.
- describe an extraordinary day you had recently. It could be extraordinarily awful or extraordinarily wonderful.
- select two fictional characters—or real people you know—and write two paragraphs: one describing similarities the characters share and one telling how the characters differ.

Ideas for Narrative Writing

You might…

- think of a real or imaginary experience that turned out better than expected and write a story about it.
- retell a familiar story or fairy tale in your own words. Change the story, adding fresh details, and give the story a surprise ending.
- write a letter to someone you have not seen for a long time, bringing that person up to date on what is happening in your life.
- think of a favorite object, plant, or animal. Pretend you are that thing and write a story about a day in your life.

Ideas for Persuasive Writing

You might…

- choose an issue and take a stand. Write about something you think should be changed. Give reasons to support your ideas.
- write an argument to persuade your parents to let you do something special, such as getting a new pet, or giving you a new privilege, such as a later weekend curfew.
- try to persuade a friend or family member to avoid an unhealthy or dangerous habit, such as smoking or eating mostly junk food.

Ideas for Expository Writing

You might…

- think of a saying or an expression you like or use frequently. Write the expression, tell what it means, and explain when and why people use it.
- choose an endangered animal or a serious environmental issue. Express your views and offer suggestions about how people can make a difference.
- design an invention that you think would help make life easier. Explain what it will look like, how it will help people, and who will use it.
- write instructions telling a classmate how to set up and care for a project, such as an aquarium or a terrarium.

Manuscript Handwriting Models

A B C D E
F G H I J K
L M N O P
Q R S T U
V W X Y Z
a b c d e f
g h i j k
l m n o p q
r s t u v
w x y z
1 2 3 4 5
6 7 8 9 10
? ! . , " " '

Cursive Handwriting Models

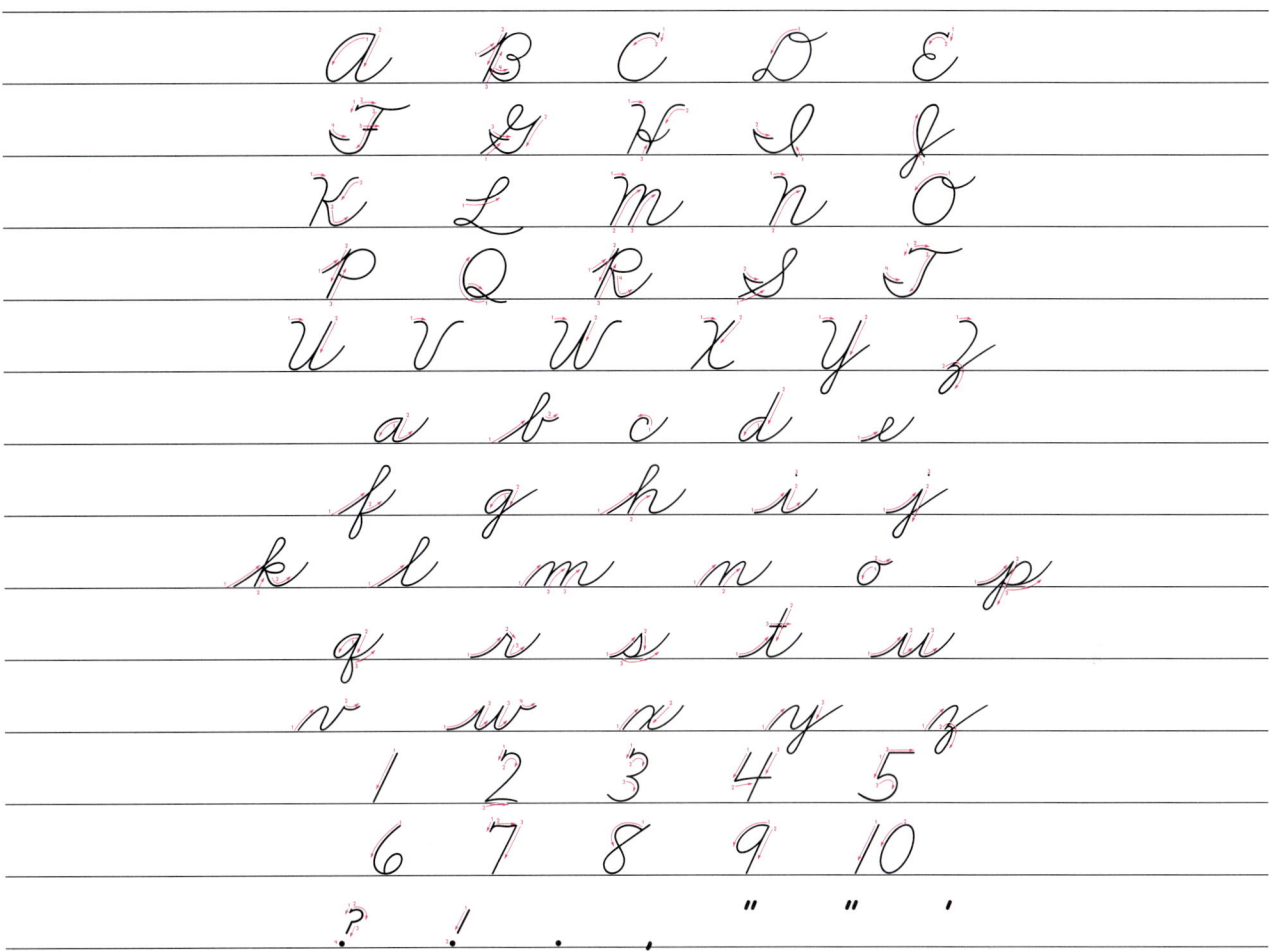

High Frequency Writing Words

A

a
about
afraid
after
again
air
all
almost
also
always
am
America
an
and
animal
animals
another
any
anything
are
around
as
ask
asked
at
ate
away

B

baby
back
bad
ball
balloons
baseball
basketball

be
bear
beautiful
because
become
bed
been
before
being
believe
best
better
big
bike
black
boat
book
books
both
boy
boys
bring
broke
brother
build
bus
but
buy
by

C

call
called
came
can
candy
can't
car
care

cars
cat
catch
caught
change
charge
children
Christmas
circus
city
class
clean
clothes
come
comes
coming
could
couldn't
country
cut

D

Dad
day
days
decided
did
didn't
died
different
dinner
do
does
doesn't
dog
dogs
doing
done

don't
door
down
dream

E

each
earth
eat
eighth
else
end
enough
even
every
everybody
everyone
everything
except
eyes

F

family
fast
father
favorite
feel
feet
fell
few
field
fight
finally
find
fire
first
fish
five

fix
food
football
for
found
four
free
Friday
friend
friends
from
front
fun
funny
future

G

game
games
gas
gave
get
gets
getting
girl
girls
give
go
God
goes
going
good
got
grade
grader
great
ground
grow

H

had
hair
half
happened
happy
hard
has
have
having
he
head
heard
help
her
here
he's
high
hill
him
his
hit
home
homework
hope
horse
horses
hot
hour
house
how
hurt

I

I
I'd
if

I'm
important
in
into
is
it
its
it's

J

job
jump
just

K

keep
kept
kids
killed
kind
knew
know

L

lady
land
last
later
learn
leave
left
let
let's
life
like
liked
likes
little

live
lived
lives
long
look
looked
looking
lost
lot
lots
love
lunch

M

mad
made
make
making
man
many
math
may
maybe
me
mean
men
might
miss
Mom
money
more
morning
most
mother
mouse
move
Mr.
Mrs.

much
music
must
my
myself

N

name
named
need
never
new
next
nice
night
no
not
nothing
now

O

of
off
oh
OK
old
on
once
one
only
or
other
our
out
outside
over
own

P

parents
park
party
people
person
pick
place
planet
play
played
playing
police
president
pretty
probably
problem
put

R

ran
read
ready
real
really
reason
red
responsibilities
rest
ride
riding
right
room
rules
run
running

High Frequency Writing Words (continued)

S

said
same
saw
say
scared
school
schools
sea
second
see
seen
set
seventh
she
ship
shot
should
show
sick
since
sister
sit
sleep
small
snow
so
some
someone
something
sometimes
soon
space
sport
sports
start
started

states
stay
still
stop
stopped
store
story
street
stuff
such
sudden
suddenly
summer
sure
swimming

T

take
talk
talking
teach
teacher
teachers
team
tell
than
Thanksgiving
that
that's
the
their
them
then
there
these
they
they're

thing
things
think
this
thought
three
through
throw
time
times
to
today
together
told
too
took
top
tree
trees
tried
trip
trouble
try
trying
turn
turned
TV
two

U

united
until
up
upon
us
use
used

V

very

W

walk
walked
walking
want
wanted
war
was
wasn't
watch
water
way
we
week
weeks
well
went
were
what
when
where
which
while
white
who
whole
why
will
win
winter
wish
with
without
woke

won
won't
work
world
would
wouldn't

Y

yard
year
years
yes
you
your
you're

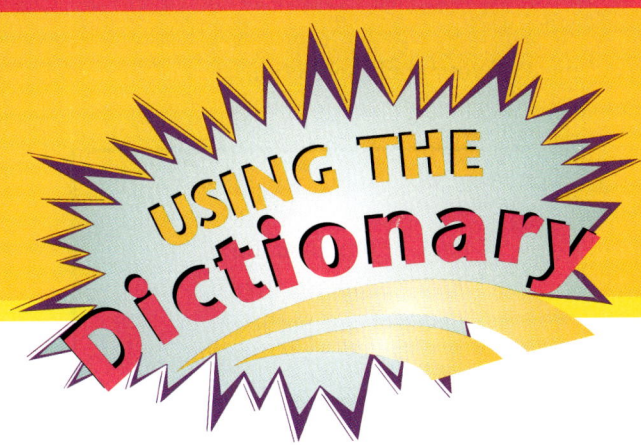

USING THE Dictionary

- The **guide words** at the top of each dictionary page show the first and last entries on the page. Think of words to spell. Practice using guide words to find each word's entry.

- Some spellings are listed with the base word. To find **calicoes**, look up **calico**. To find **occurring**, look up **occur**.

- If you do not know how to spell a word, guess the spelling and try to find the first three letters of the word. (Using just the first letter often takes too long.)

- If you can't find a word, think of alternative spellings. For example, if a word starts with the /**k**/ sound, the spelling might begin with **k, c,** or even **ch**.

Information on page 266 provides additional explanation of terms and abbreviations in your Spelling Dictionary.

entry correct spelling; bullets separate syllables

part of speech

pronunciation phonetic spelling shows correct pronunciation

field label identifies special area to which the definition applies

o•ver•ture /ō vər chŏŏr'/ *n.* **a.** *Music.* **l.** an instrumental composition intended especially as an introduction to an extended musical work, such as an opera or an oratorio. *The rousing overture prepared us for an exciting concert.* **a.2.** a similar orchestral work, such as one written as introductory music to a play or as a concert piece. **b.** an act, offer, or proposal that indicates readiness to undertake a course of action or to open a relationship. [ME < OFr. < Lat. *apertura,* opening < *aperire,* to open.]

definition Be sure you have the correct entry word!

etymology history or origin of the word

sample sentence to clarify definition

265

A pronunciation key appears on every right-hand page of your spelling dictionary.

The abbreviation for the **part of speech** of each entry word follows the phonetic spelling. These abbreviations include:

n.	noun	*adj.*	adjective	*conj.*	conjunction
pron.	pronoun	*prep.*	preposition	*interj.*	interjection
adv.	adverb	*pl.*	plural	*p.part.*	past participle
v.	verb	*sing.*	singular	*pr.part.*	present participle

Stylistic and geographic labels limit a definition to a particular level or style of usage. These labels include:

Nonstandard indicates a level of language usage that is not commonly accepted and is inappropriate for formal writing or speaking.

Slang indicates a style of language using figures of speech that are usually extravagant and overelaborate. Slang is often heard in informal conversation but is inappropriate for formal writing.

Obs. (Obsolete) indicates a term that is no longer in use.

Archaic indicates terms that were once common but are now rarely used. Archaic terms may be familiar, as they were once common in speaking and are still found in literature.

The following abbreviations also appear in your spelling dictionary.

aug. (augmentative—indicates an increase, as in size, force, or intensity, in the meaning of the original word)

comp. (comparative)

dim. (diminutive—denotes smallness, youth, or familiarity)

fem. (feminine)

freq. (frequentative—indicates that the meaning of a word is derived from the repetition of the action denoted by the original word)

perh. (perhaps)

prob. (probably)

var. (variant—indicates that a word differs slightly from the word that follows)

The **etymology,** or history of a word, appears in square brackets [ ] following the definitions. An etymology traces a word back to the language from which it is believed to have come. The symbol < means *derived from*. The abbreviations used to denote the original languages include:

AN	Anglo-Norman	*Ar.*	Arabic	*Canadian Fr.*	Canadian French
Du.	Dutch	*Fr.*	French	*MDu.*	Middle Dutch
Gk.	Greek	*Ital.*	Italian	*OProv.*	Old Provençal
G.	German	*OFr.*	Old French	*LLat.*	Late Latin
OE	Old English	*Sp.*	Spanish	*Med. Lat.*	Medieval Latin
Turk.	Turkish	*ON*	Old Norse	*Mex. Sp.*	Mexican Spanish
Lat.	Latin	*OSp.*	Old Spanish	*ME*	Middle English
Port.	Portuguese	*OItal.*	Old Italian	*MHG*	Middle High German
Prov.	Provençal	*NLat.*	New Latin	*Norman Fr.*	Norman French
OHG	Old High German			*VLat.*	Vulgar Latin

ab•di•cate /ăb′ dĭ kāt′/ *v.* (-cates, -cat•ed,
-cat•ing) **a.** to relinquish (power or responsibility) formally. **b.** to relinquish formally high
office or responsibility.

-able a suffix used to form adjectives meaning:
a. capable or worthy of: *lovable.* **b.** tending
toward: *peaceable.*

a•board[1] /ə bôrd′, ə bōrd′/ *adv.* on board a ship,
train, airplane, or other passenger vehicle.

a•board[2] /ə bôrd′, ə bōrd′/ *prep.* on board of;
on; in.

a•brupt /ə brŭpt′/ *adj.* **a.** unexpectedly sudden.
b. surprisingly curt; brusque.

ab•scis•sa /ăb sĭs′ ə/ *n.* the coordinate representing the distance of a point from the y-axis in
a plane Cartesian coordinate system, measured
along a line parallel to the x-axis.

ab•sorb /əb sôrb′, -zôrb′/ *v.* **a.** to take in; soak
in or up. **b.** to occupy the full attention, interest,
or time of; engross. **c.** *Chem. & Physics.* to
retain wholly, without reflection or transmission,
that which is taken in.

ab•surd /əb sûrd′, -zûrd′/ *adj.* **a.** ridiculously
incongruous or unreasonable. **b.** of, pertaining
to, or manifesting the view that there is no order
or value in human life or in
the universe; meaningless.

a•bun•dance /ə bŭn′ dəns/
n. **a.** a great or plentiful
amount. **b.** affluence; wealth.
[ME *aboundant* < OFr.
abondant < Lat. *abundans,*
p.part. of *abundare,*
to overflow.]

abundance

a•bun•dant /ə bŭn′ dənt/ *adj.* **a.** in plentiful
supply; ample. **b.** abounding with; rich: *a region
abundant in wildlife.*

ac•a•dem•ic[1] /ăk′ ə děm′ ĭk/ *adj.* **a.** of, pertaining to, or characteristic of a school. **b.** relating to
studies that are liberal or classical rather than
technical or vocational. **c.** based on formal education. [Lat. *Academia,* Academy < Gk. *Akadēmia,*
the school where Plato taught.]

ac•a•dem•ic[2] /ăk′ ə děm′ ĭk/ *n.* a student
or teacher.

a•cad•e•my /ə kăd′ ə mē/ *n.* (**a•cad•e•mies**
pl.) **a.** a school for special instruction. **b.** a secondary or college-preparatory school, especially
a private one. **c.** an association of scholars.
[Lat. *Academia,* Academy < Gk. *Akadēmia,* the
school where Plato taught.]

ac•cel•er•ate /ăk sĕl′ ə rāt′/ *v.* (-ates, -at•ed,
-at•ing). **a.** to increase the speed of. **b.** to move
or act faster. [Lat. *accelerare: ad-* (intensive) +
celerare, to quicken < *celer,* swift.]

ac•cen•tu•ate /ăk sĕn′ chōō āt′/ *v.* (-ates,
-at•ed, -at•ing) (**ac•cen•tu•a•tion** *n.*) **a.** to pronounce with a stress or accent. **b.** to mark with
an accent. **c.** to stress or emphasize.

ac•cep•tance /ăk sĕp′ təns/ *n.* **a.** the act or
process of accepting. **b.** the state of being
accepted or acceptable. **c.** favorable reception;
approval. **d.** belief in something; agreement.
[ME *accepten,* to accept < Lat. *acceptare,* freq.
of *accipere,* to receive: *ad-,* to + *capere,* to take.]

ac•ces•so•ry[1] /ăk sĕs′ ə rē/ *n.* (-ries *pl.*) **a.** one
who incites, aids, or abets a lawbreaker in the
commission of a crime, but is not present at the
time of the crime: *accessory before the fact.*
b. one who aids a criminal after the commission
of a crime, but was not present at the time of the
crime: *accessory after the fact.*

ac•ces•so•ry[2] /ăk sĕs′ ə rē/ *adj.* serving to aid
or abet a lawbreaker, either before or after the
commission of the crime, without being present
at the time the crime was committed.

Pronunciation Key

ă	pat	ŏ	pot	th	**th**in
ā	pay	ō	toe	*th*	**th**is
âr	care	ô	paw, for	hw	**wh**ich
ä	father	oi	n**oi**se	zh	vi**s**ion
ĕ	pet	ou	**ou**t	ə	**a**bout,
ē	be	ŏŏ	t**oo**k		**i**tem,
ĭ	pit	ōō	b**oo**t		penc**i**l,
ī	pie	ŭ	c**u**t		gall**o**p,
îr	p**ier**	ûr	**ur**ge		circ**u**s

Spelling Dictionary

ac•com•mo•date /ə kŏm′ ə dāt/ v. (**-dates,
-dat•ed, -dat•ing**) **a.** to do a favor or service
for; oblige. **b.** to provide for; supply with.
c. to contain comfortably; have space for.
[Lat. *accomodare, accomodat-,* to fit: *ad-,*
to + *commodus,* suitable.]

ac•com•plice /ə kŏm′ plĭs/ n. one who aids or
abets a lawbreaker in a criminal act, either as a
principal or an accessory.

ac•count•a•ble /ə koun′ tə bəl/ adj.
(**ac•count•a•bil•i•ty, ac•count•a•ble•ness** n.)
a. answerable. **b.** capable of being explained.

ac•cu•mu•late /ə kyo̅o̅m′ yə lāt′/ v. (**-lates,
-lat•ed, -lat•ing**) **a.** to amass or gather; pile up;
collect. **b.** to grow or increase; mount up.
[Lat. *accumulare, accumulat-: ad-,* to + *cumu-
lare,* to pile up < *cumulus,* heap.]

ac•cu•ra•cy /ăk′ yər ə sē/ n. the quality or state
of being accurate; correctness. [Lat. *accuratus,*
done with care, p.part. of *accurare,* to do with
care: *ad-,* to + *curare,* to care for < *cura,* care.]

a•chieve•ment /ə chēv′ mənt/ n. something
that has been accomplished successfully,
especially by means of exertion, skill, practice,
or perseverance.

ac•id /ăs′ ĭd/ n. any of many substances that when
dissolved in water are capable of reacting with a
base to form water and a salt. *Acids turn blue lit-
mus to red and have a characteristic sour taste.*

a•cid•ic /ə sĭd′ ĭk/ adj. **a.** acid. **b.** tending to
form an acid.

ac•knowl•edge /ăk nŏl′ ĭj/ v. (**-edg•es, -edged,
-edg•ing**) **a.1.** to confess, avow, or admit the existence, reality, or truth of. **a.2.** to recognize as
being valid or having force or power. **b.1.** to
express recognition of. **b.2.** to express thanks or
gratitude for.

ac•knowl•edg•ment also **ac•knowl•
edge•ment** /ăk nŏl′ ĭj mənt/ n. **a.** the act of
admitting something. **b.** recognition of someone's or something's existence, validity, authority, or right. **c.** an expression or token of appreciation or thanks.

a•cous•tics /ə ko̅o̅′ stĭks/ n. **a.** (*used with a
sing. verb*) the scientific study of sound. **b.** (*used
with a pl. verb*) the total effect of sound, especially as produced in an enclosed space.

ac•quaint /ə kwānt′/ v. **a.** to make familiar.
b. to inform.

ac•quain•tance /ə kwān′ təns/ n. **a.** knowledge of a person acquired by a relationship less
intimate than friendship. **b.** a person whom
one knows.

ac•quit /ə kwĭt′/ v. (**-quits, -quit•ted, -quit•ting**)
to free or clear from a charge or accusation.

a•crop•o•lis /ə krŏp′ ə lĭs/
n. the fortified height or
citadel of an ancient Greek
city, especially the citadel
of Athens. [Gk. *akropolis:
akron,* top + *polis,* city.]

acropolis

ac•ti•vate /ăk′ tə vāt′/ v.
(**-vates, -vat•ed, -vat•ing**)
to set in motion; make
active. [ME *actif,* active < OFr.< Lat. *activus <
actus,* moving, p.part of *agere,* to impel.]

ad- or **ac-** or **af-** or **ag-** or **al-** or **ap-** or **as-** or
at- a prefix meaning toward or to: *adapt.*

ad•di•tive[1] /ăd′ ĭ tĭv/ adj. marked by, produced
by, or involving addition.

ad•di•tive[2] /ăd′ ĭ tĭv/ n. a substance added in
small amounts to something else to improve,
strengthen, or otherwise alter it.

ad•ja•cent /ə jā′ sənt/ adj. **a.** close to; lying
near. **b.** next to; adjoining.

ad•join /ə join′/ v. **a.** to be next to. **b.** to attach
to; unite.

ad•journ /ə jûrn′/ v. to suspend until a later
stated time.

ad•just /ə jŭst′/ v. (**ad•just•a•ble** adj.) **a.** to
change so as to match or fit; cause to correspond. **b.** to bring into proper relationship. **c.** to
adapt or conform, as to new conditions.

ad•min•is•ter /ăd mĭn′ ĭ stər/ v. **a.** to have
charge of; manage. **b.** to manage as an
administrator.

ad•mis•si•ble /ăd mĭs′ ə bəl/ adj. **a.** capable
of being accepted; allowable. **b.** worthy of
admission.

ad•o•les•cent[1] /ăd′ l ĕs′ ənt/ n. a boy or girl,
especially a teenager, in the stage of development between childhood and adulthood.

ad•o•les•cent² /ăd′l ĕs′ ənt/ *adj.* of or going through adolescence.

ad•ver•tise /ăd′ vər tīz′/ *v.* (-tis•es, -tised, -tis•ing) **a.** to call the attention of the public to a product or business. **b.** to inquire or seek in a public notice, as in a newspaper: *advertise for an apartment.*

ad•ver•tise•ment /ăd′ vər **tīz′** mənt, ăd **vûr′** tĭs-, -tĭz-/ *n.* a notice designed to attract public attention or patronage. [ME *advertisen,* to notify < OFr. *avertir, avertiss-,* to notice.]

ad•vi•so•ry /ăd **vī′** zə rē/ *adj.* **a.** empowered to advise: *a student advisory committee.* **b.** of, pertaining to, or containing advice.

ad•vo•cate¹ /ăd′ və kāt′/ *v.* (-cates, -cat•ed, -cat•ing) to speak in favor of; recommend.

ad•vo•cate² /ăd′ və kĭt, -kāt′/ *n.* a person who argues for a cause; supporter or defender. [< ME *advocat,* lawyer < OFr. *avocat* < Lat. *advocatus,* p.part. of *advocare,* to summon for counsel: *ad-,* to + *vocare,* to call.]

af•fil•i•ate¹ /ə fĭl′ ē āt′/ *v.* (-ates, -at•ed, -at•ing) **a.** to adopt or accept as a subordinate associate. **b.** to associate or connect oneself: *a group that decided to affiliate.*

af•fil•i•ate² /ə fĭl′ ē ĭt′, -āt′/ *n.* a person or organization associated with another in a subordinate relationship.

a•gen•da /ə jĕn′ də/ *n.* (*used with a sing. verb*) a list of things to be done, especially the program for a meeting. [Lat. pl. of *agendum,* something to be done, from *agere,* to do.]

ag•gres•sion /ə grĕsh′ ən/ *n.* **a.** the act of commencing hostilities or invasion; assault. **b.** *Psychoanal.* hostile action or behavior.

a•gron•o•my /ə grŏn′ ə mē/ *n.* the application of the various soil and plant sciences to soil management and the raising of crops; scientific agriculture.

-al¹ a suffix that forms adjectives from nouns: *postal.*

-al² a suffix that forms nouns from verbs: *arrival.*

agronomy

al•ge•bra /ăl′ jə brə/ *n.* a generalization of arithmetic in which symbols, usually letters of the alphabet, represent numbers or members of a specified set of numbers and are related by operations that hold for all numbers in the set. [ME < Med. Lat. < Ar. *al-jebr,* the (science of) reuniting: *al-,* the + *jabr,* reunification.]

al•go•rithm /ăl′ gə rĭth′ əm/ *n. Math.* a mechanical or recursive computational procedure.

al•ka•li /ăl′ kə lī′/ *n. Chem.* **a.** sodium hydroxide, potassium hydroxide, or any similar compound formed from a related metal. All compounds of this kind are very strong bases. **b.** sodium carbonate, potassium carbonate, or any similar salt formed from a related metal. All salts of this kind are strong bases. **c.** any of various basic mineral salts found in natural water and in arid soil.

al•ka•line /ăl′ kə lĭn, -līn′/ *adj.* **a.** of, relating to, or containing an alkali. **b.** having a pH greater than 7.

al•le•go•ry /ăl′ ĭ gôr′ē, -gōr′ ē/ *n.* (-ries *pl.*) a literary, dramatic, or pictorial device in which each literal character, object, and event represents a symbol illustrating an idea or moral or religious principle.

al•lit•er•a•tion /ə lĭt′ ə rā′ shən/ *n.* the occurrence in a phrase or line of speech or writing of two or more words having the same initial sound, for example, *wailing in the winter wind.*

al•lo•cate /ăl′ ə kāt′/ *v.* (-cates, -cat•ed, -cat•ing) **a.** to designate for a special purpose; set apart. **b.** to distribute according to plan; allot. [Med. Lat. *allocare, allocat-:* Lat. *ad-,* to + Lat. *locare,* to place < *locus,* place.]

al•lu•sion /ə lōō′ zhən/ *n.* **a.** the act of alluding; indirect mention. **b.** an indirect, but pointed or meaningful reference.

al•pha•bet•ize /ăl′ fə bǐ tīz′/ *v.* (**-iz•es, -ized, -iz•ing**) to arrange in alphabetical order.

a•lu•mi•num /ə lōō′ mə nəm/ *n. Symbol* **Al**. a silvery-white, ductile metallic element, the most abundant in the earth's crust, but found only in combination, chiefly in bauxite. It is used to form many hard, light, corrosion-resistant alloys.

a•lum•na /ə lŭm′ nə/ *n.* (**-nae** /-nē′/ *pl.*) a female graduate or former student of a school, college, or university. [Lat., fem. of *alumnus.*]

a•lum•nus /ə lŭm′ nəs/ *n.* (**-ni** /-nī′/ *pl.*) a male graduate or former student of a school, college, or university. [Lat., pupil < *alere,* to nourish.]

am•bas•sa•dor /ăm băs′ ə dər, -dôr′/ *n.* **a.** a diplomatic official of the highest rank appointed and accredited as representative in residence by one government to another. **b.** a diplomatic official heading his or her country's permanent mission to certain international organizations, such as the United Nations. **c.** any authorized messenger or representative.

am•big•u•ous /ăm bǐg′ yōō əs/ *adj.* **a.** having two or more possible meanings. **b.** doubtful or uncertain.

ana- a prefix that means: **a.** upward; up. **b.** backward; back. **c.** again; anew.

an•a•log /ăn′ ə lôg′, -lŏg′/ *adj.* representing numerical data in continuous form, as by analogous physical magnitudes or electrical signals.

a•nal•y•sis /ə năl′ ĭ sǐs/ *n.* (**-ses** /-sēz′/ *pl.*) the process of separating a subject into its parts and studying them so as to determine its nature. [NLat. < Gk. *analysis,* a dissolving < *analyein,* to undo: *ana-,* throughout + *lyein,* to loosen.]

an•a•lyze /ăn′ ə līz′/ *v.* (**-lyz•es, -lyzed, -lyz• ing**) to separate into parts or basic principles so as to determine the nature of the whole; examine methodically.

an•ar•chy /ăn′ ər kē/ *n.* (**-chies** *pl.*) absence of any form of political authority. [Gk. *anarkhia* < *anarkhos,* without a ruler: *an-,* without + *arkhos,* ruler < *arkhein,* to rule.]

-ance a suffix that forms nouns from verbs: *resemblance.*

-ant a suffix that forms nouns and adjectives: *resultant.*

an•tic•i•pate /ăn tǐs′ ə pāt′/ *v.* (**-pates, -pat•ed, -pat•ing**) **a.** to feel or realize beforehand; foresee. **b.** to look forward to, especially with pleasure; expect. **c.** to foresee and fulfill in advance.

an•tique[1] /ăn tēk/ *adj.* **a.** of or belonging to ancient times, especially of, from, or characteristic of ancient Greece or Rome. **b.** belonging to, made in, or typical of an earlier period.

an•tique[2] /ăn tēk/ *n.* an object having special value because of its age, especially a work of art or handicraft that is more than 100 years old. [Fr.]

a•or•ta /ā ôr′ tə/ *n.* (**-tas** or **-tae** /-tē′/ *pl.*) *Anat.* the main trunk of the systemic arteries, carrying blood from the left side of the heart to the arteries of all limbs and organs except the lungs.

a•pol•o•gize /ə pŏl′ ə jīz′/ *v.* (**-giz•es, -gized, -giz•ing**) to make excuse for or regretful acknowledgment of a fault or offense.

ap•pro•pri•ate /ə prō′ prē ĭt/ *adj.* suitable for a particular person, condition, occasion, or place; proper; fitting. [ME *appropriat* < Med. Lat. *appropriatus,* p.part. of *appropriare,* to make one's own: Lat. *ad-,* to + Lat. *proprius,* own.]

ar•chae•ol•o•gy or **ar•che•ol•o•gy** /är′ kē ŏl′ ə jē/ *n.* (**ar•chae• ol•o•gist** *n.*) the systematic recovery and study of material evidence, such as graves, buildings, tools, and pottery, remaining from past human life and culture.

archaeology

ar•chi•tec•ture /är′ kǐ tĕk′ chər/ *n.* **a.** the art and science of designing and erecting buildings. **b.** architectural structures collectively. [OFr. < Lat. *architectura* < *architectus,* architect < Gk. *arkhitekton,* master builder: *arkhi-,* archi- (< *arkhein,* to rule) + *tekton,* builder.]

a•re•na /ə rē′ nə/ *n.* **a.** the area in the center of an ancient Roman amphitheater where contests and other spectacles were held. **b.** a modern auditorium for sports events.

-ary a suffix that forms adjectives from nouns: *budgetary.*

as•cend /ə sĕnd′/ *v.* **a.** to go or move upward; rise. **b.** to move upward upon or along; climb: *ascended the mountain.* [ME *ascenden* < Lat. *ascendere:* *ad-*, toward + *scandere*, to climb.]

as•cent /ə sĕnt′/ *n.* **a.** the act or process of ascending. **b.** an advancement, especially in social status.

a•sep•tic /ə sĕp′ tĭk, ā-/ *adj.* free of microorganisms that are capable of causing disease.

as•pi•ra•tion /ăs′ pə rā′ shən/ *n.* **a.** expulsion of breath in speech. **b.1.** a strong desire for high achievement. **b.2.** an object of such desire; ambitious goal. [Lat. *aspirare, aspirat-*, to breathe on: *ad-*, to + *spirare*, to breathe.]

as•pire /ə spīr′/ *v.* (**-pires, -pired, -pir•ing**) **a.** to have a great ambition; desire strongly. **b.** to strive toward an end; aim at. [ME *aspiren* < Lat. *aspirare*, to desire: *ad-*, to + *spirare*, to breathe.]

as•sent¹ /ə sĕnt′/ *v.* to express agreement; concur: *assented to his plan.*

as•sent² /ə sĕnt′/ *n.* **a.** agreement, as to a proposal; compliance. **b.** acquiescence; consent.

as•sis•tance /ə sĭs′ təns/ *n.* aid; help. [ME *assisten*, to assist < OFr. *assister* < Lat. *assistere: ad-*, near to + *sistere*, to stand.]

as•so•nance /ăs′ ə nəns/ *n.* **a.** resemblance in sound, especially in the vowel sounds of words. **b.** a partial rhyme in which the accented vowel sounds correspond but the consonants differ, as in *brave* and *vain.*

a•ston•ish /ə stŏn′ ĭsh/ *v.* to fill with sudden wonder or amazement; confound.

as•tron•o•mer /ə strŏn′ ə mər/ *n.* a scientist specializing in astronomy.

as•tron•o•my /ə strŏn′ ə mē/ *n.* the scientific study of the part of the universe that lies beyond the earth, especially the observation of stars, planets, comets, galaxies, etc.

-ate¹ a suffix that forms adjectives: *affectionate.*

-ate² a suffix that forms verbs: *pollinate.*

-ation a suffix that forms nouns from verbs: *civilization.*

at•tor•ney /ə tûr′ nē/ *n.* (**-neys** *pl.*) a person legally appointed to act for another, especially an attorney at law.

au•di•to•ri•um /ô′ də tôr′ ē əm, -tōr′-/ *n.* **a.** a room to accommodate an audience in a building such as a school or theater. **b.** a large building for public meetings or artistic performances.

auditorium

au•di•to•ry /ô′ dĭ tôr′ē, -tōr′ē/ *adj.* of or pertaining to the sense, the organs, or the experience of hearing.

au•thor•ize /ô′ thə rīz′/ *v.* (**-iz•es, -ized, -iz•ing**) **a.** to grant authority or power to. **b.** to approve or give permission for; sanction.

au•to•crat /ô′ tə krăt′/ *n.* (**au•to•crat•ic** *adj.*) a ruler having absolute or unrestricted power; despot. [Fr. *autocrate* < Gk. *autokratēs*, ruling by oneself: *auto-*, self + *kratos*, authority.]

a•vail•a•ble /ə vā′ lə bəl/ *adj.* (**a•vail•a•bil• i•ty** *n.*) accessible for use; at hand. [ME *availen*, to avail: *a-* (intensive) + OFr. *valoir, vail-*, to be worth < Lat. *valēre.*]

ax•is /ăk′ sĭs/ *n.* (**ax•es** /-sēz′/ *pl.*) **a.** a straight line about which a body or geometrical object rotates or may be conceived to rotate. **b.** *Math.* **1.** an unlimited line, half-line, or line segment serving to orient a space or geometrical object, especially a line about which the object is symmetrical. **b.2.** a reference line from which distances or angles are measured in a coordinate system.

Spelling Dictionary

B

bank•rupt•cy /bǎngk′ rŭpt′ sē, -rəp sē/ *n.*
a. the condition of being legally bankrupt.
b. impoverishment; destitution. [Fr. *banquerote,*
bankrupt < Ital. *bancarotta: banca,* money-
changer's table + *rotta,* p.part of *rompere,* to
break < Lat. *rumpere.*]

ba•roque¹ /bə rōk′/ *adj.*
a. of, pertaining to, or characteristic of a style in art
and architecture developed
in Europe from about 1550
to 1700 and typified by
elaborate and ornate
scrolls, curves, and other
symmetrical ornamentation.

baroque

b. of, pertaining to, orcharacteristic of a style of
musical composition that flourished in Europe
from about 1600 to 1750. [Fr.]

ba•roque² /bə rōk′/ *n.* the baroque style or
period in art, architecture, or music.

bat•tle•field /bǎt′ l fēld′/ *n.* a field or area
where a battle is fought.

ba•zaar /bə zär′/ *n.* **a.** an Oriental market consisting of a street lined with shops and stalls. **b.**
a fair or sale at which miscellaneous articles are
sold, often for charitable purposes.

beige¹ /bāzh/ *n.* a light grayish brown or yellowish brown to grayish yellow.

beige² /bāzh/ *adj.* light grayish brown or yellowish brown to grayish yellow.

bene- a prefix meaning well or good.

ben•e•fac•tor /běn′ ə fǎk′ tər/ *n.* one who
gives financial or other aid. [LLat. < *benefactio,*
benefaction < *bene facere,* to do well.]

ben•e•fi•cial /běn′ ə fǐsh′ əl/ *adj.* promoting a
favorable result; enhancing well-being; advanta-
geous [Fr. *bé né ficial* < LLat. *beneficialis*
< Lat. *beneficium,* benefit < *bene facere,* to
do well.]

ben•e•fi•ci•ar•y /běn′ə fǐsh′ ē ěr ē, -fǐsh′
ə rē/ *n.* (**-ies** *pl.*) **a.** one that receives a benefit.
b. *Law.* the recipient of funds, property, or other
benefits, as from an insurance policy or will.

ben•e•fit¹ /běn′ ə fǐt/ *n.* something that promotes or enhances well-being; advantage. [ME
< OFr. *bienfait* < Lat. *benefactum,* good deed
< *bene facere,* to do well.]

ben•e•fit² /běn′ ə fǐt/ *v.* **a.** to be helpful or useful to. **b.** to gain advantage; profit: *benefit from
her example.*

be•nev•o•lent /bə něv′ ə lənt/ *adj.* characterized by or suggestive of benevolence; kindly.
[ME < Lat. *benevolens,* well-wishing: *bene,* will
+ *volens,* pr.part. of *velle,* to wish.]

be•nign /bǐ nīn′/ *adj.* tending to promote well-
being; beneficial. [ME *benigne* < OFr. < Lat.
benignus: bene, well + *genus,* born.]

best sell•er /běst′ sěl′ ər/ *n.* (**best sell•ing** *adj.*)
a book or other product that is among those sold
in the largest numbers.

bi•as¹ /bī′ əs/ *n.* **a.** a preference or inclination,
especially one that inhibits impartial judgment;
prejudice. **b.** a specified instance of this.

bi•as² /bī′ əs/ *v.* to cause to have a prejudiced
view.

bi•zarre /bǐ zär′/ *adj.* strikingly unconventional
or far-fetched, as in style or appearance; odd.
[Fr. < Sp. *bizarro,* brave, prob. < Basque *bizar,*
beard.]

bo•nan•za /bə nǎn′ zə / *n.* **a.** a rich mine, vein,
or pocket of ore. **b.** a source of great wealth or
prosperity. [Sp. exaggerated good, aug. of
bueno, good < Lat. *bonus.*]

book•keep•ing /bŏŏk′ kē′ pǐng/ *n.* the art or
practice of recording the accounts and transac-
tions of a business.

bot•a•ny /bŏt′ n ē/ *n.* (**-nies** *pl.*) the biological
science of plants.

boul•e•vard /bŏŏl′ ə värd′, bŏŏ′ lə-/ *n.* a broad
city street, often tree-lined and landscaped.
[Fr. < OFr. *boloart,* rampart converted to a
promenade < MDu. *bolwerc,* bulwark < MHG.]

boy•cott¹ /boi′ kŏt′/ *v.* to abstain from using,
buying, or dealing with to express protest or to
coerce. [after Charles C. *Boycott* (1832–1897).]

boy•cott² /boi′ kŏt′/ *n.* the act or an instance of
boycotting.

bril•liant /brĭl′ yənt/ *adj.* **a.** full of light; shining. **b.** superb; wonderful. **c.** marked by extraordinary powers of intellect or invention. [Fr. *brillant*, pr.part of *briller*, to shine < Ital. *brillare*, perh. < *brillo*, beryl < Lat. *beryllus*.]

brusque /brŭsk/ *adj.* abrupt and curt in manner or speech, often to the point of rudenes; blunt. [Fr. < Ital. *brusco*.]

budg•et¹ /bŭj′ ĭt/ *n.* **a.** an itemized summary of probable expenditures and income for a given period. **b.** the total sum of money allocated for a particular purpose or time period.

budg•et² /bŭj′ ĭt/ *v.* to plan in advance the expenditure of (money, for example).

bun•ga•low /bŭng′ gə lō′/ *n.* a small cottage, usually of one story. [Hindi *banglā* < *Bengal*, a region in eastern India and Bangladesh.]

bungalow

bu•reauc•ra•cy /byoŏ rŏk′ rə sē/ *n.*(**-cies** *pl.*) **a.1.** administration of a government chiefly through bureaus staffed with nonelective officials. **a.2.** the departments and their officials as a group. **b.** an administrative system in which the need to follow complex procedures impedes effective action. [Fr. *bureaucratie*: *bureau*, office + Gk. *-kratia*, rule < *kratos*, strength.]

ca•lam•i•ty /kə lăm′ ĭ tē/ *n.* (**-ties** *pl.*) an extraordinarily serious event marked by terrible loss, lasting distress, and affliction.

cal•cu•lus /kăl′ kyə ləs/ *n. Math.* a method of analysis or calculation using a special symbolic notation.

cal•lig•ra•phy /kə lĭg′ rə fē/ *n.* **a.** the art of fine handwriting. **b.** penmanship; handwriting.

cam•paign /kăm pān′/ *n.* **a.** a series of military operations undertaken to achieve a specific objective within a given area. **b.** an operation undertaken, as by means of propaganda, to attain some political, social, or commercial goal. [Fr. *campagne* < OFr., battlefield < OItal. *campagna* < LLat. *compania*, open country < *campus*, field.]

Pronunciation Key

ă	pat	ŏ	pot	th	**th**in
ā	pay	ō	toe	*th*	**th**is
âr	c**ar**e	ô	p**aw, for**	hw	**wh**ich
ä	f**a**ther	oi	n**oi**se	zh	vi**s**ion
ĕ	pet	ou	**ou**t	ə	**a**bout,
ē	be	oŏ	t**oo**k		**i**tem,
ĭ	pit	ōō	b**oo**t		penc**i**l,
ī	pie	ŭ	c**u**t		gall**o**p,
îr	p**ier**	ûr	**ur**ge		circ**u**s

can•vas /kăn′ vəs/ *n.* **a.** a heavy, coarse, closely woven fabric of cotton, hemp, or flax, used for making tents and sails. **b.** a piece of canvas on which a painting is made, especially an oil painting.

can•vass /kăn′ vəs/ *v.* **a.** to examine carefully or discuss thoroughly; scrutinize. **b.1.** to go through (a region) or go to (persons) to solicit votes, orders, or subscriptions. **b.2.** to conduct a survey of (public opinion) on a given subject; poll.

ca•pa•bil•i•ty /kā′ pə bĭl′ ĭ tē/ *n.*(**-ties** *pl.*) **a.** the quality or condition of being capable; ability. **b.** potential ability: *lived up to her capabilities.*

ca•per¹ /kā′ pər/ *v.* to leap or frisk about; frolic.

ca•per² /kā′ pər/ *n.* a wild escapade or prank.

cap•il•lar•y¹ /kăp′ ə lĕr ē/ *adj.* **a.** having a very small internal diameter, as a tube. **b.** *Anat.* in, of, or pertaining to the capillaries.

cap•il•lar•y² /kăp′ ə lĕr ē/ *n.* (**-ies** *pl.*) *Anat.* one of the minute blood vessels that connect the arteries and veins.

car•di•ac /kär′ dē ăk′/ *adj.* of, near, or pertaining to the heart.

car•pet•ing /kär′ pĭt ĭng/ *n.* material or fabric used for carpets.

ca•tas•tro•phe /kə tăs′ trə fē/ *n.* (**cat•a•stroph•ic** *adj.*) **a.** a great and sudden calamity; disaster. **b.** a sudden violent change in the earth's surface; cataclysm.

273

Spelling Dictionary

cat•e•go•ry /kăt′ ĭ gôr′ē, -gōr′ē/ *n.* (-**ries** *pl.*) a specifically defined division in a system of classification; class.

ca•the•dral /kə thē′ drəl/ *n.* a large or important church.

ce•les•tial /sə lĕs′ chəl/ *adj.* of or pertaining to the sky or the heavens: *Planets are celestial bodies.*

cen•trif•u•gal /sĕn trĭf′ yə gəl, -trĭf′ ə-/ *adj.* moving or directed away from a center or axis.

cha•os /kā′ ŏs′/ *n.* a condition or place of total disorder or confusion.

char•i•ot /chăr′ ē ət/ *n.* an ancient horse-drawn two-wheeled vehicle used in war, races, and processions.

chem•is•try /kĕm′ ĭ strē/ *n.* (-**tries** *pl.*) the science of the composition, structure, properties, and reactions of matter, especially of atomic and molecular systems.

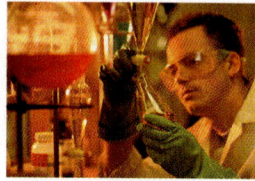
chemistry

chiv•al•ry /shĭv′ əl rē/ *n.* (-**ries** *pl.*) **a.** the medieval institution of knighthood. **b.** the qualities idealized by knighthood, such as bravery, courtesy, honor, and devotion to the weak.

chlo•ro•phyll /klôr′ ə fĭl, klōr′-/ *n.* any of a group of related green pigments found in photosynthetic organisms.

cir•cuit /sûr′ kĭt/ *n.* **a.** a closed, usually circular curve. **b.** a regular or accustomed course from place to place, as that of a salesman; round. **c.** an association of teams, clubs, or arenas of competition. [ME *circumference* < OFr. < Lat. *circuitus,* a going around < *circumire,* to go around: *circum,* around + *ire,* to go.]

cir•cu•late /sûr′ kyə lāt′/ *v.* (-**lates, -lat•ed, -lat•ing**) (**cir•cu•la•tor•y** *adj.*) **a.** to move in or flow through a circle or circuit. **b.** to move around as from person to person or place to place. **c.** to move about or flow freely. [Lat. *circulare, circulat-,* to make round < *circulus,* dim. of *circus,* circle.]

cir•cu•la•tion /sûr′ kyə lā′ shən/ *n.* **a.** movement in a circle or circuit. **b.** the movement of blood through bodily vessels as a result of the heart's pumping action. [Lat. *circulare, circulat-,* to make round < *circulus,* dim. of *circus,* circle.]

circum- a prefix meaning around or on all sides: *circumnavigate.*

cir•cum•nav•i•gate /sûr′ kəm năv′ ĭ gāt′/ *v.* (-**gates, -gat•ed, -gat•ing**) to sail completely around. [Lat. *circum,* around (< *circus,* circle) + *navigare, navigat-* to navigate: *navis,* ship + *agere,* to direct.]

cir•cum•stance /sûr′ kəm stăns′/ *n.* a condition or fact attending an event and having some bearing upon it; a determining or modifying factor. [ME < OFr. < Lat. *circumstantia* < *circumstare,* to stand around: *circum-,* around (< Lat. *circus,* circle) + *stare,* to stand.]

cir•cum•stan•tial /sûr′ kəm stăn′ shəl/ *adj.* **a.** of, pertaining to, or dependent upon circumstances. **b.** of no primary significance; incidental.

cir•cum•vent /sûr′ kəm vĕnt′/ *v.* to overcome by artful maneuvering. [Lat. *circumvenire, circumvent-: circum-,* around (< *circus,* circle) + *venire,* to come.]

civ•ic /sĭv′ ĭk/ *adj.* of, pertaining to, or belonging to a city, a citizen, or citizenship; municipal or civil. [Lat. *civicus* < *civis,* citizen.]

civ•i•li•za•tion /sĭv′ ə lĭ zā′ shən/ *n.* **a.** an advanced stage of development in the arts and sciences accompanied by corresponding social, political, and cultural complexity. **b.** the type of culture and society developed by a particular nation or region or in a particular epoch: *the civilization of ancient Rome.* [ME < Lat. *civilis* < *civis,* citizen.]

clas•si•fi•ca•tion /klăs′ ə fĭ kā′ shən/ *n. Biol.* the systematic grouping of organisms into categories based on shared characteristics or traits.

cli•ché /klē shā′/ *n.* a trite or overused expression or idea.

clo•sure /klō′ zhər/ *n.* **a.** a finish; conclusion. **b.** the property of being mathematically closed.

co•ef•fi•cient /kō′ ə fĭsh′ ənt/ *n. Math.* a numerical factor of an elementary algebraic term, as 4 in the term 4X.

co•in•ci•dence /kō ĭn′ sĭ dəns, -dĕns′/ *n.* a sequence of events that although accidental seems to have been planned or arranged.

col•i•se•um /kŏl´ĭ sē´ əm/ *n.* a large amphitheater for public entertainment or assemblies.

col•lo•qui•al /kə lō´ kwē əl/ *adj.* characteristic of or appropriate to the spoken language or to writing that seeks the effect of speech; informal.

com- a prefix meaning together, with, joint, or jointly: *compress.* Before **l** or **r, com-** becomes **col-** or **cor-.** Before vowels, **h,** or **gn,** it is reduced to **co-.** Before all other consonants except **p, b,** or **m,** it becomes **con-.**

com•mend /kə mĕnd´/ *v.* (**com•mend•a•ble** *adj.*) **a.** to represent as worthy, qualified, or desirable; recommend. **b.** to express approval of; praise.

com•mit /kə mĭt´/ *v.* (**-mits, -mit•ted, -mit•ting**) to do, perform, or perpetrate.

com•mit•tee /kə mĭt´ ē/ *n.* a group of people officially delegated to perform a function, as investigating, considering, reporting, or acting on a matter.

com•mon•place /kŏm´ ən plās´/ *adj.* not remarkable; ordinary.

com•pe•tence /kŏm´ pĭ təns/ *n.* the state or quality of being competent.

com•pe•tent /kŏm´ pĭ tənt/ *adj.* **a.** properly or well qualified; capable: *a competent worker.* **b.** adequate for the purpose; sufficient: *a competent performance.*

com•ple•men•ta•ry /kŏm´ plə mĕn´ tə rē, -trē-/ *adj.* **a.** forming or serving as a complement; completing. **b.** supplying mutual needs or lacks. **c. complementary angles** *pl. n.* two angles whose sum is 90 degrees.

com•pli•ment /kŏm´ plə mənt/ *n.* an expression of praise, admiration, or respect.

com•pli•men•ta•ry /kŏm´ plə mĕn´ tə rē, -trē-/ *adj.* expressing, using, or resembling a compliment.

com•press /kəm prĕs´/ *v.* **a.** to press or squeeze together. **b.** to shorten or condense as if by pressing or squeezing.

compress

com•pro•mise[1] /kŏm´ prə mīz´/ *n.* **a.** a settlement of differences in which each side makes concessions. **b.** something resulting from such a settlement.

com•pro•mise[2] /kŏm´ prə mīz´/ *v.* to settle by concessions.

con•cede /kən sēd´/ *v.* (**-cedes, -ced•ed, -ced•ing**) **a.** to acknowledge as true, just, or proper, often unwillingly; admit: *conceding defeat.* **b.** to yield or grant as a privilege or right [Fr. *concéder* < Lat. *concedere: com-* (intensive) + *cedere,* to yield.]

con•cept /kŏn´ sĕpt´/ *n.* **a.** a general idea or understanding, especially one derived from specific instances or occurrences. **b.** a thought or notion.

con•cer•to /kən chĕr´ tō/ *n.* a composition for an orchestra and one or more solo instruments, typically in three movements.

con•ces•sion /kən sĕsh´ ən/ *n.* **a.** the act of conceding. **b.** something conceded.

con•cise /kən sīs´/ *adj.* expressing much in few words; clear and succinct.

con•fi•dence /kŏn´ fĭ dəns/ *n.* **a.** trust or reliance. **b.** a feeling of assurance, especially of self-assurance.

con•fi•dent /kŏn´ fĭ dənt/ *adj.* (**con•fi•dent•ly** *adv.*) **a.** marked by assurance, as of success. **b.** marked by confidence in oneself; self-assured.

con•fi•den•tial /kŏn´ fĭ dĕn´ shəl/ *adj.* (**con•fi•den•tial•ly** *adv.*) **a.** done or communicated in confidence; secret. **b.** entrusted with the confidence of another: *a confidential secretary.* **c.** denoting confidence or intimacy: *a confidential tone of voice.*

con•form /kən fôrm′/ *v.* **a.** to correspond in form or character; be similar. **b.** to act or be in compliance; comply. **c.** to act in accordance with current customs or modes.

con•grat•u•late /kən grăch′ ə lāt′/ *v.* (**-lates, -lat•ed, -lat•ing**) to express joy or acknowledgment for the achievement or good fortune of. [Lat. *congratulari, congratulat-: com-,* with + *gratulari,* to rejoice < *gratus,* pleasing.]

con•grat•u•la•tion /kən grăch′ə lā′ shən/ *n.* **a.** the act of congratulating. **b.** often **congratulations**. an expression of joy or acknowledgment for the achievement or good fortune of another.

con•gress /kŏng′ grĭs/ *n.* (**con•gres•sion•al** *adj.*) **a.** a formal assembly of representatives, as of various nations, to discuss problems. **b.** the national legislative bodies of certain nations, especially of republics. **c.** *Congress.* **1.** the national legislative body of the United States, consisting of the Senate and the House of Representatives. **c.2.** the two-year session of this legislature between elections of the House of Representatives.

con•i•fer /kŏn′ ə fər, kō′ nə-/ *n.* any of various predominantly evergreen cone-bearing trees, such as a pine, spruce, hemlock, or fir.

con•junc•tion /kən jŭngk′ shən/ *n.* **a.1.** the act of joining. **a.2.** the state of being joined. **b.** *Gram.* in some languages, one of the parts of speech comprising words such as, in English, *and, but, because,* and *as,* that connect other words, phrases, clauses, or sentences.

con•se•quence /kŏn′ sĭ kwěns′, -kwəns/ *n.* **a.** something that logically or naturally follows from an action or condition; effect. **b.** a logical result or inference.

con•ser•va•tive[1] /kən sûr′ və tĭv/ *adj.* **a.1.** tending to oppose change; favoring traditional views and values. **a.2.** traditional in style; not showy: *a conservative dark suit.* **b.** moderate; cautious; restrained: *a conservative estimate.* **c.** belonging to a conservative party or political group.

con•ser•va•tive[2] /kən sûr′ və tĭv/ *n.* **a.** a person who favors traditional views and values. **b.** a person who supports political conservatism.

con•stit•u•ent[1] /kən stĭch′ ōō ənt/ *adj.* **a.** serving as part of a whole; component. **b.** empowered to elect or designate.

con•stit•u•ent[2] /kən stĭch′ ōō ənt/ *n.* **a.** someone who authorizes another to represent him; client. **b.** a member of a group represented by an elected official.

con•struc•tion /kən strŭk′ shən/ *n.* **a.** the act or process of constructing. **b.** the condition of being constructed. **c.** the business or work of building.

construction

con•sul /kŏn′ səl/ *n.* an official appointed by a government to reside in a foreign city and represent his or her government's commercial interests and give assistance to its citizens there.

con•sum•er /kən sōō′ mər/ *n.* one who acquires goods or services; buyer [ME *consumen,* to consume < Lat. *consumere: com-* (intensive) + *sumere,* to take.]

con•tem•po•rar•y[1] /kən těm′ pə rěr′ē/ *adj.* **a.** belonging to the same period of time. **b.** current; modern: *contemporary trends in design.*

con•tem•po•rar•y[2] /kən těm′ pə rěr′ē/ *n.* (**-ies** *pl.*) **a.** one of the same time or age. **b.** a person of the present age; a modern.

con•tin•u•al /kən tĭn′ yōō əl/ *adj.* (**con•tin•u•al•ly** *adv.*) **a.** repeated regularly and frequently: *the continual banging of the shutters.* **b.** not interrupted or broken; steady: *continual noise.*

con•tin•u•ous /kən tĭn′ yōō əs/ *adj.* (**con•tin•u•ous•ly** *adv.*) extending or prolonged without interruption or cessation; unceasing.

con•tra•dict /kŏn′ trə dĭkt′/ *v.* **a.** to assert or express the opposite of (a statement). **b.** to deny the statement of. [Lat. *contradicere, contradict-,* to speak against: *contra-,* against + *dicere,* to speak.]

con•tra•dic•tion /kŏn′ trə dĭk′ shən/ *n.* **a.** a denial. **b.** inconsistency or discrepancy. **c.** something that contains contradictory elements.

con•trar•y /kŏn′ trĕr′ē/ *adj.* **a.** opposed, as in character or purpose; completely different. **b.** opposite in direction or position.

con•trol[1] /kən trōl′/ *v.* (**-trols, -trolled, -trol•ing**) **a.** to exercise authority or dominating influence over; direct regulate. **b.** to hold in restraint; check.

con•trol[2] /kən trōl′/ *n.* authority or ability to regulate, direct, or dominate.

con•ven•ient /kən vēn′ yənt/ *adj.* **a.** suited or favorable to one's comfort, purpose, or needs. **b.** easy to reach; accessible.

con•ven•tion /kən věn′ shən/ *n.* a formal assembly or meeting of members, representatives, or delegates of a group, such as a political party or fraternal society.

con•ven•tion•al /kən věn′ shə nəl/ *adj.* **a.** developed, established, or approved by general usage; customary. **b.** conforming to established practice or accepted standards.

con•ver•sion /kən vûr′ zhən, -shən/ *n.* **a.1.** the act of converting. **a.2.** the state of being converted. **b.** something that is changed from one use, function, or purpose to another.

con•vinc•ing /kən vĭn′ sĭng/ *adj.* **a.** serving to convince: *a convincing argument.* **b.** believable; plausible.

co•op•er•a•tive /kō ŏp′ ə rə tĭv, -ŏp′ rə-, ə rā′ tĭv/ *adj.* **a.** done in cooperation with others: *a cooperative effort.* **b.** marked by willingness to cooperate: *a cooperative patient.*

co•pla•nar /kō plā′ nər/ *adj.* lying or occurring in the same plane.

cor•po•ra•tion /kôr′ pə rā′ shən/ *n.* **a.** a body of persons granted a charter legally recognizing them as a separate entity having its own rights, privileges, and liabilities distinct from those of its members. **b.** a group of people combined into or acting as one body.

cor•pus•cle /kôr′ pə səl, -pŭs′ əl/ *n.* **a.** a body cell, such as a red or white blood cell, that is capable of being moved about freely. **b.** a particle such as an electron or proton.

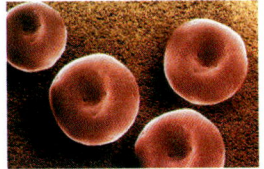

corpuscle

cor•re•la•tion /kôr′ ə lā′ shən, kŏr′-/ *n.* **a.** a relationship; systematic connection; correspondence. **b.** *Statistics.* **1.** the simultaneous increase in the value of one and decrease in the value of the other of two numerically valued random variables: *the negative correlation between age and normal vision.* **b.2.** the simultaneous increase or decrease in value of two numerically valued random variables: *the positive correlation between cigarette smoking and the incidence of lung cancer.*

cor•re•spond•ing /kôr′ ĭ spŏn′ dĭng, kŏr′-/ *adj.* **a.** agreeing or conforming, as in degree or kind. **b.** equivalent.

co•sine /kō′ sīn′/ *n.* in a right triangle, the function of an acute angle that is the ratio of the adjacent side to the hypotenuse.

cos•mo•pol•i•tan /kŏs′ mə pŏl′ ĭ tn/ *adj.* at home in all parts of the world or in many spheres of interest. [Gk. *kosmopolites, cosmopolite: kosmos,* world + *politēs,* citizen < *polis,* city.]

coun•ter•ex•am•ple /koun′ tər ĭg zăm′ pəl/ *n.* an example that refutes or disproves a hypothesis, proposition, or theorem.

coun•ter•feit¹ /koun′ tər fĭt′/ *v.* **a.** to make a copy of, usually with the intent to defraud; forge: *counterfeiting money.* **b.** to make a pretense of; feign: *counterfeited interest in the story.*

coun•ter•feit² /koun′ tər fĭt′/ *adj.* **a.** made in imitation of what is genuine with the intent to defraud: *a counterfeit dollar bill.* **b.** simulated; feigned: *a counterfeit illness.*

cre•dence /krēd′ əns/ *n.* **a.** acceptance as true or valid; belief. **b.** claim to acceptance; trustworthiness.

crim•i•nal¹ /krĭm′ ə nəl/ *adj.* of, involving, or having the nature of crime.

crim•i•nal² /krĭm′ ə nəl/ *n.* a person who has committed or been legally convicted of a crime.

cri•te•ri•on /krī tîr′ ē ən/ *n.*(-te•ri•a *pl.*) a standard, rule, or test on which a judgment or decision can be based. [Gk. *kriterion* < *krites,* judge < *krinein,* to separate.]

crit•i•cism /krĭt′ ĭ sĭz′ əm/ *n.* **a.** a critical comment or judgment. **b.1.** the art, skill, or profession of making discriminating judgments and evaluations, especially of literary or other artistic works. **b.2.** a review or other article expressing such judgment and evaluation.

cru•sade /kroo sād′/ *n.* **a.** a holy war undertaken with papal sanction. **b.** a vigorous concerted movement for a cause or against an abuse.

cul•ti•vate /kŭl′ tə vāt/ *v.* (**-vates, -vat•ed, -vat•ing**) **a.1.** to improve and prepare (land) as by plowing or fertilizing, for raising crops; till. **a.2.** to loosen or dig (soil) around growing plants. **b.** to grow or tend (a plant or crop).

cur•ric•u•lum /kə rĭk′ yə ləm/ *n.* (**-la** or **-lums** *pl.*) **a.** all the courses of study offered by an educational institution. **b.** a particular course of study, often in a special field.

da•ta /dā′ tə, dăt′ ə, dä′ tə/ *pl. n.* (*used with a sing. or pl. verb*). information, especially organized for analysis or used as the basis for a decision. [Lat., pl. of *datum*.]

da•tum /dā′ təm, dăt′ əm, dä′ təm/ *n.* (**-ta** *pl.*) an assumed, given, measured, or otherwise determined fact or proposition used to draw a conclusion or make a decision. [Lat., something given < p.part. of *dare*, to give.]

de- a prefix that means: **a.** do or make the opposite of: *decode.* **b.** remove from: *defrost.*

de•but /dā byoo′, dā′ byoo/ *n.* a first public appearance, as of an actor.

de•ceive /dĭ sēv′/ *v.* (**-ceives, -ceived, -ceiv•ing**) to cause (a person) to believe what is not true; mislead.

de•cel•er•ate /dē sĕl′ ə rāt/ *v.* (**-ates, -at•ed, -at•ing**) to decrease in velocity.

de•cid•u•ous /dĭ sĭj′ oo əs/ *adj.* **a.** falling off or shed at a specific season or stage of growth: *deciduous leaves.* **b.** shedding or losing foliage at the end of the growing season: *deciduous trees.*

deciduous

de•ci•pher /dĭ sī′ fər/ *v.* **a.** to read or interpret (something ambiguous, obscure, or illegible). **b.** to convert from a code or cipher to plain text; decode. [de + cipher < ME *cifre* < OFr. < Med. Lat. *cifra* < Ar. *sifr.*]

de•ci•sion-mak•ing /dĭ sĭzh′ ən mā′kĭng/ *n.* the act or process of reaching a conclusion, judgment, or verdict. *The students wanted to become involved in class decision-making.*

ded•i•cate /dĕd′ ĭ kāt/ *v.* (**-cates, -cat•ed, -cat•ing**) **a.** to set apart for a special use. **b.** to commit (oneself) to a particular course of thought or action. **c.** to address or inscribe (a literary work, for example) to someone as a mark of respect or affection.

ded•i•ca•tion /dĕd′ ĭ kā′ shən/ *n.* **a.** the act of dedicating or the state of being dedicated. **b.** a note prefixed to a literary, artistic, or musical composition dedicating it to someone in token of affection or esteem.

de•duce /dĭ doos′, -dyoos′/ *v.* (**-duc•es, -duced, -duc•ing**) **a.** to reach (a conclusion) by reasoning. **b.** to infer from a general principle; reason deductively. [ME *deducen* < Lat. *deducere*, to lead away: *de-*, away + *ducere*, to lead.]

de•duc•tive /dĭ dŭk′ tĭv/ *adj.* of or based on the method of logical reasoning known as deduction.

def•i•ni•tion /dĕf′ ə nĭsh′ ən/ *n.* **a.** the statement of the meaning of a work, phrase, or term. **b.** the act of making clear and distinct.

del•e•gate[1] /dĕl′ ĭ gāt, -gĭt/ *n.* **a.** a person authorized to act as representative for another; deputy or agent. **b.** a representative to a conference or convention.

del•e•gate[2] /dĕl′ ĭ gāt/ *v.* (**-gates, -gat•ed, -gat•ing**) **a.** to authorize and send (a person) as one's representative. **b.** to commit or entrust to another.

del•i•ca•tes•sen /dĕl′ ĭ kə tĕs′ ən/ *n.* a shop that sells cooked or prepared foods ready for serving. [G. *Delikatessen*, pl. of *Delkatesse*, delicacy.]

de•moc•ra•cy /dĭ mŏk′ rə sē/ *n.* (**-cies** *pl.*) **a.** government by the people, exercised either directly or through elected representatives. **b.** a political or social unit based upon democratic rule. [OFr. *democratie* < LLat. *democratia* < Gk. *dēmokratia*: *dēmos*, people + *kratia*, -cracy.]

dem•o•crat /dĕm′ ə krăt′/ *n.* **a.** an advocate of democracy. **b. Democrat.** a member of the Democratic Party. [OFr. *democrate < democratie: dēmos*, people + *kratia*, -cracy.]

de•mog•ra•phy /dĭ mŏg′ rə fē/ *n.* the study of the characteristics of human populations, as size, growth, density, distribution, and vital statistics. [Fr. *démographie:* Gk. *dēmos*, people + Fr. *-graphie*, -graphy.]

de•pend /dĭ pĕnd′/ *v.* **a.** to rely, as for support or aid. **b.** to be assured; place trust. [ME *dependen*, to hang down < OFr. *dependre* < Lat. *dependēre: de-*, down + *pendēre*, to hang.]

de•pend•ent[1] /dĭ pĕn′ dənt/ *adj.* **a.** contingent upon something or someone else. **b.** relying on or requiring the aid of another for support.

de•pend•ent[2] /dĭ pĕn′ dənt/ *n.* one who relies on another for support.

de•rive /dĭ rīv′/ *v.* (-rives, -rived, -riv•ing) **a.** to obtain or receive from a source. **b.** to arrive at by reasoning; deduce or infer: *derive a conclusion from facts.*

de•scend /dĭ sĕnd′/ *v.* **a.** to move from a higher to a lower place. **b.** to slope, extend, or incline downward. **c.** to come down from a source; derive.

de•scent /dĭ sĕnt′/ *n.* **a.** the act or an instance of descending. **b.** a downward incline or passage; slope. **c.** hereditary derivation; lineage: *of Native American descent.*

de•scribe /dĭ scrīb′/ *v.* (-scribes, -scribed, -scrib•ing) **a.** to give a verbal account of. **b.** to transmit a mental image or impression of with words.

de•scrip•tion /dĭ skrĭp′ shən/ *n.* **a.** the act, process, or technique of describing. **b.** a statement or account describing something. [ME *descripcioun* < OFr. *description* < Lat. *descriptio < descriptus*, p.part. of *describere*, to delineate: *de-*, down + *scribere*, to write.]

de•struc•tion /dĭ strŭk′ shən/ *n.* **a.** the act of destroying. **b.** heavy damage.

de•struc•tive /dĭ strŭk′ tĭv/ *adj.* causing or wreaking destruction; ruinous.

di•ag•nose /dī′ əg nōs′, -nōz′/ *v.* (-nos•es, -nosed, -nos•ing) to distinguish or identify (a disease, for example).

di•a•logue /dī′ ə lôg′, -lŏg′/ *n.* **a.** a conversation between two or more people. **b.** a conversational passage in a play or narrative. **c.** an exchange of ideas or opinions. [ME < OFr. < Lat. *dialogus* < Gk. *dialogos < dialegesthai*, to discuss: *dia-*, between + *legesthai*, to speak < *legein*, to tell.]

dic•tate[1] /dĭk′ tāt′, dĭk tāt′/ *v.* (-tates, -tat•ed, -tat•ing) **a.** to say or read aloud material to be recorded or written by another. **b.** to issue orders or commands. [Lat. *dictare, dictat-*, freq. of *dicere*, to say.]

dic•tate[2] /dĭk′ tāt′/ *n.* a directive or command.

dic•ta•tor /dĭk′ tā′ tər, dĭk tā′-/ *n.* a ruler having absolute authority and supreme jurisdiction over the government of a state.

dic•tion /dĭk′ shən/ *n.* **a.** choice and use of words in speech or writing. **b.** degree of clarity and distinctness of pronunciation in speech or singing; enunciation. [Lat. *dictio < dictus*, p.part. of *dicere*, to say.]

dig•it /dĭj′ ĭt/ *n.* **a.** a finger or a toe. **b.** any one of the ten Arabic number symbols, 0 through 9.

dig•i•tal /dĭj′ ĭ tl/ *adj.* **a.** of, relating to, or resembling a digit, especially a finger. **b.** expressed in digits, especially for use by a computer.

digital

di•lem•ma /dĭ lĕm′ ə/ *n.* **a.** a situation that requires one to choose between two equally balanced alternatives. **b.** a predicament that seemingly defies a satisfactory solution. [Lat. < Gk. *dilemma*, ambiguous proposition: *di-*, two + *lemma*, proposition.]

Spelling Dictionary

di•plo•ma•cy /dĭ **plō′** mə sē/ *n.* (**-cies** *pl.*)
a. the art or practice of conducting international
relations, as in negotiating alliances, treaties,
and agreements. **b.** tact in dealing with people.

dip•lo•mat•ic /dĭp′lə **măt′** ĭk/ *adj.* **a.** of, pertaining to, or involving diplomacy. **b.** characterized by tact and sensitivity in dealing with people.

dis- a prefix meaning: **a.** not: *dissimilar.* **b.1.**
absence of: *disinterest.* **b.2.** opposite of: *disfavor*
c. undo: do the opposite of: *disarrange.*

dis•ap•pear /dĭs′ə **pîr′**/ *v.* (**dis•ap•pear•ance**
n.) **a.** to pass out of sight; vanish. **b.** to cease to
exist. [dis + ME *aperen* < OFr. *aparoir* < Lat.
apparēre: *ad-*, to + *parēre*, to show.]

dis•ap•prove /dĭs′ə **prōōv′**/ *v.* (**-proves,**
-proved, -prov•ing) **a.** to have an unfavorable
opinion of; condemn. **b.** to refuse to approve;
reject. [dis + approve < ME *approven* < OFr.
aprover < Lat. *approbare*: *ad-*, to + *probare*, to
test < *probus*, good.]

dis•ci•pline[1] /dĭs′ə plĭn/ *n.* **a.** training that is
expected to produce a specific character or
pattern of behavior, especially training that
produces moral or mental improvement. **b.** controlled behavior resulting from disciplinary training. **c.** a branch of knowledge or of teaching.

dis•ci•pline[2] /dĭs′ə plĭn/ *v.* (**-plines, -plined,**
-plin•ing) **a.** to train by instruction and control.
b. to punish or penalize.

dis•crep•an•cy /dĭ **skrĕp′** ən sē/ *n.* (**-cies** *pl.*)
divergence or disagreement, as between facts or
claims; inconsistency.

dis•in•fec•tant[1] /dĭs′ĭn **fĕk′** tənt/ *n.* an agent
that disinfects by destroying, neutralizing, or
inhibiting the growth of harmful microorganisms.

dis•in•fec•tant[2] /dĭs′ĭn **fĕk′** tənt/ *adj.* serving
to disinfect.

dis•lo•cate /dĭs′ lō kāt′, dĭs lō′ kāt′/ *v.* (**-cates,**
-cat•ed, -cat•ing) **a.** to throw into disorder;
upset. **b.** *Pathol.* to move (a limb or organ) from
the normal position, especially to displace (a
bone) from the socket or joint. [ME *dislocare,*
dislocat-: Lat. *dis-* (reversal) + Lat. *locare*, to
place < *locus*, place.]

dis•mal /dĭz′ məl/ *adj.* **a.** causing gloom or
depression; dreary. **b.** characterized by lack
of hope.

dis•pos•a•ble /dĭ **spō′** zə bəl/ *adj.* designed to
be disposed of after use.

dis•pos•al /dĭ **spō′** zəl/ *n.* **a.** an act of throwing
out or away. **b.** an apparatus or device for dispos-
ing of something, as
garbage. **c.** the liberty
or power to dispose of
or use: *funds at our
disposal.* [ME *disposen,*
OFr. *disposer* < Lat.
disponere, to arrange: *dis-*,
apart + *ponere*, to put.]

disposal

dis•sent[1] /dĭ **sĕnt′**/ *v.* to differ in opinion or feeling; disagree.

dis•sent[2] /dĭ **sĕnt′**/ *n.* difference of opinion or
feeling; disagreement.

dis•sim•i•lar /dĭ **sĭm′** ə lər/ *adj.* unlike;
different.

dis•solve[1] /dĭ **zŏlv′**/ *v.* (**-solves, -solved, -solv•ing**)
a. to cause to pass into solution: *dissolve sugar
in water.* **b.** to bring to an end by or as if by
breaking up; terminate. **c.** to dismiss (a meeting
or parliament, for example). **d.** to shift scenes in
a motion-picture film or videotape by having one
scene fade out while the next appears behind it
and grows clearer as the first dims.

dis•solve[2] /dĭ **zŏlv′**/ *n.* a scene transition in
a motion-picture film or videotape made
by dissolving.

dis•tinct /dĭ **stĭngkt′**/ *adj.* **a.** distinguishable
from all others; separate: *on two distinct occasions.* **b.** easily perceived by the senses or intellect; clear: *a distinct flavor.*

doc•ile /dŏs′ əl/ *adj.* **a.** easily taught; teachable.
b. submissive to training or management;
tractable. [Lat. *docilis* < *docēre*, to teach.]

doc•trine /dŏk′ trĭn/ *n.* **a.** a principle or body of
principles presented for acceptance or belief, as
by a religious, political, scientific, or philo-
sophic group; dogma. **b.** a rule or principle of
law, especially when established by precedent.
[ME < OFr. < Lat. *doctrina*, teaching, learning
< *doctor,* teacher < *docēre*, to teach.]

doc•u•men•ta•ry[1] /dŏk′ yə **mĕn′** tə rē/ *adj.*
a. consisting of, concerning, or based upon documents. **b.** presenting facts objectively without
editorializing or inserting fictional matter, as in
a book or film.

doc•u•men•ta•ry[2] /dŏkʹ yə mĕnʹ tə rē/ *n.* (**-ries** *pl.*) a television or motion-picture presentation of factual, political, social, or historical events or circumstances, often consisting of actual news films accompanied by narration. [ME, precept < OFr. < Lat. *documentum,* lesson < *docēre,* to teach.]

dom•i•nant /dŏmʹ ə nənt/ *adj.* **a.** exercising the most influence or control; governing. **b.** most prominent. [OFr. < Lat. *dominans,* pr.part. of *dominare,* to dominate.]

dom•i•nate /dŏmʹ ə nātʹ/ *v.* (**-nates, -nat•ed, -nat•ing**) **a.** to control, govern, or rule by superior authority or power. **b.** to be dominant in position or authority. [Lat. *dominari,* to rule < *dominus,* lord.]

dom•i•neer /dŏmʹ ə nîrʹ/ *v.* to rule over arbitrarily or arrogantly; tyrannize. [Du. *domineren* < Fr. *dominer* < Lat. *dominari,* to dominate.]

drain•age /drāʹ nĭj/ *n.* the action or a given method of draining.

ec•cen•tric[1] /ĭk sĕnʹ trĭk/ *adj.* departing or deviating from the conventional or established norm; odd or unusual in appearance, behavior, etc.; strange, peculiar.

ec•cen•tric[2] /ĭk sĕnʹ trĭk/ *n.* an eccentric person.

e•con•o•mize /ĭ kŏnʹ ə mīzʹ/ *v.* (**-miz•es, -mized, -miz•ing**) to be thrifty; practice economy.

-eer a suffix meaning someone who works, makes, is involved in, etc.: *auctioneer.*

ef•fi•cien•cy /ĭ fĭshʹ ən sē/ *n.* (**-cies** *pl.*) the quality or property of being efficient.

ef•fi•cient /ĭ fĭshʹ ənt/ *adj.* acting or producing effectively with a minimum of waste, expense, or effort.

E•gyp•tian /ĭ jĭpʹ shən/ *n.* (**E•gyp•tian** *adj.*) a native or citizen of Egypt.

Pronunciation Key

ă	pat	ŏ	pot	th	**th**in
ā	pay	ō	toe	*th*	**th**is
âr	care	ô	paw, for	hw	**wh**ich
ä	father	oi	noise	zh	vision
ĕ	pet	ou	out	ə	about,
ē	be	ŏŏ	took		item,
ĭ	pit	ōō	boot		pencil,
ī	pie	ŭ	cut		gallop,
îr	pier	ûr	urge		circus

e•lab•o•rate /ĭ lăbʹ ə rātʹ/ *v.* (**-rates, -rat•ed, -rat•ing**) **a.** to work out with care and detail; develop thoroughly. **b.** to produce by effort; create. **c.** to express at greater length or in greater detail.

e•late /ĭ lātʹ/ *v.* (**-lates, -lat•ed, -lat•ing**) to excite pride or joy in. [Lat. *effere, elat-,* to carry out: *ex-,* out + *ferre,* to carry.]

e•lat•ed /ĭ lāʹ tĭd/ *adj.* exultant; joyful.

e•la•tion /ĭ lāʹ shən/ *n.* gladness; high spirits; feeling of great pride or joy. *The fans showed their elation by cheering and waving banners.*

e•lec•tri•cal /ĭ lĕkʹ trĭ kəl/ *adj.* of, pertaining to, or operated by electricity.

e•lec•tron•ic /ĭ lĕk trŏnʹ ĭk, ēʹ lĕk-/ *adj.* **a.** of or pertaining to electrons. **b.** of, pertaining to, based on, operated by, or otherwise involving the controlled conduction of electrons or other charge carriers, especially in a vacuum, gas, or semiconducting material. **c.** of or pertaining to electronics.

electronic

el•e•men•ta•ry /ĕlʹ ə mĕnʹ tə rē, -trē/ *adj.* **a.** fundamental, essential, or irreducible. **b.** of, involving, or introducing the fundamental or simplest aspects of a subject: *an elementary problem.* **c.** of or relating to an elementary school: *the elementary grades.*

em•bas•sy /ĕmʹ bə sē/ *n.* (**-sies** *pl.*) **a.** a mission to a foreign government headed by an ambassador. **b.** the official headquarters of an ambassador and his or her staff.

em•i•grant[1] /ĕmʹ ĭ grənt/ *n.* one who emigrates.

em•i•grant[2] /ĕmʹ ĭ grənt/ *adj.* of or pertaining to emigration or emigrants.

em•i•grate /ĕm' ĭ grāt'/ *v.* (**-grates, -grat•ed, -grat•ing**) to leave a native country or region to settle in another. [Lat. *emigrare, emigrat-: ex-,* away + *migrare,* to move.]

em•i•nent /ĕm' ə nənt/ *adj.* outstanding in performance, rank, or attainments; distinguished. [ME < OFr. or < Lat. *eminens,* pr.part. of *eminere,* to project.]

em•pha•sis /ĕm' fə sĭs/ *n.* (**-ses** /-sēz'/ *pl.*) **a.** special weight or importance placed upon something. **b.** stress applied, as to a syllable or word.

em•pha•size /ĕm' fə sīz'/ *v.* (**-siz•es, -sized, -siz•ing**) to give emphasis to; stress.

em•ploy /ĕm ploi'/ *v.* (**em•ploy•er** *n.*) to engage the services of; put to work.

en- a prefix that forms verbs: *endanger.* When **en-** is followed by **b, m,** or **p,** it becomes **em-.**

en•act /ĕn ăkt'/ *v.* **a.** to make (a bill, for example) into law. **b.** to act out, as on a stage; represent.

-ence a suffix that forms nouns from verbs: *reference.*

en•deav•or[1] /ĕn dĕv' ər/ *n.* a conscientious or concerted effort toward a given end; an earnest attempt. [ME *endevour* < *endeveren,* to make an effort: *en-,* en- + *dever,* duty < OFr. *devoir,* duty.]

en•deav•or[2] /ĕn dĕv' ər/ *v.* to make an earnest attempt.

en•sem•ble /ŏn sŏm' bəl/ *n.* a unit or group of complementary parts that contribute to a single effect, especially: **a.** a coordinated outfit or costume. **b.** a group of supporting musicians, singers, dancers, or actors who perform together. [Fr. < LLat. *insimul,* at the same time: *in,* in + *simulo,* at the same time.]

ensemble

-ent a suffix that forms adjectives and nouns: *effervescent; resident*

en•ter•prise /ĕn' tər prīz'/ *n.* **a.** an undertaking, especially one of some scope, complication, and risk. **b.** a business organization. **c.** readiness to venture; initiative.

en•tire•ly /ĕn tīr' lē/ *adv.* wholly; completely.

en•tre•pre•neur /ŏn trə prə nûr'/ *n.* a person who organizes, operates, and assumes the risk for a business venture.

en•vi•sion /ĕn vĭzh' ən/ *v.* to picture in the mind.

ep•ic /ĕp' ĭk/ *n.* **a.** an extended narrative poem in elevated or dignified language, celebrating the feats of a legendary or traditional hero. **b.** a series of events considered appropriate to an epic. **–modifier:** *an epic poem.*

ep•i•dem•ic[1] /ĕp' ĭ dĕm' ĭk/ *adj.* **a.** spreading rapidly and extensively by infection among many individuals in an area. **b.** widely prevalent.

ep•i•dem•ic[2] /ĕp' ĭ dĕm' ĭk/ *n.* **a.** an outbreak of contagious disease that spreads rapidly. **b.** a rapid spread, growth, or development. [Fr. *épidemique* < *épidémie,* an epidemic < OFr. *espydymie* < LLat. *epidemia* < Gk. *epidēmia* < *epidēmos,* prevalent: *epi-,* on + *dēmos,* people.]

ep•i•logue /ĕp' ə lôg, -lŏg'/ *n.* **a.** a short poem or speech spoken directly to the audience following the conclusion of a play. **b.** a short addition or concluding section at the end of literary work, often dealing with the future of its characters. [ME *epiloge* < OFr. *epilogue* < Lat. *epilogus* < Gk. *epilogos* < *epilegein,* to say more: *epi-,* in addition to + *legein,* to say.]

e•qual[1] /ē' kwəl/ *adj.* having the same quantity, measure, or value as another. [Lat. *aequalis* < *aequus,* even.]

e•qual[2] /ē' kwəl/ *v.* to be equal to, especially in value.

e•qual•i•ty /ĭ kwŏl' ĭ tē/ *n.* (**-ties** *pl.*) the state or quality of being equal. [ME *equalite* < OFr. *equalite* < Lat. *aequalitas* < *aequalis,* even.]

e•quate /ĭ kwāt'/ *v.* (**-quates, -quat•ed, -quat•ing**) **a.** to consider, treat, or depict as equal or equivalent. **b.** to be or seem to be equal; correspond. [ME *equaten* < Lat. *aequare* < *aequus,* even.]

e•qua•tion /ĭ kwā' zhən, -shən/ *n. Math.* a statement that two expressions are equal. (For example, 3 + 2 = 5.)

equi- a prefix meaning equal or equally: *equiangular*. [ME < Lat. *aequi* < *aequus*, equal, even.]

e•qui•lib•ri•um /ē′ kwə lĭb′ rē əm, ĕk′ wə-/ *n.* (**-ri•ums** or **-ri•a** *pl.*) **a.** a condition in which all acting influences are canceled by others, resulting in a stable, balanced, or unchanging system. **b.** mental or emotional balance; poise. [Lat. *aequilibrium: aequus*, equal + *libra*, balance.]

eq•ui•ta•ble /ĕk′ wĭ tə bəl/ *adj.* exhibiting or characterized by equity; impartial or reasonable in judgment or treatment. [Fr. *équitable* < OFr. < *équité*, equity < Lat. *aequitas* < *aequus*, even, fair.]

eq•ui•ty /ĕk′ wĭ tē/ *n.* (**-ties** *pl.*) the state, ideal, or quality of being just, impartial, and fair. [ME *equite* < OFr. < Lat. *aequitas* < *aequus*, even, fair.]

e•quiv•o•cal /ĭ kwĭv′ ə kəl/ *adj.* **a.** capable of two or more interpretations and often intended to mislead. **b.** of uncertain significance. [LLat. *aequivocus: aequus*, equal + *vocare*, to call.]

es•cape¹ /ĭ skāp′/ *v.* (**-capes,** **-caped, -cap•ing**) **a.** to break loose from confinement; get free. **b.** to issue from confinement or an enclosure; leak or seep out. **c.** to avoid capture, danger, or harm.

escape

es•cape² /ĭ skāp′/ *n.* **a.** the act or an instance of escaping. **b.** a means of obtaining temporary freedom from worry, care, or unpleasantness.

es•sence /ĕs′ əns/ *n.* **a.** the quality or qualities of a thing that give it its identity. **b.** the most important ingredient; crucial element. [ME *essencia* < Lat. *essentia* < *esse*, to be.]

es•sen•tial¹ /ĭ sĕn′ shəl/ *adj.* **a.** constituting or part of the nature of something; inherent. **b.** basic or indispensable; necessary: *essential ingredients.*

es•sen•tial² /ĭ sĕn′ shəl/ *n.* **a.** something that is fundamental. **b.** something that is necessary or indispensable.

es•tab•lish /ĭ stăb′ lĭsh/ *v.* **a.** to make firm or secure. **b.** to settle in a secure position or condition: *established her in her own business.* **c.** to cause to be recognized and accepted: *a discovery that established his reputation.*

et•i•quette /ĕt′ ĭ kĕt′, -kĭt/ *n.* the practices and forms prescribed by social convention or by authority. [Fr. *etiquette*, label < OFr. *estiquet*, label, ticket.]

et•y•mol•o•gy /ĕt′ ə mŏl′ ə jē/ *n.* (**-gies** *pl.*) the origin and historical development of a word as shown by determining its earliest known use and changes in form and meaning.

e•val•u•ate /ĭ văl′ yōō āt′/ *v.* (**-ates, -at•ed, -at•ing**) **a.** to estimate or judge the value or worth of. **b.** *Math.* to calculate or set down the numerical value of; express numerically.

ev•i•dence¹ /ĕv′ ĭ dəns/ *n.* **a.** the data on which a judgment or conclusion may be based; something that furnishes proof. **b.** *Law.* the documentary or verbal statements and the material objects admissible as testimony in a court of law.

ev•i•dence² /ĕv′ ĭ dəns/ *v.* (**-denc•es, -denced, -denc•ing**) to indicate clearly; prove. **—idiom. in evidence.** present and plainly visible; conspicuous: *He was very much in evidence at the convention.*

ev•i•dent /ĕv′ ĭ dənt/ *adj.* easily seen or understood; obvious.

e•voke /ĭ vōk′/ *v.* (**-vokes, -voked, -vok•ing**) to call to mind or memory. [Lat. *evocare: ex-*, out + *vocare*, to call.]

ev•o•lu•tion /ĕv′ ə lōō′ shən, ē′ və-/ *n.* **a.** *Biol.* the theory that groups of organisms, as species, may change with passage of time explaining why descendants become less like their ancestors. **b.** the gradual process of the development or growth of something, such as a social institution.

Spelling Dictionary

ex- a prefix meaning: **a.** out; out of. **b.** former.

ex•ag•ger•ate /ĭg zăj′ ə rāt′/ *v.* (-ates, -at•ed, -at•ing) (**ex•ag•ger•a•tion** *n.*) to distort through overstatement.

ex•ca•va•tion /ĕk′ skə vā′ shən/ *n.* **a.** the act or process of digging or hollowing out. **b.** a cavity formed by excavating.

excavation

ex•ceed /ĭk sēd′/ *v.* to go beyond the limits of. [ME *exceden* < Lat. *excedere*: *ex-*, out + *cedere*, to go.]

ex•ec•u•tive[1] /ĭg zĕk′ yə tĭv/ *n.* **a.** a person or group having administrative or managerial authority in an organization. **b.** the branch of government charged with putting into effect a country's law and the administering of its functions.

ex•ec•u•tive[2] /ĭg zĕk′ yə tĭv/ *adj.* **a.** of or pertaining to the branch of government charged with the execution and administration of the nation's laws. **b.** of or pertaining to an executive.

ex•haust[1] /ĭg zôst′/ *v.* **a.** to use up; consume. **b.** to wear out completely; tire. **c.** to deal with comprehensively: *exhaust a topic.*

ex•haust[2] /ĭg zôst′/ *n.* **a.1.** the escape or release of vaporous waste material, as from an engine. **a.2.** the fumes or gases so released. **b.** a device or part, such as a pipe, through which waste material is emitted.

ex•hil•a•rate /ĭg zĭl′ ə rāt′/ *v.* (-rates, -rat•ed, -rat•ing) **a.** to make cheerful, elate. **b.** to stimulate.

ex•hil•a•rat•ing /ĭg zĭl′ ə rā′ tĭng/ *adj.* causing exhilaration.

ex•pi•ra•tion /ĕk′ spə rā′ shən/ *n.* the act of coming to a close; termination. [ME *expiren,* to expire < Lat. *exspirare*: *ex-*, out + *spirare*, to breathe.]

ex•port[1] /ĭk spôrt′, -spōrt′, ĕk′ spôrt′, -spōrt′/ *v.* to send or carry (a commodity, for example) abroad, especially for trade or sale. (Lat. *exportate*: *ex-*, out + *portare*, to carry.]

ex•port[2] /ĕk′ spôrt′, -spōrt′/ *n.* something that is exported.

ex•pose /ĭk spōz′/ *v.* (-pos•es, -posed, -pos•ing) **a.** to lay open, as to something undesirable or injurious. **b.** to subject (a photographic film, for example) to the action of light. **c.** to make visible. **d.** to make known (a crime, for example). [ME *exposen* < OFr. *exposer* < Lat. *exponere*: *ex-*, out of + *ponere*, to place.]

ex•press[1] /ĭk sprĕs′/ *v.* **a.** to make known or set forth in words. **b.** to communicate (one's feelings, for example), especially through artistic activity. [ME *expressen,* to express < OFr. *expresser* < Med. Lat. *expressare*: Lat. *ex-*, out + Lat. *pressare*, to press, freq. of *premere,* to press.]

ex•press[2] /ĭk sprĕs′/ *adj.* **a.** definitely and explicitly stated: *his express wish.* **b.1.** sent out with or moving at high speed. **b.2.** direct, rapid, and usually nonstop: *express mail delivery.*

ex•pres•sive /ĭk sprĕs′ ĭv/ *adj.* **a.** serving to express or indicate: *actions expressive of frustration.* **b.** full of expression; significant.

ex•tinct /ĭk stĭngkt′/ *adj.* **a.** extinguished or inactive: *an extinct volcano.* **b.** no longer existing or living.

ex•traor•di•nar•y /ĭk strôr′ dn ĕr′ē-, ĕk′ strə ôr′-/ *adj.* highly exceptional; remarkable.

fac•to•ri•al[1] /făk tôr′ ē əl, -tōr′-/ *n.* the product of all the positive integers from 1 to a given number: *4 factorial, usually written 4!, is equal to 24 (1 • 2 • 3 • 4 = 24).*

fac•to•ri•al[2] /făk tôr′ ē əl, -tōr′-/ *adj.* of or relating to a factor or factorial.

fa•mil•iar[1] /fə mĭl′ yər/ *adj.* **a.** often encountered; common. **b.** having fair knowledge of something; acquainted: *was familiar with those roads.*

fa•mil•iar[2] /fə mĭl′ yər/ *n.* a close friend or associate.

fa•mil•iar•ize /fə mĭl′ yə rīz′/ *v.* (-iz•es, -ized, -iz•ing) to make known, recognized, or familiar.

farce /färs/ *n.* **a.** a comic play with a story and characters greatly exaggerated to cause laughter. **b.** something that is ridiculous or laughable, especially something supposed to be serious.

far·reach·ing /fär′ rē′ chǐng/ *adj.* having a wide range, influence, or effect.

fas·ci·nate /făs′ ə nāt′/ *v.* (**-nates, -nat·ed, -nat·ing**) to hold an intense interest or attraction for.

faux pas /fō pä′/ *n.* (**faux pas** /fō päz′/ *pl.*) a social blunder. [Fr. *faux,* false + *pas,* step.]

feign /fān/ *v.* **a.** to give a false appearance of; sham: *feign sleep.* **b.** to represent falsely; pretend to.

fi·as·co /fē ăs′ kō, -ä′ skō/ *n.* (**-coes** or **-cos** *pl.*) a complete failure. [Fr. < Ital.]

fig·u·ra·tive /fĭg′ yər ə tĭv/ *adj.* **a.** based on or making use of figures of speech; metaphorical: *figurative language.* **b.** containing many figures of speech; ornate.

fil·a·ment /fĭl′ ə mənt/ *n.* **a.** a fine or thinly spun thread, fiber, or wire. **b.** a fine wire that is enclosed in the bulb of an electric lamp and that is heated by the passage of current until it gives off light.

filament

fi·nite /fī′ nīt′/ *adj.* having bounds; limited: *a finite list of choices.*

flash·back /flăsh′ băk′/ *n.* a literary or dramatic device in which an earlier event is inserted into the normal chronological order of a narrative.

flex·i·ble /flĕk′ sə bəl/ *adj.* (**flex·i·bil·i·ty** *n.*) **a.** capable of being bent or flexed; pliable. **b.** susceptible to influence or persuasion; tractable. **c.** responsive to change; adaptable: *a flexible schedule.*

flour·ish¹ /flûr′ ĭsh, flŭr′-/ *v.* **a.** to fare well; prosper. **b.** to wield, wave, or exhibit dramatically: *flourish a baton.*

flour·ish² /flûr′ ĭsh, flŭr′-/ *n.* **a.** an act or instance of waving or brandishing. **b.** an embellishment or ornamentation.

fo·li·age /fō′ lē ĭj, fō′ lĭj/ *n.* plant leaves collectively.

for·bid /fər bĭd′, fôr-/ *v.* (**-bids, -bade** or **-bad, bid·den** or **-bid, -bid·ding**) (**for·bid·den** *adj.*) to command (someone) not to do something.

fore·cast¹ /fôr′ kăst′, fōr′-/ *v.* **a.** to estimate or calculate in advance, especially to predict (weather conditions) by analysis of meteorological data. **b.** to serve as an advance indication of; foreshadow: *price rises that forecast inflation.*

fore·cast² /fôr′ kăst′, fōr′-/ *n.* a prediction, as of coming events or conditions.

fore·head /fôr′ ĭd, fŏr′-, fôr′ hĕd′, fōr′-/ *n.* the part of the head or face between the eyebrows and the normal hairline.

for·eign /fôr′ ĭn, fŏr′-/ *adj.* **a.** of, characteristic of, or from a country other than one's own. **b.** conducted or involved with other nations or governments; not domestic: *foreign trade.* **c.** not natural; alien: *Jealousy is foreign to her nature.* [ME *forein* < OFr. *forain* < Lat. *foras,* outside.]

fore·shad·ow /fôr shăd′ ō, fōr-/ *v.* to present an indication or suggestion of beforehand.

fore·sight /fôr′ sīt′, fōr′-/ *n.* **a.** the ability to look ahead, anticipate, and plan for the future before it comes. **b.** the act of looking forward.

for·feit /fôr′ fĭt/ *n.* something surrendered as punishment for a crime, offense, error, or breach of contract; to lose or give up (something) as a penalty or fine.

for·get /fər gĕt′, fôr-/ *v.* (**-gets, -got, -got·ten** or **-got, -get·ting**) **a.** to be unable to remember. **b.** to lack concern for; neglect. **c.** to leave behind unintentionally. **d.** to fail to mention.

for•ti•fy /fôr′ tə fī′/ *v.* (**-fies, -fied, -fy•ing**) **a.** to add strength to (a structure) by reinforcement; reinforce. **b.** to impart physical strength to; invigorate. **c.** to give moral or mental strength to; encourage.

fo•rum /fôr′ əm, fōr′-/ *n.* (**fo•rums** or **fo•ra** *pl.*) **a.** the public square or marketplace of an ancient Roman city that was the assembly place for judicial and other public activity. **b.1.** a public meeting place for open discussion. **b.2.** a medium for open discussion, as a radio or television program.

forum

frag•ile /frăj′ əl, -īl′/ *adj.* (**fra•gil•i•ty** *n.*) **a.** easily broken or damaged; brittle. **b.** physically weak or delicate; frail. [OFr. < Lat. *fragilis* < *frangere*, to break.]

frame•work /frām′ wûrk′/ *n.* **a.** a structure for supporting or enclosing something, especially a skeletal support used as the basis in something being constructed. **b.** a basic arrangement, form, or set of relationships.

fran•chise[1] /frăn′ chīz′/ *n.* **a.** a privilege or right officially granted a person or a group by a government. **b.** authorization granted by a manufacturer to a distributor or dealer to sell his products.

fran•chise[2] /frăn′ chīz′/ *v.* (**-chis•es, -chised, -chis•ing**) to endow with a franchise.

fric•tion /frĭk′ shən/ *n.* **a.** the rubbing of one object or surface against another. **b.** conflict, as between persons having dissimilar ideas or interests; clash.

friv•o•lous /frĭv′ ə ləs/ *adj.* **a.** unworthy of serious attention; trivial. **b.** inappropriately silly.

-ful a suffix meaning: **a.** full of: *eventful.* **b.** characterized by: *boastful.* **c.** having a specified tendency or capability: *mournful.* **d.** an amount or quantity that will fill: *cupful.*

ful•fill /fŏŏl fĭl′/ *v.* (**ful•fill•ment** *n.*) **a.** to carry out (an order, for example). **b.** to measure up to; satisfy.

full-length /fŏŏl′ lĕngkth′, -lĕngth′/ *adj.* **a.** showing or fitted to the entire length, especially of the human body. **b.** of a normal or standard length: *a full-length novel.*

func•tion[1] /fŭngk′ shən/ *n.* **a.** the action for which a person or thing is particularly fitted or employed. **b.** an official ceremony or formal social occasion. **c.** *Math.* **1.** a variable so related to another that for each value assumed by one there is a value determined for the other. **c.2.** a rule of correspondence between two sets such that there is a unique element in one set assigned to each element in the other.

func•tion[2] /fŭngk′ shən/ *v.* to have or perform a function; serve.

fun•da•men•tal[1] /fŭn′ də mĕn′ tl/ *adj.* forming or serving as an essential component of a system or structure; basic.

fun•da•men•tal[2] /fŭn′ də mĕn′ tl/ *n.* something that is an essential or fundamental part.

G

gal•va•nize /găl′ və nīz′/ *v.* (**-niz•es, -nized, -niz•ing**) **a.** to stimulate or shock with an electric current. **b.** to arouse to awareness or action; spur. **c.** to coat (iron or steel) with rust-resistant zinc.

gen•er•a•tor /jĕn′ ə rā′ tər/ *n.* a machine that converts mechanical energy into electrical energy.

gen•re /zhän′ rə/ *n.* **a.** type; class. **b.1.** a category of artistic composition marked by a distinctive style, form, or content, especially a style of painting concerned with depicting scenes and subjects of common everyday life. **b.2.** a distinctive class or category of literary composition.

gen•u•ine /jĕn′ yŏŏ ĭn/ *adj.* not false; real; true.

ge•o•graph•ic /jē′ ə grăf′ ĭk/ *adj.* **a.** of or pertaining to geography. **b.** concerning the topography of a specific region.

ge•o•met•ric /jē′ ə mĕt′ rĭk/ *adj.* of or pertaining to geometry and its methods and principles.

ge•om•e•try /jē ŏm′ ĭ trē/ *n.* (**-tries** *pl.*) the mathematical study of the properties, measurement, and relationships of points, lines, planes, surfaces, and angles and of figures composed of combinations of them.

3. foreign (adj) - from a countr other than one's own
4. heir ( ) -
5. retrieve ( ) -
6. sovereign ( ) -
7. heirloom ( ) -
8. grieve (v) - to cause t. be sorrowful
9. veil ( ) -
10. reprieve ( ) -
11. leisurely ( ) -
12. beige (adj.) -
13. achievment ( ) -
14. percieve (v)
15. unwieldy ( ) -
16. forfeit (n) - to surrender
17. counterfeit ( ) -
18. decieve (v) -
19. convenient ( ) -
20. weirdly ( ) -

ger•und /jĕr′ ənd/ *n.* the form of the verb ending in *-ing* when it is used as a noun; a verbal noun.

glad•i•a•tor /glăd′ ē ā′ tər/ *n.* a person trained to entertain the public by engaging in mortal combat in the ancient Roman arena.

gran•deur /grăn′ jər, -jōͦr′/ *n.* the quality or condition of being grand; magnificence. [Fr.]

grieve /grēv/ *v.* (**grieves, grieved, griev•ing**) **a.** to cause to be sorrowful; distress. **b.** to experience grief; mourn.

gu•ber•na•to•ri•al /gōͦ′ bər nə tôr′ ē əl, -tōr′-, gyōͦ′-/ *adj.* of or pertaining to a governor.

ha•rangue¹ /hə răng′/ *n.* a speech or piece of writing characterized by strong feeling or expression; tirade.

ha•rangue² /hə răng′/ *v.* (**-rangues, -rangued, -rangu•ing**) to deliver a harangue.

har•mo•nize /här′ mə nīz′/ *v.* (**-niz•es, -nized, -niz•ing**) **a.** to bring into agreement or harmony; make harmonious. **b.** to provide harmony for (a melody).

haz•ard /hăz′ ərd/ *n.* a possible source of danger: *a fire hazard.*

heir /âr/ *n. Law.* a person who inherits or is entitled by law to inherit the property, rank, title, or office of another.

heir•loom /âr′ lōͦm′/ *n.* a valued possession passed down in a family through succeeding generations.

hick•o•ry /hĭk′ ə rē/ *n.* (**-ries** *pl.*) **a.** any of several chiefly North American deciduous trees that have smooth or shaggy bark, compound leaves, and hard, smooth nuts with an edible kernel. **b.** the hard, tough, heavy wood of a hickory tree. [Earlier *pohickery* < *pawcohiccora*, food prepared from crushed hickory nuts, of Algonquian orig.]

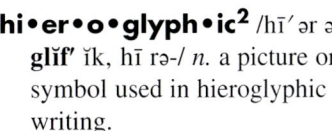

hi•er•o•glyph•ic¹ /hī′ ər ə glĭf′ ĭk, hī rə-/ *adj.* of or pertaining to a system of writing, as that of ancient Egypt, in which pictorial symbols are used to represent words or sounds.

hi•er•o•glyph•ic² /hī′ ər ə glĭf′ ĭk, hī rə-/ *n.* a picture or symbol used in hieroglyphic writing.

hieroglyphic

hon•or•a•ble /ŏn′ ər ə bəl/ *adj.* **a.** deserving or winning honor and respect. **b.** possessing and characterized by honor: *an honorable man.* **c. Honorable.** used as a title of respect for certain high officials.

hos•pi•ta•ble /hŏs′ pĭ tə bəl, hŏ spĭt′ ə bəl/ *adj.* **a.** cordial and generous to guests. **b.** favorable to growth and development: *a hospitable environment.*

hy•dro•e•lec•tric /hī′ drō ĭ lĕk′ trĭk/ *adj.* **a.** generating electricity by conversion of the energy of running water. **b.** of, pertaining to, or using electricity so generated.

-ible a form of the suffix **-able.**

-ic a suffix that forms adjectives meaning of or characteristic of: *allergic.*

id•i•om /ĭd′ ē əm/ *n.* **a.** an expression having a special meaning that cannot be understood from the usual meaning of the words. For example, *fly off the handle* (lose one's temper) is an idiom. **b.** a regional speech or dialect.

il•lu•mi•nate /ĭ **loo′** mə nāt′/ *v.* (**-nates, -nat•ed, -nat•ing**) **a.** to provide or brighten with light. **b.** to make understandable; clarify. **c.** to adorn (a page of a book, for example) with ornamental designs, miniatures, or lettering in brilliant colors or precious metals.

il•lus•tra•tion /ĭl′ ə **strā′** shən/ *n.* **a.** something used to clarify or explain. **b.** visual matter used to clarify or to decorate a text.

im•age•ry /**ĭm′** ĭj rē/ *n.* (**-ries** *pl.*) **a.** mental pictures or images. **b.** the use of figures of speech or vivid descriptions in writing or speaking to produce mental images.

i•mag•i•na•tion /ĭ măj′ə **nā′** shən/ *n.* **a.1.** the power of the mind to form a mental image or concept of something that is not real or present. **a.2.** such power of the mind used creatively. **b.** the ability to confront and deal with reality by using the creative power of the mind; resourcefulness.

im•ma•te•ri•al /ĭm′ə **tîr′** ē əl/ *adj.* of no importance or relevance; inconsequential.

im•merse /ĭ **mûrs′**/ *v.* (**-mers•es, -mersed, -mers•ing**) **a.** to cover completely in a liquid; submerge. **b.** to involve profoundly; absorb. [< Lat. *immersus*, p.part. of *immergere*, to immerse: *in-*, in + *mergere*, to dip.]

im•mi•grant /**ĭm′** ĭ grənt/ *n.* one who enters and settles in a country or region to which one is not native. [Lat. *immigrare*, *immigrat-* to go into: *in-*, in + *migrare*, to depart.]

immigrant

im•mi•nent /**ĭm′** ə nənt/ *adj.* about to occur; impending. [Lat. *imminens*, pr.part. of *imminere*, to overhang.]

im•pli•cate /**ĭm′** plĭ kāt′/ *v.* (**-cates, -cat•ed, -cat•ing**) **a.** to involve or connect intimately or incriminatingly. **b.** to imply. [Lat. *implicare*, *inplicat-*, to entangle, unite: *in-*, in + *plicare*, to fold.]

im•ply /ĭm **plī′**/ *v.* (**-plies, -plied, -ply•ing**) to say or express indirectly.

im•port¹ /ĭm **pôrt′**, **-pōrt′**, **ĭm′** pôrt′, -pōrt′/ *v.* (**-ports, -port•ed, -port•ing**) to bring or carry in from an outside source, especially to bring in (goods) from a foreign country for trade or sale. [ME *importen* < Lat. *importare*: *in-*, in + *portare*, to carry.]

im•port² /**ĭm′** pôrt′, -pōrt′/ *n.* something imported.

im•pose /ĭm **pōz′**/ *v.* (**-pos•es, -posed, -pos•ing**) **a.** to bring about by exercising authority. **b.** to take unfair advantage of something or someone. [OFr. < Lat. *impositus*, p.part. of *imponere*, to place upon: *in-*, on + *ponere*, to place.]

im•po•si•tion /ĭm pə **zĭsh′** ən/ *n.* a burdensome or unfair demand, as upon someone's time. [OFr. < Lat. *impositus*, p.part. of *imponere*, to place upon: *in-*, on + *ponere*, to place.]

im•pos•tor /ĭm **pŏs′** tər/ *n.* a person who deceives under an assumed identity. [OFr. *imposteur* < LLat. *impositor* < Lat. *impositus*, p.part. of *imponere*, to place upon: *in-*, on + *ponere*, to place.]

im•pres•sion /ĭm **prĕsh′** ən/ *n.* **a.** a marked effect, image, or feeling retained in the mind. **b.** a vague notion, remembrance, belief, idea, etc. **c.** a mark or imprint made on a surface by pressure.

im•pres•sion•a•ble /ĭm **prĕsh′** ə nə bəl/ *adj.* **a.** capable of receiving an impression; plastic. **b.** readily or easily influenced; suggestible.

im•pres•sive /ĭm **prĕs′** ĭv/ *adj.* making a strong or vivid impression; commanding attention: *an impressive ceremony.* [ME *impressen* < Lat. *impressus*, p.part. of *imprimere*: *in-*, in + *premere*, to press.]

im•pro•vise /**ĭm′** prə vīz′/ *v.* (**-vis•es, -vised, -vis•ing**) to invent, compose, or recite without preparation.

in-¹ a prefix meaning without or not: *inaccurate.* When **in-** is followed by **l** or **r**, it becomes **il-** or **ir-** respectively. Before **b, m,** or **p,** it becomes **im-**.

in-² a prefix meaning in, within, or into: *inbound.* When **in-** is followed by **l** or **r**, it becomes **il-** or **ir-** respectively. Before **b, m,** or **p,** it becomes **im-**.

in•ac•ces•si•ble /ĭn′ăk **sĕs′** ə bəl/ *adj.* not accessible; unapproachable.

in•ad•vis•a•ble /ĭn′ əd **vī′** zə bəl/ *adj.* unwise; not recommended.

in•can•des•cent /ĭn′ kən **dĕs′** ənt/ *adj.* **a.** emitting visible light as a result of being heated. **b.** shining brilliantly; very bright.

in•cen•tive¹ /ĭn sĕn′ tĭv/ *n.* something, as the fear of punishment or the expectation of reward, that incites to action or effort. [ME < Lat. *incentivum < incentivus,* inciting < *incentus,* p.part. of *incinere,* to sound: *in-,* (intensive) + *canere,* to sing.]

in•cen•tive² /ĭn sĕn′ tĭv/ *adj.* inciting; motivating.

in•come /ĭn′ kŭm′/ *n.* the amount of money or its equivalent received during a period of time in exchange for labor or services, from the sale of goods or property, or as profit from financial investments.

in•com•pat•i•ble /ĭn′ kəm păt′ ə bəl/ *adj.* **a.** not compatible; not in harmony or agreement. **b.** not capable of living or working together happily or smoothly.

in•con•gru•ous /ĭn kŏng′ grōō əs/ *adj.* **a.** made up of sharply different members, parts, or qualities. **b.** not consistent with what is logical, customary, or correct; inappropriate.

in•con•ven•ience¹ /ĭn′ kən vēn′ yəns/ *n.* **a.** the state or quality of being inconvenient. **b.** something that is inconvenient.

in•con•ven•ience² /ĭn′ kən vēn′ yəns/ *v.* **(-ienc•es, -ienced, -ienc•ing)** to cause inconvenience to or for; trouble.

in•con•ven•ient /ĭn′ kən vēn′ yənt/ *adj.* not convenient, especially: **a.** not accessible or handy. **b.** difficult or awkward to perform. **c.** inopportune; untimely.

in•cor•po•rate /ĭn kôr′ pə rāt′/ *v.* **(-rates, -rat•ed, -rat•ing) a.** to unite with or blend indistinguishably into something already in existence. **b.** to cause to merge or combine together into a united whole. [ME *incorporaten* < LLat. *incorporare,* to form into a body: Lat. *in-,* in + Lat. *corpus,* body.]

in•crim•i•nate /ĭn crĭm′ ə nāt′/ *v.* **(-nates, -nat•ed, -nat•ing)** to charge with or involve in a crime or other wrongful act.

in•de•pend•ent /ĭn′ dĭ pĕn′ dənt/ *adj.* **a.** free from the influence, guidance, or control of another or others; self-reliant. **b.** *Math.* not dependent on other variables: *an independent variable.*

in•dex¹ /ĭn′ dĕks′/ *n.* **(-dex•es** or **-di•ces** /dĭ•sēz′/ *pl.*) something that serves to guide, point out, or otherwise aid reference, especially an alphabetized listing of names, places, and subjects included in a printed work that gives for each item the page on which it is mentioned. [Lat. *index, indic-,* forefinger, pointer < *indicare,* to indicate.]

index

in•dex² /ĭn′ dĕks′/ *v.* **a.** to furnish with an index: *index a book.* **b.** to enter in an index.

in•dict•ment /ĭn dīt′ mənt/ *n. Law.* a written statement charging a party with the commission of a crime or other offense, drawn up by a prosecuting attorney and found and presented by a grand jury.

in•di•vid•u•al•i•ty /ĭn′ də vĭj′ōō ăl′ ĭ tē/ *n.* **(-ties** *pl.*) **a.** the quality of being individual; distinctness. **b.** the sum of qualities and characteristics that distinguish one person or thing from others. [ME *individual,* single, indivisible < Med. Lat. *individualis* < Lat. *individuus: in-,* not + *dividuus,* divisible < *dividere,* to divide.]

in•dom•i•ta•ble /ĭn dŏm′ ĭ tə bəl/ *adj.* incapable of being overcome, subdued, or vanquished; unconquerable. [LLat. *indomitabilis,* untameable: Lat. *in-,* not + *domitare,* to tame, freq. of *domare,* to subdue.]

in•duce /ĭn dōōs′, -dyōōs′/ *v.* **(-duc•es, -duced, -duc•ing) a.** to lead or move by influence or persuasion. **b.** to bring about the occurrence of; cause. [ME *inducen* < Lat. *inducere,* to bring in: *in-,* in + *ducere,* to lead.]

in•duct /ĭn dŭkt´/ v. **a.** to place ceremoniously or formally in an office or position; install. **b.** to admit as a member; initiate. [ME *inducten* < Lat. *inductus,* p.part. of *inducere,* to bring in: *in-,* in + *ducere,* to lead.]

in•duc•tion /ĭn dŭk´ shən/ n. **a.** the act of inducting or of being inducted. **b.** the act or process of deriving general principles from particular facts or instances.

in•dus•tri•al /ĭn dŭs´ trē əl/ adj. **a.** of, pertaining to, or derived from industry. **b.** having highly developed industries: *an industrial nation.*

in•dus•try /ĭn´ də strē/ n. (**-tries** pl.) **a.** the manufacture or production of goods on a large scale. **b.** hard work; steady effort.

in•e•qual•i•ty /ĭn´ ĭ kwŏl´ ĭ tē/ n. (**-ties** pl.) **a.** the condition of being unequal. **b.** *Math.* an algebraic statement that a quantity is greater than or is less than another quantity.

in•er•tia /ĭn ûr´ shə/ n. **a.** *Physics.* the tendency of a body at rest to remain at rest or of a body in motion to stay in motion in a straight line unless disturbed by an external force. **b.** resistance to motion, action, or change.

in•fe•ri•or /ĭn fîr´ ē ər/ adj. (**in•fe•ri•or•i•ty** n.) **a.** situated under or beneath. **b.** low or lower in order, degree, or rank. **c.** low or lower in quality, value, or estimation. [ME < Lat. *inferus,* low.]

in•fi•nite /ĭn´ fə nĭt/ adj. having no boundaries or limits.

in•fin•i•tive /ĭn fĭn´ ĭ tĭv/ n. a verb form that is not inflected to indicate person, number, or tense. In English, it is usually preceded by *to* or by an auxiliary verb.

in•flex•i•ble /ĭn flĕk´ sə bəl/ adj. **a.** not flexible; rigid. **b.** incapable of being changed; unalterable.

in•fra•red /ĭn´ frə rĕd´/ adj. having a wavelength greater than those of visible light and shorter than those of microwaves.

in•her•it /ĭn hĕr´ ĭt/ v. **a.** to receive (property) from an ancestor or another person by legal succession or will. **b.** *Biol.* to receive genetically from an ancestor.

in•i•tia•tive /ĭ nĭsh´ ə tĭv/ n. **a.** the power, ability, or instinct to begin or to follow through energetically with a plan or task; enterprise and determination. **b.** the first step; opening move: *take the initiative.*

in•no•vate /ĭn´ ə vāt´/ v. (**-vates, -vat•ed, -vat•ing**) (**in•no•va•tive** adj.) to begin or introduce something new.

in•no•va•tion /ĭn´ ə vā´ shən/ n. **a.** the act of innovating. **b.** something newly introduced.

in•or•gan•ic /ĭn ôr găn´ ĭk/ adj. involving neither organic life nor the products of organic life.

in•scribe /ĭn skrīb´/ v. (**-scribes, -scribed, -scrib•ing**) to write, print, carve, or engrave (words or letters) on or in a surface. [Lat. *inscribere: in-,* in + *scribere,* to write.]

in•scrip•tion /ĭn skrĭp´ shən/ n. something that is inscribed, as the wording on a coin, gravestone, or label. [ME *inscripcioun* < Lat. *inscriptio* < *inscribere,* to inscribe.]

inscription

in•spect /ĭn spĕkt´/ v. **a.** to examine carefully and critically, especially for flaws. **b.** to review or examine officially. [Lat. *inspectare,* freq. of *inspicere,* to look into: *in-,* in + *specere,* to look.]

in•spec•tor /ĭn spĕk´ tər/ n. **a.** a person, especially an official, who inspects. **b.** a police officer of the rank next below superintendent.

in•spi•ra•tion /ĭn´ spə rā´ shən/ n. **a.** stimulation of the mind or emotions to a high level of feeling or activity. **b.** an agency, as a person or a work of art, that moves the intellect or emotions or that prompts action or invention. **c.** something that is inspired; a sudden creative act or idea. [ME *enspiren* < OFr. *enspirer* < Lat. *inspirare: in-,* into + *spirare,* to breathe.]

in•spire /ĭn spīr´/ v. (**-spires, -spired, -spir•ing**) **a.** to fill with noble or reverent emotion; exalt. **b.** to stimulate to creativity or action. **c.** to be the cause or source of; bring about. [ME *enspiren* < OFr. *enspirer* < Lat. *inspirare: in-,* into + *spirare,* to breathe.]

in•tel•lect /ĭn´ tl ĕkt´/ n. the ability to learn and reason as distinguished from the ability to feel or will.

in•tel•lec•tu•al[1] /ĭn′tl ĕk′ chōō əl/ *adj.* of or pertaining to the intellect.

in•tel•lec•tu•al[2] /ĭn′tl ĕk′ chōō əl/ *n.* an intellectual person.

in•tel•li•gence /ĭn tĕl′ ə jəns/ *n.* **a.** the capacity to acquire and apply knowledge. **b.** the faculty of thought and reason. **c.** secret information, especially about an actual or potential enemy.

in•tel•li•gent /ĭn tĕl′ ə jənt/ *adj.* having a high degree of intelligence; mentally acute.

in•ten•si•ty /ĭn tĕn′ sĭ tē/ *n.* (-ties *pl.*) exceptionally great concentration, power, or force.

inter- a prefix meaning: **a.** between; among: *international.* **b.** mutually; together: *interact.*

in•ter•cede /ĭn′ tər sēd′/ *v.* (-cedes, -ced•ed, -ced•ing) **a.** to plead on another's behalf. **b.** to act as mediator in a dispute. [Lat. *intercedere*, to intervene: *inter-*, between + *cedere*, to go.]

in•ter•cept[1] /ĭn′ tər sĕpt′/ *v.* (-cepts, -cept•ed, -cept•ing) **a.1.** to stop, deflect, or interrupt the progress or intended course of. **a.2.** *Sports.* to take possession of by catching (an opponent's ball), especially in football. **b.** to intersect.

intercept

in•ter•cept[2] /ĭn′ tər sĕpt′/ *n. Math.* the distance from the origin of coordinates along a coordinate axis to the point at which a line, curve, or surface intersects the axis.

in•ter•change•a•ble /ĭn′ tər chān′ jə bəl/ *adj.* capable of being switched or exchanged.

in•te•ri•or /ĭn tîr′ ē ər/ *adj.* of, relating to, or located in the inside; inner.

in•ter•jec•tion /ĭn′ tər jĕk′ shən/ *n.* a word, phrase, or utterance used exclamatorily to express emotion, as *Oh!*

in•ter•lude /ĭn′ tər lōōd′/ *n.* **a.** an intervening episode, feature, or period of time. **b.** an entertainment between the acts of a play. **c.** a short musical piece inserted between the parts of a longer composition. [ME *enterlude*, a dramatic entertainment < OFr. *entrelude* < Med. Lat. *interludium*: Lat. *inter-*, between + Lat. *ludus*, play.]

in•ter•na•tion•al /ĭn′ tər năsh′ ə nəl/ *adj.* of, relating to, or involving two or more nations.

in•ter•pre•ta•tion /ĭn tûr′ prĭ tā′ shən/ *n.* **a.** the act of explaining or clarifying the meaning of something unclear. **b.** an artistic performance or presentation that expresses someone's understanding of the work. **c.** translation, especially oral translation.

in•tro•duce /ĭn′ trə dōōs′, -dyōōs′/ *v.* (-duc•es, -duced, -duc•ing) **a.** to present (a person) by name to another in order to establish an acquaintance. **b.** to propose, create, or bring into use or acceptance for the first time. **c.** to provide with a beginning knowledge or first experience of something.

in•tro•duc•to•ry /ĭn′ trə dŭk′ tə rē/ *adj.* serving to introduce.

in•tu•i•tion /ĭn′ tōō ĭsh′ ən, -tyōō-/ *n.* **a.** the act or faculty of knowing or understanding something instantly, by instinct, without having to reason it out or get proof. **b.** sharp insight.

in•verse[1] /ĭn vûrs′, ĭn′ vûrs′/ *adj.* reversed in order, nature, or effect.

in•verse[2] /ĭn′ vûrs′, ĭn′ **vûrs**′/ *n.* something that is opposite, as in sequence or character; reverse.

in•vest /ĭn vĕst′/ *v.* to commit (money or capital) in order to gain profit or interest.

in•ves•ti•gate /ĭn vĕs′ tĭ gāt′/ *v.* (-gates, -gat•ed, -gat•ing) to observe or inquire into in detail; examine systematically.

in•vest•ment /ĭn vĕst′ mənt/ *n.* **a.** the act of investing. **b.** an amount invested. **c.** property or another possession acquired for future income or benefit.

in•voice[1] /ĭn′ vois′/ *n.* a detailed list of goods shipped or services rendered, with an account of all costs; bill.

in•voice[2] /ĭn′ vois′/ *v.* (**-voic•es, -voiced, -voic•ing**) to make an invoice of; bill.

in•voke /ĭn vōk′/ *v.* (**-vokes, -voked, -vok•ing**) **a.** to call upon for assistance, support, or inspiration. **b.** to resort to; use or apply: *The governor invoked her veto power.* [OFr. *invoquer* < LLat. *invocare*: *in-*, in + *vocare*, to call.]

in•vol•un•tar•y /ĭn vŏl′ ən tĕr′ē/ *adj.* **a.** not performed willingly or deliberately. **b.** not subject to control; automatic.

i•ro•ny /ī′ rə nē/ *n.* (**-nies** *pl.*) **a.** the use of words to convey the opposite of their literal meaning. **b.** a literary style employing ironic contrasts for humorous or rhetorical effect. **c.** incongruity between what might be expected and what actually occurs.

ir•rel•e•vant /ĭ rĕl′ ə vənt/ *adj.* having no relation to the subject or situation; not applicable.

ir•re•place•a•ble /ĭr′ ĭ plā′ sə bəl/ *adj.* incapable of being replaced.

ir•re•spon•si•ble /ĭr′ ĭ spŏn′ sə bəl/ *adj.* **a.** showing no sense of responsibility or concern for consequences; not dependable, reliable, or trustworthy. **b.** not capable of being called to account for one's actions.

ir•re•vers•i•ble /ĭr′ ĭ vûr′ sə bəl/ *adj.* incapable of being reversed.

ir•ri•gate /ĭr′ ĭ gāt′/ *v.* (**-gates, -gat•ed, -gat•ing**) (**ir•ri•ga•tion** *n.*) **a.** to supply (dry land) with water by means of ditches, pipes, or streams. **b.** to wash out (a canal or wound) with water or a medicated fluid.

-ise variant of the suffix **-ize.**

-ism a suffix that forms nouns and means: **a.** an act, practice, or process. **b.** a relationship or condition. **c.** characteristic behavior or quality. **d.** a word, phrase, idiom, or usage peculiar to a language, people. **e.** a doctrine, theory, system of principles.

isth•mus /ĭs′ məs/ *n.* (**-mus•es** or **-mi** /mī/ *pl.*) a narrow strip of land connecting two larger masses of land.

i•tem•ize /ī′ tə mīz′/ *v.* (**-iz•es, -ized, -iz•ing**) to set down item by item; list.

i•tin•er•ar•y /ī tĭn′ ə rĕr′ē, ĭ tĭn′-/ *n.* (**-ies** *pl.*) **a.** a route or proposed route of a journey. **b.** an account or record of a journey. [ME *itinerarie* < LLat. *itinerarium*, course of travel < *itinerarius*, of traveling < Lat. *iter*, journey.]

-ity a suffix that forms nouns meaning a quality or condition: *authenticity.*

-ive[1] a suffix that forms adjectives meaning tending toward, performing, or accomplishing something: *disruptive.*

-ive[2] a suffix that forms nouns meaning something that performs or accomplishes something: *sedative.*

-ize a suffix that forms verbs and means: **a.** to become, cause to become, or form into: *materialize.* **b.** to treat or affect with: *magnetize.*

jar•gon /jär′ gən/ *n.* **a.** nonsensical, incoherent, or meaningless talk. **b.** the specialized or technical language of a trade, profession, or similar group.

jeal•ous /jĕl′ əs/ *adj.* **a.** fearful or wary of the loss of another's affection. **b.** resentful or bitter in rivalry; envious. **c.** vigilant in guarding something: *jealous of his good name.*

jeal•ous•y /jĕl′ ə sē/ *n.* (**-sies** *pl.*) a jealous attitude or disposition.

jer•sey /jûr′ zē/ *n.* (**-seys** *pl.*) **a.** a soft, plain-knitted fabric used for clothing. **b.** a close-fitting knitted pullover shirt, jacket, or sweater. [after *Jersey,* England.]

jodh•purs /jŏd′ pərz/ *pl. n.* wide-hipped riding breeches of heavy cloth, fitting tightly at the knees and ankles. [after *Jodhpur,* a region in India.]

jodhpurs

joust[1] /joust, jŭst, jōōst/ *n.* **a.** a combat with lances between two mounted knights or men-at-arms. **b.** personal combat or competition suggestive of a joust.

joust² /joust, jŭst, jōōst/ *v.* **a.** to engage in combat on horseback, especially with lances. **b.** to engage in personal combat or competition.

ju•di•cial /jōō dĭsh′ əl/ *adj.* **a.** of, pertaining to, or proper to courts of law or to the administration of justice. **b.** pertaining or appropriate to the office of a judge. **c.** relative to, characterized by, or expressing judgment.

kin•der•gar•ten /kĭn′ dər gär′ tn/ *n.* a program or class for four- to six-year-old children that serves as an introduction to school. [G.: *Kinder*, pl. of *Kind*, child (< OHG *kind*) + *Garten*, garden < MHG *garte* < OHG *garto*.]

knight•hood /nīt′ hŏŏd′/ *n.* the rank, profession, or dignity of a knight.

knowl•edge•a•ble /nŏl′ ĭ jə bəl/ *adj.* possessing or showing knowledge; well-informed.

la•con•ic /lə kŏn′ ĭk/ *adj.* using or marked by the use of few words; terse; concise. [Lat. *Laconicus*, Spartan < Gk. *Lakōnikos*, from the reputation of the Spartans for brevity of speech.]

lac•quer¹ /lăk′ ər/ *n.* any material that is dissolved in a solvent and can be applied to a surface, drying to leave a glossy finish. [Obs. Fr. *lacre*, sealing wax < Port. < *laca*, resin of the lac insect < Hindi *lākh*.]

lacquer

lac•quer² /lăk′ ər/ *v.* to coat with lacquer.

lec•ture¹ /lĕc′ chər/ *n.* **a.** an exposition of a given subject delivered before an audience or class, especially for the purpose of instruction. **b.** a sober admonition or reproof; reprimand.

lec•ture² /lĕc′ chər/ *v.* (**-tures, -tured, -tur•ing**) **a.** to deliver a lecture. **b.** to admonish or reprove soberly and often at length.

leg•en•dar•y /lĕj′ ən dĕr′ ē/ *adj.* of, constituting, based on, or of the nature of a legend.

le•gion¹ /lē′ jən/ *n.* **a.** the major unit of the Roman army consisting of 3,000 to 6,000 infantry troops and 100 to 200 cavalrymen. **b.** a large number; multitude.

le•gion² /lē′ jən/ *adj.* constituting a large number.

lei•sure•ly¹ /lē′ zhər lē, lĕzh′ ər-/ *adj.* without haste; unhurried.

lei•sure•ly² /lē′ zhər lē, lĕzh′ ər-/ *adv.* in an unhurried manner; slowly.

li•a•bil•i•ty /lī ə bĭl′ ĭ tē/ *n.* (**-ties** *pl.*) **a.** something for which one is liable; an obligation or debt. **b.** legal responsibility to fulfill some contract or obligation. **c.** the financial obligations entered in the balance sheet of a business enterprise. **d.** something that holds one back; handicap.

li•a•ble /lī′ ə bəl/ *adj.* **a.** legally obligated; responsible. **b.** susceptible; subject. **c.** likely. [Prob. came from AN *liable* < OFr. *lier*, to bind < Lat. *ligare*.]

li•ai•son /lē′ ā zŏn′, lē ā′-/ *n.* **a.1.** communication between different groups or units of an organization. **a.2.** a channel or means of communication: *served as the President's liaison with Congress.* **b.** a close relationship, connection, or link.

lib•er•al /lĭb′ ər əl, lĭb′ rəl/ *adj.* **a.** having, expressing, or following political views or policies that favor civil liberties, democratic reforms, and the use of governmental power to promote social progress. **b.** tolerant of the ideas or behavior of others; broad-minded.

li•chen /lī′ kən/ *n.* plants consisting of a fungus in close combination with certain green or blue-green algae, characteristically forming a crust-like, scaly, or branching growth on rocks or tree trunks.

light•ning¹ /līt′ nĭng/ *n.* **a.** a large-scale high-tension natural electric discharge in the atmos-phere. **b.** the visible flash of light accompanying such a discharge.

light•ning² /līt′ nĭng/ *v.* to discharge a flash of lightning.

light•ning³ /līt′ nĭng/ *adj.* moving with remark-able speed or suddenness.

lim•ou•sine /lĭm′ ə zēn′, lĭm′ ə zēn′/ *n.* any of various large passenger vehicles, especially a luxurious automobile usually driven by a chauffeur and sometimes having a glass parti-tion separating the passenger compartment from the driver's seat. [after *Limousin,* a region of France.]

limousine

lin•e•age /lĭn′ ē ĭj/ *n.* **a.** direct descent from a particular ancestor; ancestry. **b.** the descendants of a common ancestor considered to be the founder of the line.

lit•er•al /lĭt′ ər əl/ *adj.* **a.** in accordance with, conforming to, or upholding the exact or prima-ry meaning of a word or words. **b.** word for word; verbatim.

lit•er•ar•y /lĭt′ ə rĕr′ ē/ *adj.* **a.** of, relating to, or dealing with literature. **b.** appropriate to liter-ature rather than to everyday speech or writing. **c.** versed in or fond of literature or learning: *a literary person.*

lit•i•gate /lĭt′ ĭ gāt′/ *v.* (**-gates, -gat•ed, -gat•ing**) (**lit•i•ga•tion** *n.*) to engage in legal proceedings.

lo•cal•i•ty /lō kăl′ ĭ tē/ *n.* (**-ties** *pl.*) a particular neighborhood, place, or district. [Fr. *localité* < LLat. *localitas* < *localis,* local < Lat. *locus,* place.]

lo•co•mo•tion /lō′ kə mō′ shən/ *n.* the act of moving or the ability to move from place to place; travel. [Lat. *locus,* place + MOTION.]

long-dis•tance /lông dĭs′ təns, lŏng′-/ *adj.* **a.** located at a long distance or far away. **b.** covering a long distance. **c.** of or involving telephone communications to a distant station.

lu•mi•nes•cent /lōō′ mə nĕs′ ənt/ *adj.* capable of, exhibiting, or suitable for the emission of light from a nonthermal source.

lux•u•ry /lŭg′ zhə rē, lŭk′ shə-/ *n.* (**-ries** *pl.*) **a.** something that is not essential but that gives pleasure and comfort. **b.** something that is expensive or hard to obtain. **c.** sumptuous living or surroundings.

-ly¹ a suffix that forms adjectives and means: **a.** characteristic of: *sisterly.* **b.** appearing or occurring at specified intervals: *weekly.*

-ly² a suffix that forms adverbs and means: **a.** in a specified manner: *gradually.* **b.** at a specified interval: *hourly.*

mac•ad•am /mə kăd′ əm/ *n.* a pavement of layers of compacted broken stone, now usually bound with tar or asphalt. [after John L. *McAdam* (1756–1836).]

mack•i•naw /măk′ ə nô′/ *n.* **a.** a short, double-breasted coat of heavy, usually plaid, woolen material. **b.** the cloth from which a mackinaw coat is made, usually of wool, often with a heavy nap. [after *Mackinaw City,* Michigan.]

mag•net•ic /măg nĕt′ ĭk/ *adj.* **a.** of or relating to magnetism or magnets. **b.** operating by means of magnetism. **c.** having an unusual power or ability to attract.

maj•es•ty /măj′ ĭ stē/ *n.* (**-ties** *pl.*) **a.1.** a royal personage. **a.2. Majesty.** a title used in speaking of or to a sovereign monarch: *Your Majesty.* **b.1.** royal dignity of bearing or aspect; grandeur. **b.2.** stateliness, splendor, or magnificence, as of appearance, style, or character.

mal- a prefix meaning bad or wrongly: *malpractice.*

mal•a•dy /măl′ ə dē/ *n.* (**-dies** *pl.*) a disease, disorder, or ailment. [ME *maladie* < OFr. < *malade,* sick < Lat. *male habitus,* in poor condition.]

mal•a•prop•ism /măl′ ə prŏp ĭz′ əm/ *n.* a ludicrous misuse of a word. [after Mrs. *Malaprop,* a character in *The Rivals,* a play by Richard B. Sheridan (1751–1816).]

mal•func•tion¹ /măl fŭngk′ shən/ *v.* **a.** to fail to function. **b.** to function abnormally or imperfectly.

mal•func•tion² /măl fŭngk′ shən/ *n.* the act or an instance of malfunctioning.

mal•ice /măl′ ĭs/ *n.* a desire to harm others or to see others suffer. [ME < OFr. < Lat. *malitia* < *malus,* bad.]

ma•li•cious /mə lĭsh′ əs/ *adj.* resulting from or having the nature of malice: *malicious gossip.* [ME *malice,* malice < OFr. < Lat. *malitia* < *malus,* bad.]

ma•lign¹ /mə līn′/ *v.* to speak evil of. [ME *malignen,* to attack, < OFr. *malignier* < LLat. *malignari* < Lat. *malignus,* malign.]

ma•lign² /mə līn′/ *adj.* evil in influence; baleful.

ma•lig•nant /mə lĭg′ nənt/ *adj.* **a.** showing great malevolence; evil. **b.** highly injurious. **c.** *Pathol.* **1.** designating an abnormal growth that tends to metastasize. **c.2.** threatening to life or health: *a malignant disease.*

mal•nu•tri•tion /măl′ nōō trĭsh′ ən, -nyōō/ *n.* poor nutrition because of insufficient or poorly balanced diet or because of defective digestion or defective utilization of foods.

mal•prac•tice /măl prăk′ tĭs/ *n.* **a.** improper or careless treatment of a patient by a physician, resulting in damage or injury. **b.** improper or unethical conduct by the holder of an official or professional position.

man•age•a•ble /măn′ ĭ jə bəl/ *adj.* capable of being managed or controlled.

man•da•to•ry /măn′ də tôr′ ē, -tōr′ ē/ *adj.* required; obligatory.

ma•tri•arch /mā′ trē ärk′/ *n.* a woman who rules a family, clan, or tribe.

mat•ter-of-fact /măt′ ər əv făkt′/ *adj.* **a.** pertaining to or adhering to facts; literal. **b.** free from emotion, affection, etc.

mav•er•ick /măv′ ər ĭk, măv′ rĭk/ *n.* **a.** an unbranded or orphaned range calf or colt, traditionally considered the property of the first person who brands it. **b.** a horse or steer that has escaped from a herd. **c.** an independent-minded person who refuses to abide by the dictates of or resists adherence to a group; dissenter. [after Samuel A. *Maverick* (1803–1870).]

me•di•a•tion /mē′ dē ā′ shən/ *n. Law.* the attempt to bring about a peaceful settlement or compromise between disputing nations through the benevolent intervention of a neutral power.

me•di•e•val /mē′ dē ē′ vəl, mĕd′ ē-/ *adj.* pertaining or belonging to the Middle Ages.

me•lod•ic /mə lŏd′ ĭk/ *adj.* of, pertaining to, or containing melody.

mel•o•dra•ma /mĕl′ ə drä′ mə, -drăm′ ə/ *n.* **a.1.** a dramatic presentation characterized by heavy use of suspense, sensational episodes, romantic sentiment, and a conventionally happy ending. **a.2.** the dramatic genre characterized by this treatment. **b.** behavior or occurrences having melodramatic characteristics.

melodrama

mel•o•dy /mĕl′ ə dē / *n.* (**-dies** *pl.*) **a.** a pleasing succession or arrangement of sounds. **b.** musical quality.

mem•oir /mĕm′ wär′, -wôr′/ *n.* **a.** an account of the personal experiences of an author. **b.** often **memoirs.** an autobiography.

mem•o•ran•dum /měm′ə răn′ dəm/ *n.* (**-dums** or **-da** *pl.*) **a.** a short note written as a reminder. **b.** a written record or communication, as in a business office. [ME < Lat. *memorandus*, to be remembered < *memorare*, to remember < *memor*, mindful.]

mer•chan•dise[1] /mûr′ chən dīz′, -dīs′/ *n.* commodities or goods that may be bought or sold.

mer•chan•dise[2] /mûr′ chən dīz′/ *v.* (**-dis•es, -dised, -dis•ing**) to promote the sale of, as by advertising or display.

met•a•phor /mět′ ə fôr′, -fər/ *n.* a figure of speech in which a term is named or described as if it were something quite different, to show the likeness between the two things; for example, *the evening of life* is a metaphor.

me•te•or•ol•o•gy /mē′ tē ə rŏl′ ə jē/ *n.* (**me•te•or•ol•o•gist** *n.*) the science dealing with the phenomena of the atmosphere, especially weather and weather conditions.

me•trop•o•lis /mə trŏp ə lĭs/ *n.* **a.** a major city. **b.** a city or urban area regarded as the center of a specific activity. **c.** the largest or most important city of a country, state, or region. [LLat. < Gk. *mĕtropolis*, mother city: *mētēr*, mother + *polis*, city.]

metropolis

met•ro•pol•i•tan /mět′ rə pŏl′ ĭ tən/ *adj.* of, pertaining to, or characteristic of a metropolis. [ME < LLat. *metropolitanus* < Gk. *mētropolitēs*, citizen of a metropolis < *mētropolis*, mother city: *mētēr*, mother + *polis*, city.]

mi•gra•to•ry /mī′ grə tôr′ē, -tōr′ē/ *adj.* **a.** characterized by migration; migrating periodically: *migratory birds.* **b.** of or relating to a migration. **c.** roving; nomadic.

min•i•mum[1] /mĭn′ ə məm/ *n.* (**-mums** or **-ma** *pl.*) the least possible quantity or degree.

min•i•mum[2] /mĭn′ ə məm/ *adj.* of, consisting of, or representing the lowest possible amount or degree permissible or attainable.

mis•cel•la•ne•ous /mĭs′ ə lā′ nē əs/ *adj.* **a.** made up of a variety of parts or ingredients. **b.** concerned with diverse subjects or aspects. [Lat. *miscellaneus* < *miscere*, to mix.]

mo•men•tum /mō měn′ təm/ *n.* (**-ta** or **-tums** *pl.*) **a.** *Physics.* the product of the mass and velocity of a moving body. **b.** force or speed of motion; impetus.

mon•arch /mŏn′ ərk, -ärk′/ *n.* **a.** a sole and absolute ruler of a state. **b.** a sovereign, such as a king or emperor. [LLat. *monarcha* < Gk. *monarkhes*: *monos*, single + *arkhein*, to rule.]

mon•as•ter•y /mŏn′ ə stěr′ ē/ *n.* (**-ies** *pl.*) the dwelling place of a community of persons under religious vows, especially monks.

mon•o•logue /mŏn′ ə lôg′, -lŏg′/ *n.* **a.** a long speech made by one person, often monopolizing conversation. **b.** a long speech delivered by an actor on the stage or a character in a story or poem; a dramatic soliloquy. **c.** a continuous series of jokes or comic stories delivered by a comedian. [Fr.: Gk. *monos*, one + Gk. *logos*, speech.]

mo•nop•o•lize /mə nŏp′ ə līz′/ *v.* (**-liz•es, -lized, -liz•ing**) **a.** to gain and hold a monopoly over. **b.** to dominate by excluding others: *monopolized the conversation.* **c.** to take all of; have all to oneself.

mo•ral[1] /môr′ əl, mŏr′-/ *adj.* **a.** of or concerned with the judgment principles of right and wrong in relation to human action and character. **b.** having psychological rather than physical or concrete effects: *a moral victory.*

mo•ral[2] /môr′ əl, mŏr′-/ *n.* **a.** the lesson or principle contained in or taught by a fable, story, or event. **b.** a concisely expressed general truth; maxim.

mo•rale /mə răl′/ *n.* the state of the spirits of an individual or group as shown by confidence, cheerfulness, discipline, and willingness to perform assigned tasks.

mort•gage[1] /môr′ gĭj/ *n.* a temporary and conditional pledge of property to a creditor as security for the performance of an obligation or the repayment of a debt. [ME *morgage* < OFr.: *mort*, dead (< Lat. *mortuus* < *mors*, death) + *gage*, pledge, of Germanic orig.]

mort•gage[2] /môr′ gĭj/ *v.* (**-gag•es, -gaged, -gag•ing**) to pledge property as security for the payment of a debt.

mot•to /mŏt′ ō/ *n.* (-**toes** or -**tos** *pl.*) a brief statement used to express a principle, goal, or ideal. [Ital. *motto,* word.]

much-im•proved /mŭch ĭm **proōv′d**/ *adj.* showing a great increase in quality, value, or performance. *Extra practice sessions contributed to the team's much-improved defensive play.*

mus•tache /mŭs′ tăsh′, mə **stăsh′**/ *n.* the hair growing on the human upper lip, especially when it is cultivated and groomed.

mu•ta•tion /myoō tā′ shən/ *n.* **a.** the act or process of being altered or changed. **b.** an alteration or change, as in nature, form, or quality. **c.** *Biol.* any change in the genes or chromosomes of an organism that can be inherited by its offspring.

myth /mĭth/ *n.* a traditional story dealing with ancestors, heroes, supernatural beings, etc., and usually making an attempt to explain some belief, practice, or natural phenomenon.

myth•i•cal /mĭth′ ĭ kəl/ *adj.* **a.** having the nature of a myth. **b.** of or existing in myth: *the mythical unicorn.* **c.** imaginary; fictitious.

ne•ces•si•ty /nə sĕs′ ĭ′ tē/ *n.* (-**ties** *pl.*) something needed for the existence, success, or functioning of something; requirement. [ME *necessite* < OFr. < Lat. *necessitas* < *necesse,* necessary.]

neg•a•tive /nĕg′ ə tĭv/ *adj.* **a.** expressing, containing, or consisting of a negation, refusal, or denial. **b.** indicating opposition or resistance. **c.** *Math.* pertaining to or denoting: **1.** a quantity less than zero. **c.2.** the sign (−).

ne•go•ti•ate /nĭ gō′ shē āt′/ *v.* (-**ates,** -**at•ed,** -**at•ing**) **a.** to arrange or settle by conferring or discussing: *negotiate a union contract.* **b.** to succeed in going over, accomplishing, or coping with: *negotiate a sharp curve.* [Lat. *negotiari, negotiat-,* to transact business < *negotium,* business: *neg-,* not + *otium,* leisure.]

neu•tral /noō′ trəl, nyoō′-/ *adj.* belonging to neither side or party.

neu•tral•i•ty /noō trăl′ ĭ tē, nyoō-/ *n.* the state or policy of being neutral, especially nonparticipation in war.

nom•i•na•tion /nŏm′ ə nā′ shən/ *n.* **a.** the act or process of nominating. **b.** the state of being nominated.

non•par•ti•san /nŏn pär′ tĭ zən, -sən/ *adj.* not based on, influenced by, affiliated with, or supporting the interests or policies of a political party.

no•vel•la /nō vĕl′ ə/ *n.* (-**vel•las** or **vel•le** *pl.*) **a.** a short prose tale characterized by wit, terseness, or satire. **b.** a short novel.

nu•mer•ous /noō′ mər əs, nyoō′-/ *adj.* consisting of many persons or items.

ob- a prefix meaning toward, in front of, or against. When **ob-** is followed by **c, f,** or **p,** it becomes **oc-, of-,** or **op-,** respectively. When it is followed by **m,** it is reduced to **o-.** [NLat. < Lat., toward, against < *ob-,* toward.]

o•be•di•ent /ō bē′ dē ənt/ *adj.* obeying or carrying out a request or command; dutiful.

ob•jec•tive[1] /əb jĕk′ tĭv/ *adj.* **a.** of or having to do with a material object as distinguished from a mental concept. **b.1.** uninfluenced by emotion, or personal prejudice. **b.2.** based on observable phenomena; real, actual.

ob•jec•tive[2] /əb jĕk′ tĭv/ *n.* something worked toward or striven for; goal.

ob•ser•vance /əb zûr′ vəns/ *n.* **a.** the act or practice of observing or complying with a law, custom, command, or rule. **b.** the act or custom of keeping or celebrating a holiday or other ritual occasion. **c.** the action of watching; observation.

ob•ser•vant /əb zûr′ vənt/ *adj.* **a.** quick to perceive; alert: *an observant traveler.* **b.** diligent in observing a law, custom, duty, or principle: *observant of the speed limit.*

ob•ser•va•tion /ŏb′ zər vā′ shən/ *n.* **a.1.** the act or faculty of observing. **a.2.** the fact of being observed. **b.** the act of noting and recording something, as a phenomenon, with instruments. **c.** a comment or remark. [Lat. *observatio* < *observare*: *ob,* to + *servare,* to watch.]

ob•serve /əb zûrv′/ *v.* (**-serves, -served, -serv•ing**) **a.** to perceive; notice. **b.** to make a systematic or scientific observation of: *observe the moon's orbit.* **c.** to say casually; remark. **d.** to keep or celebrate (a holiday, for example): *observe an anniversary.* [ME *observen* < OFr. *observer* < Lat. *observare*: *ob,* to + *servare,* to watch.]

ob•sta•cle /ŏb′ stə kəl/ *n.* one that opposes, stands in the way of, or holds up progress. [ME < OFr. < Lat. *obstaculum* < *obstare,* to hinder: *ob,* against + *stare,* to stand.]

oc•ca•sion•al /ə kā′ zhə nəl/ *adj.* (**oc•ca•sion•al•ly** *adv.*) occuring from time to time. [ME *occasioun* < OFr. *occasion* < Lat. *occasio* < *occidere,* to fall: *ob,* down + *cadere,* to fall.]

oc•cu•pa•tion /ŏk′ yə pā′ shən/ *n.* **a.1.** an activity that serves as one's regular source of livelihood; vocation. **a.2.** an activity engaged in especially as a means of passing time. **b.** the act or process of holding or possessing a place.

oc•cu•py /ŏk′ yə pī′/ *v.* (**-pies, -pied, -py•ing**) **a.** to fill up (time or space). **b.** to dwell or reside in. **c.** to hold or fill (an office or position). **d.** to engage, employ, or busy (oneself). [ME *occupien* < OFr. *ocuper* < Lat. *occupare,* to seize: *ob-* (intensive) + *capere,* to take.]

od•ys•sey /ŏd′ ĭ sē/ *n.* (**-seys** *pl.*) an extended adventurous wandering. [after the *Odyssey,* a Homeric epic recounting the wanderings of Odysseus after the fall of Troy < Fr. *Odyssee* < Lat. *Odyssea* < Gk. *Odysseia* < *Odysseus,* Odysseus.]

of•fend /ə fĕnd′/ *v.* **a.** to create or excite anger, resentment, or annoyance in. **b.** to be displeasing or disagreeable to. [ME *offenden* < OFr. *ofendre* < Lat. *offendere.*]

of•fen•sive /ə fĕn′ sĭv/ *adj.* **a.** disagreeable to the senses. **b.** causing anger, displeasure, resentment, or affront. **c.** making an attack. **d.** of or pertaining to a team having possession of a ball or puck.

old-fash•ioned /ōld′ făsh′ ənd/ *adj.* **a.** of a style or method formerly in vogue; outdated. **b.** attached to or favoring methods, ideas, or customs of an earlier time.

old-fashioned

o•paque /ō pāk′/ *adj.* not capable of letting light pass through. [partly < ME *opake,* and partly < OFr. *opaque,* both < Lat. *opacus,* dark.]

op•e•ret•ta /ŏp′ ə rĕt′ ə/ *n.* a theatrical production that has many of the musical elements of opera, but is lighter and more popular in subject and style and contains spoken dialogue. [Ital., dim. of *opera,* opera < Lat., work produced < *opus,* work.]

op•po•site¹ /ŏp′ ə zĭt/ *adj.* **a.** placed or located directly across from something else or from each other: *opposite sides of a building.* **b.** facing the other way, moving or tending away from each other: *opposite directions.*

op•po•site² /ŏp′ ə zĭt/ *n.* one that is opposite or contrary to another.

op•pres•sive /ə prĕs′ ĭv/ *adv.* **a.1.** difficult to bear; harsh. **a.2.** tyrannical. **b.** weighing heavily on the spirit or senses: *oppressive heat.* [Med. Lat. *oppressivus* < Lat. *opprimere,* to press down: *ob-,* against + *premere,* to press.]

o•pus /ō′ pəs/ *n.* (**o•pe•ra** or **o•pus•es** *pl.*) a creative work, especially a musical composition numbered to designate the order of a composer's works. [Lat.]

-or¹ a suffix that forms nouns from verbs: *percolator, operator.*

-or² a suffix that forms nouns and means condition or activity: *behavior.*

or•di•nate /ôr′ dn ĭt, -āt′/ *n. Math.* the plane Cartesian coordinate representing the distance from a specified point to the *x*-axis, measured parallel to the *y*-axis.

or•gan•ic /ôr găn′ ĭk/ *adj.* **a.** of, pertaining to, or derived from living organisms. **b.** using or grown with fertilizers and mulches consisting only of animal or vegetable matter, with no use of chemical fertilizers or pesticides: *organic gardening.*

o•rig•i•nal•i•ty /ə rĭj′ ə năl′ ĭ tē/ *n.* (**-ties** *pl.*) **a.** the quality of being original. **b.** the capacity to act or think independently.

or•na•men•tal /ôr′ nə měn′ tl/ *adj.* of, pertaining to, or serving as an ornament.

-ory¹ a suffix that forms nouns and means a place of or for.

-ory² a suffix that forms adjectives and means of, involving, or tending toward.

-ous a suffix that forms adjectives and means full of or having: *joyous.*

out•come /out′ kŭm′/ *n.* a natural result; consequence.

out-of-date /out′ əv dāt′/ *adj.* outmoded; old-fashioned.

o•ver•ture /ō′ vər chŏŏr′/ *n. Mus.* **a.1.** an instrumental composition intended especially as an introduction to an extended musical work, such as an opera or an oratorio. *The rousing overture prepared us for an exciting concert.* **a.2.** a similar orchestral work, such as one written as introductory music to a play or as a concert piece. **b.** an act, offer, or proposal that indicates readiness to undertake a course of action or to open a relationship. [ME < OFr. < Lat. *apertura,* opening < *aperire,* to open.]

pag•eant•ry /păj′ ən trē/ *n.* (**-ries** *pl.*) **a.** pageants and their presentation. **b.** grand display; pomp.

pan•el•ing /păn′ ə lĭng/ *n.* a section of panels or paneled wall.

pan•ic¹ /păn′ ĭk/ *n.* a sudden, overpowering terror, often affecting many people at once. [< Fr. *panique,* terrified < Gk. *panikos* < *Pan,* Pan.]

pan•ic² /păn′ ĭk/ *v.* (**-ics, -icked, -ick•ing**) (**pan•ick•y** *adj.*) to affect or be affected with panic.

pa•py•rus /pə pī′ rəs/ *n.* **a.** a tall aquatic plant of southern Europe and northern Africa. **b.** a paper made from the pith or the stems of the papyrus, used in antiquity as a writing material.

papyrus

par•a•dox /păr′ ə dŏks′/ *n.* (**-dox•es** *pl.*) a seemingly contradictory statement that may nonetheless be true.

par•a•mount /păr′ ə mount′/ *adj.* of chief concern or importance; foremost.

parch•ment /pärch′ mənt/ *n.* the skin of a sheep or goat prepared for writing or painting on.

par•o•dy /păr′ ə dē/ *n.* a literary or artistic work that broadly mimics an author's characteristic style and holds it up to ridicule.

par•ti•ci•ple /pär′ tĭ sĭp′ əl/ *n. Gram.* either of two verb forms that are used with auxiliary verbs to indicate certain tenses and that can also function in certain cases as adjectives or nouns.

part-time /pärt′ tīm′/ *adj.* (**part-time** *adv.*) for or during less than the customary time: *a part-time job.*

pas•teur•ize /păs′ chə rīz, păs′ tə-/ *v.* (**-iz•es, -ized, -iz•ing**) to treat (a liquid) by sterilizing in order to destroy harmful germs and limit fermentation. [after Louis *Pasteur* (1822–1895).]

pat•ent¹ /păt′ nt/ *n.* a grant made by a government to an inventor, assuring him the sole right to make, use, and sell his invention for a certain period of time. [ME, unsealed < OFr. < Lat. *patens* < pr.part. of *patēre,* to be opened.]

pat•ent² /păt′ nt/ *v.* to obtain a patent on.

pa•tient¹ /pā′ shənt/ *adj.* (**pa•tient•ly** *adv.*) **a.** tolerant; understanding. **b.** persevering; constant: *a patient worker.* **c.** capable of bearing delay; not hasty. [ME *pacient* < OFr. < Lat. *patiens* < *pati,* to endure.]

pa•tient² /pā′ shənt/ *n.* one under medical treatment.

pa•tri•arch /pā′ trē ärk′/ *n.* **a.** the male leader of a family or tribe. **b.** someone regarded as the founder or original head of an enterprise, organization, or tradition. **c.** a very old and venerable man; elder. [ME *patriarche* < OFr. < LLat. *patriarcha* < Gk. *patriarkhēs: patria,* family (< *patēr,* father) + *arkhos,* ruler (< *arkhein,* to rule).]

peace•a•ble /pē′ sə bəl/ *adj.* **a.** inclined or disposed to peace; promoting calm. **b.** peaceful; undisturbed.

peace-lov•ing /pēs′ lŭv′ ĭng/ *adj.* peaceable; not hostile, aggressive, or argumentative. *Rachel was peace-loving; she always tried to settle fights between her friends.*

pe•nal•ize /pē′ nə līz′, pĕn′ ə-/ *v.* (**-iz•es, -ized, iz•ing**) to subject to a penalty, especially for infringement of a law or official regulation.

pen•dant /pĕn′ dənt/ *n.* something suspended from something else, especially an ornament or piece of jewelry attached to a necklace or bracelet. [ME *pendaunt* < OFr. *pendant* < pr.part. of *pendre,* to hang < Lat. *pendēre.*]

pendant

pen•du•lum /pĕn′ jə ləm, pĕn′ dyə-, pĕn′ də-/ *n.* an object suspended from a fixed support so that it swings freely back and forth under the influence of gravity and commonly used to regulate various devices, especially clocks. [NLat. < Lat. *pendulus,* hanging < *pendēre,* to hang.]

pen•in•su•la /pə nĭn′ syə lə, -sə lə/ *n.* a long projection of land into water, connected with the mainland by an isthmus.

per- a prefix that means thoroughly, completely, or intensely. [< Lat. *per,* through.]

per•ceive /pər sēv′/ *v.* (**-ceives, -ceived, -ceiv•ing**) **a.** to become aware of directly through any of the senses, especially to see or hear. **b.** to become aware of in one's mind; achieve understanding of.

per•en•ni•al¹ /pə rĕn′ ē əl/ *adj.* **a.** lasting or active through the year or through many years. **b.** *Bot.* having a life span of more than two years.

per•en•ni•al² /pə rĕn′ ē əl/ *n. Bot.* a perennial plant.

per•fo•rate /pûr′ fə rāt′/ *v.* (**-rates, -rat•ed, -rat•ing**) to pierce, punch, or bore a hole or holes in; penetrate [Lat. *perforare, perforat-: per* (intensive) + *forare,* to bore.]

per•ma•nence /pûr′ mə nəns/ *n.* the condition or quality of being permanent.

per•ma•nent /pûr′ mə nənt/ *adj.* fixed and changeless; lasting or meant to last indefinitely.

per•pet•u•al /pər pĕch′ ōō əl/ *adj.* **a.** lasting for an indefinitely long duration. **b.** ceaselessly repeated or continuing without interruption. [ME *perpetuel* < OFr. < Lat. *perpetualis* < *perpetuus,* continuous < *perpes,* < uninterrupted: *per-* (intensive) + *petere,* to go toward.]

per•plex /pər plĕks′/ *v.* to confuse or puzzle; bewilder. [< obs. *perplex,* perplexed < Lat. *perplexus:* (intensive) + *plectere,* to entwine.]

per•se•vere /pûr′ sə vîr′/ *v.* (**-veres, -vered, -ver•ing**) to persist in or remain constant to a purpose, idea, or task in the face of obstacles or discouragement. [ME *perseveren* < OFr. *perseverer* < Lat. *perseverare* < *perseverus,* very serious: *per-* (intensive) + *severus,* severe.]

per•sist•ence /pər sĭs′ təns, -zĭs′-/ *n.* **a.** the act of persisting. **b.** the quality of being persistent; perseverance; tenacity.

per•son•al•i•ty /pûr′ sə năl′ ĭ tē/ *n.* (**-ties** *pl.*) **a.** the totality of qualities and traits, as of character or behavior, that are peculiar to an individual person. **b.** the pattern of collective character, behavioral temperamental, emotional, and mental traits of an individual. **c.** *Informal.* a person of prominence or notoriety: *television personalities.* [ME *personalite* < LLat. *personalitas* < *personalis,* personal < Lat. *persona,* person.]

per•spi•ra•tion /pûr′ spə rā′ shən/ *n.* the saline moisture excreted through the pores of the skin by the sweat glands; sweat. [Fr. *perspirer,* to perspire < OFr. < Lat. *perspirare,* to breathe through: *per,* through + *spirare,* to breathe.]

per•suade /pər swād′/ *v.* (**-suades, -suad•ed, -suad•ing**) to cause (someone) to do something by means of argument, reasoning, or entreaty. [Lat. *persuadēre:* *per-* (intensive) + *suadēre,* to urge.]

per•ti•nent /pûr′ tn ənt/ *adj.* of, relating to, or connected with a specific matter: *a pertinent fact.* [ME < OFr. < Lat. *pertinens,* pr.part. of *pertinēre,* to pertain: *per-* (intensive) + *tenēre,* to hold.]

phar•oah /fâr′ ō, fā′ rō/ *n.* a king of ancient Egypt.

phe•nom•e•non /fĭ nŏm′ ə nŏn′, -nən/ *n.* (**-na** or **-nons** *pl.*) **a.** an occurrence or fact that is directly perceptible by the senses. **b.** an unusual, significant, or unaccountable fact or occurrence; marvel. [LLat. *phaenomenon* < Gk. *phainomenon* < *phainomenos,* pr.part. of *phainesthai,* to appear < *phainein,* to show.]

phi•los•o•phy /fĭ lŏs′ ə fē/ *n.* (**-phies** *pl.*) **a.** the study by logical reasoning of the basic truths and laws governing the universe, nature, life, morals, etc. **b.** a personal set of opinions about life, the world, etc. **c.** a basic practical rule or set of rules.

pho•net•ic /fə nĕt′ ĭk/ *adj.* representing the sounds of speech with a set of distinct symbols, each denoting a single sound: *phonetic spelling.*

pho•to•syn•the•sis /fō′ tō sĭn′ thĭ sĭs/ *n.* the chemical process by which green plants use light and cholorophyll to convert carbon dioxide and water to carbohydrates, releasing oxygen as a by-product.

phys•ics /fĭz′ ĭks/ *n.* (*used with a sing. verb*). the science of matter and energy and of interactions between the two.

pil•grim•age /pĭl′ grə mĭj/ *n.* **a.** a journey to a sacred place or shrine. **b.** a long journey or search, especially one of exalted purpose or moral significance.

plan•e•tar•i•um /plăn′ ĭ târ′ ē əm/ *n.* **a.** a device for projecting images of celestial bodies in their courses onto the inner surface of a dome. **b.** a building or room containing a planetarium, with seats for an audience.

pla•teau /plă tō′/ *n.* (**-teaus** *pl.*) an elevated and comparatively level expanse of land; tableland.

plateau

pla•ton•ic /plə tŏn′ ĭk, plā-/ *adj.* **a.** of, pertaining to, or characteristic of Plato or his philosophy. **b.** transcending physical desire and tending toward the purely spiritual or ideal. [after *Plato* (427?–347 B.C.), Greek philosopher.]

play-by-play[1] /plā′ bĭ plā′/ *adj.* consisting of a detailed running commentary or account, as of the action of a sports event.

play-by-play[2] /plā′ bĭ plā′/ *n.* a detailed running commentary.

play•er-man•ag•er /plā′ ər măn′ i jər/ *n.* a person who fills the roles of both player and manager; participant in a game or sport who also serves as a team director or supervisor. *The Stars have a great outfielder and a great leader in player-manager Theo Watson.*

pneu•mo•nia /nōō mōn′ yə, nyōō-/ *n.* an acute or chronic disease marked by inflammation of the lungs and caused by viruses, bacteria, and physical and chemical agents. [NLat. < Gk., alteration of *pleumonia* < *pleumōn,* lung.]

po•lit•i•cal /pə lĭt′ ĭ kəl/ *adj.* of, pertaining to, or dealing with the study, structure, or affairs of government, politics, or the state.

pol•i•ti•cian /pŏl′ ĭ tĭsh′ ən/ *n.* one who is actively involved in politics, especially party politics.

Spelling Dictionary

pol•i•tics /pŏl′ ĭ tĭks/ *n.* (*used with a sing. verb*). **a.** the art or science of government; political science. **b.** the activities or affairs of a government, politician, or political party. [ME *polytyk,* politic < OFr. *poilitique* < Lat. *politicus,* political < Gk. *politikos* < *politēs,* citizen < *polis,* city.]

port•a•ble /pôr′ tə bəl, pōr′-/ *adj.* **a.** capable of being carried. **b.** easily carried or moved. [ME <OFr. < LLat. *portabilis* < Lat. *portare,* to carry.]

por•trait /pôr′ trĭt, -trāt′, pōr′-/ *n.* a painting, photograph, or other likeness of a person, especially one showing the face. [Fr. < OFr. < *portraire,* to portray < Lat. *protrahere,* to reveal: *pro-,* forth + *trahere,* to draw.]

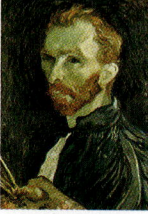

portrait

post•pone /pōst pōn′, pōs pōn′/ *v.* (**-pones, -poned, -pon•ing**) to delay until a future time; put off.

pos•tu•late /pŏs′ choō lĭt, -lāt′/ *n.* **a.** something assumed without proof as being self-evident or generally accepted, especially when used as a basis for an argument. **b.** *Math.* an axiom.

pos•ture /pŏs′ chər/ *n.* **a.** a position or attitude of the body or of bodily parts. **b.** a characteristic way of bearing one's body; carriage. [Fr. < Ital. *postura* < Lat. *positura,* position < *ponere,* to place.]

prac•ti•cal /prăk′ tĭ kəl/ *adj.* (**prac•ti•cal•i•ty** *n.*) **a.** capable of being used or put into effect; useful. **b.** designed to serve a purpose without elaboration. **c.** level-headed, efficient, and unspeculative. [< LLat. *practicus* < Gk. *praktikos* < *prattein,* to act.]

pre- a Latin prefix meaning before: *precaution.* When **pre-** is followed by a vowel, it may appear with a hyphen: *pre-empt.*

pre•cede /prĭ sēd′/ *v.* (**-cedes, -ced•ed, -ced•ing**) **a.** to come before in time. **b.** to be in a position in front of; go in advance of. [ME *preceden* < OFr. *preceder* < Lat. *praecedere: prae-,* before + *cedere,* to go.]

pre•cip•i•ta•tion /prĭ sĭp′ ĭ tā′ shən/ *n.* **a.** water droplets or ice particles condensed from atmospheric water vapor and sufficiently massive to fall to the earth's surface, such as rain or snow. **b.** the quantity of such precipitation falling in a specific area within a specific period.

pre•cise /prĭ sīs′/ *adj.* **a.** clearly expressed; definite. **b.** exactly corresponding to what is indicated; correct. **c.** strictly distinguished from others; very.

pre•dic•tion /prĭ dĭk′ shən/ *n.* something foretold or predicted; prophecy. [Lat. *praedicere, praedict-,* to predict: *prae-,* before + *dicere,* to say.]

pre•dom•i•nant /prĭ dŏm′ ə nənt/ *adj.* having greatest ascendancy, importance, influence, authority, or force. [OFr. < Med. Lat. *praedominans,* pr.part. of *praedominari,* to predominate: Lat. *prae-,* before + Lat. *dominari,* to rule < *dominus,* master.]

pre•ju•dice[1] /prĕj′ ə dĭs/ *n.* **a.1.** an adverse judgment or opinion formed beforehand or without knowledge or examination of the facts. **a.2.** a preconceived preference or idea; bias. **b.** irrational suspicion or hatred of a particular group, race, or religion.

pre•ju•dice[2] /prĕj′ ə dĭs/ *v.* (**-dic•es, -diced, -dic•ing**) **a.** to cause (someone) to judge prematurely and irrationally; bias. **b.** to affect injuriously or detrimentally by some judgment or act.

pre•lim•i•nar•y[1] /prĭ lĭm′ ə nĕr′ ē/ *adj.* leading to or preparing for the main event, action, or business. [Fr. *prē′liminaire* < Med. Lat. *praeliminarus:* Lat. *prae-,* before + Lat. *limen,* threshold.]

pre•lim•i•nar•y[2] /prĭ lĭm′ ə nĕr′ ē/ *n.* (**-ies** *pl.*) something that leads to or serves as preparation for a main event, action, or business.

prel•ude /prĕl′ yoōd′, prā′ loōd′, prē′-/ *n.* **a.** an introductory performance, event, or action preceding a more important one. **b.** *Mus.* a piece or movement serving as an introduction to a musical composition. [OFr. < Med. Lat. *praeludium* < Lat. *praeludere,* to play beforehand: *prae-,* before + *ludere,* to play < *ludus,* game.]

pre•par•a•to•ry /prĭ păr′ ə tôr′ ē, -tōr ē′, -pâr′-/ *adj.* serving to make ready or prepare; introductory. —*idiom.* **preparatory to.** in preparation for: from **prepare.** [ME *preparen* < OFr. *preparer* < Lat. *praeparare: prae-,* before + *prepare,* to make ready.]

pre•scribe /prĭ skrīb′/ *v.* (**-scribes, -scribed, -scrib•ing**) **a.** to set down as a rule or guide. **b.** *Med.* to order or recommend the use of (a drug or treatment). [Lat. *praescribere: prae-,* before + *scribere,* to write.]

pre•scrip•tion /prĭ skrĭp′ shən/ *n.* **a.** *Med.* a written instruction by a physician for the preparation and administration of a medicine. **b.** a prescribed medicine. [Lat. *praescriptio,* precept < *praescribere,* to order: *prae-,* before + *scribere,* to write.]

pre•serve[1] /prĭ zûrv′/ *v.* (**-serves, -served, -serv•ing**) **a.** to keep safe from injury, peril, or other adversity; protect. **b.** to keep in perfect or unaltered condition; maintain unchanged. [ME *preserven* < OFr. *preserver* < LLat. *praeservare:* Lat. *prae-,* before + Lat. *servare,* to guard.]

pre•serve[2] /prĭ zûrv′/ *n.* (**pres•er•va•tion** *n.*) an area maintained for the protection of wildlife or natural resources.

preserve

pres•i•den•tial /prĕz′ ĭ dĕn′ shəl/ *adj.* of or relating to a president or presidency.

pre•vent /prĭ vĕnt′/ *v.* **a.** to keep from happening; avert. **b.** to keep (someone) from doing something; impede.

pre•ven•tion /prĭ vĕn′ shən/ *n.* the act of preventing.

pri•mar•y[1] /prī′ mĕr′ē, -mə rē/ *adj.* being first or best in degree, quality, or importance.

pri•mar•y[2] /prī′ mĕr′ē, -mə rē/ *n.* (**-ies** *pl.*) a preliminary election in which the registered voters of a political party nominate candidates for office.

pro-[1] a prefix meaning: **a.** favor or support. **b.** acting as; substituting for: *pronoun.* When **pro-** is followed by a capital letter, it appears with a hyphen: *pro-American.* [ME < Lat. *pro,* for.]

pro-[2] a prefix meaning before or in front of: *prologue.* [< Gk. *pro,* before, in front of.]

prob•a•bil•i•ty /prŏb′ ə bĭl′ ĭ tē/ *n.* (**-ties** *pl.*) **a.** the quality or condition of being probable; likelihood. **b.** a probable situation, condition, or event.

prob•lem-solv•ing /prŏb′ ləm sŏlv′ ĭng/ *n.* the act or process of finding an answer or solution. *Problem-solving requires the skills of logic and creativity.*

ă	pat	ŏ	pot	th	**th**in
ā	pay	ō	toe	*th*	**th**is
âr	care	ô	paw, for	hw	**wh**ich
ä	father	oi	noise	zh	vi**s**ion
ĕ	pet	ou	**ou**t	ə	**a**bout,
ē	be	ŏŏ	took		it**e**m,
ĭ	pit	ōō	boot		penc**i**l,
ī	pie	ŭ	cut		gall**o**p,
îr	pier	ûr	**ur**ge		circ**u**s

pro•ce•dure /prə sē′ jər/ *n.* **a.** a manner of proceeding; way of performing or effecting something. **b.** a set of established forms or methods for conducting the affairs of a business, legislative body, or court of law.

pro•ceed /prō sēd′, prə-/ *v.* **a.** to go forward or onward, especially after an interruption; continue. **b.** to move in an orderly manner.

pro•duc•tion /prə dŭk′ shən, prō-/ *n.* **a.** the act or process of producing. **b.** the creation of value or wealth by producing goods and services. **c.** the total number of products; output. **d.** a public performance or showing of a play or other form of entertainment.

pro•gram•mer /prō′ grăm′ ər/ *n.* one who prepares a computer program.

pro•gres•sion /prə grĕsh′ ən/ *n.* **a.** a sequence, as of events. **b.** *Math.* a series of numbers or quantities each derived from the one before by some regular rule.

pro•logue /prō′ lôg′, -lŏg′/ *n.* **a.** the lines introducing a discourse or play. **b.** an introductory act or event. [ME *prolog* < OFr. *prologue* < Lat. *prologus* < Gk. *prologos: pro-,* before + *legein,* to speak.]

prom•i•nent /prŏm′ ə nənt/ *adj.* **a.** projecting outward from a line or surface. **b.** widely known; eminent.

pro•mote /prə mōt′/ *v.* (**-motes, -mot•ed, -mot•ing**) **a.** to raise to a more important or responsible job or rank. **b.** to contribute to the progress or growth of; further. **c.** to attempt to sell or popularize by advertising or by securing financial support.

Spelling Dictionary

pro•nun•ci•a•tion /prə nŭn′ sē ā′ shən/ *n.* the act or manner of articulating speech.

pro•verb /prŏv′ ûrb⁄/ *n.* a short, pithy saying in frequent and widespread use that expresses a well-known truth or fact.

psy•chol•o•gy /sī kŏl′ ə jē/ *n.* (**-gies** *pl.*) (**psy•chol•o•gist** *n.*) the science of mental processes and behavior.

pub•li•cize /pŭb′ lĭ sīz⁄/ *v.* (**-ciz•es, -cized, -ciz•ing**) to give publicity to. [Lat. *publicus*, public < *populus*, people.]

pul•mo•nar•y /po͞ol′ mə nĕr′ ē, pŭl′-/ *adj.* of or pertaining to the lungs.

punc•tu•al /pŭngk′ cho͞o əl/ *adj.* (**punc•tu•al•i•ty** *n.*) acting or arriving exactly at the time appointed; prompt. [Med. Lat. *punctualis* < Lat. *punctum*, point < *pungere*, to prick.]

quan•ti•ty /kwŏn′ tĭ tē/ *n.* (**-ties** *pl.*) **a.1.** a specified or indefinite number or amount. **a.2.** a considerable amount or number. **a.3.** an exact amount or number. **b.** the measurable, countable, or comparable property or aspect of a thing. **c.** *Math.* something serving as the object of a mathematical operation.

quar•an•tine[1] /kwôr′ ən tēn′, kwŏr′-/ *n.* enforced isolation or restriction of free movement imposed to prevent a contagious disease from spreading.

quar•an•tine[2] /kwôr′ ən tēn′, kwŏr′-/ *v.* (**-tines, -tined, -tin•ing**) to isolate in or as if in quarantine.

ques•tion•naire /kwĕs′ chə nâr′/ *n.* a printed form containing a set of questions, especially one addressed to a statistically significant number of subjects by way of gathering information, as for a survey. [Fr. < *questionner*, to ask < *question*, question < OFr.]

rad•i•cal[1] /răd′ ĭ kəl/ *adj.* **a.** arising from or going to a root or source; basic. **b.** carried to the utmost limit; extreme.

rad•i•cal[2] /răd′ ĭ kəl/ *n.* **a.** one who advocates political and social revolution. **b.** *Math.* the root of a quantity as indicated by the radical sign. ($\sqrt{\ }$)

ran•dom /răn′ dəm/ *adj.* **a.** having no specific pattern or objective; haphazard. **b.1.** *Statistics.* of or designating a phenomenon that does not produce the same outcome or consequences every time it occurs under identical circumstances. **b.2.** of or designating a sample drawn from a population so that each member of the population has an equal chance to be drawn.

rasp•ber•ry /răz′ bĕr′ ē/ *n.* **a.** any of various shrubby, usually prickly plants of the genus *Rubus*, bearing edible berries. **b.** the fruit of the raspberry. **c.** a moderate to dark or deep purplish red. [Obs. *raspit*, raspberry + BERRY.]

ra•tion•al•ize /răsh′ ən ə līz⁄/ *v.* (**-iz•es, -ized, -iz•ing**) **a.** to think in a rational or rationalistic way. **b.** to devise self-satisfying but incorrect reasons for one's behavior.

ra•vine /rə vēn⁄/ *n.* a deep, narrow cleft or gorge in the earth's surface, especially one worn by the flow of water.

ravine

re- a prefix meaning: **a.** again; anew: *reassemble*. **b.** back; backward: *recall*. When **re** is followed by **e,** it may appear with a hyphen: *re-elect*.

re•act /rē ăkt⁄/ *v.* **a.** to act in response to a stimulus or prompting. **b.** to act in opposition to some former condition or act. **c.** *Chem.* to undergo chemical change.

re•ac•tion /rē ăk′ shən/ *n.* **a.1.** a response to a stimulus. **a.2.** the state resulting from such a response. **b.** a reverse or opposing action.

re•bel[1] /rĭ bĕl⁄/ *v.* (**-bels, -belled, -bel•ling**) **a.** to resist or defy an authority or generally accepted convention. **b.** to feel or express strong unwillingness or repugnance.

reb•el[2] /rĕb′ əl/ *n.* a person who rebels or is in rebellion. **modifier:** *rebel soldiers; a rebel movement.*

re•bel•lion /rĭ bĕl′ yən/ *n.* **a.** an uprising or organized opposition intended to change or overthrow an existing government or ruling authority. **b.** an act or show of defiance toward an authority or established convention.

re•cede /rĭ sēd′/ *v.* (**-cedes, -ced•ed, -ced•ing**) to move back or away from a limit, point, or mark. [Lat. *recedere:* *re-*, back + *cedere,* to go away.]

rec•om•mend /rĕk′ ə mĕnd′/ *v.* **a.** to praise or commend to another as being worthy or desirable; endorse: *recommend him for the job.* **b.** to counsel or advise (that something be done). [ME *recommenden* < Med. Lat. *recommendare:* Lat. *re-* (intensive) + Lat. *commendare,* to entrust (*com-*, together + *mandare,* to order).]

re•cy•cle /rē sī′ kəl/ *v.* (**-cles, -cled, -cling**) **a.** to put or pass through a cycle again, as for further treatment. **b.** to extract and reuse (useful substances found in waste). **c.** to use again, especially to reprocess in order to use again: *recycle aluminum cans.*

re•duce /rĭ dōōs′, -dyōōs′/ *v.* (**-duc•es, -duced, duc•ing**) to lessen in extent, amount, number, degree, or price. [ME *reducen,* to bring back < Lat. *reducere: re-*, back + *ducere,* to lead.]

re•duc•tion /rĭ dŭk′ shən/ *n.* **a.** the act or process of reducing. **b.** the result of reducing. **c.** the amount by which something is lessened or diminished. [ME *reduccion,* restoration < OFr. *reduction* < Lat. *reductio* < *reducere,* to bring back: *re-*, back + *ducere,* to lead.]

re•flect /rĭ flĕkt′/ *v.* **a.** to throw or bend back (light, for example) from a surface. **b.** to form an image of (an object or figure); mirror.

re•flec•tion /rĭ flĕk′ shən/ *n.* **a.** an instance of reflecting or the state of being reflected. **b.** something reflected, as light, radiant heat, sound, or an image.

re•flex•ive[l] /rĭ flĕk′ sĭv/ *adj.* **a.** of or pertaining to a reflex. **b.** relating to or being a relation that exists between an entity and itself. **c. reflective law.**

re•flex•ive[2] /rĭ flĕk′ sĭv/ *n. Math.* the statement that any element is equal to itself.

re•gal /rē′ gəl/ *adj.* **a.** of or pertaining to a king; royal. **b.** belonging to or befitting a king: *regal attire.* [ME < OFr. < Lat. *regalis* < *rex,* king.]

regal

re•gime /rā zhēm′, rĭ-/ *n.* **a.** a system of management. **b.** a government that is in power; administration. [Fr. *régime* < Lat. *regimen* < *regere,* to rule.]

re•gret[l] /rĭ grĕt′/ *v.* (**-grets, -gret•ted, -gret•ting**) (**re•gret•ta•ble** *adj.*) to feel sorry, disappointed, or distressed about.

re•gret[2] /rĭ grĕt′/ *n.* **a.** a sense of loss and longing for someone gone. **b.** distress over a desire unfulfilled or an action performed or not performed.

reg•u•late /rĕg′ yə lāt′/ *v.* (**-lates, -lat•ed, -lat•ing**) **a.** to control or direct according to a rule. **b.** to adjust (a mechanism) for accurate and proper functioning. [Lat. *regulare, regulat-* < Lat. *regula,* a rule.]

reg•u•la•tion /rĕg′ yə lā′ shən/ *n.* **a.** the act of regulating. **b.** a principle, rule, or law designed to control or govern behavior.

re•im•burse /rē′ ĭm bûrs′/ *v.* (**-burs•es, -burs•ed, -burs•ing**) to pay back or compensate (a person) for money spent or losses or damages incurred.

re•ject[l] /rĭ jĕkt′/ *v.* **a.** to refuse to accept, recognize, or make use of. **b.** to discard as defective or useless; throw away. [ME *rejecten* < Lat. *reicere,* to throw back: *re-*, back + *jacere,* to throw.]

re•ject² /rē′ jĕkt′/ *n.* something or someone that has been rejected.

re•jec•tion /rĭ jĕk′ shən/ *n.* **a.** the act or process of rejecting. **b.** the condition of being rejected.

re•la•tion /rĭ lā′ shən/ *n.* **a.** a logical or natural association between two or more things; connection. **b.** the connection of people by blood or marriage; kinship. **c.** a person connected to another by blood or marriage; relative. **d.** the mode in which a person or thing is connected with another: *the relation of parent to child.* [Lat. *referre, relat-,* to relate: *re-,* back + *ferre,* to bear.]

rel•e•vance /rĕl′ ə vəns/ *n.* pertinence to the matter at hand.

rel•e•vant /rĕl′ ə vənt/ *adj.* related to the matter at hand; pertinent.

re•li•a•ble /rĭ lī′ ə bəl/ *adj.* that can be relied upon; dependable.

re•lieve /rĭ lēv′/ *v.* (**-lieves, -lieved, -liev•ing**) **a.** to cause a lessening of: *relieved all his symptoms.* **b.** to free from a specified duty by providing or acting as a substitute.

re•lo•cate /rē lō′ kāt′/ *v.* (**-cates, -cat•ed, -cat•ing**) to establish in a new place. [RE- + Lat. *locare, locat-,* to place < *locus,* place.]

re•or•gan•ize /rē ôr′ gə nīz′/ *v.* (**-iz•es, -ized, -iz•ing**) to undergo or effect changes in organization.

re•per•cus•sion /rē′ pər kŭsh′ ən, rĕp′ ər-/ *n.* **a.** an indirect effect, influence, or result produced by an event or action. **b.** a recoil, rebounding, or reciprocal motion after impact. **c.** a reflection, especially of sound.

rep•er•toire /rĕp′ ər twär′/ *n.* **a.** the stock of songs, plays, operas, readings, or other pieces that a player or company is prepared to perform. **b.** the range or number of skills, aptitudes, or special accomplishments, as of a person or group. [Fr. < LLat. *repertorium* < Lat. *repertus,* p.part. of *reperire,* to find out: *re-,* again + *parire,* to produce.]

rep•e•ti•tion /rĕp′ ĭ tĭsh′ ən/ *n.* the act or process or an instance of repeating or being repeated.

re•prieve¹ /rĭ prēv′/ *v.* (**-prieves, -prieved, -priev•ing**) to postpone the punishment of.

re•prieve² /rĭ prēv′/ *n.* **a.** the postponement of a punishment. **b.** a warrant for such a postponement. **c.** temporary relief, as from danger or pain.

re•print¹ /rē′ prĭnt′/ *n.* something that has been printed again, especially a new printing identical to an original.

re•print² /rē prĭnt′/ *v.* to print again.

re•pub•lic /rĭ pŭb′ lĭk/ *n.* **a.1.** a political order whose head of state is not a monarch and in modern times is usually a president. **a.2.** a nation having such a political order. **b.1.** a political order in which the supreme power lies in a body of citizens who are entitled to vote for officers and representatives responsible to them. **b.2.** a nation having such a political order. [OFr. *republique* < Lat. *respublica*: *res,* thing + *publica,* fem. of *publicus,* of the people.]

re•pub•li•can¹ /rĭ pŭb′ lĭ kən/ *adj.* **a.** of, pertaining to, or characteristic of a republic. **b. Republican.** of, pertaining to, characteristic of, or belonging to the Republican Party of the United States.

Re•pub•li•can² /rĭ pŭb′ lĭ kən/ *n.* a member of the Republican Party of the United States.

re•sem•ble /rĭ zĕm′ bəl/ *v.* (**-bles, -bled, -bling**) to have a similarity or likeness to.

res•er•va•tion /rĕz′ ər vā′ shən/ *n.* **a.** the act of reserving. **b.** something that is reserved. **c.** a limiting qualification, condition, or exception: *has reservations about the proposal.* **d.** a tract of land set apart by the federal government for a special purpose.

re•serve¹ /rĭ zûrv′/ *v.* (**-serves, -served, -serv•ing**) **a.** to keep back or save for future use or a special purpose. **b.** to keep or secure for oneself; retain.

re•serve² /rĭ zûrv′/ *n.* **a.** self-restraint in expression. **b.** a reservation of public land: *a forest reserve.* [ME *reserven* < OFr. *reserver* < Lat. *reservare,* to keep back: *re-,* back + *servare,* to keep.]

res•er•voir /rĕz′ ər vwär′, -vwôr′, -vôr′/ *n.* **a.** a body of water collected and stored for future use in a natural or artificial lake. **b.** a large supply; reserve: *a reservoir of gratitude.* [Fr. *réservoir* < *réserver,* to reserve.]

reservoir

re•spect•ful /rĭ spĕkt′ fəl/ *adj.* (**re•spect•ful•ly** *adv.*) showing or marked by proper respect.

re•spec•tive•ly /rĭ spĕk′ tĭv lē/ *adv.* singly in the order designated or mentioned: *I'm referring to each of you respectively.*

res•pi•ra•tion /rĕs′ pə rā′ shən/ *n.* the act or process of inhaling and exhaling; breathing. [ME *respiren,* to breathe again < Lat. *respirare*: *re-,* again + *spirare,* to breathe.]

re•sponse /rĭ spŏns′/ *n.* **a.** a reply or answer. **b.** a reaction, as that of an organism or mechanism, to a specific stimulus.

re•spon•si•bil•i•ty /rĭ spŏn′ sə bĭl′ ĭ tē/ *n.* (**-ties** *pl.*) **a.** the state, quality, or fact of being responsible. **b.** something for which one is responsible; duty, obligation, or burden.

re•trace /rē trās′/ *v.* (**-trac•es, -traced, -trac•ing**) **a.** to trace again. **b.** to go back over, as one's steps.

re•trieve /rĭ trēv′/ *v.* (**-trieves, -trieved, -triev•ing**) **a.** to get back; regain. **b.** to find and carry back; fetch.

retrieve

re•veal /rĭ vēl′/ *v.* **a.** to divulge or disclose; make known. **b.** to bring to view; show.

rev•e•nue /rĕv′ ə nōō, -nyōō/ *n.* **a.** the income of a government from all sources appropriated for the payment of the public expenses. **b.** a single source of income. [ME < OFr. < fem. p.part. of *revenir,* to return < Lat. *revenire*: *re-,* back + *venire,* to come.]

re•ver•ber•ate /rĭ vûr′ bə rāt′/ *v.* (**-ates, -at•ed, -at•ing**) (**re•ver•ber•a•tion** *n.*) **a.** to re-echo; resound. **b.** to be repeatedly reflected.

re•vi•sion /rĭ vĭzh′ ən/ *n.* **a.** the act or procedure of revising. **b.** a revised or new version. [Lat. *revisere,* to visit again: *re-,* again < *visere,* freq. of *vidēre,* to see.]

re•viv•al /rĭ vī′ vəl/ *n.* **a.** the act of reviving or the condition of being revived. **b.** a restoration to use, acceptance, activity, or vigor after a period of obscurity or quiescence. **c.** a new presentation of an old play, motion picture, opera, ballet, or similar theatrical vehicle.

re•vive /rĭ vīv′/ *v.* (**-vives, -vived, -viv•ing**) **a.** to bring back to life or consciousness. **b.** to restore to use, currency, activity, or notice. **c.** to present (an old play, for example) again. [ME *reviven* < OFr. *revivre* < LLat. *revivere,* to live again: Lat. *re-,* again + Lat. *vivere,* to live.]

re•voke /rĭ vōk′/ *v.* (**-vokes, -voked, -vok•ing**) to void or annul by recalling, withdrawing, or reversing. [ME *revoken* < OFr. *revoquer* < Lat. *revocare,* to call back: *re-,* back + *vocare,* to call.]

rhine•stone /rīn′ stōn′/ *n.* a colorless, artificial gem of paste or glass, often with facets that sparkle in imitation of diamond. [after the *Rhine,* a river in Europe.]

ro•mance /rō măns′, rō′ măns′/ *n.* **a.** a novel, story, or film dealing with a love affair. **b.** the class or style of fictional works about idealized love. **c.1.** a love affair. **c.2.** romantic involvement; love.

ro•man•tic¹ /rō măn′ tĭk/ *adj.* **a.** of, pertaining to, or characteristic of romance. **b.** imaginative but impractical: *romantic notions.* [Fr. *romantique* < OFr. *romans,* romance.]

ro•man•tic² /rō măn′ tĭk/ *n.* a romantic person.

ro•man•ti•cism /rō măn′ tĭ sĭz′ əm/ *n.* **a.** an artistic and intellectual movement that originated in the late 18th century and stressed strong emotion, imagination, freedom from classical correctness in art forms, and rebellion against social conventions. **b.** the spirit and attitudes characteristic of romantic thought.

ro•ta•tion /rō tā′ shən/ *n.* **a.1.** motion in which the path of every point in the moving object is a circle or circular arc with the center of all the circles the same or lying on the same straight line; spin. **a.2.** a single complete cycle of such motion; revolution. **b.** *Math.* a coordinate transformation consisting of an angular displacement or successive angular displacements of coordinate axes with the origin remaining fixed.

roy•al•ty /roi′ əl tē/ *n.* (**-ties** *pl.*) **a.1.** a person of royal rank or lineage. **a.2.** monarchs and their families collectively. **b.** the power, status, or authority of a monarch.

sa•ga /sä′ gə/ *n.* **a.** a prose narrative of the 12th and the 13th centuries recounting historical and legendary events and exploits in Iceland or Norway. **b.** a long, detailed report. [ON.]

san•i•ta•tion /săn′ ĭ tā′ shən/ *n.* the formulation and application of measures designed to protect public health.

sar•casm /sär′ kăz′ əm/ *n.* **a.** a sharply mocking or contemptuously ironic remark intended to wound another. **b.** the use of sarcasm.

sar•cas•tic /sär kăs′ tĭk/ *adj.* **a.** expressing sarcasm. **b.** given to using sarcasm.

sat•el•lite /săt′ l īt′/ *n.* **a.** *Astron.* a relatively small body orbiting a planet; moon. **b.** *Aerospace.* a manufactured object intended to orbit a celestial body.

sat•is•fac•to•ry /săt′ ĭs făk′ tə rē/ *adj.* giving satisfaction sufficient to meet a demand or requirement; adequate.

sat•u•rate /săch′ ə rāt′/ *v.* (**-rates, -rat•ed, -rat•ing**) **a.** to soak, fill, or load to capacity. **b.** *Chem.* to cause to be saturated.

scribe /skrīb/ *n.* **a.** a public clerk or secretary. **b.** a professional copyist of manuscripts and documents.

sea•son•al /sē′ zə nəl, sēz′ nəl/ *adj.* of or dependent upon a particular season. [ME *sesoun*, season < OFr. *seson*, Lat. *satio*, act of sowing < *satus*, p.part. of *serere*, to plant.]

sec•re•tar•y-treas•ur•er /sĕk′ rĭ tĕr′ ē trĕzh′ ər ər/ *n.* a person who fills the roles of both secretary and treasurer; one in charge of an organization's records and correspondence as well as the receipt and distribution of money. *Amanda was elected to be the group's secretary-treasurer.*

sen•a•to•ri•al /sĕn′ ə tôr′ ē əl, -tōr′-/ *adj.* **a.** of, concerning, or befitting a senator or a senate. **b.** composed of senators.

sen•sa•tion•al /sĕn sā′ shə nəl/ *adj.* **a.** arousing or intended to arouse strong curiosity, interest, or reaction, especially by exaggerated or lurid details. **b.** outstanding; spectacular.

sen•so•ry /sĕn′ sə rē/ *adj.* of or pertaining to the senses or sensation.

short•age /shôr′ tĭj/ *n.* a deficiency in amount; insufficiency.

shrine /shrīn/ *n.* **a.** the tomb of a saint or other venerated person. **b.** a site hallowed by a venerated object or its associations.

sig•nif•i•cance /sĭg nĭf′ ĭ kəns/ *n.* **a.** the state or quality of being significant. **b.** meaning; import.

sig•nif•i•cant /sĭg nĭf′ ĭ kənt/ *adj.* **a.** having or expressing a meaning; meaningful. **b.** notable; valuable.

sim•i•lar•i•ty /sĭm′ ə lăr′ ĭ tē/ *n.* (**-ties** *pl.*) the condition or quality of being similar; resemblance.

sim•i•le /sĭm′ ə lē/ *n.* a figure of speech in which two essentially unlike things are compared, often in a phrase introduced by like or as, as in: *He was as strong as a bull.*

sim•u•late /sĭm′ yə lāt′/ *v.* (**-lates, -lat•ed, -lat•ing**) **a.** to have or take on the appearance, form, or sound of; imitate. **b.** to make a pretense of; feign.

sine /sīn/ *n.* in a right triangle, the function of an acute angle that is the ratio of the opposite side to the hypotenuse.

snor•kel[1] /snôr′ kəl/ *n.* a breathing apparatus used by skin divers, consisting of a long tube held in the mouth. [G. *Schnorchel*, snorkel, snout < *schnarchen*, to snore.]

snorkel

snor•kel² /snôr′ kəl/ *v.* to dive using a skindiving snorkel.

so•cia•ble /sō′ shə bəl/ *adj.* **a.** pleasant, friendly, or affable. **b.** providing occasion for conversation and conviviality.

so•lil•o•quy /sə lĭl′ ə kwē/ *n.* (**-quies** *pl.*) a literary or dramatic form of discourse in which a character talks to himself or reveals his thoughts in the form of a monologue without addressing a listener. [LLat.: Lat. *solus,* along + Lat. *loqui,* to speak.]

so•lo•ist /sō′ lō ĭst/ *n.* one who performs a solo.

so•na•ta /sə nä′ tə/ *n.* an instrumental musical composition, as for the piano, consisting of three or four independent movements varying in key, mood, and tempo. [Ital. < fem. p.part. of *sonare,* to sound < Lat. *sonare.*]

sov•er•eign¹ /sŏv′ ər ĭn, sŏv′ rĭn/ *n.* the chief of state in a monarchy.

sov•er•eign² /sŏv′ ər ĭn, sŏv′ rĭn/ *adj.* **a.** having supreme rank or power. **b.** self-governing; independent: *a sovereign state.*

sphinx /sfĭngks/ *n.* (**sphinx•es** or **sphin•ges** *pl.*) **a.** *Egyptian Myth.* a figure having the body of a lion and the head of a man, ram, or hawk. **b.** *Gk. Myth.* a winged monster having the head of a woman and the body of a lion that destroyed all who could not answer its riddle. **c.** an enigmatic person.

spir•it /spĭr′ ĭt/ *n.* **a.** the vital principle or animating force traditionally believed to be within living beings. **b.1.** the part of a human being associated with the mind and feelings as distinguished from the physical body. **b.2.** the essential nature of a person. **c.** the predominant mood of an occasion or period: *"The spirit of 1776 is not dead"* (Thomas Jefferson). **d.** the real sense or significance of something: *the spirit of the law.* [ME < AN < Lat. *spiritus,* breath < *spirare,* to breathe.]

spon•ta•ne•ous /spŏn tā′ nē əs/ *adj.* **a.** happening or arising without apparent external cause. **b.** voluntary and impulsive: *spontaneous applause.* **c.** unconstrained and unstudied in manner or behavior.

spoon•er•ism /spoo′ nə rĭz′ əm/ *n.* an unintentional transposition of sounds of two or more words, as *Let me sew you to your sheet* for *Let me show you to your seat.* [after William A. Spooner (1844–1930).]

sta•bil•i•ty /stə bĭl′ ĭ tē/ *n.* (**-ties** *pl.*) **a.** resistance to sudden change or overthrow. **b.** constancy of character or purpose; steadfastness.

stan•dard•ize /stăn′ dər dīz′/ *v.* (**-iz•es, -ized, -iz•ing**) to make, cause, adjust, or adapt to fit a standard.

star•tle /stär′ tl/ *v.* (**-tles, -tled, -tling**) **a.** to cause to make a quick involuntary movement or start. **b.** to alarm, frighten, or surprise.

ster•e•o•type¹ /stĕr′ ē ə tīp′, stîr′-/ *n.* a conventional, and usually oversimplified conception, opinion, or belief.

ster•e•o•type² /stĕr′ ē ə tīp′, stîr′-/ *v.* (**-types, -typed, -typ•ing**) **a.** to develop a fixed, unvarying idea about. **b.** to make a stereotype of.

stim•u•lus /stĭm′ yə ləs/ *n.* (**-li** *pl.*) something causing or regarded as causing a response. [Lat., goad.]

stor•age /stôr′ ĭj, stōr′-/ *n.* **a.1.** the act of storing goods. **a.2.** the state of being stored. **a.3.** a space for storing goods. **b.** *Computer Sci.* the part of a computer that stores information for subsequent use or retrieval.

storage

straight•for•ward¹ /strāt fôr′ wərd/ *adj.* **a.** proceeding in a straight course; direct. **b.** honest; frank.

straight•for•ward² /strāt fôr′ wərd/ *adv.* in a straightforward course or manner.

sub- a prefix meaning: **a.** below; under; beneath: *submarine.* **b.** close to: *suburb.*

sub•merge /səb mûrj'/ *v.* (-mer•ges, -merged, -mer•ging) **a.** to place or plunge under water or other liquid. **b.** to go under or as if under water. [Lat. *submergere: sub-,* under + *mergere,* to plunge.]

sub•mit /səb mĭt'/ *v.* (-mits, -mit•ted, -mit•ting) **a.** to yield or surrender (oneself) to the will or authority of another. **b.** to subject to a condition or process. **c.** to commit (something) to the consideration or judgment of another.

sub•scribe /səb scrīb'/ *v.* (-scribes, -scribed, -scrib•ing) **a.** to express concurrence or approval; assent. **b.** to promise to pay or contribute money: *subscribe to a charity.* **c.** to contract to receive and pay for a certain number of issues of a publication. [ME *subscriben* < Lat. *subscribere: sub-,* under + *scribere,* to write.]

sub•scrip•tion /səb skrĭp' shən/ *n.* a purchase made by signed order, as for a periodical for a specified period of time or for a series of performances. [Lat. *subscriptus,* p.part. of *subscribere,* to subscribe: *sub-,* under + *scribere,* to write.]

sub•sti•tute[1] /sŭb' stĭ tōōt', -tyōōt'/ *n.* one that takes the place of another; replacement.

sub•sti•tute[2] /sŭb' stĭ tōōt', -tyōōt'/ *v.* (-tutes, -tut•ed, -tut•ing) to take the place of another.

sub•sti•tu•tion /sŭb' stĭ tōō' shən, -tyōō'/ *n.* **a.** the act or state of being substituted. **b.** that which is substituted.

sub•tle /sŭt' l/ *adj.* **a.** so slight as to be difficult to detect or analyze; elusive. **b.** not immediately obvious.

sub•urb /sŭb' ûrb'/ *n.* a usually residential area or community outlying a city. [ME < OFr. *suburbe* < Lat. *suburbium: sub-,* close to + *urbs,* city.]

suburb

sub•ur•ban /sə bûr' bən/ *adj.* **a.** of, pertaining to, or characteristic of a suburb or life in a suburb. **b.** the culture, manners, and customs typical of life in the suburbs.

suc•ceed /sək sēd'/ *v.* to accomplish something desired or intended. [ME *succeden* < OFr. *succeder* < Lat. *succedere: sub-,* after + *cedere,* to go.]

suc•ces•sion /sək sĕsh' ən/ *n.* **a.** the act or process of following in order or sequence. **b.** a group of persons or things arranged or following in order; sequence. **c.** the sequence in which one person after another succeeds to a title, throne, dignity, or estate.

suc•ces•sor /sək sĕs' ər/ *n.* one that succeeds another.

suc•cinct /sək sĭngkt'/ *adj.* **a.** clearly expressed in few words; concise; terse. **b.** characterized by brevity and clarity in speech or writing. [Lat. *succintus* < p.part. of *succingere,* to gird from below: *sub-,* below + *cingere,* to gird.]

suite /swēt/ *n. Mus.* an instrumental composition consisting of a succession of dances in the same or related keys.

super- a prefix meaning: **a.** above; over; upon: *superimpose.* **b.** superior in size, number, quality, or degree: *superfine.*

su•pe•ri•or /sōō pîr' ē ər/ *adj.* (**su•pe•ri•or•i•ty** *n.*) **a.** higher in rank, station, or authority: *a superior officer.* **b.** of a higher nature or kind. **c.** of great value or excellence; extraordinary. [ME < OFr. < Lat. *superus,* upper < *super,* over.]

su•per•sede /sōō' pər sēd'/ *v.* (-sedes, -sed•ed, -sed•ing) **a.** to take the place of; replace. **b.** to cause to be set aside or displaced. [ME *superceden,* to postpone < OFr. *superceder* < Lat. *supersedēre,* to refrain from: *super-,* above + *sedēre,* to sit.]

su•per•vise /sōō' pər vīz'/ *v.* (-vis•es, -vised, -vis•ing) (**su•per•vi•sion** *n.*) to direct and inspect the performance of; superintend. [Med. Lat. *supervidēre, supervis-,* to look over: Lat. *super-,* over + Lat. *vidēre,* to see.]

su•per•vi•sor /sōō' pər vī' zər/ *n.* a person in charge of a particular department or unit, as in a governmental agency or a school system.

sup•ple•ment[1] /sŭp' lə mənt/ *n.* (**sup•ple•men•ta•ry** *adj.*) **a.** something added to complete a thing, make up for a deficiency, or extend or strengthen the whole. **b.** the angle or arc that when added to a given angle or arc makes 180 degrees or a semicircle.

sup•ple•ment[2] /sŭp' lə mənt'/ *v.* to provide or form a supplement to. [ME < Lat. *supplementum* < *suppler,* to complete: *sub-,* from below + *plēre,* to fill.]

Spelling Dictionary

sup•press /sə prĕs′/ *v.* **a.** to put an end to forcibly; subdue. **b.** to curtail or prohibit the activities of. **c.** to hold back; check. [ME *suppressen* < Lat. *supprimere*: *sub-*, down + *premere*, to press.]

sur•face¹ /sûr′ fəs/ *n.* **a.** the outer or topmost boundary of an object. **b.** a material layer constituting such a boundary. [Fr.: *sur-*, above + *face*, face < OFr. < Lat. *facies.*]

sur•face² /sûr′ fəs/ *adj.* **a.** pertaining to, on, or at a surface. **b.** superficial.

sur•face³ /sûr′ fəs/ *v.* (-**fac•es**, -**faced**, -**fac•ing**) **a.** to rise to the surface. **b.** to emerge after concealment.

sur•geon /sûr′ jən/ *n.* a physician specializing in surgery. [ME *surgien* < Norman Fr., short for OFr. *serurgien* < *serurgie*, surgery.]

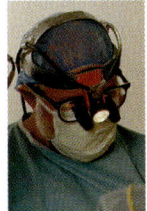

surgeon

sur•pass /sər păs′/ *v.* **a.** to go beyond the limit, powers, or extent of. **b.** to be or go beyond; exceed. [OFr. *surpasser*: *sur-*, over + *passer*, pass.]

sur•plus¹ /sûr′ pləs, -plŭs/ *adj.* being more than or in excess of what is needed or required: *surplus grain.* [ME < OFr. < Med. Lat. *super-plus*: Lat. *super-*, over + Lat. *plus*, more.]

sur•plus² /sûr′ pləs, -plŭs/ *n.* an amount or quantity in excess of what is needed.

sur•viv•al /sər vī′ vəl/ *n.* **a.** the act or process of surviving. **b.** the fact of having survived. **modifier:** *survival techniques.*

sur•vive /sər vīv′/ *v.* (-**vives**, -**vived**, -**viv•ing**) (**sur•vi•vor** *n.*) **a.** to remain alive or in existence. **b.** to live longer than; outlive. **c.** to live or persist through: *plants surviving a frost.* [ME *surviven* < Norman Fr. *survivre* < OFr. *sourvivre* < LLat. *supervivere*: Lat. *super-*, over + Lat. *vivere*, to live.]

sus•pend /sə spĕnd′/ *v.* **a.** to bar for a period from a privilege, office, or position, usually as a punishment. **b.** to cause to stop for a period; interrupt. **c.1.** to defer: *suspend judgment.* **c.2.** to render temporarily ineffective: *suspend parking regulations.* **d.** to hang so as to allow free movement. [ME *suspenden* < OFr., *suspendre* < Lat. *suspendere*, to hang up: *sub-*, from below + *pendere*, to hang.]

sus•pense /sə spĕns′/ *n.* anxiety or apprehension resulting from an uncertain, undecided, or mysterious situation. [ME < Norman Fr. < OFr. < *suspendre*, to suspend.]

sus•tain /sə stān′/ *v.* **a.** to keep in existence; maintain. **b.** to support from below; prop. **c.** to endure or withstand; bear up under: *sustain hardships.* **d.** to experience or suffer (loss or injury). [ME *susteynen* < Norman Fr. *sustein* < OFr. *sustenir* < Lat. *sustinēre*, to hold up: *sub-*, from below + *tenēre*, to hold.]

sym•bol /sĭm′ bəl/ *n.* **a.** something that represents something else, especially a material object used to represent something invisible. **b.** a printed or written sign.

sym•bol•ic /sĭm bŏl′ ĭk/ *adj.* **a.** of, pertaining to, or expressed by means of a symbol or symbols. **b.** serving as a symbol. **c.** characterized by the use of symbolism, as a work of art.

sym•bol•ism /sĭm′ bə lĭz′ əm/ *n.* **a.** the practice of representing things by means of symbols or of attributing symbolic meanings or significance to objects, events, or relationships. **b.** a symbolic meaning or representation.

sym•bol•ize /sĭm′ bə līz′/ *v.* (-**iz•es**, -**ized**, -**iz•ing**) **a.** to be or serve as a symbol of: *The dove symbolizes peace.* **b.** to represent or identify by a symbol or symbols.

sym•pa•thize /sĭm′ pə thīz′/ *v.* (-**thiz•es**, -**thized**, -**thiz•ing**) **a.** to feel or express compassion. **b.** to share or understand another's feelings or ideas.

sym•pa•thy /sĭm′ pə thē/ *n.* (**-thies** *pl.*) **a.1.** the act of or capacity for sharing or understanding the feelings of another person. **a.2.** a feeling or expression of pity or sorrow for the distress of another. **b.** favor; agreement; accord: *He is in sympathy with their beliefs.*

syn•op•sis /sĭ nŏp′ sĭs/ *n.* (**-ses** *pl.*) a brief statement or outline of a subject; abstract.

sys•tem•at•ic /sĭs′ tə măt′ ĭk/ *adj.* **a.** of, characterized by, based upon, or constituting a system. **b.** carried on in a step-by-step procedure. **c.** characterized by purposeful regularity; methodical.

tan•gent /tăn′ jənt/ *n.* **a.** a line, curve, or surface touching but not intersecting another line, curve, or surface. **b.** a function of an acute angle in a right triangle equal to the length of the side opposite the angle divided by the length of the side adjacent to the angle.

tar•get¹ /tär′ gĭt/ *n.* **a.** anything aimed or fired at. **b.** an object of criticism or attack.

tar•get² /tär′ gĭt/ *v.* to establish as a target or a goal.

tech•ni•cal /těk′ nĭ kəl/ *adj.* **a.1.** abstract or theoretical: *a technical analysis.* **a.2.** scientific. **b.** industrial and mechanical; technological. [< Gk. *tekhnikos,* of art < *tekhnē,* art.]

tech•ni•cal•i•ty /těk′ nĭ kăl′ ĭ tē/ *n.* (**-ties** *pl.*) **a.** the condition or quality of being technical. **b.** something meaningful or relevant only to a specialist.

tech•ni•cian /těk nĭsh′ ən/ *n.* an expert in a technique, as a person whose occupation requires training in a specific technical process: *a dental technician.*

tech•nique /těk nēk′/ *n.* **a.** the systematic procedure by which a complex or scientific task is accomplished. **b.** the degree of skill or command of fundamentals exhibited in any performance.

tel•e•vise /těl′ ə vīz/ *v.* (**-vis•es, -vised, -vis•ing**) to broadcast by television.

ter•race /těr′ ĭs/ *n.* **a.1.** an open colonnaded platform, as a porch or promenade. **a.2.** a platform extending outdoors from a floor of a house or apartment building. **b.** a raised bank of earth having vertical or sloping sides and a flat top: *descending terraces on the lawn.*

terrace

ter•res•tri•al¹ /tə rĕs′ trē əl/ *adj.* **a.** of or pertaining to Earth or its inhabitants. **b.** of, pertaining to, or composed of land as distinct from water or air.

ter•res•tri•al² /tə rĕs′ trē əl/ *n.* an inhabitant of Earth.

tes•ti•fy /těs′ tə fī/ *v.* (**-fies, -fied, -fy•ing**) to make a declaration of truth or fact under oath.

tex•ture /těks′ chər/ *n.* **a.** the appearance of a fabric resulting from the woven arrangement of its yarns or fibers. **b.** the representation of the structure of a surface as distinct from color or form. **c.** the composition or structure of a substance; grain. [Lat. *textura* < *textum,* that which is woven < *tegere,* to weave.]

thirst-quench•ing /thŭrst kwĕnch ĭng/ *adj.* having the ability to satisfy; subduing thirst, desire, or passion. *After exercising, I need a cold, thirst-quenching drink.*

-tion a noun suffix that means action or process.

to•bog•gan¹ /tə bŏg′ ən/ *n.* a long, narrow, runnerless sled constructed of thin boards curled upward at the front.

to•bog•gan² /tə bŏg′ ən/ *v.* (**-gans, -ganed, -gan•ing**) to coast, ride, or travel on a toboggan. [Canadian Fr. *tobagan* < *Micmac* (a tribe of native North Americans) *tobākan.*]

tol•er•ance /tŏl′ ər əns/ *n.* the capacity for or practice of recognizing and respecting the opinions, practices, or behaviors of others.

tour•na•ment /tŏor′ nə mənt/ *n.* **a.** a contest involving a number of contestants who compete in a series of elimination games or trials. **b.** a medieval martial sport in which two groups of mounted and armored contestants fought against each other with blunted lances or swords.

tra•di•tion /trə dĭsh′ ən/ *n.* the passing down of elements of a culture from generation to generation, especially orally.

tra•di•tion•al /trə dĭsh′ ə nəl/ *adj.* of, pertaining to, or in accord with tradition.

trag•e•dy /trăj′ ĭ dē/ *n.* (**-dies** *pl.*) **a.** a dramatic or literary work depicting a protagonist engaged in a morally significant struggle ending in ruin or profound disappointment. **b.** the literary genre of tragic dramatic works. **c.** a dramatic, disastrous event, especially one of moral significance.

trans- a prefix meaning: **a.** across or over: *transatlantic.* **b.** beyond: *transcend.*

trans•act /trăn săkt′, -zăkt′/ *v.* to do, carry out, perform, manage, or conduct (business, for example). [Lat. *transigere, transact-,* to carry through: *trans,* through + *agere,* to drive.]

trans•ac•tion /trăn săk′ shən, -zăk′-/ *n.* **a.** the act or process of transacting. **b.** something transacted, especially a piece of business.

trans•fer¹ /trăns fûr′, trăns′ fər/ *v.* (**-fers, -ferred, -fer•ring**) **a.** to convey or shift from one person or place to another. **b.** to move oneself from one location, job, or school to another. [ME *transferren* < OFr. *transferer* < Lat. *transferre*: *trans,* across + *ferre,* to carry.]

trans•fer² /trăns′ fər/ *n.* the removal of something from one person or place to another.

trans•form /trăns fôrm′/ *v.* **a.** to change markedly the form or appearance of. **b.** to change the nature, function, or condition of; convert. [ME *transformen* < *transformare*: *trans,* across + *forma,* shape.]

trans•for•ma•tion /trăns′ fər mā′ shən, -fôr-/ *n.* **a.1.** an act or an instance of transforming. **a.2.** the state of being transformed. **a.3.** something that has been transformed. **b.** *Math.* the replacement of the variables in an algebraic expression by their values in terms of another set of variables.

trans•form•er /trăns fôr′ mər/ *n.* a device used to transfer electric energy, usually that of an alternating current, from one circuit to another, especially by means of electromagnetic induction.

tran•sis•tor /trăn zĭs′ tər, -sĭs′-/ *n.* **a.** a three-terminal semiconductor device used for amplification, switching, and detection. **b.** a radio equipped with transistors. [TRANS(FER) + (RES)ISTOR.]

tran•si•tion /trăn zĭsh′ ən, -sĭsh′-/ *n.* the process or an instance of changing from one form, state, activity, or place to another.

tran•si•tive /trăn′ sĭ tĭv, -zĭ-/ *adj.* **a.** *Gram.* expressing an action that is carried from the subject to the object; requiring a direct object to complete meaning. **b.** *Math.* **transitive property.** The property of a mathematical relation for which it is true that if **a** bears the relationship to **b** and **b** bears the same relation to **c,** then **a** bears the same relation to **c.**

trans•late /trăns lāt′, trăns′ lāt′, trănz′-/ *v.* (**-lates, -lat•ed, -lat•ing**) **a.** to express in another language, systematically retaining the original sense. **b.** to put in simpler terms; explain. **c.** to convey from one form or style to another; convert. [ME *translaten* < Lat. *transferre, translat-*: *trans,* across + *ferre,* to carry.]

trans•la•tion /trăns lā′ shən, trănz-/ *n.* **a.** the act or process of translating, especially from one language to another. **b.** a translated version of a text. **c.** *Physics.* motion of a body in which every point moves parallel to and the same distance as every other point of the body; nonrotational displacement.

trans•la•tor /trăns lā′ tər, trănz-, trăns′ lā′ tər, trănz′-/ *n.* **a.** one who translates, especially one professionally employed to translate written works. **b.** an interpreter.

translator

trans•mit /trăns **mĭt′**, trănz-/ v. (**-mits, -mit•ted, -mit•ting**) **a.** to send from one person, thing, or place to another; convey. **b.** *Electronics.* to send (a signal), as by wire.

trans•mit•ter /trăns **mĭt′** ər, trănz-/ n. **a.** one that transmits. **b.** a telegraphic sending instrument. **c.** electronic equipment that generates and amplifies a carrier wave, modulates it with a meaningful signal, as derived from speech or other sources, and radiates the resulting signal from an antenna.

trans•par•ent /trăns **pâr′** ənt, **-păr′**-/ adj. **a.** capable of transmitting light so that objects or images can be seen as if there were no intervening material. **b.** of such fine or open texture that objects may be readily seen on the other side; diaphanous. **c.** easily understood or detected; obvious. [ME < OFr. < Med. Lat. *transparens,* pr.part. of *transparere,* to be seen through: Lat. *trans,* through + Lat. *parere,* to show.]

trans•plant[1] /trăns **plănt′**/ v. (**-plants, -plant•ed, -plant•ing**) **a.** to uproot and replant (a growing plant). **b.** to transfer from one place or residence to another; resettle; relocate. [ME *tranplaunten* < LLat. *transplantare:* Lat. *trans,* across + Lat. *plantare,* to plant.]

trans•plant[2] /**trăns′** plănt′/ v. **a.** the act or process of transplanting. **b.** something transplanted.

trans•port[1] /trăns **pôrt′**, **-pōrt′**/ v. to carry from one place to another; convey. [ME *transporten* < OFr. *transporter* < Lat. *transportare:* trans, across + *portare,* to carry.]

trans•port[2] /**trăns′** pôrt′, -pōrt′/ n. the act of transporting; conveyance.

trans•por•ta•tion /trăns′ pər **tā′** shən/ n. **a.** the act of transporting. **b.1.** a means of transport; conveyance. **b.2.** the business of transporting passengers, goods, or materials.

transportation

trans•pose /trăns **pōz′**/ v. (**-pos•es, -posed, -pos•ing**) to reverse or transfer the order or place of; interchange. [ME *transposen,* to transform < OFr. *transposer* < Lat. *transponere:* trans, across + *ponere,* to place.]

trib•u•tar•y /**trĭb′** yə těr′ ē/ n. (**-ies** pl.) a stream or river flowing into a larger stream or river.

trig•o•nom•e•try /trĭg′ ə **nŏm′** ĭ trē/ n. the study of the properties and applications of functions of an angle, such as the sine, cosine, or tangent.

trite /trīt/ adj. overused and commonplace; hackneyed.

tur•bine /**tûr′** bĭn, -bīn′/ n. any of various machines in which the kinetic energy of a moving fluid is converted to mechanical power by the impulse or reaction of the fluid with a series of buckets, paddles, or blades arrayed about the circumference of a wheel or cylinder.

tur•quoise /**tûr′** kwoiz′, -koiz′/ n. **a.** a blue to blue-green mineral of aluminum and copper, esteemed as a gemstone in its polished blue form. **b.** a light to brilliant bluish green. [ME *turkeis* < OFr. *turqueis,* Turkish < *Turc,* Turk.]

ty•phoon /tī **fōōn′**/ n. a severe tropical storm in the western Pacific or the China Sea.

ul•tra•vi•o•let /ŭl′ trə **vī′** ə lĭt/ adj. of or pertaining to the range of radiation wavelengths from about 4,000 angstroms, just beyond the violet in the visible spectrum, to about 40 angstroms, on the border of the x-ray region.

un-[1] a prefix meaning not or contrary to: *unsure.*

un-[2] a prefix meaning: **a.** reversal of an action: *untie.* **b.** release or removal from: *unleash.* **c.** intensified action: *unloose.*

un•con•trol•la•ble /ŭn′ kən **trō′** lə bəl/ adj. not able to be controlled or governed.

un•doubt•ed /ŭn dou′ tĭd/ adj. (**un•doubt•ed•ly** adv.) accepted as beyond question; undisputed.

un•for•get•ta•ble /ŭn′ fər **gět′** ə bəl/ adj. earning a permanent place in the memory; memorable.

un•i•mag•in•a•ble /ŭn′ ĭ mǎj′ ə nə bəl/ *adj.* difficult or impossible to imagine.

un•man•age•a•ble /ŭn′ mǎn′ ĭ jə bəl/ *adj.* difficult or impossible to manage or control.

un•pre•dict•a•ble /ŭn′ prĭ dĭk′ tə bəl/ *adj.* not predictable; not able to foretell.

un•so•cia•ble /ŭn′ sō′ shə bəl/ *adj.* **a.** not disposed to seek the company of others; reserved. **b.** not conducive to social exchange: *an unsociable atmosphere.*

un•wield•y /ŭn wēl′ dē/ *adj.* **a.** difficult to carry or manage because of bulk or shape. **b.** clumsy; ungainly.

up-and-com•ing /ŭp′ ən kŭm′ ĭng/ *adj.* marked for future success; promising.

up•heav•al /ŭp hē′ vəl/ *n.* **a.** the process or an instance of being heaved upward. **b.** a sudden and violent disruption or upset.

up-to-the-min•ute /ŭp′ tōō thə mĭn′ ĭt/ *adj.* information or style that extends up to the present moment. *On election night, we watched the up-to-the-minute news report.*

ur•ban /ûr′ bən/ *adj.* **a.** of or located in a city. **b.** characteristic of the city or city life. [Lat. *urbanus < urbs,* city.]

u•til•i•ty /yōō tĭl′ ĭ tē/ *n.* (**-ties** *pl.*) **a.** the condition or quality of being useful; usefulness. **b.** a public service, such as gas, electricity, water, or transportation.

u•til•ize /yōōt′ l īz′/ *v.* (**-iz•es, -ized, -iz•ing**) to put to use for a certain purpose. [Fr. *utiliser < Ital. utilizzare < utile,* useful *< Lat. utilis < uti,* to use.]

vac•ci•nate /vǎk′ sə nāt′/ *v.* (**-nates, -nat•ed, -nat•ing**) to inoculate with a vaccine in order to produce immunity to a disease, such as smallpox. [Lat. *vaccinus,* of cows *< vacca,* cow.]

var•i•a•ble¹ /vâr′ ē ə bəl, vǎr′-/ *adj.* **a.** liable or likely to vary. **b.** *Math.* having no fixed quantitative value.

var•i•a•ble² /vâr′ ē ə bəl, vǎr′-/ *n.* **a.** something that varies or is prone to variation. **b.1.** *Math.* a quantity capable of assuming any of a set of values. **b.2.** a symbol representing such a quantity.

veil¹ /vāl/ *n.* **a.1.** a piece of cloth, often wide-meshed and transparent, worn by women over the head, shoulders, and often part of the face for concealment or protection or as a token of modesty. **a.2.** a length of netting attached to a woman's hat or headdress for decoration, hanging before all or part of the face. **b.** something that conceals, separates, or screens like a curtain: *a veil of secrecy.*

veil² /vāl/ *v.* to cover, conceal, mask, or disguise with or as if with a veil.

ven•ture¹ /vĕn′ chər/ *n.* **a.** an undertaking that is dangerous, daring, or of doubtful outcome. **b.** something at hazard in a venture; stake.

ven•ture² /vĕn′ chər/ *v.* (**-tures, -tured, -tur•ing**) **a.** to expose to danger or risk. **b.** to take a risk or dare.

ves•sel /vĕs′ əl/ *n.* **a.** a hollow utensil used as a container, especially for liquids. **b.** a craft, especially one larger than a rowboat, designed to navigate on water. **c.** *Anat.* a duct, canal, or other tube for containing or circulating bodily fluid: *a blood vessel.*

vessel

vic•tim /vĭk′ tĭm/ *n.* one who is harmed by or made to suffer from an act, circumstance, agency, or condition.

vi•o•lent /vī′ ə lənt/ *adj.* **a.** marked by or resulting from great physical force or rough action. **b.** severe, intense: *a violent storm.*

vir•tue /vûr′ chōō/ *n.* **a.1.** moral excellence and righteousness; goodness. **a.2.** an example or kind of moral excellence: *the virtue of patience.* **b.** a particularly good or beneficial quality; advantage.

vir•tu•o•so /vûr′ chōō ō′ sō, -zō/ *n.* **a.** a musician with masterly ability, technique, or personal style. **b.** a person with masterly skill or technique in the arts.

vis•i•bil•i•ty /vĭz′ ə bĭl′ ĭ tē/ *n.* (**-ties** *pl.*) **a.** the fact, state, or degree of being visible. **b.** the greatest distance under given weather conditions to which it is possible to see without instrumental assistance.

vis•i•ble /vĭz′ ə bəl/ *adj.* capable of being seen. [ME < OFr. < Lat. *visibilis* < *vidēre*, to see.]

vis•ta /vĭs′ tə/ *n.* a distant view seen through an opening, as between buildings; prospect. [Ital. < *visto*, p.part. of *vedere*, to see < Lat. *vidēre*.]

vista

vi•su•al•ize /vĭzh′ ōō ə līz′/ *v.* (**-iz•es**, **-ized**, **-iz•ing**) to form a mental image of.

vi•tal /vīt′ l/ *adj.* **a.** of or characteristic of life. **b.** full of life; animated. **c.** having immediate importance; essential. [ME < OFr. < Lat. *vitalis* < *vita*, life.]

vi•tal•i•ty /vī tăl′ ĭ tē/ *n.* (**-ties** *pl.*) **a.** the characteristic that distinguishes the living from the nonliving. **b.** physical or intellectual vigor; energy. [ME < OFr. < Lat. *vitalis* < *vita*, life.]

viv•id /vĭv′ ĭd/ *adj.* **a.** perceived as bright and distinct; brilliant. **b.** having intensely bright colors. **c.1.** evoking lifelike images within the mind; heard, seen, or felt as if real: *a vivid description.* **c.2.** active in forming lifelike images: *a vivid imagination.* [Lat. *vividus* < *vivere*, to live.]

vo•cab•u•lar•y /vō kăb′ yə lăr′ ē/ *n.* (**-ies** *pl.*) **a.** all the words of a language. **b.** the sum of words used by, understood by, or at the command of a particular person or group. [Med. Lat. *vocabularium* < neuter of *vocabularius*, of words < Lat. *vocabulum*, name < *vocare*, to call.]

vo•cal /vō′ kəl/ *adj.* **a.** of or pertaining to the voice. **b.** quick to speak or criticize; outspoken. [ME < Lat. *vocalis* < *vox*, voice.]

vo•cal•ize /vō′ kə līz′/ *v.* (**-iz•es**, **-ized**, **-iz•ing**) **a.1.** to use the voice. **a.2.** to sing. **b.** to give voice to; articulate.

vo•ca•tion /vō kā′ shən/ *n.* **a.** a regular occupation or profession, especially one for which a person is specially suited or qualified. **b.** an urge or predisposition to undertake a certain kind of work. [ME *vocacioun*, divine call to a religious life < Lat. *vocatio*, a calling < *vocare*, to call.]

volt•age /vōl′ tĭj/ *n.* electromotive force or potential difference, usually expressed in volts. [after Count Alessandro *Volta* (1745–1827).]

watt•age /wŏt′ ĭj/ *n.* **a.** an amount of power, especially electric power, expressed in watts. **b.** the electric power required by an appliance or device. [after James *Watt* (1736–1819).]

weird /wîrd/ *adj.* (**weird•ly** *adv.*) **a.** unearthly; eerie. **b.** of an odd and inexplicable character; strange; fantastic.

well-in•formed /wĕl ĭn fôrm′d/ *adj.* having extensive knowledge of a subject. *Our social studies teacher makes sure we are well-informed about current events.*

with•hold /wĭth hōld′, wĭth-/ *v.* (**-holds**, **-held**, **-hold•ing**) **a.** to refrain from giving, granting, or permitting. **b.** to deduct (withholding tax) from an employee's salary.

world-fa•mous /wûrld′ fā′ məs/ *adj.* well-known throughout the world. *I had the opportunity to see a world-famous orchestra play.*

yacht /yät/ *n.* any of various relatively small sailing or mechanically propelled vessels, generally with smart, graceful lines, used for pleasure cruises or racing. [Obs. Du. *jaghte,* short for *jaghtschip: jagen,* to chase + *schip,* ship.]

zep•pe•lin /zĕp′ ə lĭn/ *n.* a rigid airship having a long, cylindrical body supported by internal gas cells. [after Count Ferdinand von *Zeppelin* (1838–1917), its inventor.]

zo•ol•o•gy /zō ŏl′ ə jē/ *n.* (**-gies** *pl.*) **a.** the biological science of animals. **b.** the animal life of a particular area.

Pronunciation Key

ă	pat	ŏ	pot	th	**th**in
ā	p**ay**	ō	toe	*th*	**th**is
âr	c**are**	ô	p**aw, for**	hw	**wh**ich
ä	f**a**ther	oi	n**oi**se	zh	vi**s**ion
ě	pet	ou	**ou**t	ə	**a**bout,
ē	be	ŏŏ	t**oo**k		item,
ǐ	pit	ōō	b**oo**t		penc**i**l,
ī	p**ie**	ŭ	c**u**t		gall**o**p,
îr	p**ier**	ûr	**ur**ge		circ**u**s

USING THE Thesaurus

The **Writing Thesaurus** provides synonyms—words that mean the same or nearly the same—and antonyms—words that mean the opposite—for your spelling words. Use this sample to identify the various parts of each thesaurus entry.

- **Entry words** are listed in alphabetical order and are printed in boldface type.
- The abbreviation for the **part of speech** of each entry word follows the boldface entry word.
- The **definition** of the entry word matches the definition of the word in your **Spelling Dictionary**. A **sample sentence** shows the correct use of the word in context.
- Each **synonym** for the entry word is listed under the entry word. Again, a sample sentence shows the correct use of the synonym in context.
- Where appropriate, **antonyms** for the entry word are listed at the end of the entry.

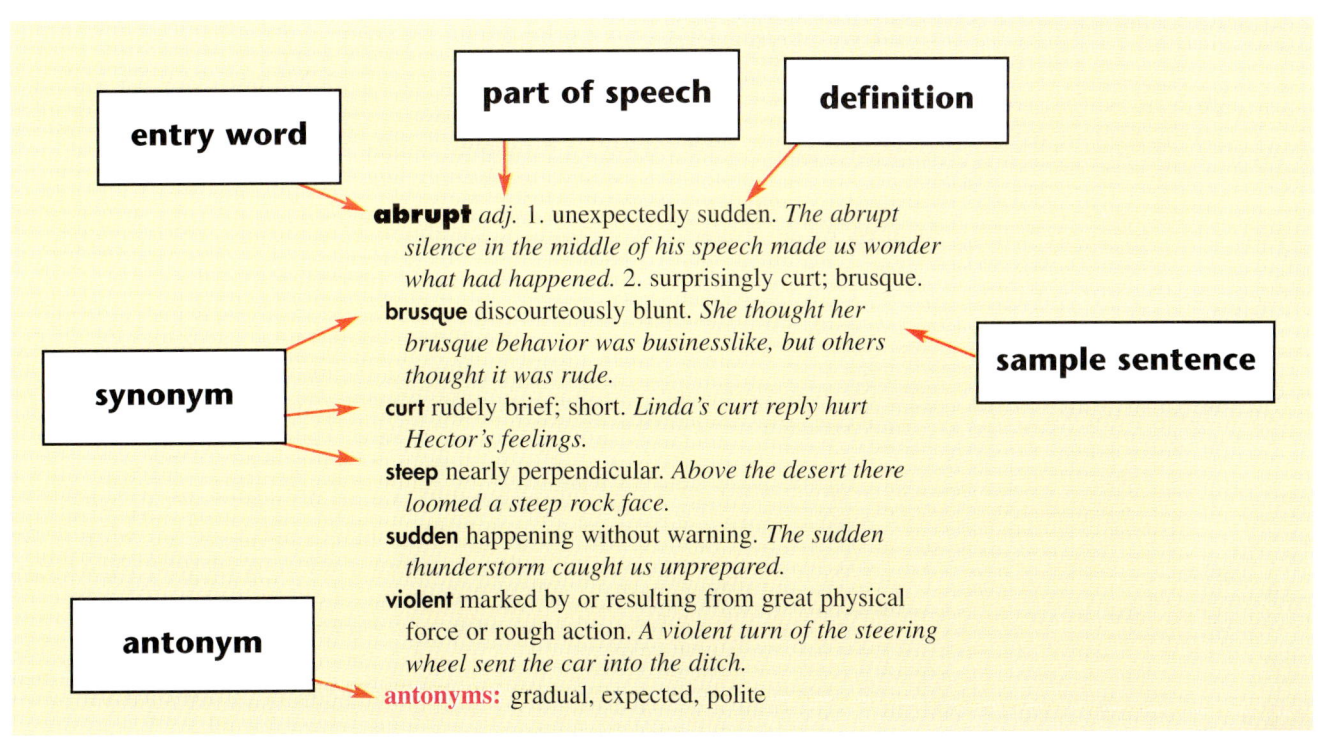

entry word | part of speech | definition

abrupt *adj.* 1. unexpectedly sudden. *The abrupt silence in the middle of his speech made us wonder what had happened.* 2. surprisingly curt; brusque.

brusque discourteously blunt. *She thought her brusque behavior was businesslike, but others thought it was rude.*

curt rudely brief; short. *Linda's curt reply hurt Hector's feelings.*

steep nearly perpendicular. *Above the desert there loomed a steep rock face.*

sudden happening without warning. *The sudden thunderstorm caught us unprepared.*

violent marked by or resulting from great physical force or rough action. *A violent turn of the steering wheel sent the car into the ditch.*

antonyms: gradual, expected, polite

synonym

sample sentence

antonym

A

abrupt *adj.* 1. unexpectedly sudden. *The abrupt silence in the middle of his speech made us wonder what had happened.* 2. surprisingly curt; brusque.

brusque discourteously blunt. *She thought her brusque behavior was businesslike, but others thought it was rude.*

curt rudely brief; short. *Linda's curt reply hurt Hector's feelings.*

steep nearly perpendicular. *Above the desert there loomed a steep rock face.*

sudden happening without warning. *The sudden thunderstorm caught us unprepared.*

violent marked by or resulting from great physical force or rough action. *A violent turn of the steering wheel sent the car into the ditch.*

antonyms: gradual, expected, polite

abundant *adj.* 1. in plentiful supply; ample. 2. abounding with; rich. *The north sector of this national forest is a region abundant in wildlife.*

ample in abundant measure. *The Wongs offered an ample reward to anyone who found their lost cat.*

plentiful abundant; more than enough. *Because of ideal growing weather, apples are plentiful this year.*

rich abounding with natural resources. *Areas rich in minerals are sometimes exploited for those riches.*

antonyms: scarce, poor

academic *adj.* of, pertaining to, or characteristic of a school. *My father enjoys the academic life of a professor.*

educational of or relating to education or learning. *We often watch television programs on the educational channel.*

scholarly characteristic of scholars or serious study. *The book is a scholarly treatment of the culture of the Navajo.*

scholastic of, pertaining to, or characteristic of schools. *This file is a record of your scholastic achievement.*

adjourn *v.* to suspend until a later stated time. *The meeting was adjourned after two hours and was reconvened in the afternoon.*

defer to put off until a later time. *They deferred making a decision about the vacation until all of the travel brochures had arrived.*

delay to postpone. *The game was delayed because of rain.*

postpone to put off. *The mayor asked the reporters to postpone the interview until the next day.*

suspend to stop for a period; interrupt. *The judge suspended the trial while a new jury was chosen.*

antonyms: convene, reconvene, continue, begin, proceed

adjust *v.* 1. to change so as to match or fit; cause to correspond. 2. to bring into proper relationship. 3. to adapt or conform, as to new conditions. *When our family moved from New Mexico to Montana, we had to adjust to snowy winters.* See **reorganize.**

adapt to adjust or change to meet a specific need. *The engineers adapted the design of the car to meet the air pollution standards.*

correct to adjust to meet a standard. *The scientists corrected the rocket's course shortly after lift-off.*

rearrange to adjust the arrangement of. *She rearranged her schedule to allow for an additional appointment.*

reconcile to adjust; settle. *The team members reconciled themselves to defeat.*

advocate *v.* to speak in favor of; recommend. *The senator advocated tax reform.*

champion to defend or support. *That organization champions animal rights.*

support to aid a cause by approving, favoring, or advocating. *The Student Council supports the change in sports eligibility rules.*

antonym: oppose

agenda *n.* a list of things to be done, especially the program for a meeting. *Everyone received an agenda prior to the meeting so that they would be prepared to discuss the listed topics.*

plan a detailed method worked out beforehand for attaining a specific goal. *The plan for the meeting included discussion of the club's new bylaws.*

program a listing of the order of events and other details of a public presentation. *According to the program, the orchestra will perform three works by Beethoven.*

schedule a listing of events or appointments. *The schedule for the tournament shows time allocated for halftime entertainment.*

analysis *n.* the process of separating a subject into its parts and studying them in order to determine the nature of the whole. *The analysis of the water showed that pollution had been reduced.*

examination inspection or analysis. *The Health Department conducted a complete examination to find the source of the virus.*

investigation process of inquiry, study, or analysis. *The committee presented the results of their investigation to the whole organization.*

anarchy *n.* absence of any form of political authority. *Anarchy followed the king's death.* See **chaos**.

antique *adj.* belonging to, made in, or typical of an earlier period. *A Model T is an antique car.* See **out-of-date**.

ancient very old; aged. *The ancient Roman coin was the most valuable part of her collection.*

antiquated very old; aged. *The antiquated law required that the school supply a slate for every child.*

old having existed for a long time. *The old pottery jar was used for canning fruits and vegetables.*

antonyms: modern, new, up-to-date, current, fresh, recent. See **up-to-the-minute**.

ascend *v.* 1. to go or move upward; rise. 2. to move upward upon or along; climb. *The campers ascended the mountain to reach their campsite.*

climb to go upward or along. *They will climb to the top of the fire tower to see the beautiful fall colors of the trees.*

mount to climb or ascend. *The lawyers, determined to win the case, mounted the courthouse steps.*

rise to go up. *When the air is still, smoke will rise straight from a campfire.*

antonym: descend

aspiration *n.* a strong desire for high achievement. *His aspiration was to read every book in the library.* See **objective**.

ambition a strong desire to achieve something. *Strong ambition is often a major ingredient in achieving high political office.*

desire something longed for. *It was their desire to visit China.*

dream an aspiration or ambition. *Sequoya realized his dream of giving his people, the Cherokee, a written language.*

assistance *n.* aid, help. *The clerk offered assistance to the customers.*

aid assistance. *Today, college students must search for sources of financial aid.*

help assistance. *In a disaster, we have come to expect help from the Red Cross.*

patronage support; encouragement. *During the eighteenth century the patronage of wealthy families enabled musicians such as Mozart to create great music.*

support assistance or encouragement. *The friends offered each other moral support in times of stress.*

antonyms: hindrance, obstruction

astonish *v.* to fill with sudden wonder or amazement; confound. *She astonished the crowd with her beautiful dives.* See **startle**.

amaze to cause surprise or great wonder. *The magician's tricks amazed us.*

astound to strike with sudden wonder. *The price of the new car astounded them.*

confound to overwhelm or confuse. *The many changes in the school building confounded the students.*

stun to overwhelm, as with emotional impact of an experience. *Even people who lost nothing were stunned by the tornado.*

stupefy to amaze or astonish. *He was stupefied by the sudden wealth winning the contest brought him.*

surprise to catch unawares. *They will surprise her with a party this year.*

antonyms: expect, anticipate

bazaar *n.* a fair or sale at which miscellaneous articles are sold, often for charitable purposes. *We donated usable items and crafts for the YMCA bazaar to raise money for new sports equipment.*

fair a place for buying and selling items. *There was a booth at the fair where you could buy, sell, or trade baseball cards.*

flea market a place for buying and selling antiques, used household items, etc. *Tanya searched the flea market for a good secondhand lamp for her desk.*

market a place where merchandise is sold. *Early Saturday morning, the farmers bring their produce to the market just south of the town square.*

benefactor *n.* one who gives financial or other aid. *An opera company must have many bene-factors to cover its financial needs.*

donor one who contributes to a cause. *Many donors are necessary to make a successful blood drive.*

patron one who supports, protects, or promotes. *All of the museum's patrons were invited to preview the new exhibit.*

philanthropist one who hopes to improve the world through donations or good works. *An anonymous philanthropist set up a series of scholarships for needy students.*

volunteer one who contributes time to a cause. *The Committee for a Clean City is looking for volunteers to help with the recycling effort.*

benign *adj.* tending to promote well-being; beneficial. *Moderate exercise is a benign activity.* See **hospitable**.

affable mild; gentle; benign. *Aunt Rosa's affable nature cheered us up when we were depressed.*

beneficent characterized by or performing acts of kindness. *The school hoped to promote a benefi-cent atmosphere.*

beneficial promoting well-being. *They thought a week at the ocean would be beneficial.*

humane having the finer qualities of human beings, such as kindness, mercy, and the like. *The organization worked for humane treatment of all animals.*

kind of a friendly nature; benign. *The kind stranger gave us directions to the airport.*

merciful compassionate; lenient. *Be merciful to yourself when you make mistakes.*

antonyms: evil, malignant, unkind, inhumane, merciless, harsh, dangerous

bias *n.* 1. a preference or inclination, especially one that inhibits impartial judgment; prejudice. *The lawyer dismissed the prospective juror because of possible bias.* 2. a specified instance of this.

inclination a tendency. *The dog shows an inclina-tion toward violence.*

narrow-mindedness bias. *The sudden display of narrow-mindedness in the newspaper caused many people to cancel their subscriptions.*

preconception a prejudice. *His decision was based on a preconception of how things should be done.*

prejudice a preconceived idea; preference; bias. *The court decided that the company's hiring practices reflected prejudice.*

proclivity an inclination or tendency; predisposi-tion. *Joe's proclivity for wasting time will be his downfall.*

tendency a demonstrated inclination to think or behave in a certain way. *I have a tendency to believe that all people are basically good.*

antonyms: open-mindedness, receptiveness, tolerance, broad-mindedness

bizarre *adj.* strikingly unconventional or far-fetched, as in style or appearance; odd. *The couple's bizarre costumes caused passersby to turn and stare.* See **extraordinary**.

curious singular; odd. *The curious combination of events made him wonder what was going on.*

eccentric departing from the normal or expected. *Walking down the sidewalk backward is eccentric behavior.*

peculiar unusual or strange. *All of the shoes on sale were either very small, very large, or some peculiar color.*

uncommon not common; rare or strange. *At our house, it is uncommon to have dinner before seven o'clock.*

unusual out of the ordinary. *The dog's unusual behavior was attributed to an illness.*

weird of an odd or unexplainable character. *The weird lighting on the stage gave everything a greenish cast.*

antonyms: usual, common, ordinary, expected, humdrum

boulevard *n.* a broad city street, often tree-lined and landscaped. *Handsome mansions lined the wide boulevards in the historic section of the city.*

avenue a wide street or thoroughfare. *Although they were designed for horse-and-buggy traffic, the city's avenues now handle the flow of motor-ized vehicles.*

parkway a broad landscaped highway sometimes having a planted median. *The state was proud of its system of beautiful parkways that allowed for a smooth flow of traffic.*

brilliant *adj.* 1. full of light; shining. 2. superb; wonderful. *The pianist gave a brilliant performance.* 3. marked by extra-ordinary powers of intellect or invention. See **intelligent, extraordinary**.

bright shining. *The bright sunlight made me squint.*

creative having the ability to create. *The creative child amazed his teachers with his original ideas.*

intellectual relating to the intellect. *The club appealed to the intellectual types who enjoy wide-ranging conversations.*

luminous full of light. *David's luminous smile brightened the gloomy day.*

magnificent grand; outstanding. *The architect's plan would result in a magnificent new building.*

splendid brilliant; glorious. *The painting was a splendid example of the new brushstroke technique.*

antonyms: dull, dark, boring, ordinary

brusque *adj.* abrupt and curt in manner or speech, often to the point of rudeness; blunt. *She thought that her brusque behavior was businesslike, but others thought it was rude.* See **abrupt, succinct**.

blunt having an abrupt and candid manner. *Rather than avoid the issue, Mr. Smith decided to be blunt.*

gruff brusque or stern in manner or speech. *His gruff reply to the invitation startled his relatives.*

insensitive unfeeling. *Insensitive passersby didn't stop to help the injured cat.*

rude ill-mannered; harsh. *That rude remark was not necessary.*

antonyms: gentle, gracious, polite, sensitive

calamity *n.* an extraordinarily serious event marked by terrible loss, lasting distress, and affliction. *An airplane crash was the latest calamity in the news.* See **catastrophe**.

caper *v.* to leap or frisk about; frolic. *The clown capered across the stage.*

cavort to bound or prance; to caper. *The cheerleaders cavorted on the sidelines.*

dance to leap or skip about in excitement. *The children danced about when they heard that they had won the contest.*

frolic to behave playfully; romp. *The colt frolicked in the tall grass.*

gambol to leap about playfully; frolic. *The kittens gamboled across the porch and fell into the bushes.*

romp to play boisterously; frolic. *The boys romped through the house and woke the baby.*

catastrophe *n.* a great and sudden calamity; disaster. *The stock market's plunge was a catastrophe for many investors.* See **fiasco**.

calamity a disaster. *One calamity after another befell the unlucky family.*

cataclysm a violent upheaval. *The revolution was an unexpected cataclysm to the many citizens.*

disaster a grave misfortune. *The hurricane was a major disaster for the Gulf Coast region.*

misfortune a distressing occurrence. *After the earthquake, it took a while to assess the magnitude of the misfortune.*

antonyms: boon, blessing, success, good luck

chaos *n.* a condition or place of total disorder or confusion. *The earthquake left the area in a state of chaos.*

anarchy absence of any form of political authority. *Anarchy followed the king's death.*

confusion a state of bewilderment. *When the electricity went out, the town fell into confusion.*

disarray a state of disorder or confusion. *After the burglary, the shop was in total disarray.*

disorder a lack of order or logical arrangement. *After hurriedly completing the difficult assignment, his desk was in complete disorder.*

pandemonium wild noise and uproar. *Pandemonium broke out when they announced the winner of the contest.*

tumult a disorderly commotion or disturbance. *The tumult of the angry crowd could be heard for blocks.*

antonyms: order, regularity, stability

circuit *n.* 1. a closed, usually circular curve. 2. a regular or accustomed course from place to place, as that of a salesman; round. *In pioneer times a preacher often followed a circuit and visited churches on a regular, but infrequent, basis.* 3. an association of teams, clubs, or arenas of competition.

circle a closed curve. *The flower beds were laid out in circles.*

course the customary sequence of events. *During the course of the service, the participants were to remain silent.*

league an association of teams or clubs who compete with each other. *Competition was tough because all of the teams in the league were playing well.*

orbit the path of one body as it circles another. *The satellite's orbit takes it directly over this city.*

round a series of acts, events, or the like ending where they began. *Letter carriers' rounds begin and end at the post office.*

tour a circular journey. *The tour of the western states began and ended in Wyoming.*

confident *adj.* 1. marked by assurance, as of success. *His confident smile as he left the meeting let us know that the deal was made.* 2. marked by confidence in oneself; self-assured.

assured confident. *The actor, knowing that he would get the part, walked onto the stage with an assured air.*

certain definite. *He was certain that he had put the tickets in his coat pocket.*

dauntless self-assured. *We marveled at the dauntless way she managed the crowd.*

self-assured confident. *The self-assured child was not at all shy with adults.*

sure without doubt. *Kim was sure that she would win the match.*

antonyms: uncertain, timid, shy, unsure, daunted, self-effacing

confidential *adj.* 1. done or communicated in confidence; secret. 2. entrusted with the confidence of another. 3. denoting confidence or intimacy. *He told me the news in a confidential tone of voice.*

covert hidden; secret. *All the spies in the novel were involved in covert activities.*

private concealed or secluded from view. *The private drive began with a locked gate.*

secret kept from general view. *The secret message described the location of the treasure.*

antonyms: open, public

contrary *adj.* opposed, as in character or purpose; completely different. *They held contrary ideas about how the room should be decorated.*

conflicting in opposition. *The three journalists on the panel held conflicting views of how to help the economy grow.*

contradictory opposite; conflicting. *The statement the mayor made on Monday and the one he made on Wednesday were contradictory.*

opposite completely different. *Our two cats have opposite personalities—one is aggressive and the other is shy.*

antonyms: similar, alike, complementary

control *v.* 1. to exercise authority or dominating influence over; direct; regulate. *This switch controls the flow of water.* 2. to hold in restraint; check.

direct to control; manage. *That officer directs traffic here every afternoon.*

manage to direct or control. *She manages a retail business.*

regulate to control or direct. *A thermostat regulates the furnace.*

restrain to hold back; control. *You must use a leash to restrain your dog.*

corporation *n.* 1. a body of persons granted a charter legally recognizing them as a separate entity having its own rights, privileges, and liabilities distinct from those of its members. *The headquarters of the corporation was moved to a suburban location.* 2. a group of people combined into or acting as one body. See **enterprise**.

business any commercial establishment. *That business specializes in car accessories.*

company a business enterprise; firm. *Who owns that company?*

conglomerate a large corporation made up of many companies that operate in different fields. *A conglomerate bought up many small, independent companies.*

firm a commercial partnership of two or more persons. *After passing the bar examination, he hoped to join a large law firm.*

organization a group of persons having specific responsibilities and joined for some purpose or work. *Mr. Cusack joined an organization specializing in real estate.*

cosmopolitan *adj.* at home in all parts of the world or in many spheres of interest. *Travel gave her a cosmopolitan outlook.*

sophisticated having worldly knowledge or refinement. *Cole Porter wrote music about sophisticated people.*

worldly sophisticated or cosmopolitan. *The worldly man was at home wherever he went.*

antonyms: provincial, rustic, unsophisticated, bucolic

criterion *n.* a standard, rule, or test on which a judgment or decision can be based. *The single criterion for winning was speed.*

model a pattern or standard to be followed. *Use this report as a model for your homework assignment.*

norm a standard. *Our teacher explained how test norms work.*

rule an established standard. *Learn the rules for playing chess from this book.*

standard an acknowledged measure of comparison. *Babe Ruth set a standard for hitting that few baseball players could live up to.*

test a criterion or standard. *Endurance is the real test for triathletes.*

yardstick a criterion or standard. *He considered productivity the only important yardstick for his employees.*

criticism *n.* 1. a critical comment or judgment. 2.a. The art, skill, or profession of making discriminating judgments and evaluations, especially of literary or other artistic works. 2.b. A review or other article expressing such judgment and evaluation. *The criticism of the play focused on the director.*

commentary a series of explanations and interpretations. *A lengthy commentary about the current show of Picasso's early works appeared in the newspaper on Sunday.*

notice a printed criticism of an artistic or literary event. *The cast of the new play waited anxiously for the notices in the early editions of the newspapers.*

review an analysis of a new work or performance. *All of the reviews of the new film agree that it is not worth seeing.*

data *n.* information, especially organized for analysis or used as the basis for a decision. *The newspaper collected data from the past twenty years to analyze voting patterns.*

evidence information on which a decision is based. *The researcher collected evidence to help the city government decide what to do about downtown traffic.*

facts things known with certainty. *They verified the facts with experiments.*

information knowledge gained through study or experience. *An almanac is a collection of information on many subjects.*

statistics numerical data. *The Census Bureau collects statistics about the makeup of the country's population.*

deceive *v.* to cause a person to believe what is not true; mislead. *How did they deceive him about the value of the necklace?*

cheat to trick or deceive. *The sudden thunderstorm cheated us out of our picnic in the park.*

con to swindle or defraud. *The swindlers conned us into believing that the coins were genuine.*

defraud to cheat or swindle. *They tried to defraud the investors in a phony stock deal.*

fool to deceive or misinform. *I fooled Ann by putting her tiny gift in a huge box.*

hoax to deceive by trickery. *The UFO report hoaxed many people.*

hoodwink to deceive or take in. *The old lady hoodwinked the salesman into believing that she was not at home.*

mislead to lead in the wrong direction. *Don't let the sunny sky mislead you; it's cold outside.*

swindle to cheat or defraud. *The unscrupulous man swindled the family out of their savings.*

decipher *v.* 1. to read or interpret something ambiguous, obscure, or illegible. *I could barely decipher his terrible handwriting.* 2. to convert from a code or cipher to plain text; decode.

decode to convert from a code into regular language. *A cryptographer's job is to decode messages.*

interpret to clear up the meaning of. *They interpreted the directions to mean that they should turn left at the next corner.*

solve to figure out; answer. *Sue solved the crossword puzzle in fifteen minutes.*

translate to explain or put in simpler terms. *He translated the complicated directions into simple steps.*

unscramble to straighten out; decipher. *He unscrambled the secret message in record time.*

dictator *n.* a ruler having absolute authority and supreme jurisdiction over the government of a state. *Joseph Stalin was a dictator in the Soviet Union during the first half of the twentieth century.* See **monarch.**

autocrat an absolute ruler. *The autocrat shared none of his power; even his so-called friends bent to his every whim.*

despot an absolute ruler; tyrant. *The despot lived in luxury while his people starved.*

tyrant any ruler having absolute power. *The tyrant was not concerned with the needs of the people.*

dilemma *n.* 1. a situation that requires one to choose between two equally balanced alternatives. 2. a predicament that seemingly defies a satisfactory solution. *He had been invited to two holiday parties, and deciding which to attend presented a real dilemma.*

difficulty something not easily solved. *Her difficulty arose from her inability to decide on a topic for her report.*

impasse a dilemma. *The discussion reached an impasse, and no one would compromise.*

plight a situation of difficulty. *Losing his job only made his plight worse.*

predicament an embarrassing or troublesome situation. *Her predicament began when her car ran out of gas.*

problem a situation or question that presents a difficulty. *Since the two bicycles cost the same, deciding which one to buy was a problem.*

quandary a condition of uncertainty. *Because of their many obligations, they were in a quandary about how to fit anything else into their schedule.*

dismal *adj.* 1. causing gloom or depression; dreary. 2. characterized by lack of hope. *The locker room was a dismal place after the loss of the game.*

bleak gloomy and somber. *Injuries made his future as a basketball player look bleak.*

cheerless without cheer; gloomy. *The decorator thought new wallpaper might brighten the cheerless room.*

depressing causing sadness or depression. *The depressing atmosphere at school was related to a streak of bad luck.*

dreary gloomy, dismal. *Three days of rain were a dreary beginning for the week.*

gloomy dark; dreary; dismal. *The gloomy basement was a poor place to have a party.*

melancholy gloomy. *The singer sang only melancholy songs until we asked for something more upbeat.*

somber melancholy; dismal. *He chose a red sweater to brighten up his somber mood.*

sorrowful full of sadness. *The actor used a sorrowful voice to tell of the catastrophe.*

antonyms: cheerful, bright, happy, gay, joyful, merry, light

dissimilar *adj.* unlike; different. *Both ideas for solving the problem were good, although they were quite dissimilar.* See **distinct**.

different distinct; separate. *We took a different route to school because of the traffic.*

mismatched unmatched; different. *Kevin didn't discover his mismatched socks until physical education class.*

antonyms: alike, similar

distinct *adj.* 1. distinguishable from all others; separate. *The suspect was observed at the scene on two distinct occasions.* 2. easily perceived by the senses or intellect; clear. See **dissimilar**.

clear easily perceived by the senses; distinct. *Her clear pronunciation helped the people in the back of the auditorium to understand her.*

definite clearly defined. *There had been a definite break in the progress toward completing the building.*

explicit clear or distinct. *Explicit written directions with diagrams helped them assemble the desks quickly.*

separate dissimilar or distinct. *Although they are identical twins, they lead completely separate lives.*

antonyms: overlapping, indistinct, unclear, muted, blurred, indefinite, fuzzy

docile *adj.* 1. easily taught; teachable. 2. submissive to training or management; tractable. *Sheep are usually docile animals.* See **peaceable**.

manageable able to be controlled. *The small group of sheep was more manageable for the dog than the larger group was.*

meek easily imposed upon. *A meek person may fail to get needed attention.*

obedient dutiful; controllable. *The obedient dog waited outside the store.*

quiet calm; making no noise. *Blue jays are seldom quiet birds.*

teachable able to be taught. *I might learn slowly, but I am teachable.*

antonyms: wild, unmanageable, disobedient, bold

dominate *v.* to control, govern, or rule by superior authority or power. *The Cardinals dominated their league for three years.*

control to exercise dominating influence over. *The small girl controlled her horse amazingly well in the jumps.*

govern to control the behavior or actions of. *I will not baby-sit for them again because I cannot govern the children.*

manage to direct or control. *The dog managed the flock of sheep with ease.*

rule to exercise control over. *The queen ruled with an iron fist.*

subdue to bring under control; quiet. *The guards finally subdued the rioting prisoners.*

subjugate to conquer or control. *The rebels were easily subjugated by the army.*

tyrannize to control with power, especially arbitrarily. *The Airedale tyrannized all the neighborhood cats.*

antonyms: obey, submit, yield, surrender

elated *adj.* exultant; joyful. *The elated fans held an impromptu party after their team won the national tournament.*

delighted filled with happiness. *A delighted expression filled the child's face when he found the lost teddy bear.*

ecstatic of, or relating to, a state of extreme delight. *The couple was ecstatic when their first grandchild was born.*

happy having or demonstrating pleasure. *She was happy when her best friend won the spelling bee.*

jubilant joyful or very happy. *Jubilant supporters surrounded the mayor when the election results were announced.*

overjoyed filled with joy or happiness. *The dog was overjoyed when its owners returned.*

antonyms: unhappy, depressed, miserable

endeavor *n.* a conscientious or concerted effort toward a given end; an earnest attempt. *Making the debating team was the next endeavor she planned.* See **enterprise**.

attempt try or endeavor. *The first attempt for a goal was unsuccessful.*

try an effort made toward a goal. *The high jumper prepared to make his final try for a world record.*

undertaking an attempt. *Climbing the rock face was an ambitious undertaking.*

enterprise *n.* 1. an undertaking, especially one of some scope, complication, and risk. *The new business they set up was a risky enterprise.* 2. a business organization. 3. readiness to venture; initiative. See **corporation**.

ambition strong desire to accomplish something. *Is his ambition sufficient to complete this difficult project?*

business any commercial undertaking. *They went into business together willing to share risks and hoping to share profits.*

drive energy; aggressiveness; initiative. *Ms. Green's drive helped her climb the corporate ladder quickly.*

initiative the instinct, power, or ability to begin or follow through on a project; enterprise or determination. *They chose him to head the project because he has a lot of initiative.*

project an undertaking requiring effort. *The new real estate project will bring jobs to the community.*

undertaking enterprise or venture. *The landscaping business was an ambitious undertaking.*

venture an undertaking that is daring or of doubtful outcome. *Their new business venture required a lot of capital.*

antonyms: timidity, fearfulness, diffidence

epidemic *n.* 1. an outbreak of contagious disease that spreads rapidly. *An epidemic of measles broke out in the city.* 2. a rapid spread, growth, or development.

contagion a disease transmitted by direct or indirect contact. *Polio is a contagion that has been controlled in this century.*

pestilence a plague or epidemic. *The story told of an evil pestilence in the land.*

plague a pestilence, affliction, or calamity. *A plague called the Black Death struck Europe in the middle of the fourteenth century.*

scourge a cause of widespread and dreaded affliction, such as war or pestilence. *Cancer is a scourge of the twentieth century.*

essential *adj.* 1. constituting a part of the nature of something; inherent. 2. basic or indispensable; necessary. *Vegetables are essential to a healthy diet.*

indispensable necessary; required. *The ability to type is almost indispensable when learning word processing.*

necessary needed for the existence or functioning of something. *Before beginning a job, collect all necessary tools.*

vital of immediate importance; essential; indispensable. *Firefighters and medics provide a vital service to the city.*

antonyms: inessential, unnecessary, unimportant, dispensable

evident *adj.* easily seen or understood; obvious. *It was quite evident that the Clinton team would win the Quiz Bowl.*

apparent readily seen or understood. *The apparent reason for the delay was the stormy weather.*

clear plain or evident. *The clear intention of the statement was to stop rumors.*

manifest clearly apparent to sight or understanding. *After a long discussion, the solution to the problem became manifest.*

obvious easily seen or understood. *Because of his ability as a leader, Mr. Ito was an obvious choice for foreman of the jury.*

patent obvious; plain. *The patent insincerity of the many compliments was offensive.*

plain clearly understood. *It was plain that he was upset by the unpleasant incident.*

antonyms: unclear, complicated, hidden, invisible, obscure, doubtful, uncertain. See **subtle**.

exceed *v.* to go beyond the limits of. *We hope to exceed last year's total in the fund drive.*

beat to go beyond. *Attendance at the ball game Saturday beat the stadium record.*

outdistance to surpass by a wide margin. *Marco routinely outdistanced his brother and his cousin in cycling events.*

outdo to surpass in performance. *We were trying to outdo last month's total in glass for recycling.*

outstrip to exceed or surpass. *The Western Region outstripped the Northeastern Region in sales.*

surpass to go beyond the limits of. *I hope to surpass the local marathon record.*

transcend to surpass or exceed. *The costume party was great; it transcended our expectations.*

antonyms: lag, trail, fall short, underachieve

exhaust *v.* 1. to use up; consume. 2. to wear out completely; tire. 3. to deal with comprehensively. *After three days of discussion, we had completely exhausted the topic.*

deplete to use up or exhaust. *We depleted the firewood supply at the camp during the cold spell.*

fatigue to wear out or exhaust. *The difficult race fatigued the runners.*

tire to wear out or exhaust. *Staying up late to baby-sit tires her.*

antonyms: refresh, revive, invigorate

extraordinary *adj.* highly exceptional; remarkable. *The resemblance between the cousins was extraordinary; they looked like twins.* See **legendary.**

amazing causing wonder. *The magician created one amazing illusion after another.*

astonishing surprising. *They couldn't pass up buying the new car because of the astonishing price.*

exceptional uncommon or extraordinary. *All the teenagers in the musical competition had exceptional talent.*

rare happening infrequently; uncommon. *A visit from Aunt Harriet is a rare treat.*

remarkable deserving notice. *Our teacher was pleased that Jill had read such a remarkable number of books over the summer.*

uncommon not common; seldom occurring. *It is uncommon to see wild animals in the city.*

unusual not usual or common. *Warm weather is unusual for this time of year.*

antonyms: ordinary, common, usual, humdrum

fascinate *v.* to hold an intense interest or attraction for. *The changing images in the kaleidoscope fascinated the child.*

attract to evoke interest. *The Reptile House at the zoo attracts some people and repels others.*

captivate to fascinate by special charm or beauty. *The spectacular performance of the ice dancers captivated the audience.*

charm to attract greatly; fascinate. *The beautiful and complicated music boxes charmed me.*

enchant to delight completely; charm. *The scenery enchanted everyone in the theater.*

interest to arouse or hold the attention of. *The history of the American West interested Kareem.*

faux pas *n.* a social blunder. *Failing to respond to the invitation was a serious faux pas.*

blunder a grave error made through carelessness. *Did you hear about the President's blunder during the press conference?*

error an incorrect action. *She felt it was an error to eat until everyone else had been served.*

gaffe a clumsy social error. *His most embarrassing gaffe was spilling his food on his companion's fancy clothes.*

mistake an error or fault. *Joe made the mistake of waxing his car in the sun.*

feign *v.* to give a false appearance of; sham. *He feigned an injury so they would leave him alone.* 2. to represent falsely; pretend to.

fake to falsify and present as genuine. *The quarterback faked a pass to fool the defense.*

pretend to feign. *He pretended to be confident to cover his nervousness.*

sham to pretend or give a false appearance of. *After the accident, she often shammed studying because her mind was on her injured mother.*

fiasco *n.* a complete failure. *The fund-raising attempt was a fiasco.*

debacle a sudden collapse; ruin. *The movement to pass a new housing law quickly became a debacle when the leaders decided to quit.*

dud a person or a thing that is disappointingly ineffective or unsuccessful. *The plan was a dud and was finally abandoned.*

flop a complete failure. *The latest film released by that studio was a total flop.*

antonym: success

forbid *v.* to command someone not to do something. *The king decided to forbid his subjects to criticize him.*

ban to prohibit. *Dogs are banned from the playground areas of the city parks.*

disallow to refuse to allow. *Pets are disallowed at my home because of my allergies.*

prevent to keep something from happening. *The rules prevented her from talking to her coach during the competition.*

prohibit to forbid with authority. *The law prohibits parking in front of the school.*

antonyms: allow, permit, let

fragile *adj.* 1. easily broken or damaged; brittle. *The antique vase was fragile.* 2. physically weak or delicate; frail.

breakable able to be broken. *The movers carefully pack all of the breakable items in many layers of paper.*

brittle likely to break. *As we age our bones get more brittle.*

delicate easily broken or damaged. *Please don't handle the delicate figurines.*

frail delicate or weak. *A character in* The Secret Garden *is a frail boy who spends most of his time in bed.*

puny weak. *The puny puppy struggled to open its eyes.*

weak without physical strength. *He felt weak for several days after having the flu.*

antonyms: strong, sturdy, hardy, resilient, flexible

franchise *n.* 1. a privilege or right officially granted a person or a group by a government. 2. authorization granted by a manufacturer to a distributor or dealer to sell its products. *My aunt and uncle have a franchise for a new fast-food restaurant.*

charter an authorization from a central organization to operate a local branch or chapter. *A charter has been granted for the establishment of a branch bank at the corner of Second and Franklin Streets.*

suffrage the privilege or right to vote; franchise. *The goal of their organization is universal suffrage.*

vote the right to vote; suffrage. *In 1920 women were given the vote throughout the United States.*

full-length *adj.* of a normal or standard length. *The current best-seller is a full-length novel.*

complete whole. *How long does it take to go through the complete program at the health spa?*

unabridged having the original length. *You will certainly find that word in an unabridged dictionary.*

antonyms: condensed, abridged, shortened, partial

galvanize *v.* to arouse to awareness or action; spur. *Their desire for change was galvanized by the rousing speeches.*

activate to set in motion; stimulate. *The coach hoped his pep talk would activate the team's resolve for victory.*

arouse to stir up or stimulate. *The conditions they saw in the poor neighborhood aroused their anger.*

awaken to rouse or stir up. *Our campaign awakened the voters to the need to pass the school levy.*

excite to stir into action. *A series of television programs excited many people about the need for environmental action.*

incite to provoke or stir up. *He hoped his appeal to civic duty incited the people to vote in the election.*

spur to incite; stimulate. *The approaching deadline spurred us to finish the project.*

stimulate to incite; activate. *Jealousy may stimulate inappropriate behavior.*

genuine *adj.* not false; real; true. *He took the ring to a jeweler to see if the diamond was genuine.*

authentic having an undisputed origin; genuine. *His collection contained only one authentic ancient coin, but he did have many good replicas.*

real authentic; genuine. *Most people prefer real to artificial flavoring in their food.*

true not false; consistent with fact and reality. *He made a true and voluntary statement about what he had witnessed.*

antonyms: false, fake, phony, untrue, inauthentic, falsified, artificial

grieve *v.* 1. to cause to be sorrowful; distress. 2. to experience grief; mourn. *The cat grieved over the disappearance of its playmate.*

bereave to leave desolate, especially by death. *The death of their pet bereaved the children.*

distress to cause suffering. *The negative reviews distressed the cast of the play.*

lament to express grief. *She lamented the bankruptcy of her business.*

languish to continue in a state of suffering. *Although he recovered from the accident physically, the psychological trauma caused him to languish for months.*

mourn to show or feel grief. *He mourned the loss of his best friend.*

suffer to feel pain or distress. *Vicki suffered from the loss of her eyesight.*

antonyms: be pleased, enjoy

harangue *n.* a speech or piece of writing characterized by strong feeling or expression; tirade. *The man's harangue about staying off his lawn frightened the neighborhood children.*

diatribe a bitter and abusive criticism. *The coach seldom lectured the team, but when he did it was a real diatribe.*

lecture a sober scolding; sermon. *The lecture to the children was about the danger of playing with matches.*

sermon a long and tedious reproof or scolding. *The committee members tired of the chairperson's daily sermons about efficiency.*

tirade a long, violent speech, especially one that denounces. *The workers could no longer endure the boss's regular tirades.*

antonyms: praise, comfort

heir *n.* a person who inherits or is entitled by law to inherit the property, rank, title, or office of another. *Prince Charles is heir to the throne.*

beneficiary one who receives funds, property, or the like from an insurance policy, will, or other settlement. *His spouse is the beneficiary on his life insurance policy.*

inheritor one who inherits; heir. *The will names three inheritors of the estate.*

successor one who follows in an office or role. *Who was his successor when he completed his term in Congress?*

honorable *adj.* 1. deserving or winning honor and respect. 2. possessing and characterized by honor. *The soldier was an honorable man.*

ethical in accord with accepted standards of right and wrong. *The deal was legal but not ethical.*

moral being or acting in accord with accepted standards of right and wrong. *The judge was known to be a deeply moral man.*

noble lofty in character. *Helping those less fortunate is considered a noble act.*

virtuous righteous; good. *The organization praised and publicly acknowledged virtuous acts by its members.*

antonyms: dishonorable, unethical, immoral, shameful

hospitable *adj.* cordial and generous to guests. *Our hosts provided a hospitable welcome for us.* See **benign**.

accommodating doing a favor or service for. *The woman was very accommodating when we asked to use her telephone.*

gracious characterized by kindness and courtesy. *One of the duties of the First Lady is to be a gracious hostess.*

magnanimous generous in forgiving; gracious; unselfish. *Opening their home to people stranded in a blizzard was a magnanimous thing to do.*

neighborly behaving in the manner of a friendly neighbor. *Helping the stranger change the flat tire was very neighborly.*

obliging doing a favor or service for. *When he explained that he was allergic to seafood, the hostess was very obliging and brought him chicken.*

welcoming receiving with pleasure and hospitality. *He greeted us with a welcoming smile.*

antonyms: inhospitable, unfriendly, rude, unaccommodating, stingy, cold

imminent *adj.* about to occur; impending. *Residents scrambled to prepare for the imminent hurricane.*

approaching coming nearer in time or space. *The approaching holiday generated an air of excitement.*

forthcoming about to appear. *The candidates bought as much TV time as they could in preparation for the forthcoming election.*

impending likely to happen soon; imminent. *The attorney was making last-minute preparations for the impending trial.*

antonyms: eventual, retreating, distant

impose *v.* to bring about by exercising authority. *The mayor imposed a curfew during the unrest.*

demand to ask for urgently, leaving no chance for refusal. *The police officer demanded to see a driver's license.*

levy to impose or collect (taxes, for example). *The President promised to levy no new taxes.*

require to demand. *The new rule required students to carry identification cards.*

inferior *adj.* low or lower in quality, value, or estimation. *The lower-priced coat is only slightly inferior in quality.*

bad poor; not good. *Those apples are so bad that we should get rid of them.*

lower beneath or inferior. *Your test scores are lower than they were last semester.*

mediocre ordinary; commonplace. *You can do better work; this project is mediocre.*

poor lacking in quality. *The chess team made a poor showing in the tournament.*

second-rate not of first quality. *Let's not go there; I hear the food there is second-rate.*

antonyms: good, first-rate, higher, high-quality, fine, excellent. See **superior**.

inscribe *v.* to write, print, carve, or engrave words or letters on or in a surface. *Someone had inscribed a personal note inside the front cover of the book.*

carve to form by cutting. *Finally, the sculptor carved his initials in the base of his new work.*

engrave to carve words, letters, or designs in a surface. *The old trophy was engraved "District Champions—1936."*

etch to make a pattern on metal or glass with acid. *The name of the dairy was etched in the old milk bottle.*

imprint to mark with words, letters, or designs. *The contractor's name was imprinted in the concrete of the sidewalk.*

print to write. *The child carefully printed her name in every book she owned.*

write to form letters or words on a surface. *Write your name on your paper.*

inspector *n.* 1. a person, especially an official, who inspects. *The health inspectors periodically check every restaurant in the city.* 2. a police officer of the rank just below superintendent.

detective a person (often a police officer) who investigates crimes or obtains evidence. *Several detectives were assigned to investigate a series of robberies.*

examiner one who inspects in detail. *She worked as tax examiner for the Internal Revenue Service.*

investigator one who investigates; a detective. *The attorney hired an investigator to find out if there had been any witnesses to the accident.*

sleuth a detective. *As a long-time and avid reader of mysteries, she thought of herself as an accomplished sleuth.*

intelligent *adj.* having a high degree of intelligence; mentally acute. *This game requires intelligent players.* See **brilliant**.

astute keen in judgment. *The chess player made an astute move.*

bright smart or intelligent. *The bright child knew the alphabet at an early age.*

clever mentally quick. *The clever animal learned the trick the first time its trainer showed how it was done.*

discerning astute. *The discerning journalist got straight to the heart of the matter.*

quick learning, understanding, or thinking with speed. *She has a very quick mind.*

sharp shrewd or astute. *The sharp businessman knew just when to raise or to lower prices.*

shrewd having keen insight. *A shrewd investor can make a lot of money.*

smart characterized as having sharp, quick thought. *Smart buyers shop around before making a major purchase.*

antonyms: unintelligent, dull, stupid, dumb, slow

introductory *adj.* serving to introduce. *At the seminar a woman made introductory remarks outlining the objectives for the day.*

beginning coming first. *The beginning activity each day at camp was raising the flag.*

opening at the beginning; introductory. *The traditional opening music of an opera is an overture.*

preliminary introductory; beginning. *Collecting background information was always the preliminary step.*

preparatory serving to make ready. *He attended a preparatory school in New England.*

antonyms: ending, final, closing, follow-up, concluding

itemize *v.* to set down item by item; list. *They itemized their expenses for tax purposes.*

inventory to make a detailed list of items. *The workers periodically inventoried the items on the store shelves.*

list to make an itemized record or reminder. *He listed all the things he needed to do before school started.*

jealousy *n.* a jealous attitude or disposition. *Because only one of the friends could be chosen to go on the special trip, the others were filled with jealousy.*

covetousness the desire to have something belonging to another. *The ideal of "keeping up with the Joneses" is a kind of covetousness.*

envy discontent at the good fortune of another. *Envy was in the face of every child at the party when the boy got a puppy as a birthday gift.*

knowledgeable *adj.* possessing or showing knowledge; well-informed. *He is quite knowledgeable about fly-fishing.* See **well-informed, academic**.

educated having knowledge. *The lecturer attracted a highly educated audience.*

erudite deeply learned; scholarly. *The program featured an erudite discussion of myths and cultures.*

wise having great learning. *The wise professor impressed all the new students.*

antonyms: uninformed, uneducated, ignorant

laconic *adj.* using or marked by the use of few words; terse; concise. *Many men in westerns are portrayed as laconic.* See **succinct**.

lecture *n.* 1. an exposition of a given subject delivered before an audience or class, especially for the purpose of instruction. *Mrs. Garcia's use of visual aids enlivened the lecture on world geography.* 2. a sober admonition or reproof; reprimand. See **harangue**.

address a formal communication. *The President made an address before Congress.*

lesson an explanation; lecture. *The teacher planned a lesson around the coming election.*

speech a talk or an address. *All of the speeches dealt with some aspect of the economy.*

talk an informal speech. *He gave a talk about endangered species.*

legendary *adj.* of, constituting, based on, or of the nature of a legend. *Paul Bunyan is a legendary character.*

heroic courageous; grand. *The movie compared the heroic deeds of the samurai with those of heroes from the American West.*

mythic having the nature of a myth. *There are so many stories about Babe Ruth that, although he was a real baseball player, he has taken on a mythic quality.*

antonyms: ordinary, realistic, humdrum

liability *n.* 1. something for which one is liable; an obligation or debt. 2. legal responsibility to fulfill some contract or obligation. *Liability for the accident was established by the court.* 3. the financial obligations entered in the balance sheet of a business enterprise. 4. something that holds one back; handicap.

accountability being answerable. *Each team member accepted personal accountability for following the training diet.*

debt something owed; liability or obligation. *When the company's major debts were taken care of, the owners were able to consider new ventures.*

disadvantage unfavorable condition. *My inability to speak Spanish was a serious disadvantage on the trip to Mexico.*

hindrance an impediment. *A broken bone can be a hindrance to many kinds of physical activity.*

obligation a duty; promise; contract. *He accepted the care of the stray dog as his obligation.*

responsibility obligation; duty. *The teacher gave each student the responsibility for selecting supplementary readings.*

antonyms: asset, advantage

locality *n.* a particular neighborhood, place, or district. *Housing costs are lower in this locality.*

area a distinct part or section. *The section north of the river has been set aside as a wildlife area.*

district an area created arbitrarily for administrative purposes. *In this district a parent or guardian must visit the school at least four times a year.*

locale a locality in reference to some event. *Artesian Park was chosen as the locale for the family reunion and picnic.*

site the place where something is, was, or is about to be located. *The northeast corner of Second and Jefferson Streets will be the site of the new stadium.*

spot a position or location. *You are standing on a spot where history was made.*

locomotion *n.* the act of moving or the ability to move from place to place; travel. *A new suspension system improved the car's locomotion at high speeds.*

ambulation the act of walking from place to place. *The blister on her foot affected her ambulation.*

mobility the ability to move from place to place. *Lack of wheelchair access in public buildings hampers the mobility of the disabled.*

movement the act of moving. *The choreographer designed every movement on the stage for the final scene.*

travel movement from one place to another. *How much travel does a glider have under these conditions?*

antonyms: motionless, stillness, immobility

malady *n.* a disease, disorder, or ailment. *He blamed his malady on the change in the weather.*

affliction a condition of pain, suffering, or distress. *Because of her affliction, she had to miss classes for a semester.*

ailment a physical or mental disorder, especially a minor one. *The common cold is usually a minor ailment.*

disease a condition in which health is impaired. *Many diseases that were once a threat are no longer in existence.*

illness sickness; disease. *Josh's illness lingered through the winter.*

sickness the condition of being sick; illness. *Flu was the most common sickness at school in January.*

antonyms: health, well-being

malice *n.* a desire to harm others or to see others suffer. *Although disputed by many, some people believe that wolves attack other animals in malice.*

resentment anger or ill will felt as a result of a real or imagined offense. *Resentment at his classmate's success prompted him to start a harmful rumor.*

spite ill will creating an urge to hurt or humiliate someone. *The child broke his playmate's toy out of spite.*

viciousness maliciousness. *The viciousness of her attacks against her opponent cost her many votes.*

antonyms: forgiveness, charity, goodness, benevolence

malign *v.* to speak evil of. *He felt that the newspaper had maligned him.*

defame to attack the good name of. *The gossip defamed all the members of the club.*

libel to make or publish defamatory remarks about. *The sports figure sued the newspaper because he felt that he had been libeled.*

slander to utter malicious reports about. *The candidate felt that his opponent had slandered him.*

antonyms: praise, glorify

maverick *n.* an independent-minded person who refuses to abide by the dictates of or resists adherence to a group; dissenter. *He remained a maverick throughout his career as a lawyer.*

dissenter one who disagrees. *During the speech, a dissenter formulated questions that might embarrass the speaker.*

dissident one who disagrees. *The dissidents gathered outside City Hall to protest the new ordinance.*

nonconformist one who refuses to abide by the accepted rules and beliefs of a group. *The poet was a nonconformist in all his opinions.*

rebel one who disagrees with or opposes established authority. *Rebels deserted from the army and attempted a coup.*

renegade one who denies one religion, cause, allegiance, or group for another. *When he left his unit, they called him a renegade.*

antonyms: conformist, sycophant

melodic *adj.* of, pertaining to, or containing melody. *The music in most Italian operas is quite melodic.*

melodious musical. *Juan worked with a vocal coach to make his voice more melodious.*

musical resembling music; melodious. *The musical song of the birds cheered her up in the morning.*

tuneful melodic, musical. *They left the show humming the most tuneful songs.*

antonyms: unmusical, dissonant, unmelodious, noisy, jarring

memorandum *n.* a short note written as a reminder. *The principal's office sent out a memorandum about cleaning out lockers.*

message a communication. *Reggie wrote himself a message regarding when his library books were due.*

note a short written message to aid memory. *Mom left a note on the refrigerator about when she would be home.*

reminder something to jog the memory. *The boss sent a reminder to all employees about the company meeting next week.*

merchandise *n.* commodities or goods that may be bought or sold. *They restocked the store with merchandise regularly.*

commodities articles of commerce, especially those that can be transported, such as mining or agricultural products. *Commodities like wheat are traded in a special kind of financial market.*

goods merchandise or wares. *In earlier times, a store that sold all kinds of goods was called a general store.*

products manufactured items that are for sale. *They created a special display of all their new products for the promotion.*

stock the total supply of merchandise of a store or business. *The clerk reported that the item was not in stock.*

wares articles of commerce; goods. *The peddler carried all of his wares with him.*

metropolitan *adj.* of, pertaining to, or characteristic of a metropolis. *Bustling crowds are part of the metropolitan atmosphere.* See **urban**.

monarch *n.* 1. a sole and absolute ruler of a state. 2. a sovereign, such as a king or emperor. *In the United States there is no monarch.*

dictator a ruler having absolute authority and supreme jurisdiction over the government of a state. *Joseph Stalin was a dictator in the Soviet Union during the first half of the twentieth century.*

potentate one who has the power and position to rule others. *The potentate of the tiny island nation rules like a kind parent.*

queen monarch or sovereign. *Victoria was queen of the United Kingdom.*

moral *adj.* of or concerned with the judgment or principles of right and wrong in relation to human action and character. *The judge was believed to be of high moral character.*

ethical in accord with accepted standards of right and wrong. *Strictly ethical behavior is required for people in this position.*

good moral. *Consideration of others is expected from a truly good person.*

honorable deserving of respect. *Her behavior was consistently honorable.*

principled motivated by morals or ethics. *The principled woman always tried to think of the best way to behave.*

respectable of or appropriate to good and correct behavior. *During the crisis, the family members tried to look respectable.*

scrupulous principled; moral. *The story told of a scrupulous king with an unscrupulous enemy.*

upright morally correct; respectable. *Each political party was searching for an upright person to run for office.*

virtuous moral. *The group rewards the virtuous behavior of its members.*

antonyms: immoral, bad, evil, dishonorable, unethical, corruptible, unprincipled, unscrupulous

mythical *adj.* 1. having the nature of a myth. 2. of or existing in myth. *She enjoyed hearing stories about the mythical unicorn.* 3. imaginary; fictitious. See **legendary**.

fabulous in the nature of a fable or myth. *The storyteller told of fabulous beasts that talked and acted like human beings.*

fictitious imaginary; unreal. *Although the characters in this book seem real, they are completely fictitious.*

imaginary existing in the imagination only; unreal. *Pegasus is an imaginary creature from Greek mythology.*

antonyms: real, actual, existing

necessity *n.* something needed for the existence, success, or functioning of something; requirement. *Oxygen is a necessity of life.*

need something required. *Our school library has a need for more books.*

requirement that which is required; a necessity. *Good swimming ability is a requirement for lifesaving.*

requisite a necessity; requirement. *Understanding plane geometry is a requisite for learning solid geometry.*

antonyms: frivolity, luxury

negotiate *v.* 1. to arrange or settle by conferring or discussing. *They hoped to negotiate a union contract in a few days.* 2. to succeed in going over, accomplishing, or coping with. *The experienced driver negotiated the sharp curve with ease.*

deal to transact business. *The used car salesperson said he was ready to deal.*

navigate to direct oneself toward a destination. *The skier carefully navigated the trail back to the comfort of the lodge.*

settle to decide by mutual agreement. *After days of discussion, the union dispute was finally settled.*

transact to do business with; negotiate. *The business deal was transacted without fuss.*

numerous *adj.* consisting of many persons or items. *When I got to my doctor's office, there were already numerous patients waiting to see her.* See **abundant**.

countless too many to be counted. *Countless people were left homeless by the earthquake.*

infinite immeasurably large. *An infinite expanse of desert stretched before us.*

innumerable too many to be counted. *Innumerable stars filled the sky.*

many consisting of a large, indefinite number. *There were so many people at the game that we couldn't find a place to sit.*

myriad amounting to a very large, indefinite number. *Myriad letters of application were received for the one job opening.*

numberless many; countless. *There were numberless wildflowers in the meadow.*

thick close-packed; having a great number of. *The tent was thick with mosquitoes.*

antonyms: few, scarce

objective *n.* something worked toward or striven for; goal. *My objective was to read five books each month for a year.*

aim intention. *Joel's aim was to get his homework done before his favorite TV program began.*

goal purpose toward which one works. *Getting across the mountains before the first snowfall was their goal.*

purpose object toward which one strives. *The number one purpose of the trip was relaxation.*

observe *v.* 1. to perceive; notice. 2. to make a systematic or scientific observation of. *His job is to observe the moon's orbit.* 3. to say casually; remark. 4. to keep or celebrate (a holiday, for example). *The couple observed their twenty-fifth wedding anniversary.*

celebrate to observe. *They celebrated Thanksgiving with the traditional turkey dinner.*

comment to remark. *The reporter asked the lawyer whether he would comment on the case.*

mention to refer to casually. *He mentioned that he and his mother were going out of town over the weekend.*

regard to observe closely. *The children regarded the model of a hydroelectric dam with interest.*

say to speak. *After ringing up the sale, Ms. Thornton would say, "Have a nice day."*

see to perceive visually. *Did you see the accident?*

study to examine carefully. *That scientist set out to study the habits of eagles.*

watch to observe. *The people eating in the sidewalk cafe watched the passersby.*

obstacle *n.* something that opposes, stands in the way of, or holds up progress. *Construction work on the highway was a serious obstacle to our prompt arrival.*

barrier anything that obstructs or prevents passage. *A barrier was erected around the newly seeded lawn to keep people from walking on it.*

hindrance something that hinders; an obstacle. *Shyness can be a significant hindrance in making friends.*

obstruction something that obstructs; an obstacle. *The Heimlich maneuver is an effective way to remove an obstruction to breathing.*

antonyms: aid, freedom. See **assistance**.

occupation *n.* an activity that serves as one's regular source of livelihood; vocation. *His occupation was nursing.* See **vocation**.

offend *v.* 1. to create or excite anger, resentment, or annoyance in. 2. to be displeasing or disagreeable to. *On some days the level of noise in the cafeteria really offends me.*

anger to enrage or provoke. *Rude treatment always angers us.*

annoy to bother or irritate. *The bees' buzzing around annoyed Mr. Ito.*

insult to offend with a remark or action. *Ramon insulted me by hanging up in the middle of our telephone conversation.*

irritate to exasperate; vex. *The prolonged delay of the flight home irritated her.*

outrage to produce resentment or anger in. *Cruel treatment of animals outrages her.*

provoke to incite anger or resentment. *The sign said, "Do not provoke the animals."*

vex to annoy or irritate. *It vexed her when the clerk ignored her and waited on someone else.*

antonyms: please, soothe, flatter, delight

old-fashioned *adj.* of a style or method formerly in vogue; outdated. *Because it was the warmest one he had, he wore the old-fashioned coat.* See **out-of-date**.

out-of-date *adj.* outmoded; old-fashioned. *Those reference books are so out-of-date that they shouldn't be used for serious research.*

dated old-fashioned; out of style. *He purposely wore dated clothing to attract attention.*

obsolete outmoded; no longer in use. *That software is obsolete; it won't work with newer computers.*

outmoded out of fashion; obsolete. *His outmoded methods of car repair were inappropriate on new cars.*

passé no longer in fashion. *Certain extreme styles of clothing become passé more quickly than others.*

antonyms: See **up-to-the-minute**.

panic *n.* a sudden, overpowering terror, often affecting many people at once. *Panic is often the first reaction in a crisis.*

alarm a sudden fear caused by perceived danger. *The thunderstorm filled the child with alarm.*

dread to fear greatly. *Dread of the upcoming tests kept Sam studying for hours.*

fear a feeling of disquiet or alarm caused by the expectation of danger, pain, or the like. *Fear of flying is very strong in some people.*

antonyms: calmness, tranquility, peacefulness

peaceable *adj.* 1. inclined or disposed to peace; promoting calm. 2. peaceful; undisturbed. *The quiet meadow was a peaceable place.* See **docile**.

calming soothing. *The calming effect of the sound of gently lapping water helped them relax.*

tranquil free from disturbance. *The tranquil rural setting was a good place to spend a relaxing weekend.*

untroubled at peace. *They envied the child's untroubled sleep.*

antonyms: upsetting, disturbing, troubled, agitating

penalize *v.* to subject to a penalty, especially for infringement of a law or official regulation. *In the last quarter of the game the referee penalized our team twice.*

castigate to punish or chastise. *The parents castigated the teens for breaking curfew.*

chastise to punish. *The teachers chastised the children for fighting on the playground.*

fine to impose a sum of money as punishment. *He fined the motorist twenty-five dollars for the parking violation.*

impose to force upon. *The court imposed a fine and one hundred hours of community service for the offense.*

punish to penalize for wrongdoing. *How will they punish the thieves?*

sentence to impose a court judgment. *The judge sentenced the man to five years in prison.*

antonyms: reward, honor, praise

perpetual *adj.* 1. lasting for an indefinitely long duration. 2. ceaselessly repeated or continuing without interruption. *The perpetual singing of the crickets filled the summer night.*

continual continuous; without interruption or end. *The big production number in the show featured continual tap dancing.*

endless without end. *Our wait in line to buy tickets for the movie seemed endless.*

eternal without interruption or end. *The memorial featured an eternal flame.*

everlasting lasting forever. *The project seemed to require an everlasting commitment.*

permanent fixed and changeless. *Civil War relics were on permanent display at the library.*

unceasing never stopping. *The unceasing noise from the construction site interfered with studying.*

antonyms: temporary, ending, fleeting, short-lived, stopping, passing, momentary

perplex *v.* to confuse or puzzle; bewilder. *The complicated code perplexed the treasure hunters.*

befuddle to confuse or perplex. *Poorly written directions will befuddle even a skilled person trying to assemble something.*

bewilder to befuddle or confuse. *The list of contradictory rules bewildered me.*

confuse to perplex or bewilder. *He confused me by beginning a new idea mid-sentence.*

mystify to perplex or bewilder. *Many phenomena in nature will mystify you.*

puzzle to cause uncertainty and indecision. *The maze of hallways puzzles most newcomers to the building.*

persevere *v.* to persist in or remain constant to a purpose, idea, or task in the face of obstacles or discouragement. *She will persevere until the difficult task is satisfactorily completed.*

continue to go on with; persist. *The child continued to ask questions even though her father wasn't listening.*

endure to carry on in spite of hardships. *The construction workers will have to endure the winter weather and finish the project on time.*

persist to continue tenaciously. *In spite of a serious headache, Jose persisted at his work until it was completed.*

antonyms: quit, give up, lapse, discontinue

personality *n.* the totality of qualities and traits, as of character or behavior, that are peculiar to an individual person. *This job calls for someone with an easygoing personality.*

character the combination of qualities that distinguishes one person, thing, or group from another. *How would you describe the character of the club?*

makeup the qualities that constitute a personality. *It's a natural part of his makeup to be aggressive.*

nature the innate qualities and characteristics of a person or thing. *Being dishonest is not part of her nature.*

phenomenon *n.* 1. an occurrence or fact that is directly perceptible by the senses. 2. an unusual, significant, or unaccountable fact or occurrence; marvel. *She was in awe at the sight of a natural phenomenon such as the northern lights.*

event an occurrence. *The next event on her calendar is visiting the art museum.*

happening an event. *People were so excited about the way things were changing that they kept a close watch for the next happening.*

incident a distinct occurrence. *Anyone who witnessed the incident at Fourth and Clark Streets involving a bicycle is asked to call the police.*

marvel something that evokes admiration, surprise, or wonder. *The ice skater's perfomance was a marvel.*

miracle something that excites awe or wonder. *The town's quick return to normal functioning after the flood was a miracle.*

occurrence something that takes place. *The next occurrence of a lunar eclipse is several years away.*

wonder something that arouses awe, surprise, or admiration. *Old Faithful is a natural wonder that should not be missed.*

portrait *n.* a painting, photograph, or other likeness of a person, especially one showing the face. *A portrait of the company president hangs in the reception area of the office.*

image a likeness. *The images of four Presidents appear on Mount Rushmore.*

likeness an image. *George Washington's likeness appears on a one-dollar bill.*

painting a picture or design in paint. *The artist's most recent painting was a humorous self-portrait.*

photograph an image made with a camera and reproduced on a photosensitive surface. *The star sent glossy photographs of himself to his fans.*

picture a visual image painted, drawn, photographed, or otherwise created on a flat surface. *Mrs. Lee has a picture of each of her children on her desk at the office.*

postpone *v.* to delay until a future time; put off. *The baseball game was postponed because of rain.* See **adjourn**.

posture *n.* 1. a position or attitude of the body or of bodily parts. *Good posture is an important element of appearance.* 2. a characteristic way of bearing one's body; carriage.

attitude a position of the body or way of carrying oneself. *She assumed an attitude of casual confidence.*

bearing the way of carrying or conducting oneself. *The monarch's bearing on state occasions was regal.*

carriage the way of holding one's head and body; posture. *Dance lessons can improve one's poise and carriage.*

demeanor the way a person behaves. *The clown pretended a dignified demeanor.*

stance the attitude or position of one's body. *The batter worked on improving his stance.*

prediction *n.* something foretold or predicted; prophecy. *We all made predictions about who would win the Academy Awards.*

forecast a prediction. *The nightly news program on television includes a weather forecast.*

prognosis a prediction about the outcome of an illness. *Dina's prognosis was for a full recovery.*

prophecy a prediction. *In Greek tragedies, characters visited oracles to receive prophecies.*

preliminary *adj.* leading to or preparing for the main event, action, or business. *We held a brief preliminary meeting to discuss strategy before the meet began.* See **introductory**.

preserve *v.* 1. to keep safe from injury, peril, or other adversity; protect. 2. to keep in perfect or unaltered condition; maintain unchanged. *They preserved the old courthouse as a historic landmark.*

conserve to protect from depletion or loss. *A marathon runner must conserve energy in order to finish the grueling race.*

guard to protect from harm. *If you camp, take certain simple precautions to guard against setting forest fires.*

keep to preserve and protect. *Keep this bracelet to remember me by.*

maintain to preserve or keep up. *The Lindstroms maintain many of the customs their ancestors followed in Sweden.*

protect to keep from harm, injury, or attack. *The Bill of Rights protects our basic freedoms.*

save to keep safe. *The company saved detailed sales records to compare one year's business to the next.*

antonyms: destroy, waste, squander, ruin, damage

primary *adj.* being first or best in degree, quality, or importance. *Milk is a primary source of calcium.*

basic underlying; fundamental. *The basic reason for the strike was low wages.*

elementary fundamental. *Ice skating is an elementary skill for a hockey player.*

fundamental elemental; basic. *The captain's fundamental concern was for the safety of those on board.*

antonym: secondary

proceed *v.* 1. to go forward or onward, especially after an interruption; continue. *After the telephone call, he proceeded with his work.* 2. to move in an orderly manner.

advance to move forward. *After a brief pause at the reviewing stand, each band will advance down the street.*

continue to go on with. *After lunch, we will continue the discussion.*

progress to advance or proceed. *We will read a chapter each week until we have progressed through the entire text.*

antonyms: stop, discontinue, retreat

punctual *adj.* acting or arriving exactly at the appointed time; prompt. *Most companies require that employees be punctual.*

on time ready at the appointed time; not late. *It is important to be on time for the concert; no one will be seated after the program begins.*

prompt on time; punctual. *Because they were often late, their prompt arrival at the airport was a relief.*

antonyms: tardy, late

questionnaire *n.* a printed form containing a set of questions, especially one addressed to a statistically significant number of subjects by way of gathering information, as for a survey. *The senator sent a questionnaire to his constituents to assess their views on issues.*

form a document for collecting information. *He had to fill out a form in order to get a new library card.*

report a statement of facts. *The officer had to complete an accident report.*

survey a list of questions meant to gather useful information. *Complete and return this marketing survey, and we will send you a free gift.*

regal *adj.* 1. of or pertaining to royalty. 2. belonging to or befitting royalty. *The gold-embroidered robes were standard regal attire.*

majestic having stateliness or dignity; regal. *The coronation music was majestic.*

royal of or pertaining to a monarch. *The royal wedding was televised.*

stately dignified; formal; majestic. *The stately woman moved with grace and dignity.*

antonyms: common, undignified

regime *n.* a government that is in power; administration. *Everyone rejoiced when the dictator's regime ended.*

administration a government that is in power. *The Lincoln administration had to deal with one of the most difficult times in the history of the United States.*

government a governing body. *The new government promised to tackle the problem of balancing the budget.*

reign the exercise of sovereign power. *The queen's reign was marked by peace and prosperity.*

regret *v.* to feel sorry, disappointed, or distressed about. *He regretted having forgotten to send a birthday card.* See **grieve**.

deplore to feel or express deep sorrow over. *She deplored the loss of her cat in the fire.*

lament to regret deeply. *He lamented the loss of his job.*

repent to feel regret or remorse for some action or inaction. *Wanda repented of her ineffective study habits before the test.*

rue to regret or feel sorry for. *She rued the opportunity lost when she was late for the audition.*

reject *v.* 1. to refuse to accept, recognize, or make use of. *The union rejected management's offer of a six percent pay increase.* 2. to discard as defective or useless; throw away.

deny to refuse to recognize or acknowledge. *The man denied having witnessed the accident.*

disavow to deny knowledge of. *The mayor disavowed any knowledge of the incident reported in the newspaper.*

discard to throw away. *He ate the banana and discarded the peel in a litter basket.*

disdain to reject with scorn. *The lion disdained the offer of food from the zookeeper.*

junk to throw away as useless. *The car was in such bad condition that the mechanic encouraged them to junk it.*

refuse to decline to accept. *The waiter refused the generous tip offered by the obnoxious diners.*

renounce to reject or disown. *The candidate renounced his press secretary after the scandal broke.*

scorn to reject with disdain. *Sam scorned her friendly overtures.*

spurn to reject scornfully. *She spurned the low-paying job.*

antonyms: accept, affirm, keep, treasure. See **preserve**.

relevant *adj.* related to the matter at hand; pertinent. *The judge ruled that the evidence was relevant to the case.*

germane having an important bearing on the matter at hand. *Limit the discussion to points germane to your thesis.*

material substantial; notable, especially of importance to an argument. *When the speaker strayed from his topic, his remarks were no longer material.*

pertinent related to the matter at hand. *Each panelist added information pertinent to the discussion.*

antonyms: irrelevant, unrelated, unimportant, immaterial

reorganize *v.* to undergo or effect changes in organization. *He reorganized his closet to make finding things easier.* See **adjust**.

rearrange to change the arrangement of. *He rearranged his schedule so that he could go to the play.*

recast to present (ideas, for example) in a new arrangement. *She recast the report by placing the events in chronological order.*

refashion to reconstruct or reorganize. *The committee refashioned the bylaws to meet the new needs of the club.*

remodel to reconstruct or reorganize. *The auditorium is being remodeled to create more seating.*

reserve *v.* 1. to keep back or save for future use or a special purpose. 2. to keep secure for oneself; retain. *You should reserve a seat early if you plan to travel over the holiday.* See **preserve**.

hoard to accumulate by saving or hiding. *When people know that something will be in short supply, they have a tendency to hoard it and thus make the problem worse.*

hold to retain. *They will hold tickets at the box office until an hour before a performance.*

keep to retain; hold. *They asked the restaurant to keep a table for us.*

retain to keep or hold. *If you retain your sales slip, you can return the merchandise if necessary.*

save to hold or hold back. *Save a seat for me at the game; I'll be a little late.*

antonyms: waste, squander, release

revive *v.* 1. to bring back to life or consciousness. *At the scene of the accident the paramedics tried to revive the unconscious woman.* 2. to restore to use, currency, activity, or notice. 3. to present (as an old play, for example) again.

reawaken to awaken again; renew. *Seeing the tennis championships on television reawakened her desire to compete.*

refresh to become fresh again; revive. *He found that a quick shower always refreshed him when he was tired.*

reinvigorate to invigorate again; revive. *A cool drink of water and a moment of rest reinvigorated the hikers.*

rejuvenate to reinvigorate. *A good night's sleep was all that was necessary to rejuvenate her.*

renew to rebuild or revive. *The television special renewed our interest in the American West.*

resuscitate to restore consciousness or life to. *In lifesaving class we learned how to resuscitate drowning victims.*

revivify to cause to revive; to revive. *Even though the child was in a coma, they felt they could revivify him.*

antonyms: See **exhaust**.

sociable *adj.* pleasant, friendly, or affable. *When feeling sociable, she'd invite several friends to her home.* See **hospitable**.

affable easy to speak to; friendly. *He was an affable man whom everyone liked.*

amiable friendly; sociable. *The club members formed an amiable group.*

convivial sociable. *The restaurant's convivial atmosphere attracted large crowds of diners.*

festive happy and friendly. *The holidays bring many festive gatherings.*

friendly in the manner of a friend. *It was a friendly conversation.*

genial having a friendly or pleasant manner. *The genial group in the theater lobby welcomed a stranger into their conversation.*

gregarious sociable. *The gregarious group in the middle of the room kept growing as newcomers were admitted to the circle.*

jovial characterized by friendliness and sociability. *The jovial couple were popular hosts.*

antonyms: unsociable, antisocial, unfriendly, hostile

startle *v.* 1. to cause to make a quick involuntary movement or start. 2. to alarm, frighten, or surprise. *The sound of a dropped book will startle everyone in the library.* See **astonish**.

alarm to cause sudden fear. *The unexpected sound of sirens will alarm many people.*

frighten to make afraid. *Bats frighten many people.*

shock to strike with surprise and agitation. *Break the news gently; it will shock everyone concerned.*

surprise to catch unawares. *They will surprise her with a party this year.*

antonyms: soothe, comfort

stimulus *n.* something causing or regarded as causing a response. *Good questions can be a stimulus for learning.*

cause reason for an effect or action. *The cause of the accident was driving too fast on slick pavement.*

impetus something that incites. *The cheering of the throng of fans was all the impetus the team required for the win.*

motive an emotion, desire, or psychological need as an incitement to action. *The police felt that the motive for the crime was revenge.*

submit *v.* 1. to yield or surrender (oneself) to the will or authority of another. *They cheerfully submitted to the silliness of the initiation to join the club.* 2. to subject to a condition or process. 3. to commit (something) to the consideration or judgment of another.

offer to present for acceptance or rejection. *The screenwriter offered her script to a producer for consideration.*

subject to submit for consideration. *The new medical treatment was subjected to rigorous tests before being approved.*

surrender to give (oneself) over to something. *Although shy at first, Les eventually surrendered to the boisterous fun of the party.*

subtle *adj.* 1. so slight as to be difficult to detect or analyze; elusive. *Her friends noticed a subtle change in the way she behaved toward them.* 2. not immediately obvious.

elusive eluding the grasp or perception. *The difference in meaning between some words is sometimes elusive.*

hinted suggestive; indirect. *A hinted criticism was all it took to get Hilda to do the assignment over.*

indirect not direct; roundabout. *He made an indirect request to go with us.*

slight minor; hard to perceive. *The new rules involved some slight changes that we had trouble grasping.*

suggestive giving a hint or suggestion; indicative. *Mom's suggestive remark about cleaning my room was not exactly an order.*

antonyms: direct, obvious, open, bold, dramatic. See **evident**.

succeed *v.* to accomplish something desired or intended. *We are working hard to succeed in the state music competition.*

prosper to thrive; succeed. *The business prospered in the new mall.*

thrive to improve steadily; prosper. *With enough enthusiastic members, the new club will thrive.*

antonyms: fail, flop

successor *n.* one that succeeds another. *He hopes to be the team captain's successor.* See **heir**.

follower one that follows or takes the place of. *Her follower will have a tough standard to live up to.*

replacement one who takes the place of another. *His replacement in the band will be a drummer from Kansas City.*

supplanter one who takes the place of another. *They worried about who the supplanter of their well-liked principal would be.*

antonym: predecessor

succinct *adj.* 1. clearly expressed in few words; concise; terse. 2. characterized by brevity and clarity in speech. *The principal's message about the crisis was succinct.* See **laconic**.

brief short. *The judge made a brief, clarifying statement at the beginning of the trial.*

compact expressed briefly; concise. *She wrote a compact press release about the mayor's condition.*

concise expressing a great deal in a few words. *A concise statement of the facts will be appreciated by the investigator.*

condensed of reduced volume. *The condensed lecture contained all the important facts, omitting some of the less important but colorful details.*

curt rudely brief; concise. *Such a curt reply caused hurt feelings.*

pithy precisely meaningful; terse. *The professor took pride in his pithy remarks.*

terse concise; succinct. *The terse report contained all of the relevant facts.*

antonyms: wordy, rambling, long, lengthy, tedious, cumbersome

superior *adj.* 1. higher in rank, station, or authority. *She worked hard throughout her training to become like her superior officers.* 2. of a higher nature or kind. 3. of great value or excellence; extraordinary.

excellent exceptionally good. *She prided herself on being an excellent bowler.*

greater superior in character or quality. *Many of the greater works of the artist are on display at the gallery.*

supervisory greater in responsibility or authority. *The supervisory personnel worked to solve the problem of staff morale.*

antonyms: inferior, poor, ordinary

surplus *adj.* being more than or in excess of what is needed or required. *The surplus grain was stored in silos.*

additional extra; supplementary. *When each student has a text, leave all the additional books on the shelf.*

excess an amount beyond what is needed. *The recipe said to pour off the excess liquid before serving.*

extra more than usual, normal, or expected. *Keep your extra pencils in your desks.*

leftover an unused remainder. *The leftover balloons were stored for use next year.*

remaining what is left; the rest. *After dinner, put the remaining food in the refrigerator.*

residual a quantity left over at the end of a process; remainder. *After she finished knitting a sweater, she put the residual yarn into a bag of scraps she used for crafts projects.*

transfer *v.* 1. to convey or shift from one person or place to another. *He transferred the call to his boss because he couldn't answer the question.* 2. to move oneself from one location, job, or school, to another.

exchange to trade or transfer. *Every year she exchanged gifts with her pen pal.*

interchange to switch two things. *At halftime the teams interchange goals.*

move to change position. *They asked her to move to a new location.*

relocate to establish in a new place. *Because of the father's career, the family was forced to relocate many times.*

shift to move from one place to another. *Shift that vase to the left to give a more balanced look to the display.*

switch to transfer, shift, or change. *At the end of the term, she switched to a new school.*

antonym: remain

transform *v.* 1. to change markedly the form or appearance of. 2. to change the nature, function, or condition of; convert. *With a lot of work, the cluttered, dirty basement was transformed into a family room.*

alter to change or make different. *They had to alter the seating plan when five people who had not been expected showed up.*

change to cause to be different. *Her new hairstyle really changed her appearance!*

convert to change into another form, substance, or state. *Heating water will convert it to steam.*

uncontrollable *adj.* not able to be controlled or governed. *She had an uncontrollable urge to run all the way home from school.*

headstrong insisting on having one's own way. *The headstrong child gave the baby-sitter a difficult time.*

ungovernable not able to be governed. *After the coup, the country proved to be ungovernable.*

unmanageable not able to be managed. *Getting four cats ready for a visit to the veterinarian was a nearly unmanageable task.*

unruly difficult to govern or control. *He never gave up trying to arrange his unruly hair.*

wild lacking control or discipline. *The wild fans tore down the goalposts after their team's victory.*

willful inclined to demand one's own will. *The rider could not control the willful young horse.*

antonyms: controllable, governable, willing, manageable, tame. See **docile**.

unpredictable *adj.* not predictable; not able to be foretold. *Until it is trained, the animal's behavior will be somewhat unpredictable.*

capricious unpredictable; playful. *Hold onto your hat or a capricious gust of wind will carry it away.*

haphazard dependent merely upon chance. *We couldn't find the book we wanted because of the haphazard arrangement of the shelves.*

random having no specific objective or pattern. *The packages were distributed in a random order.*

whimsical capricious or arbitrary. *The whimsical arrangement of items in the store made it hard to find specific things.*

antonyms: predictable, planned, organized, orderly

unwieldy *adj.* 1. difficult to carry or manage because of bulk or shape. 2. clumsy; ungainly. *A tricycle is an unwieldy thing to carry.*

awkward hard to handle. *Two shopping bags make an awkward load when you are going through a turnstile.*

bulky extremely large; unwieldy. *Although not heavy, the down coat made a bulky package.*

clumsy lacking skill or grace; awkward. *The huge clown shoes caused the child to make a clumsy entrance onto the stage.*

ungainly difficult to move or use; clumsy. *For a beginner, the sousaphone is an ungainly instrument.*

antonyms: easy, convenient, graceful

upheaval *n.* a sudden and violent disruption or upset. *The sudden drop in stock prices caused an upheaval in the financial world.* See **chaos**.

commotion a violent or turbulent motion. *One doesn't expect a commotion in a library.*

disruption interruption; confusion; disorder. *When choosing a setting for giving standardized tests, the administrator must find a place that will be free of disruption.*

disturbance an interruption, commotion, or upset. *The rowdy demonstrators created a disturbance at the statehouse.*

riot a wild or turbulent disturbance caused by a large number of people. *Because of overcrowding, the warden feared a riot.*

turbulence a violent disturbance. *The pilot warned of pockets of air turbulence and told us to remain seated with our seat belts fastened.*

turmoil complete confusion; agitation; commotion. *The fox caused turmoil in the chicken house.*

antonyms: peace, calmness

up-to-the-minute *adj.* marked by or including the most up-to-date information; current. *Have you heard an up-to-the-minute newsbreak about the space probe?*

current belonging to the present. *He disliked the current fashion of wearing very short hair.*

fashionable conforming to the current style. *It is fashionable in some circles to be late to social events.*

modern of or pertaining to the present or recent times. *Some modern automobiles have sophisticated computer systems.*

new of recent origin or lately made. *Each month he waited eagerly for the new issue of his treasure hunters' magazine.*

up-to-date reflecting the latest developments. *He turned on the radio to find up-to-date election results.*

antonyms: See **out-of-date, antique**.

urban *adj.* 1. of or located in a city. *Urban areas are often centers of cultural activities.* 2. characteristic of the city or city life.

citified having characteristics of city life. *Some residents complained that the noise and traffic of the new highway gave their town a citified feeling.*

metropolitan of, pertaining to, or characteristic of a metropolis. *Bustling crowds are part of the metropolitan atmosphere.*

utilize *v.* to put to use for a certain purpose. *The city will utilize fifty police officers for crowd control at the rally.*

devote to give entirely to a particular activity or purpose. *The newspaper will devote the front page to election results.*

employ to put to service. *To complete this assignment, you must employ at least three reference sources.*

veil *v.* to cover, conceal, mask, or disguise with or as if with a veil. *Fog veiled the valley.*

cloak to cover up; hide; conceal. *The arrangements for the meeting were cloaked in mystery.*

conceal to hide or keep from discovery. *The spy concealed the documents in the lining of his overcoat.*

cover to hide something by placing something over or in front of it. *I covered my face with my hand.*

disguise to conceal by false show; misrepresent. *She put a handkerchief over the mouthpiece of the telephone to disguise her voice.*

hide to keep or put out of sight. *Hide the gift behind the draperies.*

mask to cover for concealment or protection. *He masked his depression with a broad but insincere smile.*

obscure to conceal from view. *They were disappointed when clouds obscured the eclipse of the moon.*

antonyms: uncover, expose, reveal, unmask, exhibit, show

violent *adj.* 1. marked by or resulting from great physical force or rough action. 2. severe, intense. *The ships were tossed about by the violent storm.*

ferocious savage; violent. *The tale told of a ferocious beast that roamed the woods.*

fierce having a violent nature; ferocious. *Fierce sandstorms swept across the desert, preventing all outdoor activity.*

powerful strong. *Don't swim along this beach; there is a powerful undertow.*

savage fierce or ferocious. *The bear cub suffered a savage attack by a mountain lion.*

antonyms: gentle, calm, weak. See **peaceable**.

vista *n.* a distant view seen through an opening; prospect. *The vista from the chalet window was breathtaking.*

outlook the view seen by looking out; prospect. *The brochure for the resort claimed a spectacular mountain outlook.*

prospect the direction in which something, such as a building, faces; an outlook. *The building's prospect provided an ocean view.*

scene a place as seen by a viewer; view. *The scene from the top floor of the skyscraper made him dizzy.*

view a prospect or vista. *They asked the desk clerk for a room with a view.*

vital *adj.* 1. of or characteristic of life. *The nurse checked the patient's vital signs.* 2. full of life; animated. 3. having immediate importance; essential. See **essential**.

critical essential; necessary. *Time is the most critical factor in completing this project successfully.*

energetic full of energy; vigorous. *The football team is looking for an energetic person for the job of equipment manager.*

indispensable required. *In the rainy season an umbrella is an indispensable accessory.*

necessary vital; essential. *The mountain climbers brought only the most necessary equipment.*

antonyms: lifeless, sluggish, inessential, dispensable, unnecessary

vivid *adj.* 1. perceived as bright and distinct; brilliant. 2. having intensely bright colors. *They stood admiring the vivid sunset until night fell.* See **brilliant, distinct**.

colorful rich in variety; vivid. *We admired the author's colorful word choices.*

garish flawed by intense color or excessive decoration. *The garish hat was orange, purple, and green with bangles and feathers.*

intense having great concentration, power, or force. *It had been a very intense dream that stayed with her for days.*

antonyms: dull, plain, indistinct, pale

vocal *adj.* 1. of or pertaining to the voice. *The singer began taking lessons with a vocal coach.* 2. quick to speak or criticize; outspoken.

frank outspoken; candid. *Frank discussion of personal finances can be embarrassing.*

pronounced spoken. *Clearly pronounced words are more easily understood.*

spoken uttered. *How does spoken grammar differ from written grammar?*

straightforward outspoken; honest. *The candidate captured the people's attention with her straightforward approach.*

unreserved outspoken; frank. *The teacher's unreserved praise boosted his morale.*

antonyms: reticent, reserved

vocation *n.* a regular occupation or profession, especially one for which a person is specially suited or qualified. *All through her childhood she planned a vocation as a physician.*

calling vocation or career. *Elizabeth Blackwell's calling was medicine.*

career a life work; vocation. *She chose a military career because the discipline appealed to her.*

occupation an activity that serves as one's regular source of livelihood; vocation. *Most people change occupations at least once during their working lives.*

profession an occupation requiring advanced specialized training. *Everyone in the family was a member of the legal profession.*

weird *adj.* 1. unearthly; eerie. 2. of an odd and inexplicable character; strange; fantastic. *The weird program featured talking insects.* See **bizarre**.

au courant having up-to-date information. *A political candidate must be au courant on all topics of public interest to answer the many questions he or she will be asked.*

well-informed, *adj.* having a good background of knowledge, especially up-to-date information. *A journalist must be well-informed to do his or her job.* See **knowledgeable**.

well-read widely read. *Tyler's goal was to be a well-read person.*

well-rounded having knowledge of a wide variety of topics. *The talk show host prided himself on being well-rounded and able to discuss anything with anyone.*

antonyms: out-of-date, uninformed, ignorant

world-famous *adj.* acclaimed around the world; outstanding. *Dame Nellie Melba was a world-famous opera singer.*

outstanding superior to others of its kind. *He claimed that his car delivered outstanding performance.*

preeminent noted above all others; outstanding. *Shakespeare is the preeminent playwright in the English language.*

redoubtable worthy of respect; awesome. *No one wanted to challenge the redoubtable world champion.*

renowned widely acclaimed; famous. *The renowned British actor Sir Laurence Olivier died in 1989.*

antonyms: unknown, obscure, little-known, unworthy

yacht *n.* any of various relatively small sailing or mechanically propelled vessels, generally with smart, graceful lines, used for pleasure cruises or racing. *The yacht cut through the turquoise water toward the island.*

cruiser a large, mechanically powered boat with living quarters. *The executive liked to have business meetings aboard his cruiser whenever possible.*

sailboat a boat propelled primarily by sail. *On most summer days Lake Michigan provides an enjoyable parade of sailboats to watch.*

ship any large vessel able to navigate deep water. *The harbor was crowded with ships of all sorts.*

zeppelin *n.* a rigid airship having a long, cylindrical body supported by internal gas cells. *The zeppelin, a flying machine, was invented by Count Ferdinand von Zeppelin.*

airship a vehicle invented to transport things through the air. *Many kinds of airships have been developed since the beginning of the twentieth century.*

blimp a buoyant aircraft. *A blimp is often used to shoot aerial views of televised events such as the World Series.*

dirigible an early cylindrical lighter-than-air craft. *There were pictures of dirigibles as well as zeppelins and blimps in the article about buoyant aircraft.*